Tomorrow's Organization

Tomorrow's Organization

Crafting Winning Capabilities in a Dynamic World

Susan Albers Mohrman

Jay R. Galbraith

Edward E. Lawler III

and Associates

Jossey-Bass Publishers • San Francisco

Substantial discounts on bulk quantities of Jossey-Bass books are available to corporations, professional associations, and other organizations. For details and discount information, contact the special sales department at Jossey-Bass Inc., Publishers (415) 433–1740; Fax (800) 605–2665.

For sales outside the United States, please contact your local Simon & Schuster International Office.

Jossey-Bass Web address: http://www.josseybass.com

TCF Manufactured in the United States of America on Lyons Falls Turin Book. This paper is acid-free and 100 percent totally chlorine-free.

Library of Congress Cataloging-in-Publication Data

Mohrman, Susan Albers.
    Tomorrow's organization : crafting winning capabilities in a
dynamic world / Susan Albers Mohrman, Jay R. Galbraith, Edward E.
Lawler III, and associates.
      p.   cm. — (The Jossey-Bass business & management series)
    Includes bibliographical references and index.
    ISBN 0-7879-4004-6
    1. Industrial management. 2. Organizational effectiveness.
I. Galbraith, Jay R. II. Lawler, Edward E. III. Title.
IV. Series.
HD31.M6154 1998
658—dc21   97-42831

FIRST EDITION
HB Printing 10 9 8 7 6 5 4 3 2 1

The Jossey-Bass
Business & Management Series

Contents

Preface   xi

About the Authors   xix

Introduction: The Challenge of Change:
Organizing for Competitive Advantage   1
Jay R. Galbraith, Edward E. Lawler III

Part One: Designing Competitive Organizations   21

1   Corporate Boards: Developing
     Effectiveness at the Top   23
     Edward E. Lawler III, David Finegold, Jay A. Conger

2   Linking Customers and Products:
     Organizing for Product and Customer Focus   51
     Jay R. Galbraith

3   Designing the Networked Organization:
     Leveraging Size and Competencies   76
     Jay R. Galbraith

4   Structuring Global Organizations   103
     Jay R. Galbraith

Part Two: Enabling Competitive Performance   131

5   Organizing for Competencies and Capabilities:
     Bridging from Strategy to Effectiveness   133
     David Finegold, Edward L. Lawler III,
     Gerald E. Ledford Jr.

6   The Changing Nature of Work: Managing
     the Impact of Information Technology   154
     Susan G. Cohen, Don Mankin

7   Employee Involvement, Reengineering,
        and TQM: Focusing on Capability Development   179
        Edward E. Lawler III, Susan Albers Mohrman

**Part Three: Managing People
in the Competitive Organization   209**

8   The New Human Resources Management:
        Creating the Strategic Business Partnership   211
        Susan Albers Mohrman, Edward E. Lawler III
9   The New Learning Partnership: Sharing
        Responsibility for Building Competence   231
        David Finegold
10   Executive Education: A Critical Lever
        for Organizational Change   264
        Jay A. Conger, Katherine R. Xin
11   Strategic Pay System Design   286
        Edward E. Lawler III

Part Four: Transforming the Organization   307

12   Teams and Technology: Extending
        the Power of Collaboration   309
        Don Mankin, Susan G. Cohen, Tora K. Bikson
13   Accelerating Organizational Learning
        During Transition   330
        Ramkrishnan V. Tenkasi, Susan Albers Mohrman,
        Allan M. Mohrman Jr.
14   Catalyzing Organizational Change and Learning:
        The Role of Performance Management   362
        Allan M. Mohrman Jr., Susan Albers Mohrman
        Conclusion: Facing the Challenges of the Future   394
        Susan Albers Mohrman, Edward E. Lawler III
        References   413
        Name Index   437
        Subject Index   443

Preface

Tomorrow's Organization focuses on the new organizational designs and management approaches that are emerging as organizations transform themselves to face the challenges of continuous and relentless global competition. The book is based on two premises. The first is that the nature and intensity of competition have changed, and so organizations are now required to be simultaneously more effective and more flexible in their ability to reconfigure themselves, carry out their dynamic strategies, and make sure they are delivering value to their customers faster and better than their competitors. The second is that strategy and organization are not enough: organizations must also create new approaches to the human issues that accompany change.

Five years ago, authors from the Center for Effective Organizations (CEO) collaborated on an earlier volume, *Organizing for the Future: The New Logic for Managing Complex Organizations,* which laid out the general directions that we saw organizations taking in order to deal with the major forces of change in the environment. At that time, much of our framework was speculative; it was based on the example of some companies that were operating in new ways, as well as on our early research into organizational effectiveness. The present volume extends and further develops the ideas in the earlier book, describing how companies can transform themselves into flexible, high-performance organizations. Our research has given us in-depth exposure to the issues entailed in putting this new kind of organization in place, and this book presents the new models in greater and richer detail, going beyond the metaphors and platitudes that characterized much of the early writing on the changing directions of organizations. We report here on what is actually required for the transformation of an organization, and we provide approaches, frameworks, and guidelines to direct the journey, dealing with four arenas: the organization's form and context, enablers of continuous performance improvement, approaches to managing people, and processes for implementing change.

Organizational effectiveness is the ultimate criterion by which we judge organizational approaches. It is also a core value underpinning our work at CEO. As we conduct our research, one of our standard questions is whether an organization is effectively carrying out its mission and strategy. We search for what the organization is trying to accomplish, and we judge its effectiveness accordingly. Another value that always underpins our work concerns the impact that the organization is having on its people. Are the approaches that the organization employs fostering the development of a highly committed and competent workforce, one that is motivated to contribute to organizational performance? This book, while spending significant time examining new organizational forms and how they operate, also pays attention to human resource–related issues and to new designs for ensuring a highly qualified workforce.

Audience

Tomorrow's Organization should be useful to managers who are striving to design and lead effective organizations. It should also be helpful to practitioners and consultants who are working to aid organizations in redesigning themselves and implementing new forms. It should be of particular interest to human resource management professionals who are grappling with the people-related issues and approaches that are part of the new designs and that play a role in supporting an organization's transition. Organizational scholars should also find the book to be of value. It presents a balance of practice, research, and theory, using examples, frameworks, and suggested solutions to integrate a broad set of topics pertaining to the process and content of organizational design and change. The book derives from work conducted in a large variety of organizational settings, building on and extending theory and creating a bridge between academic research and the practical issues that organizations are facing today.

Overview of the Contents

The Introduction, by Jay R. Galbraith and Edward E. Lawler III, lays out the challenges that organizations face as they organize for competitive advantage in an environment characterized by intense and dynamic competition. Galbraith and Lawler argue that competitive advantage increasingly depends on the organization's agility and speed in developing and exercising the competencies and capabilities to achieve strategic market and technical leadership. In essence, the authors say, competitive advantage depends on organizing in new ways to overcome the inertia of the bureaucratic form. For an existing organization, the ability to organize in new ways requires the ability to fundamentally transform the way it operates and to build in the capacity for continuous transformation through time.

Part One, comprising the first four chapters, is concerned with the form and the context of the organization. Edward E. Lawler III, David L. Finegold, and Jay A. Conger make the case in Chapter One that corporate effectiveness increasingly requires a corporate board that actively influences strategy, structure, and executive staffing. The authors argue that the effectiveness of a corporate board depends on its setting up structures and processes to foster high performance as a team.

Chapters Two, Three, and Four, all by Jay R. Galbraith, deal with organizational forms that are becoming more prevalent. In these chapters, Galbraith provides many examples illustrating the various decisions that have to be made in the creation of effective new organizational designs. He also shows how to create an intertwined strategy and structure.

In Chapter Two, Galbraith describes customer-product structures. As the name implies, some of a customer-product structure's elements are organized around customers, and others are organized around products. This kind of structure represents a hybrid organizational form, one that contains aspects of both a functional structure and, in some ways, a multidivisional structure in that it has multiple profit-and-loss centers.

In Chapter Three, Galbraith describes the various design issues that have to be addressed in networked organizations. In this kind of organizational structure, which represents a shift away from vertical integration, networks of independent companies act for some purposes as if they were a single corporation. Each company does what it does best, relying on the others to carry out the other activities that make up the value chain of a business.

Chapter Four describes multiple types of global organizations. Here, Galbraith argues that competitive forces are forcing organizations to manage multiple dimensions of global integration and to maintain multiple global networks, which are enabled in turn by personal and electronic networks.

Part Two, consisting of Chapters Five, Six, and Seven, presents discussions of three major arenas where changes are being introduced to enable heightened performance. David L. Finegold, Edward E. Lawler III, and Gerald E. Ledford Jr., in Chapter Five, present a framework for guiding companies as they organize more explicitly to support the competencies and capabilities required for success. The authors stress the potential payoffs of linking organizational strategy to core competencies as well as to the knowledge of individuals.

Chapter Six, by Susan G. Cohen and Don Mankin, examines the impact of information technology on the nature of work. The authors argue that, in the Information Era of today, what lies at the heart of much work is the processing of information, which is frequently performed by teams across organizational boundaries. This type of arrangement puts a premium on flexibility, learning, interpersonal skills, and collaboration.

In Chapter Seven, Edward E. Lawler III and Susan Albers Mohrman describe the impact that three major performance-improvement frameworks have on organizations: employee involvement, total quality management, and reengineering. They argue that the new high-performance organizational model includes elements of all three frameworks. Employee involvement builds a context for involving employees in the organization's success. Total quality management sets out methods for continuous improvement of processes. Reengineering provides conceptual approaches for the integration of information technology into an organizational design enabling the organization to manage complete processes.

Part Three comprises four chapters that deal with the challenging issues of managing people in the new organization. Chapter Eight, by Susan Albers Mohrman and Edward E. Lawler III, outlines the specifications of a new human resources management.

The authors argue that the human resources function can carve out a key role for itself in helping the organization develop and implement its strategy. It must be prepared to help design effective work systems and build systems that prepare the workforce for its role in the changing organization. To realize this opportunity, the human resource function will need to make major changes in its own design and its operating focuses.

Chapter Nine, by David L. Finegold, presents a framework for conceptualizing the developmental challenges that organizations face as demands for employee performance change and with the disappearance of the traditional employee contract. Finegold argues that a key aspect of the organization's new relationship with employees is the learning contract, by which the organization provides opportunities for development so that employees can take charge of their own careers. In return, employees contribute to the organization in expanded and shifting ways. A key challenge is to determine both where the organization should apply its scarce resources for development and how to build development into the organizational fabric.

In Chapter Ten, Jay A. Conger and Katherine R. Xin describe changes in the nature of executive education, changes that include an increased focus on developing executives for the new competitive environment and the new, more lateral organizational forms. The authors argue that executive development increasingly will occur with cohorts of managers, potentially from multiple companies within organizational networks. They predict that there will be more emphasis on the integration of executive development with organizational development and on the assessment of the added value of development activities, to ensure that resources are being applied optimally.

Chapter Eleven, by Edward E. Lawler III, focuses on how pay systems can be designed to support particular strategies. Lawler stresses the importance of pay for performance in directing behavior toward strategically important areas. He also considers how pay systems can help develop strategically important competencies.

Part Four, consisting of Chapters Twelve, Thirteen, and Fourteen, offers frameworks to guide companies as they shift from a bureaucratic structure that emphasizes reliable, predictable behavior and central control to new forms that emphasize flexibility, innovation, and distributed control. Don Mankin, Susan G. Cohen, and Tora K. Bikson, in Chapter Twelve, provide useful frameworks for creating high-performing organizations through the design and implementation of new information technologies and the team-based organizations that employ them. They describe a highly participatory process involving multiple stakeholders, an iterative learning process, and the extensive use of prototyping.

In Chapter Thirteen, Ramkrishnan V. Tenkasi, Susan Albers Mohrman, and Allan M. Mohrman Jr. present an empirically based framework for understanding how to accelerate the learning process during organizational transitions that involve changes to an organization's architecture. The organization needs to engage in learning processes that enable its members to come to a new, shared understanding of its operating logic. It also needs to engage in processes that enable local units to establish structures and behaviors consistent with the new organizational design.

In Chapter Fourteen, Allan M. Mohrman Jr. and Susan Albers Mohrman argue that performance-management processes are key tools in the creation of the conditions in which organizations learn to operate in new ways. These processes include goal setting, feedback and appraisal, development, and distribution of rewards. To illustrate how these practices can impede or facilitate large-scale change, the authors build on case studies of organizations going through major change.

The Conclusion, by Susan Albers Mohrman and Edward E. Lawler III, reiterates and builds on the major messages of the book as a whole. It recounts the challenges of organizational design, people management, and transition that organizations face as they work to establish and maintain competitiveness in today's turbulent global economy. Until now, the authors argue, creating the business conditions for success has received priority in the corporate agenda, but sustained high performance depends on dealing with the need to ensure that employees are treated as important stakeholders in the new order. They conclude that organizations will have to participate in the building of a new social order, with new societal and community arrangements.

Acknowledgments

This book reflects the collaborative research model of the Center for Effective Organizations. Much of our work is carried out by teams of researchers joined in close partnership with the members of the organizations that we study and work with. Our research teams include CEO researchers and an extended group of colleagues from the Marshall School of Business at the University of Southern California, as well as colleagues from other universities and research institutes. We would like to express our appreciation to the Marshall School of Business, which has provided encouragement and a supportive home for the kinds of work we do and to the many colleagues with whom we have worked, only some of whom are listed as authors of the chapters in this book.

Support for our research comes from more than fifty companies that sponsor our center. They provide funding, ideas, and a testing ground for the usefulness of the learning and frameworks generated by our research. They often participate in our studies, providing a rich context in which to explore the unfolding design of organizations. Employees of these companies frequently serve as partners in our research. Our strong relationships with these companies and their employees keep us energized about our work and allow us to pursue our hopes of contributing to the generation of useful knowledge.

CEO is linked tightly to the Management and Organization Department of the Marshall School of Business, as well as to the Marshall School's Leadership Institute. We are especially indebted to a number of faculty members—Warren Bennis, Thomas Cummings, Larry Greiner, Jay Conger, Lisa Pelled, and Gretchen Spreitzer, to name only a few—who have contributed ideas, worked closely with us, and supported the concept of a research center bridging theory and practice.

Finally, the Operations and Technical Support staff of CEO has been integral to our process of knowledge production and dissemination. Sheldon Eng, Elizabeth Frawley, Alice Mark, Karen Mayo, Beth Neilson, and Annette Yakushi all deserve special mention for their contributions.

November 1997

SUSAN ALBERS MOHRMAN
Los Angeles, California

JAY R. GALBRAITH
Lausanne, Switzerland

EDWARD E. LAWLER III
Los Angeles, California

About the Authors

SUSAN ALBERS MOHRMAN is a senior research scientist at the Center for Effective Organizations, Marshall School of Business, University of Southern California. She received her A.B. degree in psychology from Stanford University, her M.Ed. degree from the University of Cincinnati, and her Ph.D. degree in organizational behavior from Northwestern University. Mohrman's research and publications focus on innovations in organizational design processes, team-based and other forms of lateral organization, high-involvement management, organizational learning and change, and human resource management. She has consulted with a variety of organizations, helping to introduce innovative management approaches and redesign structures and systems. Her books include *Self-Designing Organizations: Learning How to Create High Performance* (with T. G. Cummings), *Large-Scale Organizational Change* (with A. M. Mohrman Jr., G. E. Ledford Jr., T. G. Cummings, E. E. Lawler III, and Associates), *Creating High Performance Organizations: Practices and Results of Employee Involvement and Total Quality Management in Fortune 1000 Companies* (with E. E. Lawler III and G. E. Ledford Jr.), and *Designing Team-Based Organizations: New Forms for Knowledge Work* (with S. G. Cohen and A. M. Mohrman Jr.). She serves on the board of governors of the Academy of Management and on the review and editorial boards of several journals.

JAY R. GALBRAITH is professor of management at the International Institute for Management Development, in Lausanne, Switzerland. He is currently on leave from the University of Southern California, where he is professor of management and organization and a senior research scientist at the Center for Effective Organizations. Before joining the faculty at the University of Southern California, he directed his own management consulting firm, gathering significant consulting experience in the United States, Europe, Asia and South America. He has served on the faculties of the Wharton School at the University of Pennsylvania and the Sloan School of Management at Massachusetts Institute of Technology. His principal areas of research are organizational design, change, and development; strategy and organization at the corporate, business-unit, and international levels; and international partnering arrangements, including joint ventures and network-style organizations. His books include *Designing Organizations: An Executive Briefing on Strategy, Structure, and Process* and *Organizing for the Future: The New Logic for Managing Complex Organizations* (with E. E. Lawler III and Associates).

EDWARD E. LAWLER III, after graduating from the University of California at Berkeley, joined the faculty of Yale University as assistant professor of industrial administration and psychology and was promoted to associate professor three years later. He moved to the University of Michigan in 1972 as professor of psychology and also became a program director in the Survey Research Center at the Institute for Social Research. He has held a Fulbright Fellowship at the London Graduate School of Business, and in 1978 he became a professor in the Marshall School of Business at the University of Southern California. During 1979 he founded and became director of the university's Center for Effective Organizations. In 1982 he was named professor of research at the University of Southern California. He is a member of many professional organizations in his field and serves on the editorial boards of five major journals. He is also the author or coauthor of more than two hundred articles and twenty-five books. His most recent books include *The Ultimate Advantage: Creating the High-Involvement Organization, Organizing for the Future: The New Logic for Managing Complex Organizations* (with J. R. Galbraith and Associates), *Creating High Performance Organizations: Practices and Results of Employee Involvement and Total Quality Management in Fortune 1000 Companies* (with S. A. Mohrman and G. E. Ledford Jr.), and *From the Ground Up: Six Principles for Building the New Logic Corporation.*

TORA K. BIKSON is a senior research scientist in behavioral science at the RAND Corporation. She is a visiting professor at THESUS, an international business school in France, where she teaches classes on computer-supported cooperative work. She has taught at the University of Missouri, the University of California at Los Angeles, and the Stern School of Business at New York University. She heads a number of research projects, funded by the National Science Foundation and other institutions, that involve innovative technologies, with an emphasis on advanced information and communication technologies, a topic on which she has published widely. She is coauthor (with D. Mankin and S. G. Cohen) of *Teams and Technology: Fulfilling the Promise of the New Organization.*

SUSAN G. COHEN is an associate research professor at the Center for Effective Organizations, Marshall School of Business, University of Southern California. She received her B.A. degree in psychology from the State University of New York at Buffalo, her M.A. degree in applied behavioral science from Whitworth College, and her M.Phil. and Ph.D. degrees in organizational behavior from Yale University. Her research and her consulting both focus on team effectiveness and empowerment, employee involvement, human resource management, implementation of information technology, organizational development and change, and self-management. She is the coauthor of *Designing Team-Based Organizations: New Forms for Knowledge Work* (with S. A. Mohrman and A. M. Mohrman Jr.) and *Teams and Technology: Fulfilling the Promise of the New Organization* (with D. Mankin and T. K. Bikson). She has written numerous articles and book chapters on self-management and on teams and teamwork.

JAY A. CONGER is professor of management and organization, Marshall School of Business, University of Southern California. He also chairs the Marshall School's Leadership Institute. He received his B.A. degree in anthropology from Dartmouth College, his M.B.A. degree from the University of Virginia, and his D.B.A. degree in organizational behavior from the Harvard Business School. He is an active consultant, trainer, and executive coach with a worldwide clientele of private corporations and nonprofit organizations. The author of more than sixty articles and book chapters, he researches executive leadership, the management of organizational change, and the training and development of leaders and managers. His books are *Spirit at Work, Learning to Lead, The Charismatic Leader,* and *Charismatic Leadership.*

DAVID FINEGOLD is a research assistant professor at the Center for Effective Organizations, Marshall School of Business, University of Southern California. He is a graduate of Harvard University and was later a Rhodes scholar and received his D.Phil. in politics from Oxford University. He has conducted research, published, and consulted on the relationship between the skills of the workforce and economic performance in the advanced industrial countries. His particular interests include innovative approaches to managers' and workers' development, organizational design for effective use of employees' abilities, and the impact of globalization and technological change on skill demands. He is currently engaged in a series of studies, involving a matched set of establishments in the manufacturing, banking, and hotel industries in the United States and Europe, that analyze the role played by differences in skills where productivity levels are concerned. Before joining the Center for Effective Organizations, he was a social scientist at the RAND Corporation.

GERALD E. LEDFORD JR. is a research professor at the Center for Effective Organizations, Marshall School of Business, University of Southern California. He received his B.A. degree in psychology from George Washington University and his M.A. and Ph.D. degrees in psychology from the University of Michigan. He has conducted research, published, and consulted on a wide variety of approaches to improving organizational effectiveness and employee well-being, approaches that include employee involvement, reward systems, organizational design, job design, and union-management cooperation. He has done extensive research on high-involvement organizations and innovative pay systems. His published articles and book chapters number more than fifty. He is also coauthor of five books, among them *Creating High Performance Organizations: Practices and Results of Employee Involvement and TQM in Fortune 1000 Companies* (with S. A. Mohrman and E. E. Lawler III) and *Large-Scale Organizational Change* (with A. M. Mohrman Jr., S. A. Mohrman, T. G. Cummings, E. E. Lawler III, and Associates). He is an active member of the Academy of Management, the American Psychological Association, and the American Compensation Association and past chair of the Academy of Management's Organization Development and Change Division.

DON MANKIN is the dean of organizational psychology programs for the Los Angeles campus of the California School of Professional Psychology. He teaches, consults, and writes on issues of organizational design, change management, team effectiveness, and development and implementation of information technology. He is the author of *Toward a Post-Industrial Psychology: Emerging Perspectives on Technology, Work, Education, and Leisure* and coauthor of *Classics in Industrial and Organizational Psychology* and of *Teams and Technology: Fulfilling the Promise of the New Organization* (with S. G. Cohen and T. K. Bikson). He has also written many articles on these and related themes.

ALLAN M. MOHRMAN JR. is cofounder of the Center for Effective Organizations, Marshall School of Business, University of Southern California. He was formerly on the faculty of the College of Administrative Sciences at Ohio State University. He earned his B.S. degree in physics from Stanford University, his M.A. degree in secondary education from the University of Cincinnati, and his Ph.D. degree in organizational behavior from the Graduate School of Management, Northwestern University. Mohrman's major interests are performance management; organizational design, change, and learning; the design of effective systems for human resource management; and team-based organizations. He is coauthor of *Doing Research That is Useful for Theory and Practice* (with Associates), *Designing Performance Appraisal Systems: Aligning Appraisals and Organizational Realities* (with S. M. Resnick-West and E. E. Lawler III), *Large-Scale Organizational Change* (with S. A. Mohrman, G. E. Ledford Jr., T. G. Cummings, E. E. Lawler III, and Associates), and *Designing Team-Based Organizations: New Forms for Knowledge Work* (with S. A. Mohrman and S. G. Cohen).

RAMKRISHNAN V. TENKASI is research assistant professor at the Center for Effective Organizations, Marshall School of Business, University of Southern California. He received his M.S. degree in organizational development and behavior from Bowling Green State University and his Ph.D. degree in organizational behavior from Case Western Reserve University. His research and writing interests are in the areas of organizational learning and knowledge, innovation creation and diffusion processes in organizations, information technology, and organizational development and change. He has published several articles and book chapters on these topics in *Organization Science,* the *Journal of Engineering and Technology Management, the Journal of Organizational Change Management, Research in Organizational Development and Change,* and *ACM Proceedings in Computer-Supported Cooperative Work.*

KATHERINE R. XIN is assistant professor of management and organization at the Marshall School of Business, University of Southern California. She received her Ph.D. degree from the University of California at Irvine. She has also earned an M.A. degree in applied linguistics and an M.B.A. degree. She was formerly on the faculty of the graduate school of the Chinese Academy of Sciences, Beijing, and has served as visiting scholar at Chinese University of Hong Kong, University College (Dublin), and the Hong Kong University of Science and Technology. Her research focuses on how executives in Asia and the United States use interpersonal networks to connect with forces outside their organizations and on the importance of these connections to organizational performance. She also studies the processes by which managers establish effective work relationships inside organizations, whether through processes of social identification, seeking effective feedback, or conflict resolution. Currently studying adult learning and its relationship to executive education, she has made presentations to academic conferences and has written articles addressing these topics. In addition to her research and teaching, she has worked as a business consultant including assignments for Fortune 500 firms in the automobile, construction, and high-technology manufacturing industries.

Tomorrow's Organization

The Challenge of Change
Organizing for Competitive Advantage

Jay R. Galbraith
Edward E. Lawler III

The search is on for new, more effective approaches to organizing. Organization design and management has gone from a "Me, too" issue to one in which innovation is valued, and in which organizations can gain significant competitive advantage by advancing the state of the art. This trend began in the 1970s and gained major momentum in the late 1980s and 1990s. There is no reason to believe that the situation will be any different in the next millennium. It is increasingly apparent that corporations, in order to be competitive, must continuously improve—indeed, at times dramatically improve—the way they organize their management. How organizations are structured, how people are paid, how performance is measured, how individuals are trained and developed: increasingly, these are proving to be areas in which successful innovation can lead to improved performance and to sustainable competitive advantage.

The New Competitive Strategies

The need for new and more effective approaches to organizing has its origins in the new competitive business strategies. These new strategies are based on changes in both the nature and the intensity of competition. Cooper (1995) suggests that the new competition results from the spread of lean enterprises.

Over the past thirty to forty years, the lean enterprise originally developed by Toyota has spread throughout Japan and the West (Womack, Jones, and Roos, 1990). When lean enterprise competes against lean enterprise, product advantages are short-lived. All these enterprises have state-of-the-art technologies and short product-development cycles. Any product advantage is quickly matched by all firms; no advantage is sustainable. In the past, a firm could avoid competition by differentiating its products, thereby creating a temporary position of monopoly. The firm could then invest in brands and technology to sustain its advantage. But when advantages are short-lived, a firm must confront competition, not avoid it (Cooper, 1995). The firm can still differentiate its products, but it must recognize that long-term advantage results from a *series* of short-term advantages.

To survive in this environment, a firm must actively manage the triplet of cost, quality, and product or service features through systems like total quality management, design for manufacturing, activity-based costing, target pricing, and so on. As the basis of competition changes, these integrated systems allow the firm to move from one dimension of the triplet to another. Another, similar view is that of Werther and Kerr (1995), who see competition today as resulting from ever decreasing cycles of innovation, imitation, and equilibrium. To be a leader, a firm cannot just match the latest innovation. It must also develop new competencies so that it can create the next innovation and regain the initiative. What results is a constantly shifting strategy requiring multiple and combinable competencies. No advantage lasts in this strategy-shifting framework, and the intensity of the competition is driven by the rate at which new sources of advantage can be found and countered.

The leaders in this type of thinking have been Hamel and Prahalad (1994). They too believe that there is no such thing as a sustainable advantage; leadership must be continuously invented and reinvented. They conceive of strategy as a quest to proactively configure nascent industries, and/or to reconfigure existing industries, to one's own advantage. The thinking for this kind of strategy is very different from conventional thinking about sustainable advantage. The new thinking is based on the gaining of intellectual leadership where future possibilities are concerned, and then on the preemptive building of the ability to be the first to reach those future possibilities.

D'Aveni (1994) has elaborated on the thinking just described. He also sees the thinking about creating and sustaining advantage as out of date in those industries that he describes as "hypercompetitive." These are the industries in which advantage is rapidly eroded by the intensity and speed of "hypercompetitors." D'Aveni says that trying to sustain an advantage in a hypercompetitive industry is actually counterproductive: advantage-sustaining strategies consume time, energy, and resources that should go into creating new advantages. Efforts to sustain an advantage give competitors valuable time in which to be first in launching the next advantage and establishing themselves on the high ground. A sustainer also becomes predictable—a major *disadvantage* in a hypercompetitive industry.

The company that thrives is the one that *disrupts* rather than sustains the current advantage (even if that advantage is the company's own). The thriving company changes the rules of the game, takes the initiative, seizes the high ground, and then immediately begins preparing the next disruption. Again, long-term success results from a string of temporary advantages.

All these authors describe a similar competitive situation. The leading firms are future-oriented and create the ability to satisfy the evolving needs of their customer. Then, rather than sustain the current advantage, these firms move quickly to combine the ability to disrupt the current advantage and the ability to create a series of short-term advantages. The leaders outmaneuver their competitors by stringing together series of moves and countermoves. The companies most likely to win are those with the ability to demonstrate flexible responses and a variety of moves over time. In short, firms compete to see who is fastest and most flexible.

Are all industries hypercompetitive? Are there no sustainable advantages anywhere? We think that there are some lasting advantages, and that industries vary in how durable these advantages are. The continuum shown in Figure 1 portrays advantages as varying between long cycles and short cycles (Williams, 1992). On the left-hand side are long-cycle industries, in which advantages last for decades. Some of the firms characterized by long duration of advantage are legal monopolies like the Swiss PTT (Post, Telephone and Telegraph), or they are heavily protected industries like NTT (Nippon Telephone and Telegraph). Other companies in this category have unique resources. An example is Aramco (the Saudi

Figure 1. Sustainability of Advantages.

Characteristics

Stable	Dynamic
Increasing prices/high margins	Decreasing prices and margins
Long product-life and development cycles	Short product-life and development cycles
Long-lasting success formulas	New competitive rules
Traditional competitors	Non-traditional competitors
Traditional industry boundaries	Blurred boundaries

Time

Decades　　　　Years　　　　Months

Long Cycle ⟶　　　⟶　　　⟶ Short Cycle

Strategy

Avoid competition	Confront competition
Sustain advantage	Disrupt advantage
Erect barriers	Change the rules
	Develop organizational capabilities

Industries

Protected, state-owned telecommunication companies

Autos, appliances　　　Packaged consumer tools　　　Electronics, investment banking Products

Source: Williams, 1992. Copyright 1992 by The Regents of the University of California. Reprinted from the *California Management Review,* Vol. 34, No. 3. By permission of The Regents

Arabian Oil Company), which has vast petroleum reserves unmatched anywhere else in the world and enjoys cheap access to them. Still other companies in this group have skills and reputations like those of Sotheby's; another firm could duplicate these skills and this reputation only by repeating the long development process by which Sotheby's created them. And there are industries like the Swiss private banking industry, which combines all these factors. The Swiss private banks exist in a country with investor-friendly banking laws and a stable, appreciating currency. These firms have existed for hundreds of years. They know the ins and outs of the banking laws as well as the lawmakers. They have relationships with wealthy families who trust them with their money and their secrets. They also get first choice and insider information on many investment opportunities. Therefore, although we will focus in this book on organizations belonging to the dynamic right-hand side of Figure 1, we should keep in mind that other industries are still characterized by low to moderate levels of competition.

In this book we have chosen to focus on the right-hand side of the continuum in Figure 1 for an important reason: more and more industries are characterized by the new competition. The arrows in the figure indicate the trend for more industries to see the decay of certain advantages, such as the advantage of brands where consumer-goods companies are concerned. This trend is driven by a number of factors: the increasing openness to trade; global competition; the emergence of capitalism around the globe; deregulation, privatization, and commodification; disintermediation, or bypass of traditional providers; technological breakthroughs; and, of course, the digital revolution. These factors, in various combinations, disintegrate traditional boundaries within and among industries and open competition up to many nontraditional competitors. Both the intensity and the nature of competition change—and, again, traditional advantages (product features, patents, brands, and scale, for example) are no longer sustainable, so that even thinking about this kind of sustainability becomes a step toward failure.

The industries shown on the right-hand side of the figure— the hypercompetitive industries—are the ones in which firms begin to compete on the basis of organizational capabilities. If product advantages do not last, then new ones must be continually created, and competition revolves around who has the best and fastest product-development *process* or capability. The best process is the one that integrates the firm's technical, operational, marketing, and distribution skills.

Indeed, to be effective, an organization often needs more than one organizational capability. In highly competitive environments, the organizations that win are the ones that succeed in combining difficult-to-combine organizational capabilities. In the auto industry, for example, Japanese manufacturers gained significant competitive advantage in the 1970s and 1980s by being able to combine low cost, high quality, and brief time to market. Companies like

Benetton, Nike, and Reebok have gained competitive advantage through their ability to be simultaneously large and small. They have all the purchasing, marketing, and advertising advantages of being large, but they are small when it comes to introducing shifts in products and production. They are able to combine these advantages because of their unique organizational design (often referred to as the *network approach*; see Chapter Three).

Figure 2 highlights the arguments that we have presented so far. It shows how organizational effectiveness is the result of combining the four elements in the diamond depicted in the figure. One point on the diamond represents the organizational competencies that Prahalad and Hamel emphasize (1990). They include an organization's technical knowledge and its intellectual capital with respect to technology and customers. Another point on the diamond represents an organization's ability to operate in specific ways as an organization. Lawler (1996), Ulrich and Lake (1990), and Galbraith (1994) have argued that such organizational capabilities as those involving time to market, quality, and the capacity to be both global and local are potential sources of competitive advantage. The diamond model also depicts the business environ-

Figure 2. The Diamond Model.

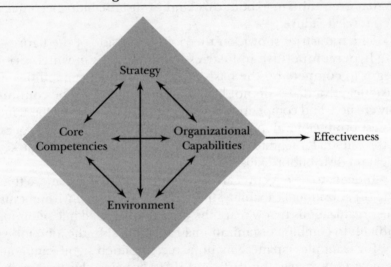

ment and the corporation's strategy as critical elements of organizational effectiveness. It is a "fit" model in the sense that it shows how organizational effectiveness comes about only when all four points of the diamond are in alignment. This means that the organization's business strategy has to fit with the environment, and that competencies and capabilities need to fit with the business strategy. The model is also dynamic in the sense that as the environment changes, the strategies, capabilities, and competencies also need to change.

The design issues involved in creating an organization with the right competencies and capabilities are highlighted by the decades-old star model, presented in Figure 3, which specifies the five key elements of the organization: strategy, structure, processes, rewards, and people. The fit among the five points on the star is crucial to determining how the organization actually operates. In short, the design of these five key elements determines the capabilities that the organization ultimately develops. Getting the elements of the star model into correct alignment with the business strategy is what creates an organization that is able to enact its strategy effectively.

The Competitive Organization

The most familiar approach to organizing is hierarchical organization. How to structure a hierarchical organization is well known, as is how to reward the individuals who work in it. The kinds of

Figure 3. The Star Model.

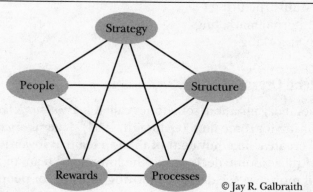

© Jay R. Galbraith

information a hierarchical organization needs, the measurement processes it requires, and the kinds of people it requires are also well known. In fact, just because the hierarchical approach is so well known, it is not an approach that is likely to provide a competitive advantage.

But this is the least of its problems. The most serious problem involved in the hierarchical approach is its inability to create an organization that can combine speed, cost effectiveness, product quality, and learning. In many respects, the search for the fast, flexible organization is a search to overcome the disadvantages of a hierarchical structure. These disadvantages result from the limited capacity at the top of the organization to coordinate the organization's activities. All hierarchies get narrow at the top. No matter how intelligent the senior executives are, and no matter how effective their teamwork may be, there is a limit to their problem-solving capacity and their ability to respond quickly. In hypercompetitive industries, there are simply too many demands on management's time, too many decisions to be made, and too many constituencies to satisfy.

This situation calls for a new approach to how corporate boards are organized and staffed (see Chapter One). It is also leading organizations to structure themselves differently, and in this area there have been four major developments, which will be introduced here and then discussed in more detail in Chapters Two, Three, and Four:

- Lateral organization
- Multistructuring
- Internal marketing
- Networking

Lateral Organization

Lateral organization, sometimes called *internal networking*, has been evolving for some time (Galbraith, 1994). Lateral organization simply creates the equivalent of the top team at lower levels and decentralizes some decisions to the lower-level team or teams. More and more, we see decisions moving to teams of people who have direct contact with products and customers. With the aid of modern information technology, these teams can be formed around products, processes, projects, customers, or purchased commodities, as shown in Figure 4. When numerous issues can be addressed simultaneously and quickly, the organization gains flexibility and speed.

Today's organizational design issues revolve around complex team structures. Some companies have created cross-functional teams for speeding products to market, and for designing with an eye to ease of manufacturing. The same companies have also created cross-functional, cross-product commodity teams, which design the same components from the same suppliers into their products, thereby producing higher volumes from fewer suppliers and lowering costs. When an organization uses cross-functional, cross-product teams, opportunities for conflict are numerous. The firm that can create interteam communication and decision processes to resolve conflicts quickly and effectively will simultaneously lower costs and increase its speed to market. That is the kind of organizational capability that can give the firm a competitive advantage.

Figure 4. Lateral Organization.

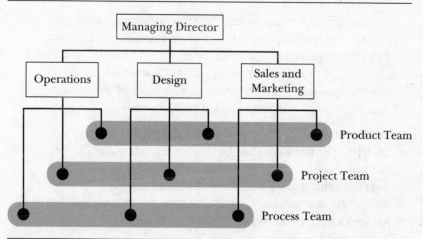

Source: J. R. Galbraith, *Competing with Flexible Lateral Organizations* (adapted from figure 1.2, page 6). © 1994 by Addison Wesley Publishing Company, Inc. Reprinted by permission of Addison-Wesley Longman Inc.

Multistructuring

Multistructures result from the creation of many multifunctional units. When a company is using linked product and commodity teams, it is a logical step for the company to add teams dedicated to particular customers, channels, and market segments and thereby shift its competitive focus as the need arises. Let us look at a case example of an extremely flexible organization: a bakery-product manufacturing company that uses multistructures to implement a strategy of shifting and disruption.

This company has a competence in brand management. It has a network of bakeries that covers North America. It also has a distribution system that can deliver fresh products directly from the bakeries to retail stores, bypassing the retailers' warehouse. (Only three other companies can deliver nationwide directly to stores: Frito-Lay, Coca-Cola, and PepsiCo).

The company came under competitive pressure in the 1980s, with its brands under attack on two fronts. First, retailers could easily duplicate the company's products and use their own private labeling. Second, and worse, the company's products were becoming less popular because they were high in fat and calories, and health-conscious consumers were avoiding them.

The company's resurgence began with the discovery of a low-fat ingredient that maintained the products' taste. After this ingredient was approved by the Food and Drug Administration, the company began reformulating its most popular brands. It focused promotions on the health-conscious segment of its consumer base, and the products flew off the shelves. The reformulation revived the company's brands and undercut the private labels.

To capitalize further on its products' popularity, the company expanded into all possible distribution channels. Different channels require different packaging, however, and so the company created partnerships with independent manufacturers, called *copackers*, to provide multiple kinds of packaging (for example, enormous boxes for such club stores, as well as single-serving portions for vending machines).

The company next took the low-fat ingredient into new categories, such as breakfast products and snacks, where it could create an advantage. New products were created for these categories, often with partners because some of the products (like granola bars) were not baked. This expansion provided new business in different aisles of grocery stores. With its delivery system, the company could also ensure that the new products were kept fresh (other manufacturers of breakfast foods did not have this capability).

Next, the company created partnerships with two of its large customers, in an approach called *category management*. Through this arrangement, these two retailers turned the management of their cookie-and-cracker aisles over to the baking company. The company's skills in brand management, its sophisticated analysis of bar-code data, and its knowledge of the cookie-and-cracker category allowed it and its two large customers to increase their profits. The coordination of product and cash flows between the bakeries and the stores also allowed for a minimum of working capital. Each of the company's two retail customers is now interested in having its own unique packaging for the company's products. The company, with its packaging flexibility, is able to meet their needs.

In summary, the company in the preceding example created an advantage through its discovery of a low-fat ingredient that maintains the taste of its products. Using its existing capabilities in logistics and brand management, it successfully targeted and dominated the health-conscious segment of its consumer base. It then created a multichannel, multipackaging capability to enlarge the population it could reach, and it used its new low-fat ingredient, as well as its capability in logistics, to enter a new category (breakfast foods). The advantage that the company enjoyed because of its low-fat ingredient bought it time to build up its knowledge in the new category. Finally, the company's enhanced reputation, its expertise in brand management and logistics, and its flexible packaging capabilities made it an attractive partner for two large retailers. In short, this company created a series of advantages by combining and recombining old and new capabilities in the areas of new products, new market segments, new marketing channels, and new customer relationships. This sequence of actions is a good example of what happens when a company disrupts the current advantages and moves on to new ones.

What will come next for this company? It may decide to develop some new market segments (such as for products geared to Asian or Hispanic tastes). But another development on the horizon is a new ingredient that is both low in fat and low in calories.

The company will then repeat the sequence of disrupting the current advantages and moving on to new ones. But this strategy can be effective only if the company has an organization that can execute it.

Before the discovery of its new low-fat ingredient, the company had been organized functionally. It achieved cross-functional coordination through teams dedicated to new products and projects. The brand managers in the marketing department also had responsibility for the coordination and profitability of their brands, and they maintained informal contacts across functions, with the executive committee of the top team serving as the primary forum for integration and for the setting of priorities.

Cross-functional teams have now been created for each of the strategic initiatives. Each team is chaired by a vice president, and members from each functional area have been assigned. The members from the functional areas are to have the information, the authority, and the time (at least 50 percent) to represent their functions in team decisions. The vice presidents are full-time. The functional representatives on the New Channel and New Category teams are also full-time and are dedicated to the work of their teams, reporting to their teams' respective vice presidents. In this way, the new initiatives are supported by permanent structures, which are also profit-and-loss centers.

This is what is called a *multidimensional* organization. It has cross-functional teams for products and new categories, and it has cross-function and cross-product units for market segments, customers, and channels. These cross-functional relationships, built up over the last few years in the project-management system, are what allow the company its organizational flexibility: with a good interpersonal network across functions, it can organize in any way that suits it. This is the kind of organizational flexibility that is needed to execute today's disruptive strategies.

Internal Marketing

A third change is toward greater use of pricing and internal markets to coordinate the services used by the line organization (Halal, 1993). This approach is the internal equivalent of deregulation.

It appears that open season has been declared on all monopolies. In the past, a company mandated the use of internal providers, and it charged a tax on everyone to pay for them. Today internal providers must compete for the company's business, offer their services at market rates, and even make a profit while doing so. As a result, providers are more responsive and competitive, users have more choice, and organizations are faster and more flexible.

Companies vary in how completely they adopt this model. Some companies start by determining what the real costs of the services are. They introduce something like activity-based costing systems, and then managers (rather than individual contributors) are put in charge of the service units, which then contract with users to determine how much service will be provided at what price and at what level of quality.

The contracting process is intended to do several things: get service providers to see and treat users as customers; increase users' influence over how much and what kinds of service they get; and educate providers and users about each other's activities. Some companies, in addition to using contracts, have adopted internal service guarantees to back the contracts up. In some Dun & Bradstreet divisions, for example, such guarantees are in place between providers and users of information technology (IT), and one IT group that failed to fulfill the terms of its contract in one particular month had to forgo that month's charge and find some other way to make up the resulting $30,000 budget deficit. Some companies stop at contracting processes; others use contracting as a step toward more open markets, in which case management usually gives internal providers some time to get competitive and then allows internal users to choose between internal and external providers. At this point, when providers must meet external standards, true competition results: internal providers have to be competitive on cost and quality and responsive to users' demands for service.

Still other firms use marketlike approaches to staff projects. For example, in some areas of Merck's research and development unit, at TRW's Space Park, and at Oticon (the Danish hearing-aid designer), management selects projects, appoints project managers, and sets the ground rules; the project managers must then attract and bid for the talent to staff the projects. Resource allocation is decentralized to users, providers, professionals, and project managers rather than determined by a management-led decision process: those who do the work discuss and negotiate how the resources will be allocated. The point is to free up management, have providers treat users as customers, and motivate professionals to stay in demand so that they can work on desirable projects.

Another aspect of internal marketing involves the decision to allow some internal providers to sell their services externally (and, again, the providers must meet a market standard). This step may be taken when the provision of a particular service does not constitute a unique advantage for the firm. It can lead to a new revenue stream for the company, and it may be a source of energy for the people who provide the service. For example, one function that has been greatly affected by this trend is the human resources function (see Chapter Eight), which is being dramatically transformed by large corporations that increasingly outsource this function or treat it as an internal small business. This trend has produced the need for new skills in the human resources function. It has also produced a new mind-set about what it means to be a human resources executive and about how the human resources function can become a meaningful business partner.

Networking

The driving force today is competition. Firms are discovering that they cannot perform every activity at the world-class standard, and yet in the hypercompetitive industries they must perform all activities at that standard or suffer from the deficiency. If a company cannot be the best in an activity, then it needs to partner with the company that is. The result is a network of independent companies, with each network competing as if it were a single company.

Benetton, a company in the fast-moving fashion business, where product advantages do not last from season to season, is a good example of a networked organization. It can use (and has used) Japanese designers to adapt to shifts in fashion. It uses joint ventures with local distributors in places like China and Turkey, where its own system of agents may not work well. In still other countries, it licenses its designs. When new materials, products, or channels appear, Benetton can establish relationships with new subcontractors or partners (for example, when Swatch wristwatches became popular, Benetton found subcontractors to create its own fashion watches).

A networked organization like Benetton is flexible enough to reconfigure itself for the next round in the game of shifting strategies. Its management must be quick to move, and it must be skilled at selecting and working with partners when they or their organizations have capabilities that can provide an important competitive advantage.

Benetton's network, in addition to being reconfigurable, is a high-energy network. What creates the energy and the drive to succeed is a combination of factors: processes for selection and socialization, the design of incentives, the distribution of ownership, and the creation of small units. A big, inflexible company finds this kind of energy hard to match. The combination of high energy and reconfigurability are the organizational capabilities with which to compete in the area of nonsustainable advantages.

Benetton created its network in the 1980s. The company sold off some of its factories to its own managers. It was now designing the merchandise, doing the necessary product management, performing the difficult capital-intensive work, and delegating the labor-intensive portions to some three hundred small, independent subcontractors who, like the factory owners, were also former Benetton employees. (Typically, a person would join the organization and, after about five years, would become a subcontractor.) If the subcontractors worked hard and performed well, they got more work. Benetton set the standard and paid cost plus 10 percent; subcontractors who could beat that standard made more. One result was that less educated people in remote parts of Italy found themselves owning their own companies and making more money than they ever dreamed of making.

A similar situation was created on the distribution side. An agent, initially a friend of Luciano Benetton, would be selected for his or her entrepreneurial drive and sense of fashion and would be given exclusive rights to a territory. The agent would recruit store owners from the general population but preferred people with no retail experience, who could be taught the Benetton way. The successful store owners were people who had been Benetton receptionists

or truck drivers, for example, and they might eventually come to own three
to five stores. An agent might have two hundred to three hundred stores in
a territory and might also own about twenty stores. The agents got 4 percent
of the volume in their areas. The store owners got what was left after their
costs. Growth goals were aligned for agents, store owners, and Benetton: the
more volume, the more profit. Agents found themselves making $300,000 to
$400,000 a year. Successful store owners, like the subcontractors, were making
more money than they had ever thought they could earn—in this case, up to
$100,000.

In competitive situations—characterized by rapid change in
products and services, by the emergence of new markets and channels, and by the blurring of boundaries between industries and
competitors—vertical integration reduces flexibility. The purpose
of a network is to make a firm not only more competitive but also
more flexible. The use of partnerships to develop suppliers and
channels gives a firm the core flexibility and reconfigurability to
shift its strategy as the need or opportunity arises.

Designing a networked organization (see Chapter Three) involves answering several questions and becoming skilled at leading
with them:

1. What is our outsourcing strategy? What activities and services
   should we perform, own, and control? What activities and services should we buy? For which activities and services should
   we seek a partner?
2. What is our network role? Will we integrate and manage our
   own network, as Boeing does? Or, like Roadway Express, will we
   specialize in logistics and participate in a number of networks?
3. What criteria and processes will we use in selecting partners?
4. What kinds of relationships should we establish with partners?
   What will hold the network together?
5. How will we develop and change the network over time?

In summary, then, the organization's ability to reconfigure itself has four aspects, used in various combinations:

1. Lateral organization
2. Multistructuring
3. Internal marketing
4. Networking

The competitive organizations are developing a mastery of all four aspects of reconfigurabilty.

Rewards and Work Design

Motivation of the workforce has always been an important topic. Today it is receiving renewed interest. More companies are finally realizing that, in the mix of ingredients for being competitive, having highly motivated, knowledgeable, talented people who can work together is the most important one.

One source of motivation is an actionable strategy. An actionable strategy is necessary before choice can be decentralized to the points of product and customer contact, because people need an understanding of the business direction before they can make appropriate trade-offs and decisions. But all the effort that today's companies make to put meaning into people's work—through mission statements and attention to vision and values—is also going to have an emotional impact on people. Today's firm wants the employee to serve a purpose, not just to have a job.

A second source of motivation is a work design that can be implemented by a small group of people. As will be discussed in Chapters Six and Seven, tasks in which people have responsibility, control, autonomy, and feedback are highly motivating when what is desired is challenging work. For example, the combination of automation and information technology now allows a complete piece of work to be performed by fewer people than in the past, and decision making can be decentralized more easily to a group performing a task with beginning-to-end responsibility. When processes are correctly reengineered, outcomes are controlled by the group and are therefore more manageable and more measurable.

A third approach to motivating employees is the reward system. As will be discussed in Chapter Eleven, in order for a reward system to motivate the building of the right kinds of capabilities it has to be "nimble" and focused on performance. Spreading ownership among the people working in a company is one way to focus employees' attention on performance. The ability to create owners in small units is a major advantage of the networked organization (as long as the interests of all its subsidiary units are aligned). The use of stock-ownership plans is particularly popular in software and other technology companies around the world, and the Silicon

Valley start-up, in which a small group receives venture capital and creates its own company, has now become the model for a high-energy software company. To take one example, the very successful German software company SAP began with venture capital and a small team; it has grown rapidly but still uses small teams and stock ownership to attract and motivate its software engineers. To take another example, Softboy, the Japanese computer software and services company that owns Comdex (the annual computer trade show in Las Vegas), creates teams of ten people to run different software ventures in Japan. The use of stock options as a motivator is limited by the Japanese commercial code, but the owner of Softboy is diluting his own stock in order to spread ownership around the company. There are other examples, too. Acer Computer, in Taiwan, has more than twenty-five subsidiaries that assemble Acer computers in local markets. Acer holds the majority of the stock in each subsidiary, but the rest is shared with management, and a portion of it is floated on the local stock exchange. Infosys, in Bangalore, India, was started in 1981 by seven founders. Foreign investors own 23 percent of this $18 million company, but the rest is owned by the founders and by the company's two hundred recruits, and about half the stock is dedicated to the employees. In all these examples, small units of talented people own the company. The ability to use ownership is an important feature of the networked organization. When its subsidiaries are aligned in their goals and interests, it can put enormous energy behind an effort and can usually outperform a vertically integrated company.

Human Resources

The demands that organizations face to be more competitive have direct implications for individuals. The trends we have been discussing have had a dramatic impact on the kinds of work that individuals do, and so they have significantly affected the kinds of skills that individuals need. Today people need the skills and ability to work in self-managing teams, but these skills also have to be aligned with the organization's strategy. As will be discussed in later chapters, this situation offers significant challenges and opportunities to human resources management, both for the organization and for individuals. As Capelli and others have noted, what this means for the individual is that he or she may increasingly need a skill set whose market value justifies compensation by the organization: in the absence of these justifiably compensable skills, the work that the individual does is likely to be sent to an outsourcer, where it will be done at a lower wage.

The new emphasis on skills has also led to the development of new employment relationships, which are significantly different from the relationships that inform the traditional "lifetime employment" model at the core of the bureaucratic approach to organizing. Rapid change and the development of new competencies and capabilities require a fungible workforce, as well as an organizational structure whose components and design are also fungible. If an existing workforce needs to be changed, it can either be replaced or change its skills. Both approaches are feasible; the challenge for the organization is to figure out which approach is most suitable to its situation and (as will be discussed in Chapter Nine) how to best manage that approach.

Change Management

Change, change, and still more change: that seems to be the agenda for the successful organizations of the future. Success will depend on constant alteration of organizational structures, reward systems, skills, information systems, and business strategies. The ultimate organizational capability, particularly in a complex organization, may be change management. As indicated by the star model depicted in Figure 3, change management is not a simple process. In most cases, it requires changing all the points on the star in order to maintain a good fit between the rapidly changing environment and the organization's competencies, capabilities, and strategies. As will be discussed in the Conclusion of this volume, change management must also take account of rapid changes in technology and in global and political conditions. Fortunately, there is an emerging set of principles, ideas, research, and theory that can help guide organizational change. Creating an organization that uses these principles is also not a simple task, but it is one with potentially high payoffs for the organization. An organization that is capable of change is much less likely to develop into a corporate dinosaur and is much more likely to be able to reinvent itself.

The examples of IBM, Xerox, AT&T, Harley-Davidson, and Hewlett-Packard all show that corporate reinvention is possible if difficult. In a rapidly changing environment, the competitive advantage moves to the organization that does not have an "experience handicap." The organization that reverts to old perceptions and traditional habits is increasingly losing to the newcomer that has the advantage of designing itself for today's environment and today's strategies. The newcomer doesn't arrive at the table with traditional structures, reward systems, skills, and so on. As a result, it can often invent new and better ways of doing things. The key seems to lie in developing highly customer-oriented internal processes, speeding products to market, and valuing new products that supersede obsolete existing ones.

It is increasingly apparent that, in this era of rapid and complex change, the ability to organize complex processes is the ultimate source of competitive advantage. But new forms of organization can provide a powerful competitive advantage only if they are continually improved and updated—and, in many cases, they often have to be reinvented themselves. In a changing world, no advantage is sustainable forever. Therefore, the challenge is to continually improve the organization's ability to develop new and different approaches to structure, reward systems, human resources management, and business processes. As will be seen in the chapters to come, there is a growing portfolio of ideas and practices. A major change is taking place, one that promises to shape and reshape the very nature of complex organizations.

Part One

Designing Competitive Organizations

Corporate Boards

Developing Effectiveness at the Top

Edward E. Lawler III
David Finegold
Jay A. Conger

Corporate boards are assigned a critical role in the governance of corporations. Therefore, it is not surprising that the higher performance demands placed on corporations today have increasingly led to a greater focus on board effectiveness. Much of this focus on board structure and behavior in the United States has resulted from the growing activism of institutional shareholders, who now own over 50 percent of the stock in many large American corporations. They are increasingly demanding that boards be independent of management, and that boards add value by acting in the best interests of shareholders (Useem, 1993). Meanwhile employees, the general public, and governments are questioning whether the focus on maximizing shareholders' value, a focus often associated with major downsizing initiatives, is coming at the expense of the corporations' other stakeholders: employees, communities, and consumers.

The debate about the effectiveness of boards is fueled by well-publicized examples of their failure to act in the face of major corporate performance problems. There are numerous examples of boards that have tolerated years of subpar performance by corporations, or that were ill prepared for crises. The boards in question were so staffed and structured that they were powerless to question the decisions of their companies' senior executives (Lear and

Yavitz, 1995). Further, the sharp rise in pay for chief executive officers (CEOs), often in companies that have failed to match the performance of their peers, has led many to question whether boards are truly holding management accountable or are simply "rubber stamping" CEOs' decisions and requests.

A growing body of academic research attempts to relate characteristics of corporate boards to companies' performance (Johnson, Daily, and Ellstand, 1996; Zahra and Pearce, 1989). There also have been a number of surveys describing how boards currently operate (Korn/Ferry International, 1996; National Association of Corporate Directors, 1995a; Lorsch and MacIver, 1989), as well as sets of guidelines on how boards should be operating (National Association of Corporate Directors, 1995b, 1995c). Often, however, the lists of "best practices" that boards come under pressure to adopt have no theoretical justification, nor is there any empirical evidence that these practices actually can enhance board effectiveness. The focus of this chapter is on the development of a framework for understanding the factors that contribute to the effectiveness of corporate boards, and on specific principles and practices that can contribute to board effectiveness. We need to look first at the key activities that boards engage in and then briefly review the key elements of group effectiveness.

Key Areas of Board Activity

Numerous academic disciplines deal with the role of the corporate board. Agency theorists, for example, emphasize the role of the board in monitoring the behavior and performance of executives (Jensen and Meckling, 1976; Fama and Jensen, 1983). Resource-dependence theory argues that boards, through their members' networks with other organizations, help corporations obtain key resources, such as capital and business partnerships (Pfeffer and Salancik, 1978). Legal scholars focus on the roles that a board must play in fulfilling its responsibilities as the overseer of the corporation (Bainbridge, 1993; Budnitz, 1990). These roles include representing the interests of shareholders, selecting and replacing the CEO, and guarding against infringements of the law. Scholars concerned with business and society expect boards to focus on the impact that their corporations have on such diverse stakeholders as

communities, employees, and the environment. Organization theorists argue that boards need to be sensitive to the changes that take
place in the competitive business environment, and that they have
to be able to provide their corporations with the type of leadership
that ensures constant improvement in corporate effectiveness, so
that their corporations will stay current with the organizational designs and competitive advantages associated with high performance.
Management experts (for example, see Lorsch and MacIver, 1989)
stress the crucial service role that boards can play in providing
strategic advice to top managers and in promoting the company's
reputation externally. What these different theoretical perspectives
often neglect, however, is the potential for conflict among these
roles: a board composed of individuals with strong connections to
the corporation (for example, the firm's banker, lawyer, key customer, and so forth) may be well designed to bring in resources but
may lack the independence needed to exercise effective control of
the CEO.

The directors themselves have differing and, often, ill-defined
views of their proper roles on boards (Thain and Leighton, 1992a).
For example, when board members of the Fortune 1000 companies were surveyed (Korn/Ferry International, 1996), outside directors were more than twice as likely as chairpersons, and three
times as likely as inside directors, to attach maximum importance
to the task of reviewing the CEO's performance. Inside directors
placed more emphasis on their responsibility to shareholders than
the outsiders did, whereas outside directors placed more importance on their duty to employees than the insiders did. (These results are based on additional analyses of the Korn/Ferry survey
data, available from the authors.)

In an environment where corporations are increasingly global
and are radically redesigning themselves to be more agile, there is
no substitute for a board that understands the business and can
guide changes in business strategy and responses to major new business opportunities or crises. To accomplish these objectives, however, boards must resolve some of the conflicting tensions in their
missions and must carefully set priorities among their roles. Legally,
corporate boards have responsibility for the overall governance and
operation of their corporations, and yet it is impractical for board
members to be involved in their corporations' day-to-day operations

and decisions. Board members may be unfamiliar with specific corporate issues and often lack detailed knowledge of the industries in which their corporations operate. They are in a unique position to influence the direction and mission of corporations; at the same time, however, there are constraints: the time and real power available to them is quite limited.

The stage of a company's development may dictate which of the board's roles receives the most emphasis. A growing high-tech start-up, for example, is more likely to emphasize the resource and service functions of the board than is a large public corporation owned predominantly by institutional shareholders; in the latter setting, the board's legal and agency roles take precedence.

Overall, the key question for the board's effectiveness involves the activities that the board should engage in to optimize its contribution to organizational effectiveness. It is crucial that the board's activities focus on areas where the board can have the greatest impact on enhancing organizational performance. Using the criteria of high leverage, practicality, and legal oversight, we have identified six areas in which boards should be active:

1. Strategic direction
2. Strategy implementation
3. CEO development and evaluation
4. Development of the senior management team
5. Legal and ethical performance
6. Crisis management

Strategic Direction

Fundamental to the operation of any business is its strategy. The board is rarely in a position to develop a detailed strategy, but it should be in an excellent position to offer advice on the strategic direction that the CEO and the senior management team develop for the corporation. Because of its special relationship with the company, the board can be trusted to keep information and plans confidential, and it has a strong vested interest in seeing that the plans are successful. Board members can bring opinions and information to bear on strategic plans and can offer perspectives that are not always readily available to the corporation's managers. Particularly when board members come from different backgrounds, and when they spend their time in different countries, companies, and types of organizations, they can provide a wealth of information about the potential effectiveness of a strategy. Because they are not involved in the strategy's day-to-day development, they can provide a rigorous reality test and an outsider's viewpoint.

Strategy Implementation

Research on organizational effectiveness strongly suggests that developing a valid strategy is only the first step in creating an effective organization. Many strategies fail, not because they are flawed in concept, but because they are poorly implemented. Therefore, it is crucial for boards to play a role in advising on and evaluating implementation plans. Many board members are CEOs or former CEOs who can draw on a history of implementation experience. Because of their ability to take a relatively detached look at the performance of an organization, they are potentially in an excellent position to evaluate how effectively a strategy is being implemented. In the case of a failing or failed strategy, they may be in a position to challenge senior management to change strategies or, at the very least, to change the approaches that are being used to implement the strategy. Whether a board can distinguish between a strategy that is failing because it is a poor strategy and a strategy that is failing because it is being poorly implemented will depend on the quality and objectivity of the information that the board receives, as well as on how personally committed the board's members are to the top management team and its strategy. If implementation is a problem, the board can give advice on how implementation can be improved and on the appropriate organizational design changes and change strategies that can help.

CEO Development and Evaluation

Business environments are changing rapidly, and the performance demands facing organizations are changing with equal speed. Therefore, boards need to be proactive with respect to stimulating change in their organizations. This reality is perhaps most apparent in the case of an underperforming CEO and senior executive group. The board that simply waits for the retirement or succession process to take effect is increasingly subject to criticism, as more and more stakeholders believe that it is the board's duty to replace underperforming senior executives.

If it is able to maintain its independence from the CEO, the board is uniquely positioned to evaluate and facilitate his or her development. An effective board should have the knowledge about the organization's performance and about the CEO's performance that will allow it to conduct a candid and realistic evaluation of the CEO. The board should also be able to help the CEO recognize the areas in which he or she needs improvement. Nowhere else in the organization or in the stakeholder community does there exist a comparable combination of the legal mandate, the information about the company and its executives, and the expertise needed to select, evaluate, and develop a CEO.

Development of the Senior Management Team

The board's responsibility for evaluating and developing executive talent does not and should not stop with the CEO. The board also needs to look at the entire senior management of the organization and to be involved in planning senior executives' development. This responsibility is directly tied to the board's responsibility for selecting the CEO and ensuring that the organization has a continuing internal supply of senior managerial talent. Again, the board should have within it the expertise to evaluate senior management comparatively and to determine whether the correct investments are being made in the development of managerial talent.

Legal and Ethical Performance

Monitoring the ethical and legal behavior of senior management and of the corporation is an activity that must be done by boards. The members of the board should have access to information about the company's ethical and legal behavior, and they must take action if problems occur. Therefore, they need to be a visible and proactive check on the way senior management and the corporation do business. The board's effective fulfillment of this responsibility is crucial to its protecting against outsiders (for example, lawyers representing shareholders and employees, or government agencies) becoming involved in identifying and correcting problems. It is much more disruptive and dysfunctional for an organization to have to respond to external groups challenging its behavior than to have to respond to its own board. Further, given their insider status, board members can often recognize the early signs of unethical and illegal behavior before they precipitate a major problem for the organization.

Crisis Management

In these turbulent times for business, corporations often face unexpected developments and even crises, ranging from hostile takeovers to major product defects. When a major crisis strikes, particularly if it involves the incapacitating of a senior executive, the board must be prepared to act swiftly and effectively. Members of the board may have to commit a significant portion of their time and educate themselves quickly about aspects of the company's operations.

Keys to Group Effectiveness

Having examined the main roles that a board should play, the challenge is to specify how this type of group can be structured, trained, organized, staffed, and developed so that it can operate effectively. The research on organizational and team effectiveness (see Lawler, 1992; Mohrman, Cohen, and Mohrman, 1995) suggests that any team or group doing knowledge work needs five attributes to perform effectively:

1. Knowledge
2. Information
3. Power
4. Motivation
5. Opportunity/time

Let us take a moment to define precisely what is meant by each of these five attributes.

Knowledge concerns the expertise and understanding that is resident in a group or an individual. In the case of a board, of course, it involves expertise about such areas as business strategy, management succession, finance, government, technology, society, and organizational functioning.

Information has to do with data involving the occurrences, events, and activities that affect a business. In the case of a board, it specifically means information about the operations and management of the organization, as well as information about the business environment and the performance and activities of competitors.

Power is the ability to make and influence decisions. In the case of a board, it means the ability to reach decisions about the key issues facing the company, as well as the ability to have its decisions accepted and implemented by the members of the corporation.

Motivation involves the willingness of individuals to commit their energy to the performance of particular tasks. In the case of a board, it means the willingness to attend meetings, do any necessary preparation, spend time on corporate activities, and, of course, make decisions that will contribute to the organization's effectiveness.

Opportunity/time involves a group's having the chance to make sound decisions and perform effectively. It is a necessary precondition for effective use of the knowledge, information, power, and motivation that exist in a team or work group. In the case of a board, opportunity involves the availability of time for meetings, to prepare for meetings and deliberate about important decisions.

The absence of any of these five elements is enough to render a group ineffective. Therefore, it is not enough for a board simply to have knowledgeable or highly motivated members. The board's members must, in combination, form a work group that has the right level, mix, and kinds of knowledge, information, power, motivation, as well as the opportunity to use them in a way that contributes to organizational effectiveness. Finally, the board's members must be able to work together as an effective decision-making group.

Given the differences among boards, as well as how difficult it is for researchers to gain access to boardrooms and observe sensitive meetings, it is impossible to specify precisely what is needed in order to create all the conditions for board effectiveness. Most of the learning and research about effectiveness has not focused on either senior managers or boards. Hautaluoma, Donkersgoed, and Kaman (1995) have even suggested that there are major structural barriers that often prevent them from becoming effective teams. Because of their special situation, it probably is true that boards are unlikely to be as effective as many other types of teams, but this point only serves to emphasize the importance of doing everything possible to make boards effective. Small improvements in a board's effectiveness can have a large impact on the corporation's performance because of the crucial role that the board plays.

We believe it is possible, by using insights from the literature on group process and the research on board effectiveness, to suggest some conditions and practices that can lead to a board's having an effective mix of knowledge, information, power, motivation, and opportunity/time. To think about creating boards that have the right mix of attributes, it is important to look both at boards' membership and at how boards function. Our discussion will focus first on board membership and then turn to how boards need to operate in order to be effective.

Board Membership

Membership issues are critical because they determine the knowledge that is available on the board, as well as the time that board members have available for participating in the board's activities. Board membership is also critical to the power base of the board and to its ability to challenge management. We will look at each of these issues separately.

Much of the academic research on boards has focused on the issue of insider versus outsider members (Bainbridge, 1993; Daily and Dalton, 1994; Finkelstein and D'Aveni, 1994; Zahra and Pearce, 1989). Most experts, regulators, and institutional shareholders argue for boards made up largely of independent directors, so that they will not be dominated by corporate executives. The results of the research attempting to link boards' composition to corporate performance are ambiguous, however, and provide no clear support for increasing the percentage of outsiders. Several early studies (Vance, 1964; Cochran, Wood, and Jones, 1985; Kesner, 1987) found that a higher percentage of insiders on a board is associated with better financial performance, whereas some more recent work (Pearce and Zahra, 1992; Schellenger, Wood, and Tashakori, 1989) suggests that companies perform better when they have boards with a higher percentage of outsiders. One of the most comprehensive recent studies found no consistent relationship between a variety of measures of firm performance and the percentage of inside directors (Bhagat and Black, 1996). Another study suggests that the right balance of members can be important, with companies performing best if they have a majority of outsiders balanced by a few inside directors who bring more detailed information and knowledge of the company to the board (Pfeffer and Salancik, 1978).

Knowledge and Membership

Because of the complexity of most businesses, it is impossible for anyone, or even for any small number of individuals, to understand all the issues that are likely to come before a board. These range from financial and legal issues through issues having to do with technology, human resources, and organizational development. Nevertheless, it is important for a board to be knowledgeable enough to discuss all these issues intelligently and offer guidance. Therefore, in the selection process, the expertise and knowledge of prospective members should be taken into consideration so that the board as a whole will have the ability to understand the business, develop key executives, contribute to the design and management of the organization, and understand the technological and governmental regulatory environments of the organization.

A board should be built on the basis of complementary skills and backgrounds. In the ideal case, the competencies and knowledge that each member brings will help to form an entity with a base of expertise that covers all the key organizational issues.

The effort to build a board with the right knowledge base should begin with the identification of key areas in which the board will need to be knowledgeable. These areas typically include business strategy, executive development, relevant technology, organizational design, change management, globalization, finance, government affairs, and business law. Historically, boards have often had members with good knowledge of finance, law, and technology, but they have not had individuals with in-depth knowledge about business strategy, change management, organizational design, and globalization.

For example, many corporations based in the United States now obtain the majority of their sales and see most of their growth potential in foreign markets, but in a recent survey only 17 percent of the largest U.S. firms had even one non-U.S. native on their boards (Korn/Ferry International, 1996). Although it is possible to recruit U.S. natives with international expertise, it is difficult to become a truly global enterprise when people from only a single country are serving on the board. There are practical difficulties, of course, in having foreign nationals regularly attend board meetings, but some companies have overcome these difficulties by recruiting individuals who are heads of U.S. subsidiaries, using teleconferences, and setting different attendance expectations for those living abroad.

In today's competitive environment, where organizational capabilities are often major sources of competitive advantage, it seems particularly important that boards include experts in organizational change and organizational design (Lawler, 1996), especially in organizations that differentiate themselves from their competitors on the basis of speed, quality, customer service, and other such organizational capacities.

Each organization needs to develop its own list of key knowledge areas and staff its board accordingly. One important staffing criterion should be that each board member bring at least one key competency to the board, and that the board as a whole, on the basis of its members' complementary areas of expertise, have knowledge of all the key organizational issues.

It is often desirable for a board's members to include several sitting or former CEOs from organizations of comparable size and complexity. This arrangement provides "peers" for the CEO to talk to, and from whom to get advice and coaching. These board-member CEOs may not be subject-matter experts, but their perspective can help integrate the knowledge areas represented by the other members of the board. It is also useful to have board members who have knowledge of key organizational stakeholders—customers, employees, major investors, vendors, the public, and the government. Individual board members need not represent these stakeholders—on the contrary, if board members view themselves as representing particular groups rather than the interests of the corporation as a whole, the internal dynamics of the board may suffer disastrously. There is a need, however, to ensure that each stakeholder group is understood by at least one individual on the board, who is also able to present that group's views when issues relevant to it are discussed by the board.

Most boards in the United States do not have members who are attuned to issues of importance to employees or to other corporate stakeholders, such as customers, suppliers, and communities (Johnson, Daily, and Ellstrand, 1996; Lorsch and MacIver, 1989). For a variety of reasons, this situation is no longer acceptable.

It is common in Europe to have a representative of the workforce on the corporate board, and a small number of U.S. corporations have also adopted this practice. In a company whose employees own a significant share of the stock, it makes sense to have a representative of the general workforce on the board: in this case, the employee on the board represents not only an important group of stakeholders but also the views of employee stockholders and forms a link between them and the board. To provide the necessary kind of leadership, boards need to understand their corporations' major stakeholders—particularly employees, in the case of a corporation that intends to gain competitive advantage through organizational excellence and execution. Organizational effectiveness inevitably requires leadership from a board that fully and accurately reflects the organization's performance demands and implements policies and practices that will allow the organization to meet them.

The selection of a board also needs to take account of its prospective members' ability to work together. In many respects, a board is a team that assembles occasionally and must perform complex work effectively during its relatively short meeting time. This is a very tough challenge, so it is important to do as much as possible to ensure that board members have good team operating skills. Major conflicts on the board that are due its members' insufficient team skills can be a major detriment to the board's effectiveness.

One way to help ensure a blend of talents on a board is to develop an expertise matrix or chart to be used in selecting board members. This matrix should feature board members on one axis and key knowledge areas on the other, a conceptualization that allows a board to assess its knowledge gaps quickly and take them into consideration in future appointments. In developing such a matrix, it is crucial to identify the knowledge areas that should be represented on the board. Certain skills (for example, team skills and financial analysis) need to be present in most if not all board members; other skills may need to be present in only a few. As already mentioned, expertise is often missing in organizational design, management development, change management, and business strategy (Lorsch and MacIver, 1989). In thinking about the right number and mix of competencies to be represented in the matrix, it is also important to consider the company's size and age: the roles and skills required of a board depend on the company's stage of development.

Power and Membership

A board cannot exercise its responsibility to govern a corporation if it does not have a degree of independence from senior management (Lorsch and MacIver, 1989; Bainbridge, 1993). Independence, particularly combined with knowledge, can put directors in a position to exert considerable influence over key corporate decisions. In many cases where boards have failed to replace poorly performing senior management teams, the boards were made up of individuals who were either subordinate to CEOs or dependent in other ways on senior management. One increasingly popular way to address this problem is to have boards staffed by independent outside directors. For example, an analysis of proxy data indicates that over 80 percent of board members of the Fortune 1000 are now outside (nonemployee) directors (Korn/Ferry International, 1996). On average, large companies have just two inside directors, down from five in 1973 (Korn/Ferry International, 1996).

For a board to be effective, not all its members need to be completely independent; indeed, as mentioned earlier, former insiders, because of their knowledge of the company and of where the skeletons are buried, are often able to ask the most penetrating questions of all. When a clear majority of members are not independent, however, it is difficult for a board to make tough decisions about executives' compensation, the evaluation of senior managers, and, of course, the appointment of individuals to senior management positions. It is also difficult for the board to mount an effective challenge to new strategic thrusts in the business and to deal with malfeasance and subpar behavior on the part of senior managers. Guidelines from the Securities and Exchange Commission and pressure from major investors suggest the advisability of moving away from a board's inclusion of "affiliated directors" who are personally dependent on the firm's management.

An independent director is, at the very least, someone who is not a full-time employee of the corporation. Beyond this criterion, an independent director is someone who does not have family ties, close business relationships, or charitable-activity associations with members of senior management. Independence also requires that CEOs not sit on one another's boards. Finally, it goes without saying that board members lose their independence if they have extensive relationships with the corporation that include payment for their services, because their remuneration could be jeopardized by their taking positions against senior management at board meetings.

Opportunity/Time and Membership

Even though it is obvious that board members cannot exercise their responsibilities unless they have adequate time, this point is still worth mentioning. All too often, individuals serve on multiple boards in addition to holding full-time demanding jobs. As a result, they simply cannot find the time to perform their regular duties as board members, much less to respond in times of crisis, when extensive amounts of time may have to be spent.

Very few corporations currently limit the number of board memberships that their directors and executives can hold. More than 75 percent of directors of the Fortune 1000 companies believe that there should be a limit on the number of outside boards on which a CEO can serve, but only 11 percent report that their companies actually do impose such a limit (Korn/Ferry International, 1996). This can be a major problem, given the increasing demands that organizations and boards face. Creating an effective organization is not a simple task, and so it is difficult to understand how even the most talented director can grasp the complexities of more than three or four corporations.

It is critical that boards be able to respond quickly and effectively to the major crises and changes that corporations face. At times a board may need to spend several days studying strategy issues and considering major organizational and business changes, a situation that argues for there being at least some board members who are semiretired and not heavily burdened with other commitments. Often individuals in these positions can put in days of effort, at relatively short notice, to deal with major organizational events.

Board Operations

Specifying how a board should operate is a complex challenge. To actually be effective, a board needs to operate so that it has the time necessary to achieve its mandate and so that it uses its members' skills, knowledge, and judgment to make good decisions. In discussing board operations, we will look at how to ensure that the board has the correct knowledge, the correct information, sufficient power, proper motivation, and the necessary time to be effective. All five of these factors can be strongly influenced by how the board operates and is managed. Boards need to be designed for effectiveness. Indeed, to help create and guide a high-performance organization, a board itself needs to understand what is required in order to create such an organization and be a best-practice example. Again, leadership and organizational effectiveness start at the top. If a board operates with processes and practices that are inconsistent with the creation of a high-performance organization, it can be a significant limiting factor with respect to the organization's ability to develop high-performance practices and designs.

Knowledge and Board Operations

Ensuring that a board has the right knowledge to do its job begins with the selection process but should not end there. It is not reasonable to expect all board members to come to the board with the knowledge that they will need in order to operate effectively as members of the group. Therefore, the board needs to take steps to build the knowledge base of its members and of the board as a totality.

Board members tend to be selected for their in-depth knowledge in certain areas. As a result, they may not have the breadth of knowledge necessary to understand some information that is presented to the board. Thus it is important to bring all members of the board up to a minimum level of knowledge about the key issues that they are likely to face as board members.

Often board members have useful knowledge with respect to the key business issues that face the corporation. Where there are gaps in their knowledge, these can be filled by site visits to key parts of the corporation or by top executives making presentations. Development efforts should also focus on the key technologies of the organization, on what the organization's competitors are doing, and on how the organization measures its performance.

One way to focus development efforts is to provide board members with opportunities to attend company-run training programs and give them a budget for attending development programs of their choice. Sessions can be run as tutorials or as presentations for the entire board. In some cases, it may be best to use the courses for new board members that are offered by universities, consulting firms, and professional associations. In addition, it is helpful to provide directors with information on "best in class" practices that look beyond the company's own industry and that benchmark the firm against top performers from multiple industries on a national or global basis.

One area that is consistently overlooked where boards are concerned has to do with knowledge about group behavior. Building knowledge in this area can significantly aid the board's responsiveness and overall efficacy. Group decision making is an extremely complex activity. It is particularly difficult when individuals spend only a few hours together and are expected to make complex decisions. It is also difficult when they come to the group with different backgrounds and different perspectives on issues. Individuals often have different beliefs about how a group should operate and about how decisions should be made. Therefore, it is important for a board to spend some time on a regular basis deciding how it wants to operate in terms of decision making, general group discussions, and interpersonal relations.

Even when individuals are skilled in group process, having them engage in some team building can be a useful exercise.

There are certain group processes that must be developed with an intact group. Process training and group development may seem to be an unwise use of time, but it can save time because it improves the decision-making efficiency of the group and, as a result, pays off in quicker and better decisions in the long term.

A number of practices in addition to training have been found to play a role in a team's effectiveness (Mohrman, Cohen, and Mohrman, 1995)—for example, the practice of regularly assessing effectiveness through systematic self-appraisal. Providing the board with an expert group-process facilitator is another possibility suggested by the research on group effectiveness. This kind of facilitation is often provided to other work groups, but it may be difficult to find someone to serve as a facilitator for a board. The key issues involve confidentiality and the willingness of the board to accept an outsider. One possibility is to develop the role of board secretary in this direction, so that the secretary can act as a facilitator. At present, however, board secretaries typically are not trained or skilled in group-process facilitation.

Knowledge of group process is particularly crucial in the case of a crisis, when time is of the essence. External events often shape the need for a board's crisis meetings, and there is little time for the board to decide how it will operate after the event has already occurred. Therefore, it may be desirable for the board to develop likely crisis scenarios, such as the death of a CEO, and for board members to reach agreement on what the appropriate response will be to different scenarios.

It could be beneficial to use techniques like assumption-based planning, which can help identify previously unknown threats (Dewar, Builder, Hix, and Levin, 1993). The board, with its responsibility for the long-run health of the corporation and its distance from day-to-day operations, is well placed to focus on future success factors for the corporation and to be proactive in identifying and preparing for potentially destabilizing situations.

It is important for board members to decide in advance how they will operate in a crisis. For example, they may decide to designate an outsider to call and chair a crisis meeting in case something disables the regular chair or the board secretary. A board's chair may not always call a board meeting in response to a crisis, particularly if the crisis involves the chair in a way that is unfavorable to him or her; in this case, the chair may decide to ignore the board. Therefore, it is important for an outside director to have the authority to call a board meeting even when the board chair is able to call one but chooses not to.

Information and Board Operations

To be effective, the board needs a broad range of information about the condition of the corporation. It needs to be particularly concerned with the kind of information it gets, as well as with the sources of that information, so that it can judge the information's validity. Good decision making is impossible without comprehensive data. Given the limited time available to board members, as well as the immense amount of information available on company performance, it is vital that this information be presented clearly and concisely.

There are a number of sources for data about corporate performance; using only a few is potentially dangerous and misleading (Zahra and Pearce, 1989). Often corporate performance is seen differently by individuals who hold different positions or use different measurement approaches. For a board to have a comprehensive view of corporate performance, it needs multiple data sources. In particular, the board often needs to combine its own observations of corporate performance with reports from corporate staff and outsiders who are retained to gather specific data about the company's performance.

A "balanced scorecard" approach is one way to obtain data on the relevant areas of corporate performance (Kaplan and Norton, 1996). The scorecard should include measurements of how the company is dealing with its multiple stakeholders (customers, employees, vendors, and communities). It should also include information about financial performance, with a focus on how assets are being employed. Finally, measures of operational effectiveness (for example, cycle time and quality) and data on the introduction of new products and on the kinds and types of products and services being developed are all important.

It is particularly important that board members review operational measures. Without these it is impossible to judge the effectiveness of important organizational change initiatives (for example, total quality management programs and reengineering efforts). Often the impact of a strategic or organizational design initiative shows up in measures of quality and operational efficiency before it shows up in accounting data. These measures can serve as early-warning systems, and so access to them is critical to the board's assuming a leadership role in creating a high-performance organization.

In addition to having the board look at financial, operational, and other measures reporting on corporate performance, it is desirable for board members to receive other kinds of information on the organization. For example, they need to talk with employees in their workplaces. They also need to meet with the organization's major suppliers and find out how the organization acts as a customer. It is also very important for board members to interact with customers and, as appropriate, be customers themselves. Gathering data on customer relationships is particularly crucial because how the organization deals with customers is a major determinant of its long-term success and is something that is often hard to ascertain simply from looking at numbers.

It is also important that board members have ready access to information about the corporation's legal and ethical behavior. Board members, because of their position in the corporation, often are the last people to whom a disgruntled employee, customer, or supplier will go with a complaint about management and the organization, short of going to someone outside the corporation. One way to help board members get information about organizational executives' unethical and dysfunctional performance is to provide convenient, secure channels for employees, vendors, and customers to communicate directly with the board about cases of fraud or misbehavior or to express their concerns about how the company is performing. A secure voice-mail system or a designated mailing address can be established for this purpose. It can also be useful to identify a lead outside director, a highly credible and trustworthy individual, as the one to whom stakeholders can report actions that they feel violate legal or corporate standards.

Staffing senior management positions and developing key executives is a very important part of the board's role. Succession activities are becoming increasingly important as organizations develop high-performance approaches to organizing and as they place greater emphasis on having effective leaders. In order to play this role well, a board needs regular information about the development and performance of managers in the corporation. The board needs to review the development plans and appraisals that exist for key executives in the corporation, and it needs to develop a succession plan, regularly reviewed and updated, for filling top management positions. This plan should include information about who the main candidates are (not limited to the top few managers) for the key strategic positions and about how these candidates are being prepared for their potential new responsibilities.

Boards increasingly need to look for executives who have the leadership skills and ability to take the corporation in the strategically correct direction. This means potential executives' understanding of complex organizational design issues needs to be assessed, as well as their ability to interact with and lead employees. To assess executive candidates, a board needs to see key executives perform in the senior management arena. They need to understand how the executives behave as leaders. The behavior of executives can be observed if they are invited to give presentations to the board and if they host visits by board members to company locations. Data on how they interact with their subordinates is more difficult to gather, but it can be obtained with 360-degree leadership assessment tools. Key executives can also be sent to leadership development and leadership assessment programs.

Power and Board Operations

To ensure that the board has the independence to govern the actions of corporate management, having the board made up predominantly of independent directors is necessary but not sufficient. An effective board needs a supportive chief executive, as well as specific operating principles and practices that give outside board members a chance to have direct influence and control over how the board operates and over the decisions it makes.

Our research has confirmed earlier findings (Lorsch and MacIver, 1989) that initiatives to empower boards depend heavily on the support of the CEO. CEOs who build superior boards tend to welcome constructive feedback and to be generally secure and open to new ideas and perspectives. They enjoy debate, challenge, and a healthy measure of guidance. They also believe in continual and thoughtful evaluation that opens the door to board members, influencing them as well as key corporate decisions.

Outsiders (even when they are a clear majority) are best positioned to exercise power on boards when they can develop action plans and positions. It may be that they can discuss sensitive issues concerning executive succession and corporate performance, or develop strong positions that are contrary to the stated preferences of senior management, only when they meet in the absence of company executives. Therefore, it is important that they have the opportunity to get together independently of their formal board meetings. There are a number of ways to create this opportunity. One possibility is to have all the outside directors gather several hours before or after a scheduled board meeting. Another option is to schedule a regular meeting and/or phone conference just for outside directors.

Our analysis of the Korn/Ferry survey of directors (Korn/Ferry International, 1996) suggests that they perceive the process of evaluating the chief executive's performance to be more effective when they have at least some board meetings without the CEO and other insiders present. The key is to develop a good level of communication among the outside board members so that they are in a position to make their own judgments and exercise their own influence with respect to how the corporation is run. In the absence of an effective communication process among the board members themselves, the power to run the corporation is likely to rest solely with senior management.

Besides needing opportunities to meet, outside board members need to be able to call a board meeting when they feel that one is warranted. If the authority to call a board meeting rests only with an insider who is the chair, then the chair can effectively control the decision-making process by not calling meetings, or by canceling meetings that have been scheduled. Closely related to the issue of calling board meetings is control over the agenda of the board. Again, if control over the agenda for board meetings rests solely with the CEO, it may be very difficult for outside board members to influence decisions. They may know which issues need to be addressed but be unable to address those matters because they cannot get the issues onto the agenda.

One solution is to designate a lead outside director who is responsible for working with the chair to call board meetings and develop the agenda. There is some evidence that this kind of designation is a growing trend: one survey of boards found that 27 percent of companies had such a lead director in 1995, up from 22 percent the previous year, and another 8 percent of respondents from boards without a lead director indicated that their boards were considering such an appointment (Korn/Ferry International, 1996). Our analysis of this survey reveals that companies with lead directors are significantly more likely to have instituted a formal process for reviewing board performance.

A more radical step is to separate the chairman and CEO positions and appoint an outside board member to run board meetings. This is the clearest way to ensure that a CEO does not dominate the board, and it is a common practice in some countries, such as the United Kingdom (Committee on the Financial Aspects of Corporate Governance and Gee & Company, 1992), but it is very rare in the United States, where only 3 percent of board members report this arrangement (Korn/Ferry International, 1996).

One clear way in which outside board members can shape corporate performance is by influencing the CEO. This influence process needs to be multifaceted, but one part of it should be the outside directors' annual review of the CEO's performance relative to that of CEOs in comparable organizations (National Association of Corporate Directors, 1994), and the results of this annual review should play an important role in determining the CEO's total compensation (salary plus stock options, cash bonuses, and other major rewards).

The evaluation process needs to include goals for the annual performance of the CEO as well as a systematic evaluation of how well the goals have been accomplished. The CEO's goals should include personal development objectives in addition to targets for organizational performance and development. The CEO review should be done by the outside directors and should have a direct impact on compensation. Stock option awards, cash bonuses, and the other major rewards that the CEO receives should be clearly tied to the results of a formal appraisal where the CEO's performance is judged against peers in comparable organizations.

This kind of evaluation practice is becoming more common: over 75 percent of major corporations conducted formal evaluations of their CEOs in 1995, up from 67 percent in 1994. In most cases these evaluations did not include formal written feedback to the CEOs, but when it did, inside and outside directors were significantly more likely to report that the evaluation process was effective (Korn/Ferry International, 1996, with additional analysis of the data).

What is being called for here with respect to the performance of the CEO is not different from what all the organization's other employees should experience: being held accountable for their own or their teams' performance as part of the regular performance review (Lawler, 1990). In this way, individuals and organizations are made accountable for how well they perform. This is also a step toward the creation of an organization that strives for high performance. Indeed, our interviews in companies that have instituted this kind of process confirm that it can become a powerful tool in making the company's strategic goals more concrete for senior management. It also typically leads to a CEO's ensuring that key strategic goals are embodied in the performance objectives of the management team.

Much of the crucial work of a board gets done in its committees. Therefore, committee memberships are very important in determining how much influence independent directors will have over a company's operations. The three most important committees—those for audit, compensation, and nominating—should be completely or predominantly made up of outside directors. In the absence of a majority of outside directors on the nominating committee, or on whatever other committee is responsible for selecting new directors, there is a great danger that the CEO and other internal board members will pick and retain only those directors who they feel are "safe" (that is, likely to share their viewpoints). It is also crucial for board members to understand that remaining on the board means being a good member of the board in the eyes of outside and inside directors, and so board members should be selected and evaluated by outside directors.

At present, most compensation and audit committees are made up exclusively of nonemployee directors. This approach is a good way to help ensure effective monitoring by independent directors. (American Society of Corporate Secretaries, 1996). The same is not true, however, of nominating committees: fewer than half of all U.S. corporate boards staff their nominating committees exclusively with independent directors (American Society of Corporate Secretaries, 1996), although the vast majority of the Fortune 1000 companies do exclude inside directors from nominating committees.

Committees are a vital mechanism for getting through the board's workload, but there is a danger that they can become separate fiefdoms and undermine the board as a whole. Therefore, it is important to ensure that regular communication takes place about committees' decisions and that committee memberships are rotated so that all board members are involved, and so that all board members have the chance to serve on different committees.

Motivation and Board Operations

The financial rewards that board members receive are only one of several reasons why individuals join boards. Likewise, financial rewards are only one of the ways in which board members can be motivated to be effective in their roles. Nevertheless, it is important that financial rewards be used as much as possible to motivate effective behavior on the part of board members and to align their interests with those of the key stakeholders in the corporation.

The best way to ensure that board members effectively represent the interests of shareholders is to put board members in the same financial position as the shareholders of the corporation—that is, to tie their compensation to changes in the value that shareholders receive. This is one way to ensure that the thoughts, behavior, and actions of board members will be in alignment with the interests of the shareholders. It is also a possible way to motivate board members to behave effectively *as* board members. Indeed, more and more directors are required to own stock in their corporations, and their compensation increasingly includes stock or stock options.

As of 1995, approximately 65 percent of directors were being required by their corporations to own stock (American Society of Corporate Secretaries, 1996) and 71 percent of the largest companies were paying board members with some form of stock (Korn/Ferry International, 1996). In many respects it is surprising that these figures are not higher and that it has taken so long for corporations to require directors to own and be compensated with stock. Board members need to take a multistakeholder, long-term view of the effectiveness and performance of the organization. This point argues for incentive compensation that reflects the company's long-term performance. Stock programs must have a long-term orientation. Stock options, for example, should be exercisable only after several years, and stock should be held for several years. Short-term cash incentives can be offered for performance that focuses on goals associated with employees, communities, and customers.

The performance of a board is best measured at the collective level rather than at the individual level. Research on team effectiveness clearly indicates that when individuals are interdependent in team situations, it is important to evaluate the effectiveness of the team overall; in the absence of a team performance evaluation, individuals tend to focus on optimizing their own performance rather than attending to how they contribute to and support the team's overall effectiveness (Mohrman, Cohen, and Mohrman, 1995). More than one-third (36 percent) of the largest U.S. companies regularly conducted formal evaluations of their boards in 1995, up from 26 percent in 1994 (Korn/Ferry International, 1996). Our analyses of these data show that directors on boards in companies that conduct formal evaluations rate overall board effectiveness significantly higher than directors on boards in companies that do not conduct formal evaluations.

The easiest way to facilitate the performance evaluation of a board is to have board members fill out questionnaires dealing with how they see the board and its committees operating. These data can be used at a board meeting to generate ideas and suggestions for improving the board's performance. In many respects, however, this kind of evaluation is not sufficient; data on the board's performance are also needed from key stakeholders. It is particularly important to gather data from major investors who have some insight into how the board has performed. Large institutional stockholders and employees can also be surveyed on their perceptions of the board's performance, and this information can be included in the evaluation portfolio. All the data that are gathered should of course be given to the board so that board members can use this information in their discussions of their performance.

Research evidence indicates that individual directors are not systematically evaluated in most corporations. In two recent surveys, for example, only 15 percent and 17 percent, respectively, of large corporations assessed individual directors' performance (American Society of Corporate Secretaries, 1996; Korn/Ferry International, 1996). Our interviews show that many directors and CEOs are opposed to individual evaluations, which they view as potentially divisive and as a waste of time. In the absence of a formal evaluation process, however, individual board members cannot be held accountable for their performance. All too often board members are evaluated informally, in a "hit or miss" process that does not provide good feedback or valid data. Our analysis of the Korn/Ferry International survey data (1996) shows that in companies where individual board members are evaluated, directors have significantly more positive ratings of boards' overall effectiveness.

The people who can most appropriately evaluate a board member are typically other members of the board, which suggests a peer process in which board members evaluate one another. Peer evaluation can be conducted once a year through the distribution of forms to all board members. The forms can be filled out anonymously, and then the results can be summarized and given to the individual board members. The evaluation data should include the developmental needs of the board member as well as information about his or her contributions to the board. Some boards conduct this type of process only when board members are up for reelection. This is a step in the right direction, but in several respects it is inadequate. Its most important drawback is that it fails to give the board member continuous feedback on his or her performance and thus does not offer a chance to correct behavior before the critical decision is made about his or her continuing membership on the board (Thain and Leighton, 1992b; National Association of Corporate Directors, 1994).

It is important that the results of performance appraisals be made available to whatever committee is responsible for nominating individuals to the board. In this way, poorly performing board members can be replaced. All that is needed in this respect is a simple pass/fail evaluation that does not divert attention from the board's overall performance. At the present time, board members are rarely replaced for poor performance; instead, boards simply wait until poorly performing members are forced to retire (Korn/ Ferry International, 1996).

Opportunity/Time and Board Operations

To be effective, a board needs to have the time and the opportunity to influence decisions. Other principles have touched on elements of what a board needs to do to ensure that board members do have the opportunity to influence key decisions. For example, the decisions concerning the ability of outsiders to control agendas and meet independently falls into this category. Nevertheless, several other practices must be in place to ensure that boards have the opportunity and time necessary to perform effectively.

There is no magic number of board meetings that can be stated as being necessary, but in most cases at least eight to ten one-day meetings per year, along with a number of committee meetings, seem to be necessary. On the average, directors estimate, they spend almost a month of regular work time (163 hours) on a single board's business each year, with chairpersons devoting even more time (an average of 176 hours) (Korn/Ferry International, 1996). It is possible to save some time by taking advantage of modern information technology and holding virtual or electronic meetings via phone or video conferencing. This practice is growing, but our interviews indicate that most board members agree that it should supplement rather than replace regular face-to-face meetings.

To make the best use of the board's meeting times, members should have the chance to study relevant information before meetings because a meeting itself is typically not the best setting in which to communicate information; meeting time is more appropriately reserved for discussing information and reaching decisions. Therefore, board members should be sent relevant information before meetings so that they can arrive prepared to discuss crucial issues. Because members of the board may need help interpreting business information, it is advisable that someone in the corporation be made available to provide clarification of the most important business data.

Even when board meetings are run with maximum efficiency, the typical half-day or even full-day session often does not allow time for in-depth discussion of corporate strategy. To provide an opportunity for this key task, more and more companies schedule a two-day board retreat each year and reserve this time exclusively for long-term strategic issues. The retreat can also be an occasion for the board to interact with and assess the senior management team as the senior managers give presentations about their areas of the corporation.

Conclusion

Establishing an effective board is not easy. It requires a substantial investment of time, dollars, and thought, but the cost of an ineffective board often far outweighs the investment in building an effective one. In an era when shareholders' activism is continuously increasing and corporate performance is so critical, an effective corporate board is not an option for a major corporation. It is a necessity.

The board is in a unique position to influence the structure of the corporation, as well as its business strategy and executive staffing. Organizational effectiveness increasingly relies on innovation and creativity in these areas, and so it is particularly important that the board itself practice the behaviors and approaches that the organization needs to adopt in order to be effective. In essence, the board is a critical potential source of leadership in the area of organizational effectiveness. To be effective with respect to the five key areas of board activity identified at the beginning of this chapter, boards need the right combination of the five key attributes—knowledge, information, power, motivation, and opportunity/time. Unfortunately, the research evidence suggests that at this moment in boardrooms across America, many of the practices and conditions needed to create effective boards are not present. Therefore, a strong argument can be made that to add value effectively in the future, boards need to change the way they do business.

Chapter Two

Linking Customers and Products

Organizing for Product and Customer Focus

Jay R. Galbraith

A new, hybrid organizational structure is gaining considerable popularity and appears to be an approach whose popularity will continue to grow. This structure is partially focused on customer segments and partially focused on types of products or services. It is partly like the multidivisional structure and partly like the functional structure. This customer-product hybrid, or *front-back approach,* is like the multidivisional structure in that it has multiple profit-and-loss centers. Unlike the multidivisional structure, however, it allows customers to buy all products, and it allows all products to be supplied to all customers. In order to accomplish this, the profit centers need to be more interdependent than the usual business units in the multidivisional structure. Thus, it is a hybrid because it requires the same cross-functional coordination of front and back units as in a single business, while its diverse products and markets demand the more decentralized approach found in multidivisional businesses.

Because customer-product structures are hybrids combining aspects of the single-business structure and the multibusiness structure, their effective execution is a major management challenge. When mastered, however, it can become an organizational capability that provides a significant competitive advantage because it allows a firm to be simultaneously profit center–driven and coordinated.

This chapter focuses on three questions concerning customer-product structures:

1. What, exactly, are these hybrid structures? What do they look like?
2. Why are companies choosing to organize in this way?
3. How do we make these hybrid structures work effectively?

What Is a Customer-Product Structure?

The front-back organization is a combination of customer structures and product structures. Specifically, it consists of a front-end structure focused on customers, customer segments, channels, industries, or geographies, according to how the company segments its markets. The other part is a back-end structure that is focused on products and technologies. Both the customer and the product portions are multifunctional and profit-and-loss measurable. An example is IBM's structure, created by CEO Lou Gerstner; an abbreviated version of it shown in Figure 2.1.

On the right-hand side of the figure are the customer units, which are based on the industries in which customers compete.

Figure 2.1. IBM's Front-Back Structure.

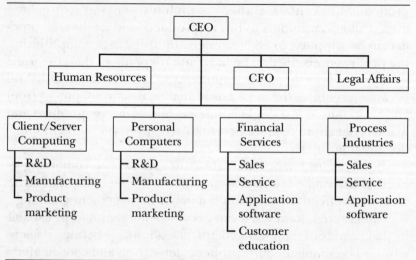

Financial services and process industries are shown in the figure, but other industries (such as retailing and consumer goods) could also be featured. Each industry segment contains functions for sales and service, along with units for developing or sourcing software for customers' unique applications. Other units could be added, and these would also be specific to the industries being served.

On the left side of Figure 2.1 are the product units. One unit develops and manufactures computer hardware for client/server applications. Another unit develops and manufactures personal desktop and laptop computers. Other units for software and storage products could also be included but are not shown in the figure; these units contain R&D, manufacturing, and product marketing. When accounting systems are designed appropriately, revenues and costs can be assigned both to customer units and to product units, so that they can be made profit-measurable.

A customer-product structure differs from a strategic business-unit structure because all products can go to all the markets served by the company's front end: each part of the front end can sell all of that company's products. This difference is shown in Figures 2.2 and 2.3, which depict IBM's customer-product structure and General Electric's strategic business unit (SBU) structure. The product flows illustrate the difference.

Whereas IBM's product units make products for all customer sets, GE's SBUs make products for their unique customer sets. As a

Figure 2.2. IBM's Customer-Product Structure.

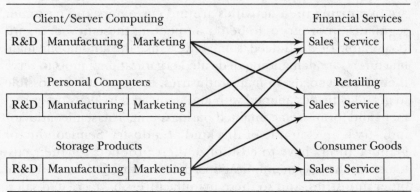

Figure 2.3. GE's SBU Structure.

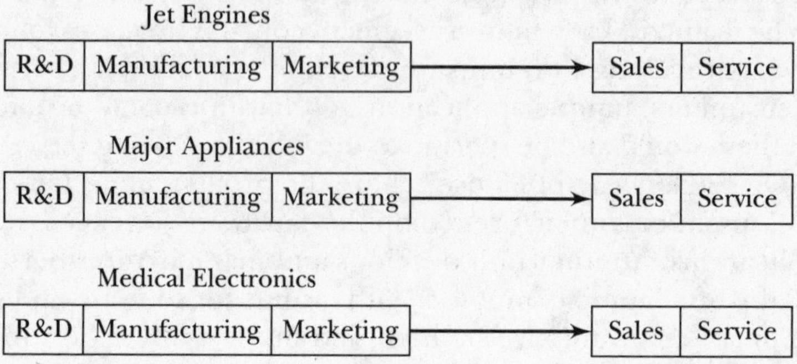

Jet Engines

| R&D | Manufacturing | Marketing |

| Sales | Service |

Major Appliances

| R&D | Manufacturing | Marketing |

| Sales | Service |

Medical Electronics

| R&D | Manufacturing | Marketing |

| Sales | Service |

result, GE's SBUs are more self-contained and autonomous. Because the product designs and product flows at IBM must be coordinated, the customer-product structure is a complicated management challenge.

Why Adopt a Customer-Product Structure?

If the customer-product structure is so complicated, why do companies adopt it? There are a number of forces pushing companies into the customer-product structure but the main force is the customer. A major effect of global competition has been a shift of power to the buyer in the buyer-seller relationship. By now, buyers have learned how to use their power and are demanding more value and more responsiveness to their needs. In return, sellers are organizing their activities around customers and customer segments, in order to do better at meeting these new demands (Galbraith, 1995). Indeed, some buyers, like the automobile manufacturers, are demanding dedicated organizational units to serve their unique needs. In many industries, however, it is impossible to get all activities aligned with and dedicated to a customer segment and form a self-contained business unit. The semiconductor industry is an example of this kind of industry. Semiconductor manufacturers have to customize their products for their customers in the telecommunications, defense, automobile, and computer industries, and so these manufacturers have created sales, service, and product-design units dedicated to their customers in these industries. A semiconductor factory now costs $1 billion, however, and so it is impossible to build a separate factory for each customer segment. Therefore, product- and process-focused factories and units are created to supply all customer segments. The product units, based on common processes, achieve scale, and the customer units achieve focus. And that is the primary objective of this structure: to achieve customer focus and responsiveness and, simultaneously, product excellence and scale.

The pressure for a market focus (and a separate customer structure) starts when customers buy—or can buy—all products. (If the products are all purchased by different customers, there is no pressure for a separate customer structure.) When customers are buying all products, there arises the question of whether each product group needs its own sales force (with each separate sales force calling on the same customer). Would it not be more economical to have one sales force selling all products to all customers? In part, the answer will depend on how customers want to do business. Some customers have different buyers purchasing different products from the same vendor, and these companies may prefer to have separate product-knowledgeable salespeople calling on separate product-knowledgeable buyers. Some products may be sold to end users within the customer's workforce, and not at all to buyers from purchasing departments. Nevertheless, more customers are preferring to pool their purchases and negotiate total single contracts with multiproduct vendors. What these customers want within the vendor organization is a single point of contact with which they can communicate and negotiate. These single interfaces are the beginning of the front-end customer structure.

More and more customers are adopting sourcing policies, as in the automobile industry—that is, they prefer to have fewer, closer, and longer-term vendor relationships. This kind of customer will choose one or two vendors for a product and dedicate its entire volume to those vendors who become its partners. In exchange, the customer may prefer (or insist) that such a vendor put a strong manager or organizational unit in place so that the customer can conduct business with that manager or unit. The activities of this manager or unit become front-end customer functions.

Some customers want to buy systems rather than products. For example, Wells Fargo Bank buys products when it orders 250 personal computers from IBM, but Wells Fargo may also want to buy a consumer banking system. A system like this will consist of many products (desktop computers, teller terminals, automatic teller machines, high-volume-transaction processors, disk-drive storage systems, and so on), all of them manufactured by different units at IBM. When it is buying a consumer banking system, Wells Fargo does not want a collection of products; it wants a system that works, and so IBM will perform the systems integration for Wells Fargo. Therefore, a vendor like IBM needs systems-integration capability, which also becomes a front-end customer function.

On occasion, with customers who currently do not buy all a vendor's products, there may be cross-selling opportunities for the vendor. By packaging (or *bundling*) products together for a single package price, the vendor may win a larger share of the customer's business. Software companies create "suites" of programs in this way for selected segments. The cross-selling and bundling usually require a single unit in the front end to create and price the package for the customer.

The preceding examples illustrate how more value-adding activities are being created that are best located in the front-end customer structure. In the past, sales was the activity that was organized around the customer; today, more customer-specific software and services are being added. For example, IBM and Digital used to have sales and after-sales equipment service in their front-end customer organizations; today they have added application software, customer education, consulting, and systems integration, and they will even run a customer's entire information technology function. PPG used to sell paint to automobile manufacturers; today, PPG sells paint, provides application software for choosing paints, and runs the entire painting operation for General Motors.

As the economies of the developed countries become service and information economies, companies will continue to add software and services as sources of growth. These services typically require customization for market segments and customers. As a result, these services are also being located in front-end customer structures.

Finally, many companies are recognizing that a customer or customer-segment structure gives them access to superior information and knowledge about customers and allows them to form closer relationships with them. If this kind of knowledge and these relationships can be converted into superior products and services, the customer-segment focus will become a competitive advantage. The total benefit to the successfully executed hybrid organization is what can be achieved through a combination of market and product structures. In short, as customers continue to demand unique products and services and to expect responsiveness, the customer-product structure should continue to increase in popularity, but continued use of this hybrid structure is contingent upon organizations' learning how to implement it effectively. Implementation of the customer-product hybrid will be one of the major challenges facing management over the next decade.

The Customer-Product Structure in Practice

For a detailed illustration of a hybrid structure, let us consider a braking-system supplier to the automotive industry. Until the late 1980s this supplier provided a relatively complete line of brake components to auto assemblers like Chrysler and Ford. The supplier manufactured disc brakes and drum brakes for front and rear wheels. It also designed and manufactured pumps and hydraulic-actuation components for power brakes. Finally, it manufactured the friction materials for the brake pads. The supplier considered the brake unit to be a multiproduct single business, a single profit center managed through the functional organization shown in Figure 2.4.

The activities that are circled in the figure are those dedicated to Chrysler. In addition to the usual sales function there is a function for liaison engineers, who rotate through that position every two to three years; liaison engineers usually have offices at Chrysler facilities. There is also project management for the design of the Chrysler minivan's brakes. People in other functions have contacts with Chrysler as well, but the functions just mentioned are the only Chrysler-dedicated ones in the old functional structure. This pattern of dedication was similar to the pattern for all this supplier's customers in the late 1980s.

When the auto industry began adopting the Toyota-style lean manufacturing system in all its dimensions (Womack, Jones, and Roos, 1990), Chrysler and Fiat began selecting one brake supplier for each of its car programs (or *platforms*). Therefore, there was

**Figure 2.4. Brake Supplier's
Single-Business Functional Organization.**

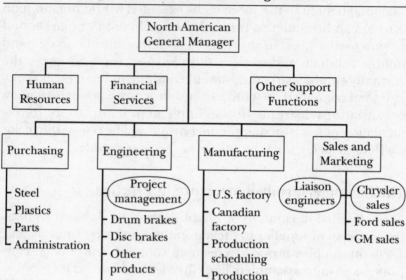

now one supplier for Chrysler's Neon, for example, and that supplier was chosen for the life of the program (eight to ten years). Chrysler also asked its individual-platform brake suppliers to do more design, and to manufacture whole braking systems, not just components. The suppliers did more systems integration and acquired competence in antilock braking systems (ABS). Fiat and Chrysler began using simultaneous engineering to reduce their product-development time, and they demanded the same of their suppliers. They also created much stronger platform managers for the Neon. These stronger managers were needed for greater cross-functional coordination on new product platforms. Once again, Fiat and Chrysler demanded the same changes from their suppliers.

Figure 2.5 shows the structure for the braking-system supplier after all these changes were made. This structure is quite different from the functional structure shown in Figure 2.4. What is shown in Figure 2.5 is a customer-product hybrid structure. Multifunction

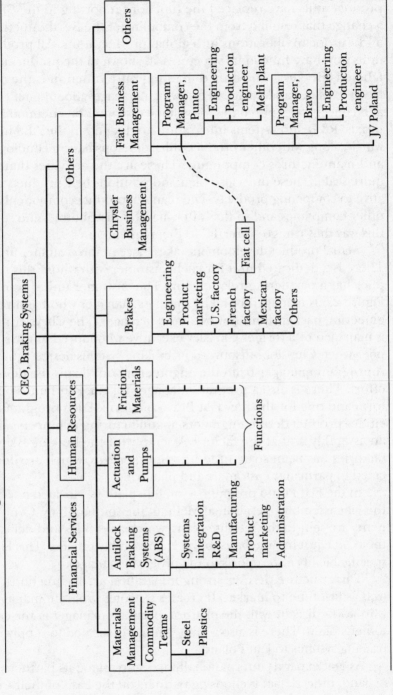

Figure 2.5. Brake Supplier's Customer-Product Structure.

product units have replaced the functions reporting to the CEO, a change that resulted from the combining of the North American and European operations into global product units. All product units now have functional structures, as shown in the product unit labeled "Brakes." The only remaining pure function is the one labeled "Materials Management," which manages the supplier base and concentrates purchases for volume discounts on common materials. R&D and systems integration are lodged in the ABS unit, which, along with other product units, develops basic technologies and manufactures components. These are the activities that require scale. These units also plan and position their products relative to competing products. They can sell product components to other companies and to the "after market" distributors, and so in this way they can go "directly" to the market.

Actual product development takes place in the customer units. There is a dedicated unit for each customer with whom this supplier has a partnering relationship. The customer unit shown in Figure 2.5 is managed by a Fiat business manager who has an engineering background, not by a sales manager. The Chrysler unit is managed by a former Chrysler executive who moved to the supplier when Chrysler outsourced its braking-systems design activity. A program manager from the engineering unit leads the design effort. There is also a program manager for the Fiat Punto platform and one for the new Fiat Bravo platform. Each program includes product-design engineers, manufacturing engineers, and an assembly unit at the factory. Assembly for the braking-system factories has been structured into lines, or *cells,* which are dedicated to particular customers and platforms.

In the Fiat Punto program, a satellite plant was located next to the Fiat assembly operation at Melfi, in the south of Italy. Components are sent to the satellite plant, which assembles and delivers them on a just-in-time basis to the Fiat assembly process. This Fiat-specific facility also reports to the program manager.

This structure permits strong integration across functions, as well as fast time to market. It creates a strong program manager who works directly with the platform program manager at the customer's plant. There is also a joint venture dedicated to supplying braking systems to Fiat Poland.

As Fiat expands internationally, it is also asking its partners to expand. Indeed, Fiat is choosing partners on the basis of their willingness and ability to support Fiat's expansion not just into Poland but also into Turkey, Argentina, Mexico, and Brazil. In Poland, the braking-system supplier was encouraged to take a local partner and form a satellite plant near the Fiat assembly factory. The satellite plant will take on more manufacturing as it improves and will supply Fiat Poland as well as Fiat's other plants in Europe. This Fiat-specific unit is also part of the Fiat business manager's organization.

Automotive suppliers using this approach can create customer-specific units that are profit-measurable. They can move many activities into customer-focused units. The customer facilitates the process by granting a partner global volume for a platform. The volume justifies the overhead that is necessary for the organizational units. The customer unit is very responsive to the unique needs of the particular customer because all activities report to a customer business manager. In the case of Fiat, this manager is the single point of contact for Fiat's top management. The manager can discuss, for example, the strategic decision to have the supplier invest in a new plant to supply Fiat South America. The Fiat platform program manager has an equivalent program manager at the supplier's site, who has all functions reporting to him.

Not all activities are placed in customer-specific units. For example, scale manufacturing of components is shared across all customers, and the R&D investment in developing the next generation of braking systems is also placed in product-specific units and shared across customers. The supplier has to continue developing new technologies and maintaining product excellence: the superiority of this supplier's product was one of the reasons why the supplier was chosen by Fiat in the first place, and if product excellence is not maintained, Fiat will be less interested in choosing this supplier for future platforms. Therefore, the supplier's customer-product structure is intended to maintain product excellence and advanced technologies in its product units while maintaining superior customer knowledge, relationships, and responsiveness in the customer units.

This extended example, which has focused on a braking-system supplier, illustrated the reasons for moving from a *single-business functional* structure to a customer-product hybrid structure. A second example, this one focusing on Hewlett-Packard, will show the change from a *multibusiness divisional* structure to a customer-product hybrid structure.

Hewlett-Packard has announced a corporate strategy called "MC^2" (measurement, computing, and communications). No other company has all these core competencies to provide solutions for customers. Hewlett-Packard is currently organized mostly around product lines, which form divisions and groups of divisions.

One of the automobile companies has given Hewlett-Packard an MC^2 project: to supply all its certified service and repair facilities worldwide with automotive electronic test equipment. This equipment is to be linked to Hewlett-Packard personal computers and printers at each facility, for diagnostic purposes, and each facility is to be linked via a private telecommunications network to the auto company's technical centers in North America and Europe. These centers will provide consulting services and data to the remote repair sites. Eventually, from their own locations, they may also perform difficult software repairs. The repair and service databases are to be accessible from the whole network. The auto company would like Hewlett-Packard eventually to take over its entire electronic testing operation.

The project is an important source of growth for Hewlett-Packard. It is also a major challenge: about twenty-five different Hewlett-Packard divisions are involved, and the customer does not want to establish twenty-five separate contacts; the customer wants Hewlett-Packard to do the integration and provide a single point of contact. To do so, Hewlett-Packard has created a customer organization unit containing sales representatives, systems integrators, information consultants, software engineers, acquirers of third-party software, managers for various partner liaisons, managers on loan from the various product divisions that are involved, and some administrative personnel. The unit is on its way to becoming a profit-measurable customer unit, and other projects are being considered for it. As other customers come to want similar solutions, the customer unit may evolve into a unit dedicated to the auto industry, and as other customer units are added, Hewlett-Packard could move to a customer-product structure like IBM's.

How Do We Make a Customer-Product Structure Work?

Whether the popularity of the customer-product structure continues or does not continue to grow will depend on whether the challenges of managing it can be mastered. In many ways the customer-product structure contains the complexities of a matrix organization. As a result, we should expect many management teams to fail at the customer-product structure, just as many management teams have failed at the matrix style of organization (Davis and Lawrence, 1977; Galbraith, 1994). But those who master the customer-product structure will gain an advantage in superior products and responsiveness to customers.

There are four major design issues to be resolved in mastering the customer-product organization:

Deciding where to locate marketing

Defining roles and responsibilities

Managing contention

Establishing front-back linkages

Marketing

The question always arises of whether to put marketing in the customer unit or in the product unit. As it turns out, marketing goes in both the front and the back. Segment or customer marketing goes in the customer front end and focuses on segmenting the customer population. It concentrates on creating packages or products, creating unique services for segments, setting prices for packages, selecting channels, and supporting the sales force. Product marketing goes in the product back end and focuses on product positioning, product pricing, new-product development, and product features. The two marketing activities also play key roles in linking front and back, as we will see shortly.

Roles and Responsibilities

The second design issue concerns the respective roles and responsibilities of the front and the back. If these roles are not clarified, there is great potential for conflict because just about any management decision can create contention over who sets prices, who does forecasts, who is responsible for the inventory, and so on. (It is usually quite helpful to use a tool like the responsibility chart; see Galbraith, 1995.) The most contentious of these issues concerns which end, front or back, will be the profit center; some management teams want to emphasize one end or the other (for example, in its recent reorganization of its commercial banking business, Citibank chose customers first, over products like foreign exchange, cash management, and so on). It is also possible to design both ends as profit centers and manage them with a matrix, as shown in Figure 2.6.

The first assumption behind the customer-product profit matrix is that an accounting system can separate revenues and costs into distinct customer and product categories, and that these revenues can then be posted in the matrix to display various products' profitability with various customers. In this matrix a sale is counted once, and both accounts are credited, so that profits are not split and arguments about percentages of split profits are avoided. Managers for market segments like the automotive segment can negotiate and plan with managers from the product lines to decide what can be sold for each product, and this negotiation constitutes the process for planning and budgeting. With a matrix displaying outcomes, management has a useful management tool for implementing the customer-product structure. The matrix yields a consistent set of targets for both sides to try to meet, and it resolves the differences between the two sides by establishing one target for which both sides are accountable.

Contention

The third of the four major design issues to be resolved in mastering a customer-product structure is the management of contention. Even if people agree on roles and responsibilities, there

Figure 2.6. Customer-Product Profit Matrix.

| Product Segments | Market Segments | | | |
	Automotive	Defense	Telecommunications	Consumer Goods
Microprocessor				
Memory				
Logic				

is still a natural level of contention, as we saw in the discussion of the customer-product profit matrix. The front end sees the world through market-oriented eyes and wants unique things for its customers; the back end sees the world through product-oriented eyes and wants scale and equal treatment of all customers. Management, as we will see, needs to create processes for using conflict to learn about customers and products and to resolve issues in a timely fashion.

Front-Back Linkages

The fourth major design issue involves management's linking the customer unit with the product unit for key work-flow processes. Orders need to enter at the front and be filled at the back; products need to be developed at the back and sold at the front. The two types of structures should not lead to two separate companies. A tight link is needed, regardless of any potential contention. The time and effort that management devotes to resolving conflicts and linking the front and the back are the major costs in implementing the customer-product model of organization.

Two Examples of a Customer-Product Structure

The combination of structures and lateral processes that will be needed for successful execution of the customer-product model is illustrated by the following two examples. The first is drawn from the area of financial services, and the second is drawn from the area of consumer products.

Example 1: Financial Services

The company in this example delivers financial services to consumers. Its structure is shown in Figure 2.7.

This company offers products in insurance, mutual funds, and savings certificates. These products are organized as multifunctional businesses (with the exception of the sales unit, which forms the product-focused back-end structure). The customer-focused front-end structure consists of multiple sales channels, segment marketing, and regional coordination units that serve to link products and

Figure 2.7. Hybrid Structure for Financial Services.

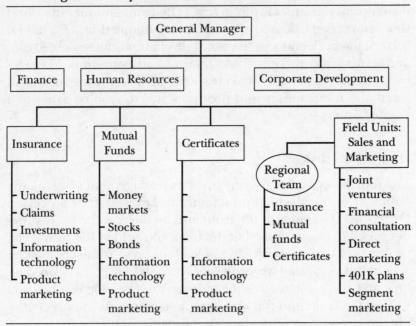

channels. The main channel is constituted by the five thousand geographically dispersed financial consultants who provide financial advice and sell investment products; additional channels are direct mail and toll-free numbers. The company recently trained financial consultants for companies offering 401k pension plans to their employees. All products are sold through all channels. The concept is to focus the business both on markets and on products. Successful execution of the front-back structure will enable the company to achieve the benefits of both a product and a market structure.

The company has created three different mechanisms for integrating the front and the back and for managing inherent contention: regional teams, a marketing council, and a career system.

Regional Teams

The regional teams (see Figure 2.8) are groups of people from the product and market segments who are co-located and are dedicated to groups of financial consultants in the field. The consultants get

Figure 2.8. Front-Back Linkage: Regional Teams.

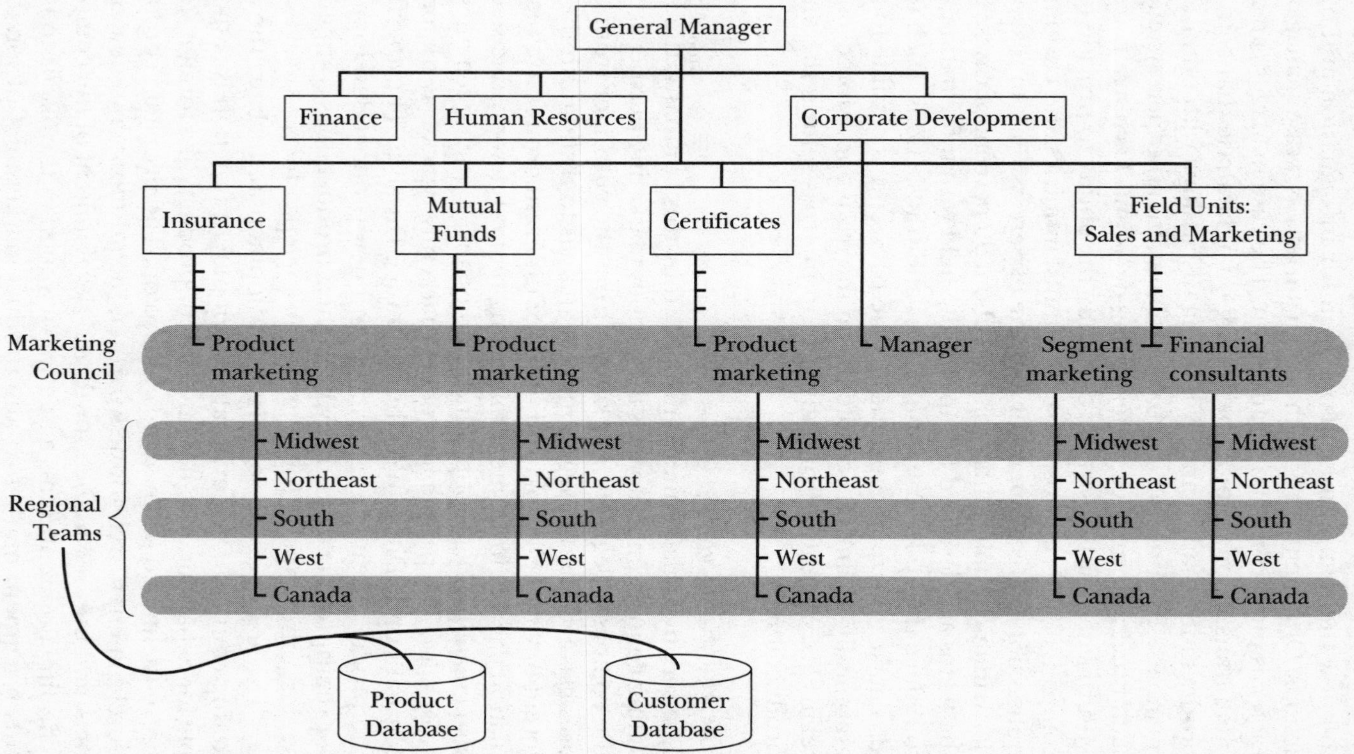

to know the teams and call on them for information and transactions. One member of each such team acts as a case manager for
each customer-consultant transaction. The case manager can complete transactions rapidly by relying on a database that contains
product information and by holding discussions with other team
members. The product database also contains an expert system for
such issues as insurance underwriting decisions. Each team, armed
with this database, gives the company the ability to provide total-
company, rapid responses to consultants' inquiries and customers'
transactions: a team member and the expert system can make underwriting commitments rapidly in about 90 percent of cases. Thus
the teams are designed to support the field with information, and
to reduce the cycle time for inquiries and transactions. Each team
also makes the total capacities of the back end accessible to geographically organized consultants on the front end. Moreover, the
teams are capable of providing help in cross-selling the entire
product line.

The Marketing Council

The second linkage mechanism used by this company, the marketing council, encompasses the various marketing perspectives in
the company. Segment marketing, from the customer front end,
uses classical market-segmentation analysis to distinguish the different buying behaviors and needs of different groups in the population. People in segment marketing request new products. They
also create packages of products and establish pricing schemes for
cross-sales. The people in product marketing typically work for the
Mutual Funds Division or the Insurance Division. They perform
the product positioning, pricing, and new-product development
for their product lines. They keep their product lines competitive
against other mutual funds and insurance products.

The leader of the corporate development unit chairs the marketing council. The corporate development function is responsible for expansion into new investment products like foreign stocks
or funds, limited partnerships, and so on. The people in corporate
development search for new partners, acquisitions, and new channels, and they see to the growth and development of the company.
This function represents a neutral viewpoint in the discussions between segment marketing and product marketing. Corporate de-

velopment searches for the best way in which the company can profit from a product, a segment, or a channel position.

The marketing council is the main forum for design and discussion of product packages, channel choices, new products, and pricing schemes. It is also the main forum for managing conflict. For example, the segment marketing people are enthusiastic about cross-selling, and the product marketing people are usually unenthusiastic about having their products be loss leaders. Some customers may not want packages of products; they may want to shop for the best products and prices regardless of the company that is offering them. Other customers may not have the time or the skill to shop for financial products, and so they rely on consultants to do it for them. How does the company reach these different customers? Should there be different product features? The company that is smartest about customers and fastest with superior products will be the winner, and so the key to this structure is to have debate, triggered by inherent contention, lead to the design and pricing of superior offerings, as well as to the company's becoming smarter about customers, products, packages of products, and channels.

Of course, the situation could degenerate and lead to hostility and politics rather than learning and innovation. Council members could bargain by withholding information instead of sharing it for problem solving. To generate learning rather than politics, this company has organized itself according to a design that supports the strategy of selling multiple products to multiple segments.

The Career System

The company's career system is crucial to its developing the necessary marketing talent. The company starts by recruiting and selecting students of finance who have marketing aptitude and can solve problems effectively in groups. Several schools have been developed as sources of new talent, and the company provides them with summer internships, study projects, and speakers for classes.

New hires begin their relationship with the company on a rotation system that starts with a product-marketing assignment. They learn about their products, and then they move on to the regional teams. On the teams, they represent their products, learn about other products, and receive exposure to the marketplace. The system is flexible, but the preferred sequence is to move the new hires next to segment marketing and have them package products for segments. The final assignment is corporate development, where the new hires get a total view of this function and learn about new-business development. From corporate development they can go anywhere in product marketing or segment marketing, or they can run one of the regional teams. Eventually they may find their way to running one of the marketing divisions or becoming general manager for a product line.

Remarks

This company's career system is an integrated set of policies, running from selection to promotion, that unfold over a period of years. By the time the marketing managers get to the marketing council, they have learned the various facets of the business. Training in group problem solving is also acquired, usually before the new hire goes on to a regional team. Because the company selects those who perform the best in groups, the people who are selected are likely to succeed on the marketing council, and they are trained, developed, and evaluated so that they do in fact succeed. The marketing council is led by the head of corporate development, who is likewise a graduate of the career system. This key leader facilitates discussion and sets the climate for openness in problem solving.

The information system is another feature of the organization's design. It makes the same data available to everyone, in keeping with a saying that has been adopted by the company: "People are entitled to their own opinions, but not to their own data." The company continues to develop extensive databases and software programs that support the regional teams and the marketing council. These databases bring information about products, product packages, customers, channels, and segments to the problem-solving process, and this link to information is the path by which conflicts are escalated for resolution by top management. Escalation helps keep top managers informed about the tough issues that require their input and policy decisions. Top managers also formulate strategy and articulate criteria for guiding the marketing council's decisions.

The organization has been evolving toward the creation of marketing-segment profit centers. Originally the product lines were the profit centers, and they are still measured on a profit-and-loss basis, but they are being joined by the marketing segments. The segments get some freedom in package pricing, but the product lines get credited with a standard price, regardless of what the segments are doing with prices. This pricing scheme eliminates some potential areas of conflict.

The reward system is designed to give people a companywide perspective rather than a parochial product- or segment-oriented view. For example, every manager receives a bonus that is based on the performance of the company as a whole, not on his or her performance with a particular product or segment.

Overall, the company has organized itself according to a design that gives it a focus on products and customers. The front-back hybrid structure, along with the regional teams and the marketing council, coordinate the product and customer segments. The career system, the information system–linked committees, and the systems for profit measurement and rewards all support the management of inherent contention. The management systems channel this contention into learning about customers and into the creation of new offerings for customers.

Example 2: Consumer Goods

The manufacturing company shown in Figure 2.9 was originally structured around product lines and categories. In the late 1980s, however, the company's customers (mass merchandisers) began to change. These mass retailers' power was increased by the volume buying and acquired intelligence that had become possible through the use of bar-code data scanned at checkout counters. Some of these retailers now demanded a single interface, along with just-in-time supply relationships. Others, however, were experiencing considerable variety in the buying habits of the ethnic groups in the regions that they served, and these retailers were moving in the opposite direction: they were doing less central buying, and they were even moving buying decisions down to the level of the individual store.

Figure 2.9. Group Structure of a Consumer-Products Company.

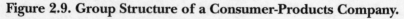

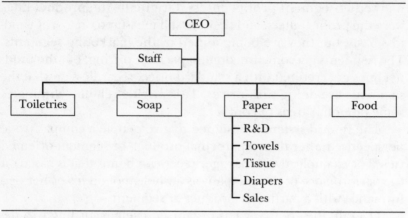

Packaged-goods manufacturers have responded differently to these forces. One company, attempting to acquire an advantage by being responsive to all types of customers, has added a dual (regional and national) front-end customer structure (see Figure 2.10). The regional and customer teams are all multifunctional and are staffed by people who come from the product groups. Customer teams are created for customers who are large enough to justify that effort and who want to coordinate their operations very closely. Some customer teams are situated at customers' headquarters. The teams consist of several functions. First there are the people from the marketing function, who work with customers' marketing departments to analyze bar-code data and use promotions to move products. Then there are the people from the sales function, who talk directly with buyers in the customers' merchandising functions. Next there are people from the distribution and information technology functions, who link producers' and retailers' logistics functions. Sometimes factory people also join a team, to discuss such issues as applying bar codes and prices in the factory rather than in the stores. The people from the financial function on both sides discuss ways to speed the turnover of inventory and accounts receivable and to minimize cash.

The entire cross-functional team works for a customer-team leader, who is a senior manager from either sales or marketing.

Figure 2.10. Front-End Structure.

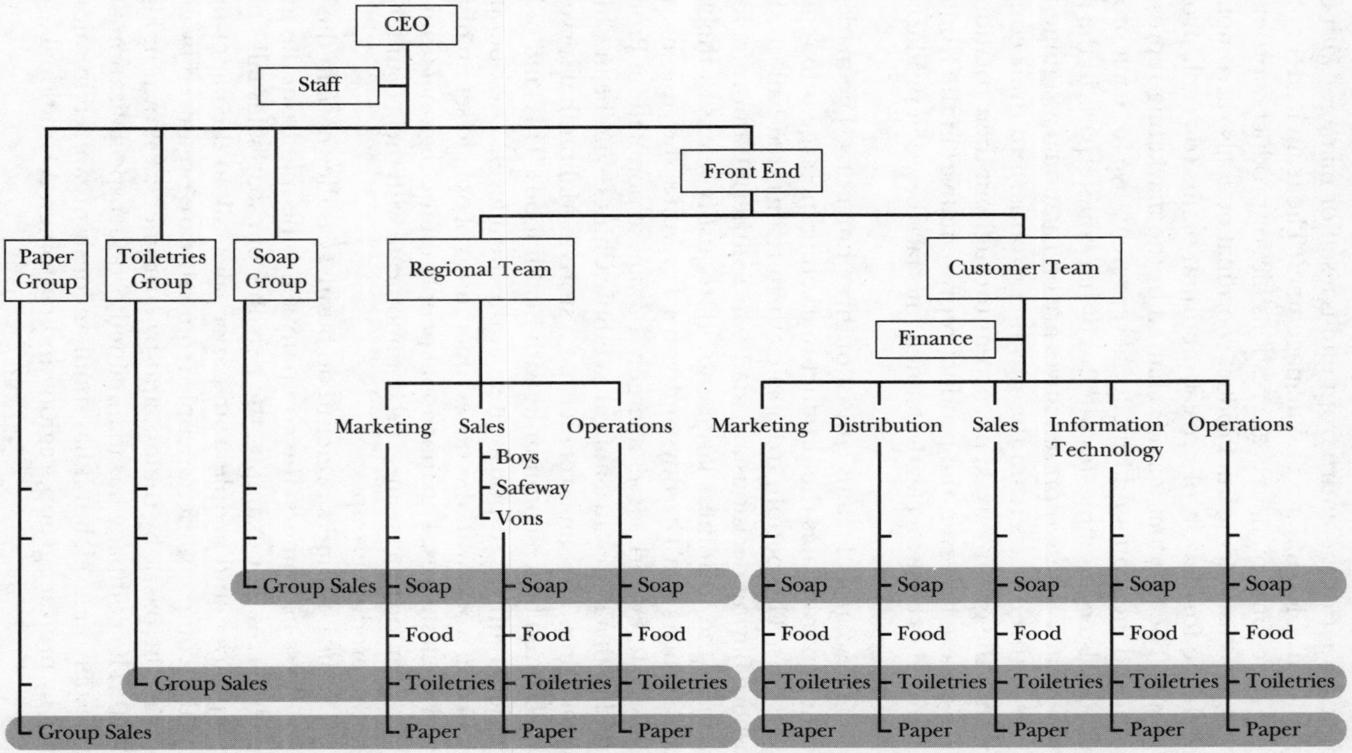

The leader of the entire front end is a senior manager with experience in sales and general management. The team leader and the top functional managers are responsible for product coordination within a customer team. Product coordination is also accomplished with the formation of cross-functional teams for each product group. The product team is chaired by the marketing representative, and the front-end functional representative for each product group also communicates with his or her counterparts in the product groups. These representatives are on rotational assignments of two to three years from the product groups, and their contacts within the groups are kept current throughout their rotations. In every case, however, the product representatives in the front end are used to create a clearly defined interface between products and customers.

The regional teams consist of three functions. The marketing function translates the product marketing message into regional versions. The people from sales form teams that call on stores where buying decisions are made. In Southern California, for example, the customers large enough to justify teams of their own are retailers like The Boys and Von's. For Von's, the store manager in Monterey Park serves a largely Taiwanese population. Products sold in that store must appeal to ethnic Chinese and be in Chinese packaging. The same retailer has a store in Malibu that serves the specialized beach community with health foods. This kind of local variety requires responsiveness at the local level. The operations function works with the stores' operations people to set up displays and stock shelves. The functional people on the regional teams can also form product teams and communicate with their counterparts in the product groups.

Some customers prefer to do business as they have in the past. For these customers, the company sends people from the group sales forces. For example, the person from soap sales talks to the soap buyer, and people from paper sales talk to the paper buyer. At this company, then, people from sales are organized by group (as in the past), by region, and by customer, as shown in Figure 2.10. The company has maintained product specialization at the salesperson level, but it has simultaneously organized its salespeople by product group, region, and customer. A rotational assignment process helps them learn to see all three sides of the issues at hand and to maintain their personal networks.

Different customers prefer different relationships, and one strength of this front-back design is that it allows the company to do business the way its customers want to do business. Another strength of this design is its clear identification of product people and product teams at the front end. These groups can communicate and coordinate both at the front end and with the back end.

This structure makes things easy for customers, but it can make things complex for producers. As always, predictable conflicts exist between customer teams and product lines, and the different interfaces with different customers make things difficult to manage and coordinate. If the company can manage the conflict and the complexity, it has achieved a competitive advantage. Competitors cannot easily copy and execute an entire customer-product organization. Therefore, to make these structures work effectively, the company must implement systems for profit accounting, systems for planning and budgeting, and front-back linkages in the form of teams, rewards, bonus systems, and human resources practices that fit the company's structure and strategy. If any of these elements are missing, internal conflicts can drain the managers' energy.

Conclusion

In industry after industry, the demands of strong customers are causing companies to create customer-focused organizational units. Not all activities can be or should be organized on the basis of customers' demands, however. Some are scale activities that are specific to products, not to customers. Increasingly, therefore, companies are adopting a customer-product hybrid structure to get both customer responsiveness and product scale. The challenge for management is to implement this hybrid design, with the biggest challenge being to manage natural conflict and create a comprehensive organizational design.

Chapter Three

Designing the Networked Organization
Leveraging Size and Competencies
Jay R. Galbraith

The networked organization is created through extensive contracting out for activities typically performed in house. The new information technology facilitates the networked organization by allowing independent firms to join together in networks, which then act as if they were a single corporation. There are compelling reasons for choosing this kind of design. Offsetting the advantages, though, are some negatives that need to be understood and managed.

What Is a Networked Organization?

The networked organization reflects an organizational design option that has considerable merit (Miles and Snow, 1986). It is the exact opposite of the vertically integrated style of organization. The networked organization, instead of owning all the activities (from obtaining raw materials to contacts with consumers) that make up a business, contracts for many of these activities (Nohria and Eccles, 1992). As a result, a network of independent companies, each one doing what it does best, acts as if it were virtually a single corporation.

The networked organization (or the virtual corporation, as some call it) is a reflection of the trend toward contracting. The old model was for a company to own and control all the activities that created value for its customers. The trend toward contracting began with the subcontracting of peripheral activities (such as the management of the company cafeteria) in order to reduce costs. Cost reduction continues to be a motivating factor, but today's company recognizes that it is not and cannot be the best at all activities—and yet a company in today's highly competitive environment does have to be the best at everything. Therefore, the company does what it actually does best, and it seeks to buy or partner with other companies that are doing what they do best, in order to get the best total offering for its customers. Some companies are also realizing that they cannot afford to be the best at all activities, and these companies are reserving their investments in research and development and equipment for those activities that are necessary for the company's competitive advantage.

Another argument for the networked organization is the issue of organizational size. Some suggest that in today's economy—characterized by variety, change and speed—large size is no longer an advantage and is probably even a disadvantage, and that the future belongs to the small entrepreneurial niche firm. Indeed, there are more and more situations in which small is beautiful. But there is also the example of the automobile industry, where small niche firms like Jaguar, Saab, and Mazda are being taken over by larger firms that have more scale and deeper pockets. The networked organization provides the ultimate answer to the size issue. The networked organization can be large when it is an advantage to be large, and it can be small when it is an advantage to be small. For example, it is an advantage for an organization to be large when it is buying: volume discounts and better terms can be secured. Therefore, the network of independent companies comprising the networked organization can pool purchases, with one company (usually the lead company) buying for all the others.

Benetton, the Italian fashion house, follows this approach: it contracts most of its manufacturing out to some 350 small firms, but Benetton buys the materials for all these small firms. Benetton has now become the world's largest purchaser of wool thread, and it exercises considerable leverage in that market. As a networked organization, it is able to gain scale without mass. At the same time, being small and independent is a good thing when fast-moving, flexible responses are needed, and so the labor-intensive operations of sewing and packing are performed for Benetton by firms of fifteen to twenty-five employees. Collectively, these small companies can handle the variety and flexibility that are needed in rapidly supplying fashion merchandise to a fickle market.

Flexible sourcing is another factor that argues for the use of networks of independent firms. In the past decade, for example, five different printing technologies and four different storage technologies have been in use on personal computers. For example, Compaq, by contracting out for components, has avoided building separate factories for dot-matrix printers and floppy disk drives. If flash memories replace hard disk drives, Compaq can quickly shift to the new storage devices by establishing a new contracted source. In fast-moving and fast-changing industries, the networked organizational form is an advantage.

The networked organization, as already mentioned, is made possible largely by the new information technology. To return to the example of Benetton, that company has designed an international telecommunications network that ties together all its franchise store owners and all its subcontracted factories. These 7,000 franchisees and 350 factory owners interact via an extensive worldwide network that any Fortune 500 company would be proud to own. Instead of being held together by their ownership of all their activities, networked organizations are held together by telecommunications and intelligence.

The networked form of organization, like any organizational form, has its downside. Its biggest disadvantage is the possible loss of proprietary knowledge. In order for a company to work with other companies, information has to be exchanged. If important information is transmitted and used by others, the company may create new competitors. For example, Apple taught independent software vendors about its Macintosh operating system so that they could write application programs that would run on the Mac. One of those vendors was Microsoft, and Microsoft did indeed write programs for the Mac, but it also incorporated what it had learned about the Mac into its own Windows operating system. After Microsoft Windows 3.0 appeared, Apple lost much of its competitive advantage. To take another example, Schwinn contracted its manufacturing out to a Taiwanese firm. After learning the U.S. bicycle business, the Taiwanese subcontractor sidestepped Schwinn and went directly to mass merchandisers like Wal-Mart. Schwinn is now emerging from Chapter 11 reorganization.

Another possible negative is loss of control over parts of the business. For example, if a disagreement arises between Benetton and one of its network partners, the Benetton manager cannot fire anyone in the other firm; one firm cannot force another to do anything, and so the issues must be negotiated, which means that disagreements can lead to endless discussion. As we will see, however, a company can minimize these negatives by becoming skillful at the partnering process.

Designing the Organization

The design of any organization should follow from the organization's strategy; in the case of the networked organization, the partnering strategy should lead the design. In the following discussion of organizational design, the element that will be discussed in greatest detail is the element of external relationships. This issue is the one that can make or break the designing of a networked organization.

Strategy

The strategy of primary interest is the partnering strategy. The partnering strategy is what has an impact on lateral relationships between and among the companies in the network. This strategy delineates the company's role in the network, and it determines which activities each company performs. In turn, the organizational design should influence how the contracted activities are coordinated.

Company Role

A company can play different roles in a network. These roles may vary from the role of a specialist to the role of a network integrator for the entire business. A specialist performs one or a few activities and provides the relevant service or services to everyone. A network integrator coordinates the activities performed by many firms, including itself, in order to create value for the ultimate customer.

The specialist focuses on a few activities and attempts to become the best in the world at these few activities. For example, SCI manufactures printed circuit boards. It manufactures more boards and invests more in process research and development than anyone else does. SCI then sells its services to network integrators in all industries, and in all countries. Why would any other company want to manufacture printed circuit boards when they can be bought from SCI? Federal Express does the same thing where distribution is concerned, and Automatic Data Processing (ADP) does likewise with payroll processing. Each company is an expert and is usually the lowest-cost provider in its specialty, gaining enormous scale by working for everyone.

The network integrator is a firm that coordinates the decisions and actions of the companies that make up the network. This firm takes the lead and manages the network as if it were a vertically integrated company. It formulates the strategy for the network, chooses member firms, and links them by way of a telecommunications system. For example, Nike, like Benetton, coordinates the work performed by independent factories (for Nike, these are in Asia) and by the retailers in all the markets that Nike serves. A firm can choose to perform the entire integrating task, as Nike, Benetton, and Compaq do, or it may integrate portions of these activities. If it integrates a portion of the total business, it may choose to link up with peer firms, integrating complementary portions. Thus a company's partnering strategy starts with its choice of the roles that it will play in the networked organization.

What's In and What's Out

A company playing some type of integrating role has a choice of which activities it will perform, own, and control and which ones it will contract out. A company typically chooses to perform the following activities:

- Those that its customers find important
- Those for which there are few outside suppliers
- Those that involve scale
- Those that are central to a product's performance
- Those that integrate the members of the network
- Those that influence a brand
- Those that give the company an opportunity to have a competitive advantage

Commodities and inputs that can be obtained from plentiful and/or superior suppliers are contracted out.

A difficult choice for a network integrator occurs when an activity is important in the eyes of a customer but outside suppliers are superior. The company can then make an investment to improve its own capability or it can form a close relationship with an outside supplier in order to manage its dependence and perhaps learn some of the skills it needs. (The choice of forming a relationship to manage its dependence will be described shortly.)

Boeing is an example of a network integrator. For its aircraft, over the years, Boeing has managed the systems-integration function, the difficult work of customer relationships, the manufacture of the cockpit (where all systems converge), and as much of the wing-manufacturing function as it can retain. The rest of the work is subcontracted out to specialists and low-cost assemblers around the world (a procedure that helps to sell airplanes to airlines owned by governments). In this way, Boeing has positioned itself strategically to integrate its business in every aspect, from raw materials to customer relationships, while performing about 20 percent of the actual work.

External Relationships

Once a company has chosen its role in the network and decided which activities to perform and which to contract out, it needs to design processes for coordinating the activities that are performed by others. Communication and joint decision processes are needed to manage the interdependence between the companies in the network. These external relationships have many similarities to the relationships involved in the lateral processes that take place between organizational units inside the firm. As in these internal lateral processes, the type and amount of coordination varies from very little to a great deal, and again as in the internal relationships, the task of the organizational designer is to match type and amount of coordination with the appropriate types and numbers of external lateral relationships.

The design choice can be represented by a strength continuum of types of external relationships (Contractor and Lorange, 1988). These take various forms: a marketing relationship between buyer and seller, a contracting relationship between parties, arrangements for sourcing and alliances, equity-based relationships, and outright ownership, for example. The continuum is shown in Figure 3.1, which links relationships with the amount of coordination required and with the amount of dependence on the outside firm. Relationships nearer to the top of the list are the cheapest and easiest ones to use. As the designer proceeds down the list, relationships become more complex and require more managerial time and effort. The designer should proceed down the list to the point where the amount of coordination required by the partnering strategy is reached.

Marketing Relationships

Markets, like contracts, are standard mechanisms for mediating economic transactions. Figure 3.1 shows that relationships mediated by markets require little coordination and communication between parties; indeed, the purchase of commodities from spot markets takes place without buyer and seller even knowing each other's identity. Markets are used to obtain products and services that are standard and freely available.

Contracting Relationships

In the somewhat more involved relationship of a contract, buyer and seller periodically communicate and negotiate terms, with little subsequent contact unless exceptions arise. Contracts are needed when

Figure 3.1. External Relationships and Coordination Requirements.

Relationships	Relative Strength	Coordination	Dependence
	Weak		
Market		None	Zero
Contract		Occasional/Some	Minimum
Sourcing/Alliance		Substantial	Moderate
Equity		Great Deal	High
Ownership		Great Deal	Critical
	Strong		

the items being acquired are not standard and are not always available. Some items may need to be customized. Others may be standard, like dynamic random-access memory (DRAM) chips for personal computers, but subject to shortages. A contract guarantees the source of supply for the length of the contract and specifies the customization.

Arrangements for Sourcing and Alliances

Sourcing involves contracts but also fewer, closer, longer-term relationships between buyers and sellers. Usually the parties exchange long-term plans and participate jointly in developing products and services. The automobile companies are becoming more like network integrators and are forming sourcing relationships with suppliers. For example, Ford chooses TRW to supply all its passenger-restraint and passenger-safety equipment (seat belts, airbags, and so on). TRW, in order to be chosen, had to share its technology and development. Ford in turn had to share its plans for automobile development with TRW so that TRW could design the safety features, and TRW had to invest in special equipment in order to make these unique products.

This kind of sourcing relationship is characterized by several features. One of these features is substantial customizing by the supplier, to the customer's unique advantage. In return, the customer makes the customizer a preferred supplier, an arrangement that reduces the supplier's risk and grants the volume to pay for the extra effort. Sourcing relationships, as we saw in the example of Ford and TRW, also involve a great deal of communication about future plans and coordination in developing unique products, usually through a formal product-development team with members representing both parties. As in internal product-development processes, these efforts have a leader (usually a product manager from the vendor's company), and the partners from both companies share the same computer-aided design system and design information. After the product is designed, ordering and supplying are also handled electronically.

Although there is no standard terminology, similar relationships between competitors (as opposed to relationships between suppliers and customers) are referred to as *alliances* (or, in the aerospace industry, as *teaming*). As in a sourcing relationship, the parties to an alliance also exchange information and commitments and then jointly perform an activity and share the outcome. For example, IBM and Siemens formed an alliance for jointly developing the process technology for manufacturing 16-megabit DRAM chips. Each company then produced and marketed the product independently. Motorola and Toshiba formed an alliance to exchange technologies. Toshiba provided manufacturing-process technology for DRAM chips, and Motorola provided microprocessor technology. The technologies were then transferred during the joint development of products that used these technologies. Each case involved a team or teams staffed by both partners. A project manager coordinated the joint effort and managed the relationship.

Equity Relationships

Relationships that involve the transfer of equity are of three main types. In one type, the network integrator becomes a minority shareholder in a supplier. For example, Ford invested in Cummins Engine for a 20 percent stake and in Mazda for a 25 percent stake. In a second type, each member takes a small stake in the others. For example, Swiss Air, Delta Airlines, and Singapore Airlines each bought 5 percent of one another in order to seal their alliance for coordinating schedules and sharing facilities. Such cross-share holdings, by contrast with an investment by a dominant member, are used in alliances among equals. A third kind of equity relationship is the joint venture. In this type of relationship, a separate company is created with equity of its own, and the equity is usually split more or less equally among the parties.

Equity relationships are like alliances, and there may be as much need for coordination and communication as in an alliance, but there is more control for both parties. One or both partners to an equity relationship may also be more dependent and more vulnerable, and so the exchange of equity symbolizes both a greater commitment and a longer-term commitment. The equity relationship is usually more difficult to dissolve than an alliance, which may even have a termination date.

Often equity relationships are used when dependence cannot be covered by normal contractual terms and conditions. For example, advantages that endure, are critical, or cannot easily be copied usually need more protection, and in certain cases one of the partners may have an enormous incentive to use proprietary information. In circumstances like these an equity exchange, which is intended to be a long-term bond of trust, aligns the partners' interests and gives them more control over their relationship.

Outright Ownership

The ultimate form of control is 100 percent ownership of an activity. If one partner's vulnerability is too great, or if the opportunity for profit is too great to share, one partner may need to own the other. The application software unit of Apple is a good example of this situation. When the Macintosh operating system first appeared, little application software was available for it, and so Apple started its own software unit. Developers outside Apple then became interested in creating software for the Macintosh platform, but they were reluctant to share information with Apple because Apple's in-house unit was a competitor.

Therefore, Apple decided to make its software unit, called Claris, into a separate company but to maintain a minority interest in it. Just before the initial public stock offering, however, Apple pulled Claris back into the company: Microsoft had introduced its Windows operating system, and Claris was the company that had the most experience in writing programs for Windows-type operating systems. Because there were ten times as many computers capable of running Windows as there were Macintosh personal computers, Claris's incentive as a publicly owned company would have been to write primarily for the Windows platform and secondarily for the Macintosh platform. As a wholly owned unit of Apple, however, Claris could support the Macintosh platform first. Apple needed full control of Claris in order to align its own interests with those of Claris.

External Relationships: Summary

Two factors, coordination and vulnerability, drive companies to choose more complex forms of relationships. Alliances and sourcing relationships are adopted to achieve the coordination needed for executing customization and joint development; markets and simple contracts are insufficient by themselves. But working jointly with other companies increases a firm's vulnerability, whereas equity exchanges reduce vulnerability and increase the firm's commitment and control. The combination of greater coordination and lower vulnerability drives organizational designers to choose the more complex relationships.

It is important to match the type of relationship with the amount of coordination and protection that will be needed. If a contract will provide the communication and protection necessary in a transaction, an alliance should not be used because it takes more time and effort and is more expensive than a contract. A company can err, however, by creating too weak a relationship. Recall Schwinn's vulnerability when its Taiwanese alliance partner learned the bicycle business and technology and bypassed Schwinn in the distribution channel. If the effort had been a joint venture in which Schwinn had majority ownership, Schwinn might have had enough control to prevent the competition. Thus a company can err either with too much effort and cost or with too little protection and communication.

Companies need, over time, to learn how to match types of relationships with the necessary degrees of coordination and protection. Often relationships start out on a very simple basis, with a contract between the parties. Then, building on success, the partners to the contract form an alliance that leads to a joint venture. In other situations, no amount of control is sufficient to overcome a misalignment of goals and intentions, and there can be no partnership. Ultimately, relationships in alliances and joint ventures depend on a minimum amount of trust. But, as Killing (1994, p. 131) points out, "You do not start with trust. Trust is built through shared experiences over time."

Partner Selection

The choice of partners is crucial in any networked organization. Vulnerability is best managed through the selection of partners whose goals and intentions are compatible with a company's own goals and intentions. Firms that are skilled at forming alliances and equity ventures evaluate their potential partners continuously and thoroughly.

The first priority in selecting a partner is to understand the potential partner's strategic intentions. The partner's intention may be to develop a relationship in which the first company becomes its supplier, but the partner's intention may also be to use the partnership for the purpose of learning the supplier's technology. The partner could then gain the ability to supply its own needs internally, or it could use its internal capability to negotiate lower prices from the supplier (having stripped the supplier of its technical edge). Knowing these intentions in advance is the key to partner selection. Then there are the other factors, such as compatibility of goals, values, styles, time horizons, and so on.

Corning, for example, is skilled at continuously uncovering potential partners and assigning research on them to its officers. Top managers investigate a partner candidate by having a consulting firm analyze the candidate company and its history. Corning has found that adversity can reveal more about a company's values, and so the company investigates what the candidate partner has done during a plant closure, a hazardous-waste spill, and similar events. Corning's managers get to know the partner candidate's managers. Corning invites them to speak at meetings and attend Corning's annual officers' meeting with their spouses. A small joint project may come next. Each test is a screening operation. If a candidate passes all the tests, then Corning may try an alliance. If the first alliance is successful, Corning may try another, larger alliance, moving toward an equity relationship and, eventually, a joint venture. The selection process requires much time and effort, and this degree of effort is characteristic of successful partnering. The process brings to mind the saying "Pay me now, or pay me later": issues that are not discovered during courtship will arise later on, when they will be more difficult to resolve and when the partnership will be more difficult to dissolve.

The evaluation of partner candidates is getting easier, however. More and more companies now have partnering histories that can be examined. Indeed, in the future, being seen as an attractive partner will be a requirement for competitiveness, and the desire for a good reputation as a partner can actually control certain temptations to behave opportunistically in alliances.

Partnership Structures

Alliances, sourcing relationships, and joint ventures, unlike purchases and contracts, are partnerships that need to be structured. The alliance, relationship, or venture itself is probably a functional structure focused on developing and supplying a product, a service, or a technology. Representatives of both partner companies form a board to supervise the joint activity, as shown in Figure 3.2, which depicts a basic model for structuring an alliance, sourcing relationship, or joint venture.

Within this general model there are three more specific possibilities for structuring partnerships like these (Killing, 1983). In the *operator* model, one partner takes on managerial responsibility for the joint activity. In the *shared-responsibility* model, responsibility is divided between the two partners. In the *autonomous* model, as its name implies, the joint activity can be autonomously conducted by the joint venture.

The Operator Model

The operator model (see Figure 3.3) is used in sourcing arrangements and sometimes in alliances and joint ventures. One company serves as the operator and manages product development. The other company may contribute participants to work on the product and managers to serve on the joint board, but the alliance manager and the key functional managers are from the operator company. In the General Motors/Toyota joint venture, for example, Toyota was the operator. Toyota wanted to learn how to manage in the United States and how to partner with the United Auto Workers. General Motors wanted to learn Toyota's production sys-

Figure 3.2. Basic Model for Structuring a Partnership, Sourcing Relationship, or Joint Venture.

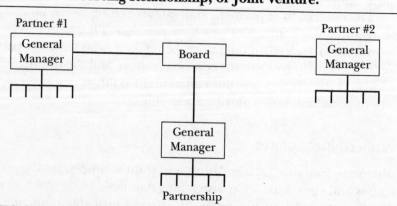

Figure 3.3. The Operator Model for Structuring a Partnership.

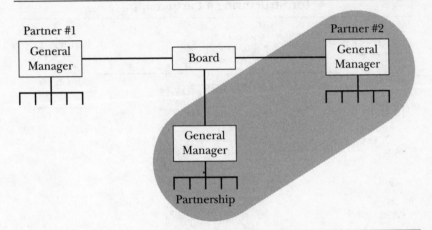

tem. Both objectives were served by having Toyota manage the joint venture, even though ownership of the joint venture was shared equally. In the operator model, the joint board acts much as a normal board of directors does—reviewing work, approving investments, agreeing to the selection of key people, and so forth. The shading in Figure 3.3. illustrates the decision-making orientation in this model.

In general, the operator model has been more successful than the shared-responsibility model. The operator model makes one company responsible and minimizes conflicts. It leads to faster decisions. It is preferred when one partner has the ability to manage the joint effort. It also works best when the operator role can be alternated between the partners.

The Shared-Responsibility Model

The shared-responsibility model (see Figure 3.4) is used in many alliances and joint ventures. It is preferred when each partner brings a complementary skill. For example, when Ford and Mazda form an alliance to make a new car, they share the responsibility. Mazda has the skills in product development, engineering design, and manufacturing to create small cars, whereas Ford has competency in styling, purchasing, finance, and marketing. The two companies

Figure 3.4. The Shared-Responsibility Model
for Structuring a Partnership.

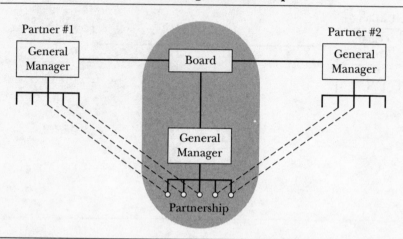

divide the work on the basis of their skills, and they share the over-all responsibility for management. In this model, the focal point of decision making can shift, as illustrated by the dots in the shaded area of Figure 3.4.

The shared-responsibility model is characterized by a small and active board. Usually the board consists of four or five (but no more than seven) people. It is staffed with two managers from each of the partner companies and the general manager of the partnership. This general manager is a member of one of the part-ner companies, and a manager from the other partner chairs the board.

The difficulty with the shared-responsibility model lies in the potential for conflict or indecision between the partners. Indeci-sion is likely if managers in the partner organizations interfere in-stead of using the joint board as the focal point for decisions. Issues and conflicts are best handled within the venture, not between the partners. If the partners are skilled at alliances and joint ventures, and if the board is active, the partnership can capitalize on the partners' complementary skills.

The Autonomous Model

The autonomous model is shown in Figure 3.5. In this model, decisions are placed within the venture itself, which becomes independent of its parent organizations. Usually this model is adopted by joint ventures. Often a venture begins by using the operator or shared-responsibility model and then moves toward the autonomous model. As the venture becomes successful and grows its own talent, it becomes less dependent on its parents. Its board becomes a normal board, and major decisions continue to be made within the venture, which can then react more quickly to changing business situations.

Supportive Policies

The design of the networked organization is completed by the creation of supportive policies in the selection and development of people and in the distribution of rewards. Both these aspects of the organization's activities should be designed to create behaviors, values, and norms that support the partnering process.

**Figure 3.5. The Autonomous Model
for Structuring a Partnership.**

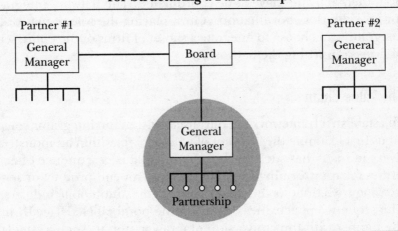

Many of the same skills that facilitate lateral internal processes also facilitate processes between companies. Particularly key are the ability to influence without authority and the ability to work with people from different cultures. In the course of their development, people often can move from participating in internal processes to participating in external ones.

Another "people" issue is the selection and development of those who can deal with the dilemma of partnering: namely, that people need to reveal information and cooperate with the organization's partners, but that they should not reveal certain critical pieces of information. On the one hand, this issue involves selecting people who can comfortably walk that fine line. On the other, it involves training employees to understand what aspects of the company's strategy and core competencies should not be revealed.

The reward system must also be designed to encourage employees to look for win-win outcomes. For example, managers at Corning can all relate a story of the boss who reprimanded them for not looking for benefits for their partners. Partnering has to be good for both parties, and companies that partner effectively promote the seeing of situations through their partners' eyes.

Leading and Integrating a Networked Organization

For independent companies to act as if they were a single corporation, their activities have to be coordinated. The network integrator provides this coordination. A firm playing the role of network integrator can choose to integrate a subset of firms or the entire set of firms comprising the network.

The Value Chain

To establish a framework for our discussion of the integrator role, let us first examine the concept of a *value chain* within an industry. Every industry has such a value chain—that is, a sequence of activities for transforming raw materials into an end product or service. Figure 3.6 shows the value chain for the automobile industry. The sequence of activities begins (at the point labeled Tier III in the figure) with the conversion of a raw material (such as steel) into parts (for example, brake drums). The parts (at the point

Figure 3.6. Value Chain for the Automobile Industry.

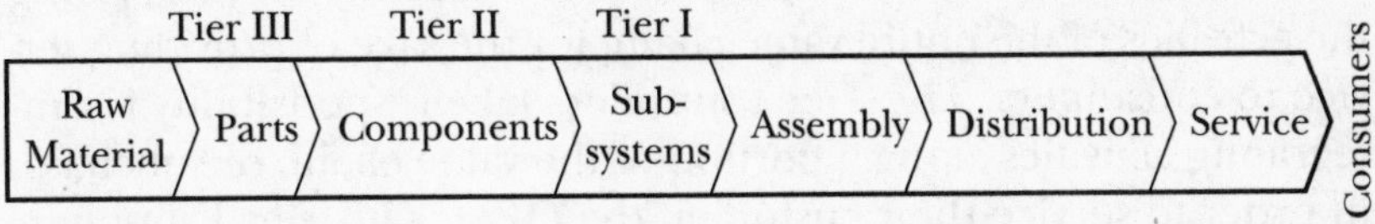

	Tier III		Tier II		Tier I				
Raw Material	Parts	Components	Sub-systems	Assembly	Distribution	Service	Consumers

labeled Tier II) are converted into components (for example, front-wheel brakes), and (at the point labeled Tier I) the components are converted into subsystems (for example, antilock braking systems). The assembly process creates automobiles, which are distributed to dealers. After-sales service completes the process when the automobiles have been purchased by consumers.

In the networked organization, different companies perform activities along an industry's value chain. The network integrator coordinates these activities and the flow of work across the value chain for the particular industry (Gerlach, 1992). The integrator usually chooses the firms that will constitute the virtual corporation and assumes responsibility for the network's maintenance.

Historically, original equipment manufacturers (OEMs) like Ford and General Motors vertically integrated and owned all the activities along the chain except for the activities of the dealers who distributed and serviced the end products. Henry Ford even integrated backwards, to the point of running his own steel mills at the River Rouge complex outside Detroit. Today, OEMs are vertically *dis*integrating. For example, Chrysler adds only about 30 percent of the total value to the cars it makes, and it subcontracts for the remaining 70 percent (Dyer, 1996). Nevertheless, Chrysler does take on the task of integrating its supply network along the chain from raw materials to consumers. It contracts out whole subsystems when it can. Tier I suppliers integrate the activities along the value chain, from raw materials to delivery to the OEM. For example, Chrysler would like to have Tier I suppliers handle the entire braking subsystem (including front-wheel brakes, rear-wheel brakes, power hydraulics, and antilock braking systems). These Tier I suppliers are integrators for the activities along their portion of the value chain, which runs from raw materials to delivery to the OEM. These suppliers might even have joint responsibility for the warranty system as it involves brakes, and they might participate in supplying after-sales service. Thus Chrysler assumes responsibility for integrating the activities of the entire value chain, for the sake of providing service to consumers. The Tier I suppliers take responsibility for integrating activities along a portion of the value chain, or subchain, in order to service their customer, the OEM. The Tier I suppliers and the OEM both play the role of integrator for the activities along their respective portions of the value chain. There are also Tier II and Tier III suppliers who could integrate activities in the subsection of the chain that runs from raw materials to the Tier I supplier.

Performing the Integrator Role

Companies choose to play the integrator role because there are benefits to integrating vertically along the value chain. When work flows are coordinated, all firms along the value chain can minimize their inventories and speed product flow. When information and forecasts are shared, suppliers can plan and coordinate capacity investments. With joint development of products and services, the firms can increase speed to market. By working together, they can reduce duplication and total network costs. These are the benefits of vertical integration.

The integrator role usually allows a firm to earn superior returns—but the role itself must be earned, and often the leader's position changes along with changes in the structure of its particular industry. The integrator must have the skills and ability to lead the other firms, and its leadership must result in significant rewards for all the firms along the chain. Otherwise, those firms will not accept the integrator's leadership.

Negotiating Leverage

The networked organization is held together by constant negotiation. At Boeing, every new airplane represents an opportunity to renegotiate the relationships that make up the network. At Chrysler, every new-car platform likewise represents an opportunity to renegotiate, just as every new style of shoe does at Nike. The firm that plays the integrator role, besides being a good negotiator and knowing how to make deals, must have a power base from which to negotiate.

Very often the integrator uses its size for leverage in dealing with other members of the network. For example, Chrysler is the largest entity in its network, and it uses its buying power to its own and its network's advantage. Chrysler may influence one supplier to specialize in front-wheel brakes, another to specialize in rear-wheel brakes, and both to reduce redundant research and development, as well as other expenses. The network thereby lowers its total costs, and Chrysler awards its volume to those who comply with its suggestions.

The integrator may also create a power base by keeping its options open when it is dealing with many suppliers and customers. Recall that Nike spreads its manufacturing among factories in Korea, Taiwan, China, and Indonesia, and that Benetton uses 350 small manufacturers and sells through 100 agents and 6,000 stores. The suppliers need Nike and Benetton more than these integrators need the suppliers. The integrator also needs credibility, however, and its suppliers' trust, as we shall see later. The integrator is better off not having to use its leverage: the benefit of leverage, like that of veto power, lies in the threat that it represents, not in its use.

Leverage can also be gained through proprietary technology. For example, Apple acts as a network integrator, using its size and its proprietary technology to gain leverage. It integrates the work of the twelve thousand small developers who write software that runs on the Macintosh platform. These developers depend on Apple to use its size in getting shelf space for them in retail outlets and in making sales calls on large buyers. But Microsoft also writes software for the Macintosh, and Apple also uses Sony and Canon as suppliers. In each case, Apple uses its superior design technology to maintain its suppliers' dependence and get negotiating leverage. Apple designs its own disks and printers, and it leads Sony and Canon, who are willing to learn from Apple. Apple protects itself with nondisclosure agreements, noncompete clauses, and rapid movement to new technologies when the agreements expire.

Knowledge and Information

To integrate all the activities in a network, the integrator must have knowledge of and information about all the activities in its industry's value chain. The integrator uses this knowledge and information for several purposes: to formulate strategies for the networked organization as a whole; to conceive of winning products and services; and to coordinate work flows, costs, and prices within the network. The integrator must have the ability to help the firms comprising the network achieve superior collective performance by comparison with the firms comprising other networks, with collections of independents, and with vertically integrated single companies.

New technology offers many opportunities for integrating the activities along the value chain through the creation of information. The network integrator needs to know where to find opportunities for reducing costs and creating value anywhere along the chain. Benetton, for example, has created an information system that records bar-code data from sales in all its franchises and coordinates work flows to keep all the stores supplied. All the subcontractor factories in Benetton's network have computers wired into the system, so that work-flow information for all Benetton's products comes into the factories from all the stores. With this information system, Benetton has total visibility into its work flow, from the processing of raw materials to the ultimate contact with consumers. Benetton also has ten stores of its own in key trend-setting markets, as well as two of its own factories. Through these facilities, Benetton can understand cost structures and margins at each stage of the value chain. Thus Benetton stays informed enough to negotiate with the members of its network, coordinate work flows for customers' benefit, and spot trends for new products. Because Benetton also manages the working capital for its network, the network's costs are lower, and its cash flows are faster than its competitors'.

Another way to capture information and profit from it is to embed intelligence in the products offered for sale—for example, by placing microprocessors and value-added software into them. Thus an elevator manufacturer can sell service contracts, elevators can be monitored continuously from remote sites, and repairs can be made to the elevators' software without the need for on-site monitoring: when sensors detect a breakdown, repair crews can be dispatched. In this way, the elevator manufacturer can control the reliability and servicing of its product and coordinate a network of repair businesses. The same kind of service can be provided for any piece of capital equipment or any durable good that requires after-sales service.

Access to data on a product's performance allows the manufacturer to integrate direct information from customers into the network, and this information in turn allows for the manufacture of a better product and for the design of self-correcting features into frequently failing components. Similarly, toll-free numbers that bring inquiries and information from customers give manufacturers information that is usually reserved for the stages of service and repair, which come later in the value chain.

The best location for the integrator of the activities along a value chain is at that point on the chain where scale is highest and access to information is most easily obtained. This location varies by industry, and even within an industry it can change over time. To take one example, the value chain for mass-marketed fiction is shown in Figure 3.7. By contrast with other areas of book publishing, in which the raw material is manuscripts (and even the ideas that eventually find form in manuscripts), the raw material of mass-marketed fiction is authors, who are analogous to brand names. The authors may be represented by agents who establish contracts with book publishers. The publishers, after editing the authors' manuscripts, pass them on to the typesetters, printers, and binders who produce the bound books that are distributed to and sold in bookstores. In the past the activities along this value chain were integrated by book publishers. They searched for book ideas that they believed would have a market, and they knew how to match

Figure 3.7. The Value Chain for Mass-Marketed Fiction.

| Authors | Agents | Publishers | Typesetters, Printers and Binders | Bookstores | Consumers |

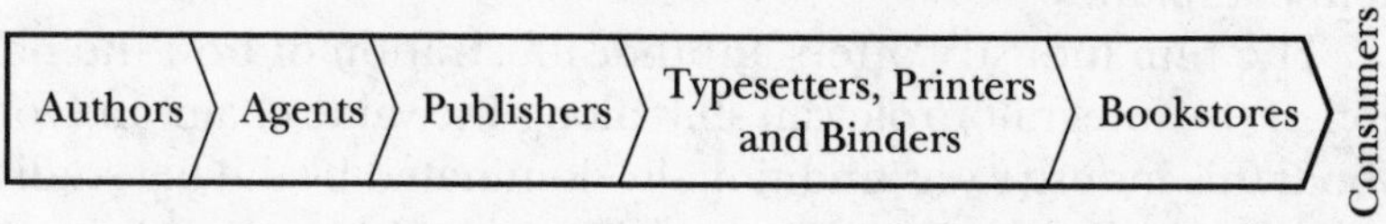

those ideas with authors, and how to match authors with the interests and tastes of the market. The publishers took the risks. They managed the promotion, and they were usually the largest entity in the value chain (with the possible exception of the printers).

Today, as small bookstores continue to be replaced by superstores, leverage has shifted to these larger stores, without which publishers cannot have blockbusters. Waldenbooks has responded to this trend by trying to integrate the activities along the value chain. With its presence in so many markets, its bar-code data, and its direct access to customers, Waldenbooks thinks it is better positioned than most book publishers are to match authors with markets. Waldenbooks can go directly to best-selling authors like Danielle Steel and Sidney Sheldon and strike deals that give Waldenbooks a three-month exclusive on sales, bypassing book publishers altogether. Waldenbooks also thinks it can do a better job of choosing titles, designing jackets, setting prices, and promoting books. In short, Waldenbooks is contesting the integrating role of book publishers, using its buying leverage and knowledge of the market to integrate the activities along the value chain for mass-marketed fiction in a way that may be more effective. With the rise of the Internet, companies like Amazon Books (http://www.amazon.com) are challenging the superstores, and the dominant position along the value chain may shift yet again.

Financial Capability

The network integrator often brings the ability to finance projects or deals for other members of the network. For example, Benetton initially had difficulty getting Italian banks to finance the owners of its small stores and factories. Therefore, Benetton established a subsidiary to finance the accounts receivable of its stores. It also established subsidiaries to finance the inventories and equipment purchases of its suppliers. In this way, instead of owning all the activities along the value chain, Benetton is the banker to independent companies.

The film industry offers another illustration of how the position of the integrator role can shift along the value chain. In Hollywood, this industry was traditionally dominated by the big studios, which vertically integrated the activities along the value chain. Actors and writers signed on with the studios, which marketed, distributed, and financed the movies that eventually were shown in studio-owned theaters. A combination of two factors broke up the studio system: the antitrust laws, and the phenomenon of independent producers. Yet the studios were still able to play the integrator role through their control of distribution, their knowledge of what would sell, and their ability to finance expensive projects. They became skilled at creating limited partnerships and ownership structures for individual films and packages of films.

Today this integrator role is also being contested. Superagencies like Creative Artists Agency (CAA) and the William Morris Agency can put together film packages on their own. CAA, for example, using talent that it represents, can sign writers, composers, directors, producers, and actors and create its own films. It can hold the rights to the work and then hire the studios to distribute it. If a superagency is big enough to create a whole package and is positioned to know which actors and scripts will match the public's taste, it can integrate the activities along the value chain. The step now being taken by CAA and William Morris is the creation of a capability in investment banking for the purpose of financing and taking risks. Studios will now have to compete with superagencies even at the earliest stages of a film's development.

Credibility

It is very important for the integrator to have the trust of the other network participants. These participants are independent companies; they have to choose to follow the leadership of the integrator. The integrator must use its superior size, information, and capital to benefit the network rather than exploit it, or else it will lose its members. Therefore, the integrator must look for network opportunities, see the fate of all the network's members, and search for win-win situations.

Among the Big Three car makers, Chrysler is the most skilled at playing the role of integrator. Chrysler has a motto: "My enemy is my suppliers' costs, not my suppliers' margins. Therefore, what can I do to help my suppliers reduce their (and ultimately my) costs?" Chrysler wants its suppliers to be financially healthy and to expand when it expands, and so Chrysler includes its suppliers in its steel contracts: a supplier pays the same price as Chrysler does for an amount of steel equal to the supplier's volume to Chrysler, and Chrysler then negotiates with the supplier about how to allocate the savings realized from this discount. As a result, Chrysler profits from the success of its Tier I suppliers.

The integrator that has the trust and confidence of its network members greatly reduces its negotiating costs, as measured in the time and effort of its managers. The credible integrator is more likely to get better information from its partners, as well as better and more flexible terms and conditions in its contracts; it can avoid constraining conditions and covenants. Therefore, being seen as a good partner is a competitive advantage.

Responsibility for the Network

The integrator needs an awareness of and a willingness to improve or perform all the activities carried out by the networked organization. The delivery of value to customers depends on superior performance by all the network participants along the value chain. The integrator (often the owner of a brand, such as Apple or Coca-Cola) *assumes responsibility* for all the value chain's activities, whether or not the integrator itself *performs* those activities well. As necessary, the integrator takes corrective action, which may begin with assistance to a weak member of the network but may end with that member's expulsion. The integrator may send help in the form of people from its own organization to provide consulting and training. The integrator may also arrange visits to superior performers in the network. Ultimately, however, the integrator must replace a poor performer or perform that member's activity itself.

Once again, Apple provides a good example. In Europe, Apple distributes through franchises called Apple Centers. These centers were having difficulty finding computer-literate salespeople, and so Apple took responsibility for recruiting computer-literate salespeople from universities. Apple also created Apple University, which does the training that the individual franchises cannot do on their own.

To take another example, Coca-Cola distributes its product through independently owned bottlers. Often a third- or fourth-generation owner is incompetent or takes cash out of the business rather than growing the bottler's market share. Ultimately, Coca-Cola buys out the poor performer, fixes the franchise, brings in new leadership, and resells the equity. Again, although a network integrator does not perform all the activities along the value chain, the integrator assumes responsibility for seeing that all the activities are performed well.

Brand Management

The integrator, as already mentioned, often assumes responsibility for managing a brand of product or service. There is often intellectual property or some design feature that distinguishes the product or service, and a brand franchise is necessary in order to capture higher margins. Consumer-goods companies like Nike, Benetton, Apple, and Nintendo all manage all the activities along their respective value chains, to ensure the value of their brand franchises.

The networked organization does require some management of its independent members, and the firms playing the role of network integrator (for all or portions of the activities along the value chain) provide that management, as well as leadership. They achieve efficiencies along the value chain that uncoordinated independents cannot achieve, and although the benefits of these efficiencies are distributed along the value chain, the lion's share goes to the integrator. This is why there is some competition for the integrator role. The firms most likely to execute this role are those that have the following attributes:

- Leverage
- Knowledge
- Information about the entire value chain
- Access to capital
- Credibility with other network members
- Willingness and ability to take responsibility for all the activities of the value chain
- Brand-management capability

The competition for this role is continuous and is characterized by shifts in the position of this role along the chain as industry structures change.

The Future of the Networked Organization

The term *networked organization* is a new name for a group of companies acting collectively. The key choices for an individual firm concern its role in the network and the specific activities that it will perform, own, and control. The key choices for organizational design involve the selection of partners, the types of relationships established with them, the structuring of joint efforts, and methods for developing employees who can participate in partnerships.

There is little doubt that the future will see the development of more and more networked organizations. They are an effective response to the many changes taking place in the business environment, particularly because they can create the advantages of a large organization without creating the large organization itself. Therefore, organizations are likely to prosper if they develop the capabilities associated with being an effective member of a network. Networked organizations are relatively new, and so there is a great deal to be learned about making them even more effective, as well as about how their members should behave. Organizations that are fast learners are likely to have a competitive advantage when it comes to creating and being part of a networked organization.

Chapter Four

Structuring Global Organizations

Jay R. Galbraith

How does a company organize its global operations? The answer to the question is obviously "It depends." There are four major factors on which the choice depends:

- The company's level of international development
- The amount of cross-border coordination required by the company's strategy
- The amount of host governments' activity in the economic process
- The diversity of the firm's global business portfolio

To a lesser extent, the choice will also depend on the history and timing of the company's international expansion and on the size of the company's market in the home country. In this chapter we will examine all these factors, and then we will consider the major approaches to organizing, as well as where those approaches fit.

Major Factors Influencing the Design of a Global Organization

Company's Level of International Development

The usual measure that companies use to gauge how global they are is the percentage of their sales outside the home country. Why is this a poor measure of a company's level of international development? There are two interrelated reasons.

The first reason involves the organizational challenges that arise from the attempt to transfer a firm's competitive advantages to a new geographical area and build a business around them. Subsidiaries play a critical role in a company's international development, a role that can vary from that of being a sales office to that of being a fully functional business. Subsidiaries also play different roles in the creation of competitive advantages. What typically happens at a lower level of international development is that advantages are created in the home country and transferred to foreign subsidiaries (Lorenz, 1995), which then become implementers. A company is more developed internationally, however, when its subsidiaries can take a leadership role in creating new competitive advantages. These advantages are then transferred to the global network, and even back into the home country.

The other, related reason involves the challenges that come with the attempt to integrate all the activities being carried out by people in different countries who are speaking different languages and working in different time zones. A company becomes more developed in a geographical area when it adds more value locally by using its own assets and people in that location. This challenge is different from the challenge of using exporters and local distributors.

Before it can play a leadership role by creating and transferring competitive advantages, a subsidiary needs assets, people, and power. A company becomes more internationally developed as it creates more assets and employees outside the home country, thereby enlarging the role that its subsidiaries can play in contributing and leading in the creation of the firm's advantages. Therefore, the measure of international development that will be used here is the proportion of the firm's assets and employees that is located outside the home country. Table 4.1 shows four different levels representing different proportions of a firm's out-of-country assets and employees. It also lists four different roles for subsidiaries and indicates the type of organization appropriate at each level and for each kind of subsidiary role.

The firm at level I is a national company with some international business (usually in the form of exports or licenses). It has a single profit center, as well as a functional organization (if it is a

Table 4.1. Levels of International Development.

Level	Proportion of Assets and Employees Outside of the Home Country	Role of the Subsidiary	Type of International Organization
I	Zero	None	National company
II	Low	Startup	International geographical division
III	Moderate	Implementer	Multidimensional network
IV	High	Leader	Transnational organization

single business) or a divisional multiprofit-center structure (if it has diversified into multiple businesses).

At level II the firm is beginning to participate in international markets. The typical organization at this level is an international division that has been added to the company's domestic structure.

As more assets and employees are created in more geographical locations, the international division disappears, and a network of multiple dimensions appears at level III. If the company at level III is a single business, a network of functions and countries is used. If the company is a multibusiness enterprise, a network of functions, countries, and businesses is used. For example, consumer-goods companies like Nestlé use geography as their central dimension. whereas high-technology enterprises use either functions or businesses (the choice depends on whether the company is a single-business entity or a multibusiness entity).

The transnational organization of level IV appears when the role of some subsidiaries is changed so that they can generate competitive advantages and take regional or global leadership for an activity (Bartlett and Ghoshal, 1989). When a company at level III uses functions or businesses as the central dimension of its network, the company headquarters those businesses and functions in the home country. In the transnational model the company still works with a multidimensional network, but headquarters for some businesses and/or activities will move to the best locations in the world for them. (The form of organization is also called the *distributed-headquarters model.*)

It is tempting to suggest that a firm will start at level I and progress sequentially to level IV, but there is only inconclusive evidence on whether there exists a fixed sequence of stages of internationalization. A company may start at level I and move sequentially through the other levels, but no assumption is made here that this is the only or necessary sequence to be followed. For example, many new companies starting up today begin at level IV, and it is likely that movement between and among levels will be different for different companies in different industries. Thus one company moving from level I to level II could go through substages, whereas another company could make an acquisition and move directly from level I to level II, and still another company could move from level II back to level I. In the early 1980s Westinghouse moved to level III as a multidimensional organization, but by 1995 the company had sold off its subsidiaries and moved back to level I as a national company with international business in the form of exports.

There is no imperative to move to level IV as the pinnacle of international development. It is quite possible to be effective by staying at level I as a national company with exports. It is also possible for a firm to be at different levels of international development in different parts of the world. For example, Western companies have vast experience in western Europe and North America, and yet they are newcomers to Asia. Ford's reorganization, taking place in the late 1990s, is not really a global reorganization; it is an integration of the company's European and North American operations and a move toward the transnational model (level IV) in those parts of the world, with Europe as the headquarters for small front-wheel-drive vehicles and standard transmissions, and with North America as the headquarters for sport/utility vehicles and automatic transmissions. Meanwhile, Ford is operating at the geographical-division stage (level II) in Latin America and Asia. Thus a company's level of development in a particular geographical location influences the company's choice of organizational style in that location.

Need for Cross-Border Coordination

The second factor influencing the type of international organization that will be appropriate is the amount of cross-border coordination required by the firm's international strategy (Prahalad and
Doz, 1987; Bartlett and Ghoshal, 1989). When there is a minimal
amount of cross-border coordination (as in food retailing, for
example), country subsidiaries are the main profit centers, and
geography becomes the principal axis around which the global network operates. Alternatively, when cross-border coordination is
central, the business unit and/or function becomes the principal
axis. The amount of cross-border coordination that will be necessary is determined by several factors all acting together:

• The level of the firm's fixed costs
• The nature of the firm's products, markets, and brands
• The concentration of the firm's customers, competitors, and
  suppliers

High fixed costs result from large investments in research and
development, capital-intensive operations, and expenses for promotion and advertising. For example, the semiconductor, computer, and pharmaceutical industries have investments in research
and development accounting for 10 to 15 percent of sales. They
cannot afford to duplicate those investments in each region of the
world. Instead, they use cross-border product-development processes to invest once in a product or technology and then transfer
that product or technology across borders. To take another example, in 1996 Procter and Gamble spent $3.5 billion on advertising.
The company might want one ad from one agency to be translated and transferred around the world for a global brand, and so
one common package for a common brand in eastern Europe is
designed and then translated and printed in fourteen languages,
to save on design and packaging costs. In both of these examples,
the company has to concentrate its investments in one place and
then transfer technology, products, services, or ads, as the case may
be, across borders, using a cross-border strategy to guide its investments. The company also has to accomplish coordination
across subsidiaries in order to achieve the volume to cover fixed

costs. This kind of coordination is carried out within a business unit or function.

In order for markets to be supplied with products or services across borders, the markets must be relatively homogeneous and must use common products. Over time, effective international companies become skilled at developing products and services that are mostly standard but easily adapted to local differences in taste. Rarely are markets truly homogeneous, but they can be supplied with standardized products and services that are designed from the beginning for easy localization. Thus the strategic factor here is the degree of markets' homogeneity and the degree of brands' and products' ability to be standardized.

Cross-border coordination is required when customers are in different locations around the world and want a single contract for all their subsidiaries. It is also needed when the company itself is a global customer that shops around the world and wants a single global supplier to serve all its subsidiaries. Subsidiaries, too, need to coordinate across borders when a global competitor is encountered in multiple markets: it is important to share information about global competitors, and competitive moves and counter-moves often need to be synchronized across subsidiaries in order to be effective. Therefore, cross-border coordination will be required when there are global customers, global suppliers, or global competitors. By contrast, when there are local customers, local suppliers, and local competitors, what is required is within-border coordination. The most likely scenario, however, is that some customers will be global, some will be regional, and some will be local. The firm will inevitably be both global and local in its orientation if it hopes to serve all its customers (Prahalad and Doz, 1987).

These factors tend to work together for some companies. Intel, to take one example, invested around $6 billion in research and development, manufacturing plants, and working capital before seeing any revenue from its Pentium chip. Therefore, in order to recover the fixed costs, Intel had to design this product for sale in all world markets. Global customers like Compaq and Acer buy the Pentium chip for their subsidiaries around the world, and Intel also competes with global competitors like Motorola and NEC. Therefore, the design, manufacture, and sale of Intel's Pentium chip is a global business that is driven across borders by a global business manager. Nestlé, by contrast, has thousands of different brands of foods and beverages in hundreds of local markets. These products are designed for local tastes and are produced in local or regional plants, with less than 1 percent of Nestlé's sales revenues reinvested in research and development. Therefore, Nestlé is run by many country managers, with a minimum of cross-border coordination.

The trend in the 1990s has been toward more cross-border trade and coordination. If the trend toward free trade and free-trade areas continues, we can expect to see even more cross-border coordination, which will mean a continuing shift of power away from country managers to regional, business, and functional managers. Governments are still mostly country-based, however, and are still capable of making trade less free.

Activity of Host Governments

As long as there are country governments, unions, and other such institutions, there will be country managers in some form (Doz, 1988). The more active the host government is in the country's economic activities, the stronger the country manager must be in order to deal with the host government. When there is a high need for both cross-border coordination and local responsiveness to active host governments, the preferred organizational type is a matrix that balances the power of the country manager and the business manager.

The trend has been away from strong country managers, however, because the trends toward free trade, global capital markets, deregulation, and privatization in turn have been reducing the influence of governments in the economic process and encouraging more cross-border trade. If these trends continue, businesses will grow stronger, with country governments (and country managers) growing weaker. If a backlash to globalization occurs, however, along with a return to protectionism, country governments and geographical factors will regain their strength.

Diversity of the Firm's International Business Portfolio

The fourth major factor influencing the design of a global organization is the diversity of the firm's international business portfolio (Stopford and Wells, 1972). In general, the more diverse the portfolio, the stronger the business manager, and the weaker the country manager. At General Electric, for example, the portfolio of twelve businesses includes financial services, major appliances, jet engines, and locomotives. General Electric's country managers cannot be experts on such a broad range of businesses; they are essentially ambassadors representing the firm to host governments, and the expertise resides in General Electric's business unit. When a firm's business portfolio is diverse, there is also less need for coordination across businesses within a country (unless the host government treats all these businesses as a single company).

At Nestlé the situation is reversed. Nestlé has a broad range of products, but they are predominantly foods and beverages. Therefore, Nestlé's country managers can easily comprehend the company's range of businesses. Moreover, there is often cross-business coordination within a country by means of common distribution systems serving common customers. Food products are consumer products, which represent marketing businesses. Markets are different from country to country, and so the expertise resides mostly in the individual countries, with marketing-oriented country managers.

Other Factors Influencing the Design of a Global Organization

Size of the Firm's Home-Country Market

A company in a large country usually expands domestically before going into international markets, and its home-country operations always play a large role. For example, companies from the United States, Japan, and Germany are often less international and can face the domination dangers of the domestic business versus an international business. Companies from small countries go international very quickly—they have no choice. They are usually more internationally minded, and their home-country operations play less of a role. They are also the most likely firms to become transnationals. Therefore, the size of an international firm's home-country market can moderate the effects of the four major factors influencing organizational design.

History of the Firm

A firm's history also plays a role in the design of a global organization (Bartlett and Ghoshal, 1989). Many European firms expanded internationally early in this century. They established country-based subsidiaries during a time of two world wars, protectionism, and virtually no cross-border trade. Each subsidiary was self-sufficient and autonomous, and so with the arrival of free trade and the creation of the European Economic Community these companies were not immediately free to integrate across borders. Their country-based subsidiaries and country managers were sources of considerable inertia.

Japanese and German companies expanded internationally in the 1970s and 1980s, during a time of free trade and free-trade institutions like GATT. When integration was needed across borders, these companies were free to create integrated businesses rather than country-based subsidiaries.

Today, as already mentioned, many companies virtually start up at level IV, as transnationals. They immediately open sales companies in Europe, North America, and Japan, and they put manufacturing in Taiwan and software in India. Therefore, the timing of a firm's international expansion can also moderate the effects of the four major factors influencing organizational design.

Approaches to Organizing

International or Geographical Division

The first approach to international organization, at level II, is the international or geographical division. For companies just beginning to create value-adding activities in other countries, the usual form of organization is an international division. The company that already has some international business and experience but is entering a new area—say, China—may form a China division and add it to the existing structure while the Chinese operation is in start-up mode.

This form of organization is chosen at this point for several reasons. First, it gathers all the company's international activities in one place and gives them a focus, separating them from domestic activities and allowing them to be uniquely developed for an international market. Second, it gives the international activities a critical mass so that they can compete for scarce resources. Third, a talented manager can be assigned to lead the international division and report to top management so that the division has a voice in resource-allocation decisions. Fourth, it economizes on a scarce resource: general managers with international experience.

The international or geographical division has several tasks. The first is to transfer the firm's competitive advantages to the new geographical area, modify them to fit the local circumstances, and build a business around them. This task is a crucial one. A firm entering a new country enters at a competitive disadvantage. In addition to being foreign, the firm has no knowledge about doing business locally, no local relationships, and no local reputation. To overcome this disadvantage, it must bring advantages from its home country that the local firms do not have. These advantages are rarely transferable in full; some adjustments, even substantial modifications, may be needed. For example, one advantage that McDonald's now enjoys is its supply network, but when the company was expanding into Europe, its supply network had to be built from scratch. It had to be built all over again in Japan, and it is being built yet again in China, Russia, and wherever else McDonald's is expanding. As a result, McDonald's now has a new advantage: its ability to build a supply network from scratch anywhere in the world. International expansion is all about transferring competitive advantages (Yu, 1992).

The second task of the international or geographical division is to maintain a continuous dialogue with the home-country operation. It is not always clear which aspects of a firm's success formula will be transferable and which will require modification, and so there are often surprises. A dialogue is necessary in order for the adjustments to be made. Some changes will be needed in the home country, and some will be needed in the new international subsidiary. Ultimately, however, this dialogue has to lead to learning about how to transfer competitive advantages from the home country to the new area.

The international or geographical division's third task is to build management systems in each new geographical area. For the subsidiary to be integrated into a corporate network, it needs compatible financial and information systems. Again, some adaptation to local conditions is usually needed; for example, human resources policies are rarely transferable without adaptation. The international division plays a mediating role in discussions about these adaptations: it needs to explain to the local subsidiary why it must use the corporate system, and it needs to explain to the home-country corporation why the corporate system has to be modified.

A key organizational decision is the amount of autonomy to grant the subsidiary. Usually there is more autonomy for a start-up than for a subsidiary that is being integrated into the global network. There are always questions of balance, however. For example, more autonomy is needed when there is a need for substantial adaptations to local circumstances, and so the greater the cultural differences between the home country and the new country, the more autonomy for the subsidiary. Autonomy is usually achieved if an expatriate start-up team is sent to work with the local nationals to make the adaptations in real time.

If the home-country firm maintains few assets and employees outside the country or in the new geographical area, the international or geographical division often remains intact. If more resources are created in the subsidiary, however, it becomes a stand-alone in a geographical structure or it is divided up and allocated to the worldwide businesses or, what is more likely, it undergoes some combination of these two changes.

Multidimensional Network

The second approach to international organization, represented by the multidimensional network, at level III, encompasses businesses, geographical areas, and functions. Usually one of these three dimensions becomes the axis around which most activity revolves. Which dimension becomes the axis and which dimensions become supplementary are issues whose resolution depends on the interplay of key strategic factors (cross-border coordination, diversity of the firm's international business portfolio, and the economic activities of host governments, as already described).

Single-Business Organization

The single-business organization is a network of functions and geographical areas. The issue of whether the functions or the geographical area will become the axis depends on the amount of cross-border coordination that is needed.

In the prescription pharmaceuticals business, for instance, there is a great deal of cross-border coordination. About 15 percent of sales revenues in this industry are reinvested in research and development: it costs several hundred million dollars to get a new drug approved, and once it is approved, the same product or active ingredient is used around the world. A pharmaceuticals company has to make the same efficacy claims to ministries of health all around the world, and its competitors are mostly also global.

Pharmaceuticals research laboratories are located all over the world, but they all form a single global function for research or discovery: the idea is to eliminate expensive duplication and speed the flow of information worldwide. The situation is similar with the development of a new drug application (NDA). As already mentioned, it costs enormous amounts of money to get a new drug approved, and so the development unit wants to share results worldwide, create a common NDA process, and decide where it would be best to get approvals, with minimum duplication of effort.

Pharmaceuticals manufacturing is a sophisticated, stringent, quality-oriented activity. Therefore, important buying and sourcing decisions are centralized, although packaging processes may be decentralized to individual countries. Likewise, each country has to certify a new pharmaceutical and decide on its form (tablet, capsule, powder, liquid, skin patch), and there is also great variation in levels of the active ingredient. Customers are local (and are often the local government itself).

In the prescription pharmaceuticals industry, then, local activities include sales, marketing, packaging, and some manufacturing; the most critical cross-border coordination takes place in research and development and in the greater portion of the manufacturing function. Another critical activity, product development, takes place across functions and across borders, with the strategic marketing function participating in this key process by gathering information from all the local-country markets. What this means is that the functions become the axis in the prescription pharmaceuticals business, given the high need for cross-border coordination.

When there is little need for cross-border coordination, the geographical area becomes the axis. For example, cement companies organize on the basis of geographical areas. Cement is a product with low value and high transport costs, and so each country or region is self-sufficient. There is very little research and development in this industry, and customers are local, as are competitors. Ideas, best practices, and money are moved across borders, but little else is mobile. Geographical areas are the profit centers.

Multibusiness Company

The multibusiness company adds another dimension to the question of organizational structure. In this section we will look at examples of two extremes (Nestlé and Hewlett-Packard) among such companies, as well as at one balanced matrix (Asea Brown Boveri).

Nestlé. Nestlé has often been mentioned as an example of a company whose axis is geography and countries. Its products are foods and beverages, and so its business portfolio is not very diverse. The products vary considerably with national tastes. The customers are local food retailers. The fixed costs associated with research and development and with factories are low by comparison with fixed costs in the pharmaceuticals industry. Nestlé has thousands of local brands that are unique to particular countries, and so there is minimal cross-border coordination; the country or region is the basic building block of the company.

The countries in which Nestlé operates are grouped into zones, but the countries themselves are the profit centers. They are divided into business units (confections, ice cream, coffee, and so on). There are also central business units for coordinating the few global brands and the businesses worldwide. These central business units pass on best practices, and they influence the development of new products, but they have no formal authority; they can only persuade and influence the countries. The functions of research and development, finance, and human resources do coordinate across borders, and they too have influence, but final decisions are made at the level of the countries and zones.

Hewlett-Packard. Hewlett-Packard is an example of a company whose axis is worldwide business units. The businesses of Hewlett-Packard are intensely focused on research and development: about 75 percent of Hewlett-Packard's sales are from products newer than two years old. A new product (such as a computer, a printer, or a test instrument) costs several hundred million dollars to launch, and a product's life cycle is often less than a year. Therefore, global volume is needed to cover the fixed costs.

Hewlett-Packard's customers are often global, and they purchase on a global basis. For example, Mitsubishi Trading Company may want the same hardware, the same software, and the same network to be delivered on the same day in Singapore, Tokyo, New York, and London. Hewlett-Packard's competitors are usually global as well, and so most of the coordination that takes place occurs within a business and across borders.

Hewlett-Packard does have a geographical axis. There are local issues having to do with taxes and financial consolidation, and there is often a country-specific human resources function. Many issues involving salaries, pensions, and other benefits also vary by country. Regional and company managers play a largely ambassadorial role, however, representing the company to governments, unions, and customers. Hewlett-Packard's business decisions are made within the products' profit centers.

Asea Brown Boveri. Asea Brown Boveri (ABB) is one organization that has struck a balance between using business and using geographical areas as its axis. ABB is a matrix organization.

Like Hewlett-Packard, ABB has businesses that are intensely focused on research and development. The company invests about 8 percent of revenues in research and development, and it continuously generates new products. Its competitors are usually global, and its customers are commercial users. Nevertheless, ABB's customers—utilities, railroads, steel mills, cement plants—are also very local, and more than 50 percent of the company's revenues come from local governments or from government-influenced purchases. These customers prefer local vendors, or vendors that add value locally, and the customers buy products from more than one business area. As a result, ABB coordinates across borders, but it also coordinates across products within borders. It tries to add value locally and be a good local citizen. The outcome is a balance of power between the functional and geographical axes. ABB's matrix structure is shown in Figure 4.1.

The businesses, based on product lines, are grouped into business segments (an example would be the segment dedicated to power generation), and the segments in turn are divided into about fifty business areas (for example, areas like gas turbines, steam turbines, hydroelectric power, and nuclear power in the business segment dedicated to power generation). The regions in which the company operates are standard (the Americas, for example, a region that is divided into country-specific units like the United States, Mexico, Brazil, Argentina, and so on). A key role is played by the business segment or the business area within a country. Here is where the two axes of the matrix converge, and each manager has two bosses. Below this business/country level is the usual hierarchical organization.

ABB's matrix is supported by information systems, human resource practices, and role definitions. Immediately after creating its matrix organization, ABB created an accounting system for measuring profit and loss on the basis of both geographical and business factors. Thus the company can report profits for gas turbines across borders, and for Brazil across businesses. The planning process operates to achieve alignment of the company's profit goals across the two sides of the matrix. People are also rotated across countries within a business, and across businesses within a

Figure 4.1. The Matrix Structure of Asea Brown Boveri.

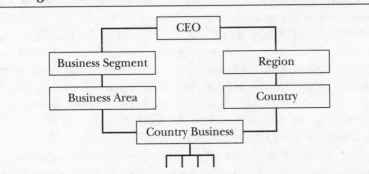

country. Therefore, the company carefully selects and develops employees who can function in a cross-border matrix.

The roles of the two sides are also carefully defined so that there is as little confusion and conflict as possible. The premise is established that roles on the two sides are complementary. One side knows the business, and the other knows the country; together they can make a success of a business in a country. The business side is responsible for cross-border strategy, product development, assignment of markets to factories, purchasing, and cross-border profit and loss. The geographical side is responsible for regional and customer-based strategy; relations with governments, unions, and universities; day-to-day supervision of businesses; human resources within a country; and country-specific profit and loss. There are certainly occasions when roles conflict, but these situations are resolved quickly by the business manager, the country manager, and the country business manager. The functions also coordinate their activities across businesses and across borders. They can often assist in resolving conflicts, but their influence is informal.

Lateral Networking

The coordination and communication that take place across borders are not necessarily brought about through the hierarchical organization (Galbraith, 1994). An increasingly important activity is coordination and communication across basic structures. Recall the example of the pharmaceuticals industry, where the key process is new-product development that coordinates activities across functions and across borders. This and other processes that operate across borders constitute the *lateral networking* aspect of the multidimensional organization.

Networking activity, built on the foundation of the interpersonal network that exists across businesses and countries, constitutes the ability to communicate and coordinate across organizational units. This kind of communication is most effective when people know one another and have relationships, and these relationships are built over time as people interact. Indeed, companies are recognizing that they conduct a number of activities for one purpose, but that a by-product of these activities is the creation of interpersonal networks, and today the by-product is often the main product.

In addition to cross-border assignments, there are management-development courses, management meetings, functional conferences, and especially social events. Short-sighted management sees such events as opportunities to cut costs; astute management sees them as investments in international organizational capability.

These relationships can be used initially on a simple, voluntary basis. For example, the head of Nestlé's coffee business unit in Germany calls or visits the head of the coffee business in France to exchange best practices, and this sort of contact can be encouraged by the company. In fact, many companies with twenty-five to thirty plants producing the same products publish performance data, and the implicit message—which may become explicit—is that people from low-performing plants should visit the high-performing plants and learn from them. More and more, the trend is toward calling the framework for these voluntary practices *self-organizing networks* (Eccles and Crane, 1988).

As companies experience the need for more cross-border coordination, lateral networking can be reinforced for the purpose of enabling more cross-border decisions. Thus the company can increasingly shift decision-making power from the geographical axis to the business axis, and vice versa. Figure 4.2 shows how the distribution of power can be shifted through the use of different cross-unit coordination mechanisms. At the far left side, the figure shows that some power can be shifted to the business side through the voluntary coordination of the business-unit managers in the countries. This move is represented by the circled numeral 1 on the far left side of Figure 4.2.

More coordination can be achieved through the formation of virtual teams—that is, all the managers of Nestlé's ice-cream factories can be linked electronically via an intranet, for example. They can have discussions on electronic bulletin boards, or they can hold computer conferences on various topics. They can have a continuing exchange about their experiences with self-managing work teams, for example, or hold a computer conference on their experiences with various pieces of equipment.

The next step is the move to formal teams, represented on the far left side of Figure 4.2 by the circled numeral 3. Nestlé, for example, might create cross-country formal teams for new-product development for Pan-European or global brands. The creation of

Figure 4.2. Distribution of Power Between Axes.

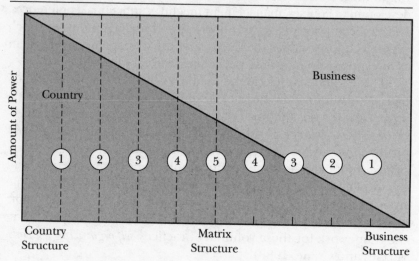

1. Voluntary organization (self-organizing networks)
2. Virtual teams
3. Formal teams
4. Business or country manager as full-time team leader
5. Matrix organization

formal teams builds in specific goals and accountability (Galbraith, 1973, 1994, 1995; Mohrman, Cohen, and Mohrman, 1995; Mankin, Cohen, and Bikson, 1996).

The question of team leadership always arises, and the usual solution is eventually to appoint a full-time business-team leader (represented by the circled numeral 4 on the far left side of Figure 4.2). This leader can chair the team and suggest changes, but it is the country managers who make the decisions. The team leader has no formal authority, although he or she may have particular influence when a decision has to do with an investment in research and development, capacity expansion, or a new product. The challenge is to find a person with the skills of a general manager who can play this role without a general manager's formal authority and who can exert this kind of delicate influence as an aspect of cross-border coordination. Success in this role depends on interpersonal skills and persuasion. If a company begins building international managerial capability at the beginning of its international expansion, it can develop people who have the skills needed to exert influence without authority.

The next increase in business power would be to move to a matrix organization like ABB's, an increase represented at the midpoint of Figure 4.2 by the circled numeral 5. At point 5, the businesses in the countries report both to their country managers and to their business managers, and there is a balance of power between the axes. If one more step were taken to have the businesses within a country report to a worldwide business manager, and to have a dotted line to the country manager, the power would shift to point 4 on the right-hand side of the diagram. This point best describes the Hewlett-Packard organization. The model is completed by moving to points 3, 2 and 1 on the right hand-side of diagram. They represent worldwide a business unit structure with formal country teams 3, with virtual country teams 2, and finally informal or voluntary country coordination. Thus power can be shifted between the two axes as circumstances shift the degree of cross-border coordination, the amount of host governments' economic activity, or the level of diversity in a firm's international business portfolio. The same reasoning can be extended to three dimensions when the functions are included.

Figure 4.3 is a summary of the points made so far. At the bottom of Figure 4.3 are arrayed three of the factors influencing the distribution of power in the multidimensional network: the need for cross-border coordination, the amount of economic activity conducted by host-country governments, and the diversity of the firm's international business portfolio. A company's location on the chart represented in Figure 4.3 is the result of the impact of these three factors, and a change in one of the factors may give management cause to fine-tune the distribution of power. Recently the force represented by the need for cross-border coordination has been the one moving most companies toward the use of stronger business managers—indeed, fifteen years ago Hewlett-Packard was operating at the point where Nestlé operates today— but the distribution of power can move in either direction as business conditions change.

Figure 4.3.

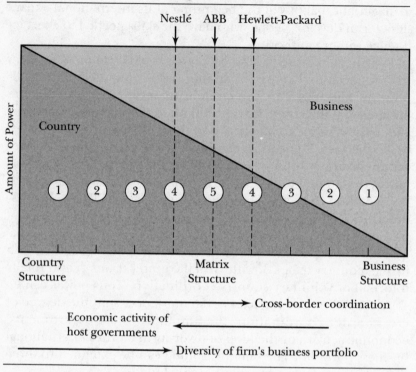

Today most companies operate at level II or level III of international development, with operations in the home country serving as the source of competitive advantages that are transferred around the world. Subsidiaries may be very sizable and effective, but their role is still one of implementing the advantages and strategies that come from the home country. In other words, most so-called global companies have a definite national bias. For example, if the U.S. domestic economy accounts for 20 percent of the world economy, then a company calling itself global could be expected to have 80 percent of its assets and employees outside the United States. Instead, however, the average global U.S. company actually has 60 percent of its assets within the United States (Yu, 1995). A study of the global Fortune 500 (Ruigrok and van Tulder, 1996) has found only eighteen companies worldwide with a majority of their assets outside their home countries, and these companies are headquartered in small countries like Switzerland. The record is even more revealing where research and development are concerned, with only about 10 percent of a company's research and development taking place outside the home country (Yu, 1992; Patel, 1995), and usually that 10 percent is for localization and customer support; advanced research and development, like new-product development, remains in the home country. A company's move to level IV occurs only when such major value-adding activities as these take place in other countries and begin to generate advantages that can be used throughout the network (which would include the home country). Some argue that a move to level IV is unlikely (Yu, 1992); others see it as inevitable (Bartlett and Ghoshal, 1989).

Transnational Organization

The third approach to international organization is the transnational organization (Bartlett and Ghoshal, 1989). At level IV, a company has substantial assets and people outside the home country, and it uses some of its subsidiaries as creators of advantages, not just as implementers. There is also formal designation of those subsidiaries as leaders in their particular activities and as headquarters for their particular businesses. For example, DuPont has headquartered its agrichemicals business in France, where agriculture is quite advanced. France is a lead market for the types of products that DuPont makes; therefore, what happens in France today will happen in other markets tomorrow, and the new products and technologies generated in France will serve the rest of DuPont's business network.

Two forces drive companies toward the transnational model. The first is the variation in excellence, across countries, in particular industries and skills. Historical, governmental, geographical, and cultural variables have made some countries or regions into centers of excellence (Porter, 1990). One finds in those countries or regions the most advanced and demanding customers, the toughest competitors, and the most vigorous competition. Usually a supportive infrastructure—networks of suppliers, trade associations, specialty courses and research in local universities, apprenticeship programs, governmental support for exports—has grown up around a center of excellence. The second force is the intense competition in many industries, which forces companies to search for the best skills along their value chains. Therefore, global companies search for the centers of excellence that are key to their businesses: if they do not compete by using the best resources, their competitors will.

The price of worldwide excellence is a more complicated organization. For example, a multidimensional network, whose subsidiaries implement competitive advantages developed in the home country, looks like the hub-and-spoke model shown on the left-hand side of Figure 4.4—a simpler model than the transnational model depicted on the right-hand side of the figure. In the hub-and-spoke model, most communication and control come from headquarters in the home country, and communication is mostly in one-to-one mode. Subsidiaries are staffed with locals, and the subsidiaries' performance is measured with respect to the local bottom line. In the transnational model, by contrast, the multidimensional network is a peer network in which communication is much more intensive. Its subsidiaries may also be staffed with locals, but they need international experience and skill in working with the global network, and so the transnational organization's subsidiaries find their performance measured on both a local and a global basis. Another contrast is that the hub-and-spoke model runs on a one-to-one leadership style, whereas the transnational model requires a team. But because the members of the trans-

Figure 4.4. Hub-and-Spoke Model Versus Transnational Model.

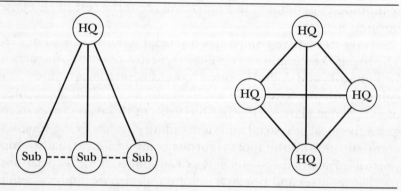

national's team are likely to be remotely located and made up of people of different nationalities, the transnational model requires a high degree of communication and integration, which this diversity of locations and nationalities makes difficult to attain. What makes a transnational organization so sophisticated and such a challenge is that it is a multidimensional network with the added feature of distributed headquarters. (For a detailed example of the distributed-headquarters model, see Galbraith, 1994, chap. 6).

A number of companies are adopting the transnational form, at least in part. For example, the French chemical company Rhône-Poulenc has several businesses headquartered in the United States, and Hewlett-Packard has its business in personal computers headquartered in Grenoble, France. Some companies are retreating from this model, however. For instance, a few years after Nestlé placed the headquarters for its global confectionery business in the United Kingdom, having acquired the British firm Rowntree, the British managers themselves requested that the Rowntree headquarters be moved to Nestlé headquarters in Vevey, Switzerland, because they believed they could work better with the Nestlé system if they were in the same location as the other Nestlé businesses and functions. Other companies have found the transnational organizational model too complicated, and still others have been finding that overhead expenses mount as each remote headquarters adds its own staff and infrastructure. In one case a destructive debate took place between the business units in the United States and those in Germany. The issue was which one would be the global leader, and the damage from that clash is still being repaired. Thus the transnational model is not without its costs.

Nevertheless, the transnational model does appear to be the one being chosen by most of the young companies that are now expanding internationally. In fact, as already observed, many of these companies start out as international companies and become transnational organizations within a few years. Take the case of Verifone, a U.S. manufacturer of hardware and software for the verification and authorization of credit-card purchases. The company started up in the United States, the world's largest user of credit cards, but it has expanded and now has its high-end equipment manufacturing in the United States and its low-cost equipment manufacturing in Taiwan and, increasingly, in China. The company's software is developed in the United States and in Bangalore, India. The sales function exists in all the countries where credit cards are in use. The product-development center for credit cards is in the United States, but the development center for "smart cards" (credit cards with embedded semiconductor chips) is in Paris. (Europe, and France in particular, are far ahead of the United States in smart-card use and development.) The center for stored-value cards is in Singapore. (Asia does not have well-developed telecommunication systems for credit-card verification, and so Asian markets use pre-paid cards that store cash equivalents in a magnetic strip.) Thus Verifone has located its development centers in lead markets, and its hardware and software creation in the world's centers of excellence.

A question naturally arises: What holds an organization like this one together? Verifone's answer is that it is held together by a common value system and an integrated communication network. Having articulated a set of values, the organization lives, hires, and promotes by them, and the company reinforces these values and its network with constant travel. For example, Verifone's CEO travels nearly half a million miles every year, and at any one time 40 percent of Verifone's people are also traveling. Face-to-face meetings are augmented by an electronic mail system that everyone uses, especially the CEO. The "glue" for this company is made up of common values, a shared understanding of the business strategy, and constant communication.

Future Challenges

Just as it is today, it will be a challenge in the future to implement the current forms of global organization. Most companies already have difficulty with the two-dimensional matrix, and the transnational model presents an even higher degree of difficulty. Progress is being made as companies build multidimensional accounting systems, adopt cross-border planning processes, and develop global processes for product development, but there are never enough people with international business skills and experience, not to mention people with leadership ability. Every cross-border team represents an effort to overcome barriers of culture, language, and time; few companies are happy with their ability to measure and reward performance in a multidimensional context. Therefore, although progress is being made, mastery of the multidimensional organization is still an enormous challenge.

While companies are still struggling to implement two- and three-dimensional forms of organization, the trend is toward adding yet more dimensions. To take one example, commercial and investment banks are facing the challenge of four dimensions. For years they have been geographically organized and run by country managers, but today they have to provide their cross-border customers with services like foreign exchange and cash management, and they must introduce strong functions for information technology, risk management, and human resources. Thus commercial and investment banks are implementing organizations that are networks of customers, products, countries, and functions.

At Asea Brown Boveri, the three-dimensional network that has been in use is now being extended to cover two new dimensions. The first new dimension is for megaprojects. As developing countries build infrastructure, they initiate projects costing more than $1 billion (power plants, hydroelectric dams, desalination plants, and so on). These projects involve a dozen or more business areas within the organization, and so they must be coordinated across businesses and across borders. The second new dimension involves ABB's global customers who want to negotiate single contracts with vendors certified as global suppliers. Once again there are multiple ABB businesses that come into play, and a global account manager must coordinate across businesses and countries to serve ABB's global customers. Thus ABB is becoming a five-dimensional network of businesses, countries, functions, projects, and customers.

In addition to (or often because of) the global-customer dimension, other dimensions and processes may need to be implemented—for example, a global-process dimension led by a global-process owner, or a common global order-fulfillment process to serve the global-customer dimension. Other relationships may also require special attention. For instance, Sony is a customer, supplier, partner, and competitor of Philips; a company will often appoint a manager to coordinate these relationships across the company. New electronic channels are making distribution channels yet another new dimension. Companies are also identifying core competencies and coordinating investments in them across units, functions, divisions, businesses, and countries. It seems there is no end to the number of interdependent dimensions that can profitably be identified and coordinated, and they add to the already complex challenge of coordination that multinational corporations face. How are they coping with the new demands?

One method is to set priorities for these dimensions during the strategy-making process. For example, more than one bank has given top priority to global customers and lower priority to products, functions, and countries. The bank's customer is now the primary profit-and-loss account, and countries are no longer profit-and-loss centers. The setting of priorities brings some clarity and reduces complexity for managers throughout the organization.

Other forms of assistance present themselves as technological barriers continue to fall. In the past, the positive impact of information technology (IT) was oversold. The new IT was supposed to bridge gaps of time and space and lead to so-called location-free organizations, but linguistic and cultural gaps persisted (O'Hara-Devereaux and Johansen, 1994). There was also the reality of incompatibility between computer systems, not to mention regulated and antiquated telecommunication infrastructures. If the potential of moving to location-free organizations was overestimated, the difficulty of doing so was underestimated. But today deregulation, wireless and satellite systems, the Internet, and the new technologies appearing daily are removing the technical barriers to low-cost cross-border communication. The most powerful new tool appears to be the organizational intranet, which can integrate the previously incompatible, inaccessible systems of subsidiaries into one unified, low-cost network. Intranets and advances in groupware have moved the formation of virtual teams into the realm of reality.

The removal of technical barriers has been accompanied by changes on the human side as well. In all countries, business school–educated young people are taking positions of responsibility. These managers are multilingual and computer-fluent; an intranet seems to them like a natural tool for communication. In addition, more leaders are also seeing one of their tasks to be the building of personal networks throughout the company. Again, Verifone serves as a good example of this trend: the company's leaders, as already described, promote the use of electronic communication, but they also promote a common value system and business understanding, and the company's electronic network is supported by face-to-face encounters that renew relationships. The same three factors—electronic networks, personal networks, and common value systems—must be built to support coordination processes in the cross-border firms of the future.

Conclusion

It should be obvious that no one type of organization embodies the right answer for all companies. Rather, the multinational corporation needs to be a multidimensional network of businesses, countries, and functions. Which dimension forms its primary axis will depend on the corporation's level of international development, its need for cross-border coordination, the diversity of its international business portfolio, and the amount of economic activity undertaken by the governments where the corporation does business. The form of the multinational network should also be influenced by the history of the company's international activity and by the size of its home market.

Competitive pressures continuously create new challenges that call for more complexity. To use their best resources in competition, companies are moving their locations and their leadership to areas that are centers of excellence for particular activities. Global customers demanding single points of business contact are now forcing companies into four-and five-dimensional networks. The company that can build interpersonal networks and combine them with electronic networks is the company best positioned to meet this challenge. The virtual teams that can be formed from these networks will allow companies to continue organizing and reorganizing along any new dimensions that may yet be called for.

Part Two

Enabling Competitive Performance

Organizing for Competencies and Capabilities

Bridging from Strategy to Effectiveness

David Finegold
Edward E. Lawler III
Gerald E. Ledford Jr.

Competency, a term rarely mentioned in the management literature a decade ago, is a commonplace concept today. Signs of the growing interest in competencies abound. A number of large international conferences have focused on competencies, and numerous consulting firms offer competency models to companies as a means of enhancing individual and organizational performance. National governments, too, are devoting millions of dollars to the development of competency-based skill standards (see Keltner, Finegold, and Pager, 1996; National Center on Education and the Economy and National Alliance of Business, 1994). Prahalad and Hamel (1990), in a widely disseminated article, argue that competencies should play a vital role in corporate strategy.

Is this attention to competencies another management fad, or is it a more fundamental and lasting change in the theory and practice of managing organizations and individuals? Answering this question entails, first, defining competencies and identifying the forces that have driven the increased interest in them, and, second,

Note: This chapter is based in part on Lawler and Ledford (1997).

analyzing whether the new competency models offer solutions to the challenges facing individuals and organizations. This analysis is complicated by the fact that there is no single competency movement. Rather, there are at least three quite distinct approaches. It is only by understanding each of these different approaches, as well as the tensions among them, that we can begin to assess the impact that the interest in competencies is likely to have on organizations in the future.

Core Competencies

As companies seek to develop the flexibility needed to cope with vital competitive challenges, the traditional bureaucratic approach to organizing has come under heavy criticism. According to its critics, the traditional bureaucratic approach does not produce the high levels of speed, quality, and productivity that are needed in highly competitive global businesses, nor does it create organizations that can change rapidly and adapt easily to the increasingly turbulent business environment. The key principles of the bureaucratic model include a high degree of specialization, the division of labor down to the level of the job, dependence on hierarchical authority, and reliance on formal rules and standard operating procedures. These design elements create and maintain top-down management control and organizational stability. In an era of constant change and demand for ever higher levels of performance, bureaucratic designs appear clumsy and lethargic. At this point, it is not clear that any one approach has emerged as the clear successor to the bureaucratic model. Most organizations still embrace such key features of the traditional bureaucratic model as individual jobs, hierarchical relationships, and individual accountability.

The concept of competency as an alternative basis for managing organizations has gained visibility partly as a result of its use in the business strategy literature, which increasingly calls for a focus on the core competencies and capabilities of organizations as the principal sources of competitive advantage. Prahalad and Hamel (1990), the leading proponents of this core competencies perspective, argue that corporations can identify a relatively small number of underlying competencies that give them a sustainable strategic edge in the marketplace. For example, Sony's core competencies in miniaturization and precision manufacturing provide competitive advantages across a large number of product lines and markets.

Stalk, Evans, and Shulman (1992) have presented a variation on this approach that focuses on "strategic capabilities," which are organizational and operational rather than technical in nature. They cite Wal-Mart's strategic capabilities in distribution, marketing, and information systems as an example of this source of competitive advantage. Later writings of both Prahalad and Hamel (for example, Hamel, 1994) have absorbed this approach into the core competencies stream.

There are several key characteristics of core competencies (Hamel, 1994; Rumelt, 1994). First, competencies represent a complex bundle of skills and technologies that span multiple businesses and products (for example, precision manufacturing). Second, competencies are more stable and evolve more slowly than the products and markets that have been the traditional focus of strategy. Third, core competencies are difficult to imitate. Witness the unsuccessful attempts of automakers around the world to match the productivity and quality of the Toyota production system during the past two decades. Fourth, core competencies (rather than markets or products) are the true battleground of interfirm competition.

Lado and Wilson (1994) distinguish among four types of competencies. *Managerial competencies* include articulating a strategic vision and enacting (managing) the environment. *Input-based competencies* include exploiting imperfections in the labor market, creating an internal labor market, and investing in firm-specific human capital. *Transformational competencies* include harnessing innovation and entrepreneurship, fostering organizational learning, and promoting organizational culture. *Output-based competencies* include building a corporate reputation, building product or service quality, and building customer loyalty.

Ulrich and Lake (1990) and Lawler (1996) argue for the importance of organizational capabilities. They suggest that organizational capabilities allow organizations to perform in particular ways that are critical to business performance. Quality, speed, low-cost operations, learning, innovation, and customer focus are examples of these kinds of capabilities. According to Lawler (1996), these capabilities do not reside in any one individual or, for that matter, in any one area of technological excellence. Instead, they reside in the systems, structures, cumulative knowledge, and mind-set of the organization. As a result, they are hard to develop and hard to duplicate, but they are potentially a significant source of competitive advantage. In essence, they are the key to allowing organizations to turn their important technological and operational core competencies into products and services that are superior to those offered by competing organizations. In the case of Wal-Mart, for example, the organizational capabilities argument is that its competitive advantage is not just in its distribution, marketing, and information system capabilities; it is also in Wal-Mart's ability to operate a customer-focused organization, a capability that resides in the company's communication, reward, leadership, involvement, and training practices.

Individual Competencies

The strategy-based view of core competencies and organizational capabilities is very different from the competency approaches, which are rooted in the human resources tradition. The latter tradition is "bottom up"—that is, it was built through identification and reinforcement of the competencies that are associated with high individual performance. Most research in this tradition has taken the form of validity studies in the tradition of industrial psychology. These studies attempt to identify competencies that distinguish high from low individual performers in an organization (Spencer and Spencer, 1993). For example, Boyatzis (1982) has identified twenty-one competencies (such as conceptualization, memory, objectivity, and self-confidence) that distinguish high- from low-performing managers. A number of studies have focused on the human resources function in particular. For example, Ulrich, Brockbank, Yeung, and Lake (1995) have found that the colleagues, supervisors, and clients of human resources managers rate the performance of these managers more favorably to the extent that these managers display competencies in business knowledge, in delivery of human resources services, and in management of change.

An important advantage of the individual-competencies approach is that it provides some specific guidance about ways to enhance performance. Whereas the *core* competencies identified by strategists are somewhat mysterious and difficult to manage, writers concerned with *individual* competencies typically connect competencies directly to human resources systems that promote such competencies. Selection systems are designed to help in hiring those who possess more of the needed competencies, and pay systems are also designed to reward those who display the needed competencies.

Nevertheless, there are three important shortcomings of the individual-competencies approach. First, managers and even researchers typically assume that organizational effectiveness is enhanced when key individual competencies are fostered, but there is little research evidence to demonstrate these effects on organizational performance. For a number of reasons, greater individual performance does not always translate into higher organizational performance. Second, organizations increasingly are purchasing prepackaged "one size fits all" competency models that probably do not offer a competitive advantage. For example, competency-based pay systems commonly reward individuals for competencies (such as communication skills) that certainly are not "core" competencies (as strategists use the term) and are too generic to provide competitive success (Zingheim, Ledford, and Schuster, 1996). Indeed, to the extent that the competency model is widely used across firms, it cannot offer a competitive advantage. Third, the individual-competencies approach has a historical focus in the sense that it identifies competencies that have led individuals to be successful in the past. For example, selection methods are validated on the basis of employees' current and past performance. In a rapidly changing business, this type of validation may be misleading because new competencies may be needed.

The interest of human resources specialists in individual competencies has grown in direct proportion to the decline of the "job", the cornerstone on which companies traditionally have built their human resources practices. A number of related forces have been reducing the relevance of the job in today's competitive environment (Bridges, 1994). The rapid pace of technological and organizational change makes it increasingly difficult to define a stable set of tasks that an individual will be hired to perform and will be measured against. The move toward more team-based work has also made it harder to isolate individuals' jobs and their contributions to organizational performance (see Mohrman, Cohen, and Mohrman, 1995). Moreover, as corporations become flatter, opportunities to move into a higher-level job become rarer, and so organizations are seeking ways to motivate and reward high performers without promoting them. Competencies have not yet emerged as a clear successor to the job as the basis of human resources practices. Nevertheless, using competencies and new skills as the basis on which individuals are hired, developed, and rewarded appears to be a possible solution to the needs of many organizations.

There has been relatively little research to date on the ways in which companies are using individual-level competencies for organizing their human resources systems or employees' careers. The movement appears to be most advanced in Europe, where numerous individual case studies of competency experiments are appearing. In the United States, the dominant method involves studying high performers and attempting to identify the characteristics that distinguish them from average and low performers. This procedure focuses on existing individual competencies, using a bottom-up analytical procedure analogous to job analysis. It tends to be very complex and precise, and it focuses on the competencies of successful *individuals* rather than on the *pattern* of individual competencies that are needed to make an *organization* successful.

This method is applicable to many situations, but it may be disastrous in others. For example, it is not based on business strategy, which means that many firms paying consultants to create "customized" competency models could end up with virtually identical lists of competencies (Zingheim, Ledford, and Schuster, 1996). Moreover, in environments that are rapidly changing, a much more nimble, anticipatory, temporary structure of competencies may be more appropriate than the elaborate, job analysis–like systems of competencies that so far appear prevalent (Ledford, 1995). Some firms, for instance, use a "learning contracts" approach, in which employees redefine learning objectives each year in performance appraisals with their supervisors. These learning contracts marry individual needs and interests with organizational needs and strategic directions.

We also know relatively little about the extent to which companies are adopting competency systems and the effectiveness of these efforts. The only U.S. study of any scope is a survey of 217 companies that are using 148 different competency models (American Compensation Association, 1996). This survey found that most of the competency-based plans for staffing, training and development, performance management, and compensation had been in place for less than a year or were still in development. Of the few firms that had been using competency-based programs for more than a year, most reported positive effects in such areas as communicating valued behaviors, raising the competency level of employees, emphasizing person-based characteristics, and reinforcing new values, but few were able to show improvements in performance.

National Competency Systems

Like the competency systems developed within firms, the national systems of industry-specific skill standards, which many countries have developed or are in the process of establishing, focus on individual-level competencies. In contrast with the company-based systems, the national systems are explicitly concerned with generic competencies that can be transferred from one enterprise to another rather than with those that are distinctive to any one enterprise. The recent growth in national competency-based standards stems from policymakers' recognition that if the advanced industrial countries are to maintain their levels of employment and their standards of living in the face of growing international competition, it is essential for them to foster the continuous development of their workforces (Reich, 1991).

National systems of skill standards are intended to address the problem of imperfect labor-market information. This problem can arise in unregulated labor markets where there is no clear and externally verified information on individuals' skills and abilities. In the absence of such information, employers tend to discount the value of the skills that individuals acquired before being hired. Therefore, individuals have less incentive to invest in their own skills. This is a particular difficulty in the United States, where the lack of well-recognized national standards, either for general education or for occupational skills, has meant that employers tend to pay little attention to the credentials of people who are not college graduates, and where young people who are not planning to attend selective colleges have little incentive to work hard in school (Bishop, 1993). This situation has also contributed to the problem of "churning" in the U.S. sub-baccalaureate labor market, which lacks clear career pathways for young people (Osterman, 1988; Klerman and Karoly, 1994; National Alliance of Business, 1995).

The U.S. youth labor market may be an extreme case of the effects of imperfect information, but all industrialized countries are struggling with the twin challenges posed by the growing importance attached to competencies and by the increasing instability of the employment relationship (see Chapter Nine). Certain competencies (such as working in teams and problem solving), which employers in many sectors are demanding, may be taught most effectively in real work settings (Streeck, 1989), and yet they are more difficult to assess and certify than traditional academic or technical skills. Likewise, increased competitive pressures have made the "job for life" a thing of the past. In the course of their working lives, most employees will work not just for a number of different firms but also, potentially, in a number of different occupations and industries. Therefore, national systems of skill standards may support both upward mobility (through recognition of the competencies that individuals have developed in the workplace) and lateral mobility (through support for the development of broadly recognized and transferable qualifications) (Wills, 1994; Tucker, 1996). These types of support in turn entail the establishment of quality-control mechanisms so that employers can be confident in individual qualifications as a fair representation of individuals' actual competencies.

In an effort to improve labor-market information and better prepare workers for the rapidly changing global economy, in 1994 the United States set up the National Skills Standards Board (NSSB) as part of the Goals 2000 Act. The NSSB is charged with bringing major stakeholders (employers, organized labor, and education providers) together to develop a voluntary national system of skill standards. The United States, with an abundance of separate professional and occupational standards, has been relatively late to recognize the potential importance of such a national system

(Hoachlander and Rahn, 1994). The Germanic countries have well-established national standards for skills in most occupations, standards that form an integral part of youth training (Finegold, 1993; Hamilton, 1990). Likewise, Canada and Japan have designed craft-certification systems through which individual workers can gain recognition for competencies that fall outside the needs of their employers (Wills, 1994).

More recently, Great Britain, Australia, and New Zealand have adopted frameworks for national standards of skills. What distinguishes these frameworks from more traditional qualification systems is that they are comprehensive, covering all levels of ability from unskilled labor to managerial and professional skills, and that they are competency-based. This entails "precise objectives stated in behavioral terms; explicit and public criteria for actual assessment; and a rejection both of set times for learning and being assessed, and of entrance requirements for candidates. Only the exit requirements associated with competence displayed should matter" (Wolf, 1995, p. 5; see also Jessup, 1991).

The appeal of the competency-based approach is that it offers individuals greater flexibility by allowing them to learn at their own pace. At the same time, it stimulates innovation among the providers of education and training (Tucker, 1996). Competency-based standards, like the use of performance specifications rather than design specifications in making a purchasing decision, do not assume that there is one best way to create a given set of skills; instead, they encourage providers to determine the best way to meet an individual's or an employer's skill requirements. This is particularly important in times of rapid advances in education and training technologies (multimedia self-study packages, for example, and Internet-based education networks).

Qualifications in these national frameworks are defined in terms of performance outcomes, with major input from firms to ensure that qualifications reflect the actual demands of the workplace. The qualifications must include the occupationally specific competencies needed for a particular function (for example, blueprint reading) and more general or "core" skills (for example, arithmetical and communication skills). To obtain a qualification, an individual must demonstrate in a real or simulated work setting that he or she has the required competencies.

It is this form of competency- or performance-based model that the United States seems likely to adopt (Tucker, 1996; Vickers, 1994; Wills, 1994). Ironically, the theory and assessment practices that underlie the British and Australian competency systems were first developed in the United States in the 1970s, in an effort to raise the quality and accountability of teacher education and certification (Andrews, 1972). This effort, which faded as federal funding for education was cut in the early 1980s, attempted first to specify the behaviors, or competencies, needed to be an effective teacher and then to design new training programs that could develop these competencies (Wolf, 1995).

Tensions Among the Competency Approaches

There are some major tensions among the different competency-based approaches. The first area of tension is a product of the three very different literatures (on corporate strategy, industrial psychology/human resources, and education/public policy) from which these competency-based approaches emerged. Not surprisingly, there are marked differences in how these three approaches define competencies. The second fundamental conflict concerns what these approaches intend to achieve and how they set about accomplishing their goals. For example, it is common practice among human resources consultants, hired to create individual-level competencies for a company, to present a prepackaged list of competencies to the client and let the client pick those that are desired. This practice is anathema to those who embrace the strategic approach because it negates the entire idea of an organization's developing competencies that are distinctive and therefore able to provide a unique competitive advantage.

It will be difficult to resolve such tensions, but it is also unlikely that the separate competency movements will succeed unless these issues are addressed. Organizational strategies designed to create core competencies must be translated into the right set of individual-level capabilities and incentives if they are to yield lasting competitive advantages. Likewise, national systems of skill standards rely heavily on employers to help define relevant competencies, provide individuals with opportunities for developing these competencies, and reward individuals who attain them. Nevertheless, employers are unlikely to want to participate in such systems if their investment in and certification of general skills fails to improve organizational performance, or if it makes it easier for competitors to hire away skilled employees. Indeed, this very problem is one of the principal stumbling blocks that is preventing the use of national skill standards in the United Kingdom and in Australia (Keltner, Finegold, and Pager, 1996).

It does seem possible, however, for companies to reconcile these three approaches to competency. Instead of paying consultants to reinvent the wheel by creating largely generic sets of competencies, they can start by embracing industry-specific skill standards (where these are available) as the basis for recruiting. This move could reduce hiring costs and improve the quality of new recruits by improving the flow of information between educators and employers and by creating a mechanism for holding educational institutions accountable for the competencies of their graduates. By carefully analyzing their own strategic organizational requirements, companies can determine what distinctive individual competencies they need to add to national standards. The following section discusses how these distinctive competencies can be embedded in the core elements of an organization.

Organizational Design and Effectiveness

The business strategy literature on core competencies and capabilities leads to some rather straightforward predictions about when an organization will be effective. Essentially, this literature argues that an organization will be effective when it has the competencies and capabilities to implement a well-developed business strategy—that is, when the organization can execute the kinds of behavior necessary for it to deal effectively with its business environment. It is also worth noting here that the resources available to an organization may also come into play in determinations of how effective the organization is.

The diamond model (see Figure 2 in the Introduction) captures the relationship between organizational effectiveness and strategy. It shows organizational effectiveness as being the result of a good fit among the organizational strategy, competencies, capabilities, and environment. The diamond model depicts the environment as an important part of this relationship for two reasons: first, an organization may do a wonderful job of executing its strategy, but the strategy may not fit the business environment; and, second, as the environment changes, the organization may need to change its strategies, capabilities, and competencies. In this respect, the environment, like the existing competencies, capabilities, and resources of the organization, should be an important factor in strategy development.

Whereas the business strategy literature is relatively silent about how organizations can be designed for the right mix of core competencies, the literature on organizational capabilities is much more concerned with how organizations should be designed (Lawler, 1994; Lawler and Ledford, 1997). This is hardly surprising because, in many respects, an organization's capabilities tend to reside more in its design and its systems than core competencies do. In order for either of these approaches to be useful and testable, it must ultimately be tied to how the organization can be designed to produce particular competencies and capabilities. The star model (Figure 3 in the Introduction) depicts the fit among organizational strategy, structure, processes, people, and rewards (Galbraith, 1973). The star model (like the Leavitt diamond and the McKinsey "Seven S" model) can be a helpful aid to thinking about how competencies and capabilities can be developed in an organization. Once the strategy has been defined, and once the competencies and capabilities needed to implement the strategy have been identified, it becomes a matter of identifying and developing the structures, processes, reward systems, and human resources management practices that will produce the needed competencies and capabilities. In terms of the points on the star, what are the implications of the competencies/capabilities approach for conceptualizing and operationalizing these elements?

Structure

The structural component of the star model addresses structure at the micro or job-design level as well as at the macro or organizational-architecture level. Perhaps the most interesting and potentially radical implication of the competencies/capabilities approach has already been noted: its implications for job design. The job is the organizational atom in bureaucratic designs. It is the lowest level of organizational structure, the point at which the division of labor stops. The entire organization is built on the basis of job descriptions and individual accountability for job performance. Job descriptions are also the basis for the design of all major human resources systems, including selection, training, pay, career development, and performance management (Ash, Levine, and Sistrunk, 1983).

The rate of organizational change is currently so great that the well-defined stable job appears to be a historical anachronism (Bridges, 1994; Lawler, 1996; Lawler and Ledford, 1992). The focus on speed to market, quality, and lateral processes, and the use of downsizing, reengineering, work redesign, team-based designs, and other changes, have made the conventional job obsolete in many companies. Increasingly, employees do not have discrete, stable jobs; instead, they have a constantly changing mix of tasks to perform. These changes are especially common and significant in the case of managers and professionals, whose work has always been the most difficult to capture in job descriptions. Even when the job continues to be a relevant concept, the downsized human resources function may be unable to administer job-based systems that include extensive job descriptions. Therefore, firms are increasingly abandoning job descriptions and careful job analyses: they lack the personnel to create and maintain them.

A number of authors (for example, Lawler, 1990) have argued that the focus should be on individuals' skills and knowledge rather than on the nature of their jobs. This argument leads directly to the idea of replacing a job description with a description of skills and knowledge, or of individual competency. To be useful, this kind of description has to identify what technical and organizational skills and knowledge an individual needs. It also has to identify how an individual's possession of these skills and knowledge can be determined. As will be discussed in Chapter Eleven, this is a critical element for any reward system that is focused on rewarding individuals for developing skills and knowledge.

The literature on teams has argued that it may not make sense for organizations to focus on and measure individual performance in team-based environments (for example, see Mohrman, Cohen, and Mohrman, 1995). Instead, it has been argued, performance is best measured at the level of the team or business unit because this is where performance can be measured most objectively, and where measurement of performance can best create key lateral processes. It is also often argued in this approach that tasks should be assigned to groups, teams, or parts of an organization. For this kind of task-assignment process to be an informed one, however, the organization must be able to identify the skills and knowledge of each participating individual—and before the organization can be adequately staffed for the performance of its key business tasks, of course, it must ensure that individuals develop the right sets of skills and the right kinds of knowledge.

The competency/capability approach also has some interesting implications for macro-level organizational design—indeed, this level of the organization's structure is where this approach may already be having its greatest impact. Some current trends in organizational design—for example, the trends discussed in Chapters Two, Three, and Four, especially the trend away from corporations with multiple unrelated businesses—may be the result of this impact. Such corporations typically find it difficult to develop any particular distinguishing competencies and capabilities. As a result, their effectiveness and reasons for being (as contrasted to the effectiveness and reason for being of a single-business corporation) are hard to defend. Approaches like front-back and process organizing, however, seem to be growing in popularity partly because they allow the organization to develop capabilities in quality, speed to market, and customer focus (see Chapters Two, Three, and Four).

A good guess is that focusing on the kinds of competencies and capabilities that a particular organizational structure generates will lead, over time, to some innovative approaches to organizational design. The bureaucratic approach to thinking about the macro level of organization focuses on functional expertise, the achievement of organizational growth, and control, whereas focusing on the development of competencies and capabilities provides a significantly different starting point for organizational design. In essence, it provides a new set of lenses through which to view the world of organizational design. Therefore, it seems possible that it will lead not just away from the functional bureaucratic organization but also toward the invention of macro-organizational structures that provide competitive advantage through the creation of new and different capabilities.

Processes

Perhaps the most direct implications of the competencies/capabilities approach for organizational effectiveness concern measurement. In the bureaucratic model, measurement processes are focused on operational and financial results in ways that fit an individually oriented bureaucratic approach to control. The alternative is to focus on measuring the level of organizational performance around such capabilities and competencies as speed to market, technical expertise, quality, and whatever else is crucial to the organization's effectiveness.

Organizations that have adopted the thinking of total quality management provide an interesting example of how a focus on developing a particular capability leads to changes in information processes. Almost without exception, these organizations have changed their measurement systems to focus more on product quality and customer satisfaction. The reengineering approach, with its emphasis on cycle time (and, of course, on staffing levels) has also often changed the nature of the information and communication processes in organizations. The reengineering approach asks different questions about organizational performance; as a result, it too has suggested different kinds of measurement.

The different competency-based approaches also suggest that the organization needs, again, to be very aware of the skills and knowledge of each individual employee. It needs to be able to develop an information system that includes data on what individuals need to know as well as on their current knowledge. This approach fits well with a human resources information system keyed to the performance capabilities of each individual. There already are a few organizations with information systems whereby managers at every level can access a database and determine the competencies, knowledge, and experience of individuals throughout the organization. This kind of access to information enables them not only to make staffing decisions but also to obtain an overall sense of how able the organization is to staff particular projects and perform in particular ways.

Reward Systems

The approaches to structure and processes that are suggested by competencies/capabilities thinking have significant implications for the design of reward systems. As will be discussed further in Chapter Eleven, these approaches argue strongly for the use of skill- or competency-based pay and for pay-for-performance systems that focus on collective rather than individual performance. Both reward systems follow directly from the types of structures and the kinds of information and measurement processes that fit the competencies/capabilities approach.

There already is a significant increase in the use of skill- or competency-based pay (Jenkins, Ledford, Gupta, and Doty, 1992; Lawler, Mohrman, and Ledford, 1995). In most cases, it is being used in manufacturing and in nonexempt white-collar work because these are areas where teams are being introduced and where the competencies needed for specific tasks are most easily identified and measured. Nevertheless, there is also growing interest in using competency-based pay for knowledge workers and managers (Ledford, 1995; O'Neal, 1993–1994; Tucker and Cofsky, 1994). This trend follows from the movement away from jobs. It is the logical way to support the development of particular competencies and capabilities in an organization. It encourages employees to develop the skills and knowledge that create the organization's competencies and capabilities. Competency-based pay also may be the best way to determine the actual market value of individuals. As organizations increasingly look for individuals with particular performance capabilities, it follows that the market value of individuals is likely to be determined by what they can do, not by what jobs they are doing (Lawler, 1990). Therefore, a logical alternative to paying individuals for what they do in their jobs is to pay individuals for what they *can* do by assessing and determining the market value of their skills, knowledge, and competencies.

Individual performance-based pay or merit pay is a staple of the traditional bureaucratic approach to organizing. It fits the logic of the bureaucratic approach because it targets individual performance effectiveness as the key behavior. This approach offers only a poor fit, however, with most of the capabilities and competencies that organizations want to develop. Competencies and capabilities often involve complex behavior on the part of multiple individuals, and the effectiveness of all this complex behavior is often visible only at the collective level. It is not surprising, then, that over the last decade there has been increased use of profit sharing, stock ownership, gainsharing, and other reward systems that pay for collective behavior (Lawler, Mohrman, and Ledford, 1995). Often these collective reward systems focus on performance measures that reflect such capabilities as speed to market, customer satisfaction, and innovation.

People

The competencies/capabilities approach to organizing suggests a very different approach to thinking about an organization's human resources management systems. The absence of jobs makes most such traditional systems unusable because they rest on the foundation of good job descriptions. These traditional systems pay individuals on the basis of the number of their job responsibilities and the quality of their job performance. They select individuals for particular jobs, and they train and develop individuals to do jobs or a series of jobs during their careers. Earlier we suggested that, in the new approach, a set of individual competencies should be substituted for the individual job description and should form the basis for the organization's human resources management systems. It should also be used as a basis for the selection process, as well as for the purposes of training and development and pay.

Where the organization's hiring decisions are concerned, the competency/capabilities approach suggests a different starting point from the one that is traditionally used. Instead of simply hiring somebody to fill a job, the organization needs to view itself as hiring a new organizational employee (Bowen, Ledford, and Nathan, 1991). Another way to put this is to say that individuals are hired to become members of the organization, not to fill jobs. The organization needs to look at the kinds of skills and capabilities it needs *as an organization* and determine how a job applicant's existing skills and knowledge will contribute to the organization's necessary capabilities and competencies, as well as how likely the individual is to develop the skills needed to support the organization's competencies and capabilities. The implication is that it will be helpful to use realistic job (work and organization) previews, team-based selection processes, extensive hiring and entry processes, and, perhaps most important, a focus on an individual's ability to develop new skills and competencies.

The selection process needs to be supported by the kind of human resources information system that carefully catalogues and enables the development of individuals' skills and knowledge and that links the selection process to the kinds of competencies and capabilities called for by the organization's strategy. Another implication is that there should be a career-management system in which individuals make career moves aimed at their developing the skills and knowledge they need in order to contribute to the organization's key capabilities. For example, if mastery of lateral processes is a key capability, then cross-functional career moves need to be an important part of the career-management system (Galbraith, 1994)—indeed, cross-functional moves, in this case, need to be built into the systems for career management, rewards, and information; individuals should be provided with extensive information about career opportunities, and cross-functional moves should be directly rewarded.

The competencies/capabilities approach also has some interesting implications for employment stability and security. Many of the competencies and capabilities that provide such competitive advantages as quality and speed to market require effective relationships among many individuals. The suggestion here is that relatively permanent employees are needed because employment stability is a necessary precondition for the development of effective working relationships. This is not an argument that everyone should be "guaranteed" a job for life—quite the contrary. The necessary organizational competencies and capabilities may change as the environment changes and as the business strategy changes. Under these conditions, it is important that the organization either be able to develop existing employees so that they have the necessary new skills and knowledge or that it be able to hire replacement employees who have the kinds of skills and capabilities that are needed to support the new organizational requirements.

As will be discussed further in Chapter Nine, what is called for here is nothing less than a new kind of learning contract between the organization and the individual.

There already exists some research on the relationship between competencies and employment stability. For example, Capelli and Crocker-Hefter (1996) compared several pairs of competitors. In each pair, one member (for example, Pepsi) pursued flexible, entrepreneurial, "prospector" strategies, and the other (for example, Coca-Cola) pursued "defender" strategies aimed at protecting established market niches. The prospector firms consistently emphasized the hiring of employees who brought advanced skills, whereas the defender firms devoted far more resources to employee development and emphasized employment stability to a greater degree.

The competencies/capabilities approach is compatible with a "ring of defense" approach to employment stability (Handy, 1990, 1994). This strategy involves establishing a core group of employees as relatively permanent members of the organization. Individuals outside the core have less job security and, at the extreme, may be temporary employees or consultants. If an organization is going to compete on its technical competencies or its organizational capabilities, then it needs to protect those individuals who are most important to its key competencies and capabilities. A clear implication is that decisions about layoffs or terminations ought to take account of how important individuals are to the organization's key competencies and capabilities; such decisions should not be based on individuals' seniority or positions in the organizational hierarchy.

The challenge in implementing the "ring of defense" approach is to identify the individuals who are crucial to those competencies and capabilities that the organization has identified as its competitive advantage. This approach also requires decisions about which kinds of knowledge are best provided by members of the organization and which kinds are best purchased from consultants or temporary employees. As a general rule, the more important a competency or capability is to an organization's competitive advantage, the less sense it makes to purchase the relevant knowledge from a vendor. It is risky to depend on vendors because most of them are free to sell the same services and resources to an organization's competitors.

Fit

Central to the star model is the concept of *fit*. Organizational effectiveness depends not only on the proper design of each point of the star but also on the fit among the points. Historically, the whole concept of fit has been very attractive to organizational theorists, but it is sometimes difficult to put into operation. Saying that fit is important does not give the kind of detailed specifications needed to design reward systems for particular types of organizational structures, nor does it indicate the kinds of individual skills and abilities that are needed to operate particular information systems. The idea of competencies and capabilities certainly does not provide these answers, but it can help in specifying what constitutes an adequate fit because it allows each element of the star to be tested on its alignment with the kinds of competencies and capabilities that the organization needs. For example, as will be discussed in Chapter Eleven, the idea of competencies and capabilities is directly related to the issue of whether the right kinds of individual skills and competencies are being rewarded, and whether these are likely to produce the organizational capabilities that are needed for the effective implementation of a strategy.

Conclusion

The work done so far on competencies and capabilities represents an interesting convergence of work done at the individual level and work done at the organization's strategic level. In many respects, this is its most interesting and potentially most significant feature. It holds the promise of linking traditionally non-strategic processes (such as human resources management) to organizational strategy, in a meaningful and coherent way. It is one vehicle that may in fact help the human resources function achieve its frequently stated goal of becoming a strategic business partner.

Perhaps the best way to summarize the situation with respect to competencies and capabilities is to say that the ideas are promising and the work is interesting, but in many respects the ideas and the empirical research are in their infancy. As a result, there are still no operational systems that would allow an organization to go directly from a strategy calling for particular competencies to organizational systems in which particular competencies could be developed. To remedy this lack, research is needed on the behavior and effectiveness of organizations that adopt structures like those discussed in Chapters Two, Three, and Four. Work is also needed on the other four points of the star.

A growing body of research is focusing on the competencies/capabilities approach, and so there is good reason to believe that this approach may develop as a principal organizing logic in the future (Lawler, 1994; Lawler and Ledford, 1997). It is less clear how national standards for skills and competencies will develop, and how critical their development will be to the use of the competencies/capabilities approach in the design of organizations. National standards clearly have the potential to be helpful to individuals and organizations alike. If they were to become well developed, for example, they could ease human resources management challenges by helping with the selection and development processes, both inside and outside firms. In the best-case scenario, national standards could provide foundational skills and knowledge on which organizations could build as they developed the unique competencies and capabilities constituting competitive advantages.

Any company inevitably looks for an edge over its competitors where organizational design is concerned. Therefore, a company is not likely to support a competency system that expects it to invest in general skills that are not potential sources of competitive advantage. One way to make the system useful is to place heavy emphasis on the basic skills that employees will need in order to operate in the modern business environment. If these skills can be certified and are widely present in the employee population, then an organization can go on to structure its own unique training programs for producing the core competencies and organizational capabilities that will provide a differentiating advantage. What kinds of capabilities might form the basis on which an organization could build its own individual competencies? A number of them clearly have to do with interpersonal processes, communication, business understanding, economical and financial analysis, problem solving, and a host of others that have been identified by various reports on the future of work and educational reform. The challenge is not to define these competencies but to create the learning environments—in schools, in colleges, and in the workplace—where they can be developed effectively.

Chapter Six

The Changing Nature of Work
Managing the Impact of Information Technology

Susan G. Cohen
Don Mankin

New information technologies, combined with the global competitive pressures discussed throughout this book, have fundamentally changed the nature of work. Work is now more abstract than physical, more likely to be designed for teams than for individuals, and more likely to cross boundaries than to be confined within particular organizations, departments, or functions. As a result, organizations have become more flexible, empowering, and team-based. Information technology (IT) has enabled these changes. Personal computers, company networks, multimedia capacity, and the Internet provide and distribute the information and the analytical tools required for individual and team-based work. More people can have access to the information and knowledge needed to produce new products and services more quickly than the competition, and at a higher level of quality. Processing information to produce knowledge is at the heart of how the nature of work has fundamentally changed. The implications are profound. Individuals and organizations must successfully adapt to them if they are to survive in this postindustrial economy.

Note: Material for this chapter has been adapted and excerpted from Mankin, Cohen, and Bikson (1996).

The Information Age

Computers are everywhere. They are on just about every desk, in every office, and on every factory floor. Computers and communication systems continue to grow in sophistication while decreasing in price. They are smaller, more powerful, and networked, connecting individuals within and across organizations. The amount of money that organizations spend on computer systems is staggering. Corporate spending for IT hardware has doubled in the last five years—and each dollar buys more computing power. In 1995, corporations spent $225 billion dollars on IT hardware, and this figure does not include the cost of software or services (Stewart, 1995). Although computers are expected to be even more widespread in the twenty-first century, everyday experience strongly suggests that the Information Age is already here.

Information technology has changed its emphasis from stand-alone computation to collaboration and connection (Chatterjee, 1991). The number of North American home/office users of the Internet in 1996 was estimated at 17.6 million, and estimates of the worldwide Internet user base ranged from as low as 23.5 million to as high as 60 million. The number of computers connected directly to the Internet has nearly doubled in just the last year (Bott, 1996). More and more companies are setting up company intranets (frequently linked to the Internet), connecting employees to one another and to massive databases. For example, in 1994 Hewlett-Packard's ninety-seven thousand employees exchanged twenty million e-mail messages (and seventy thousand more outside the company), shared three trillion characters of data (for example, engineering specs), and executed more than a quarter of a million electronic transactions each month with customers and suppliers (Stewart, 1994).

If present trends continue, we will have supercomputing power at our fingertips by the beginning of the next century. This will have a dramatic impact on how we communicate with one another. Multimedia transmission—the simultaneous communication of text, pictures, voice, and movies—requires state-of-the-art hardware and high-bandwidth data highways. Portable systems—laptop computers, cellular phones, faxes, and pen-based computers—provide multimedia capacity to users regardless of time and space, and the use of portable systems is growing. As the information revolution continues, there will be an almost unlimited capacity to simultaneously sense, manipulate, store, display, and communicate large amounts of information (Van der Spiegel, 1995). Clearly, IT helps organizations respond to the new competitive environment. What may not be so clear is that it will continue to do so by fundamentally changing the nature of work.

The Changing Nature of Work: From the Physical to the Abstract

Work in industrial economies requires metal, steel, machinery, and muscle. The sheer physicality of the work is its defining characteristic. In postindustrial economies, the raw material is information, the product is knowledge, the machinery is the computer, and physical labor is replaced by intellectual effort. Most knowledge-based work involves the manipulation of symbols and abstractions, not of things. The production machinery is software, not assembly lines. Inventory and stores are represented by databases that are on disks several inches in diameter, not by warehouses covering acres of land. The defining characteristic of postindustrial work, in short, is its *lack* of physicality. Nowadays it often involves little more than eyes scanning a computer screen, fingers moving across a keyboard, and the occasional furrowing of a brow. Of course, not all work in the modern economy is knowledge-based, and some physical work does remain; more than ever, though, people work with their heads and not with their hands. Most people provide services, and some make products, but everyone's work has been influenced by information technology.

The design of knowledge-based work is not constrained by unwieldy physical materials and objects. The raw material, information, is infinitely manipulable. Even the machinery is flexible and can be "retooled" by the writing of new software code. Work can thus be designed, structured, and organized in any number of ways. Information technology creates many options, and this fact has several implications for the nature and quality of work today.

Deskilling Versus Upgrading Work

Computer-based systems can be used to deskill work (by automatically generating decisions) or upgrade work (by providing information to help individuals or teams make the decisions themselves). To use Zuboff's terms (1984), computers can automate work or "informate" it by providing data about underlying productive and administrative processes. Employees can use this computer-generated stream of information to make decisions that add value to the production of goods and to the delivery of services.

A recent reengineering project in a telephone company illustrates how computer systems can upgrade the skills of employees by "informating" their work:

> An expert system was placed in the company's repair centers to enable the new maintenance administrators to test telephone lines during customer calls. About half of the new maintenance administrators had worked previously as customer service representatives. Before reengineering, customer service representatives had performed only data-processing tasks: they entered the customer's name, address, and phone number into the computer system, along with a description of the nature of the problem. After the work processes had been reengineered, the new work maintenance administrators received training in the use of the expert system and were then able to perform the telephone-line testing themselves and decide, while talking with the customer, whether a repair worker needed to be dispatched to the customer's site. The former customer service representatives saw the new system as augmenting their capabilities. Although some were intimidated by the new technical challenges, most enjoyed being able to solve problems for customers. They reported increased job satisfaction and a higher quality of work life.

External Control Versus Self-Management

The flexibility of computer-based work extends to the systems that organizations use to control behavior and performance. Managers can use computers as instruments of control or as means of enabling self-control. Managers can closely monitor employees' behavior by using computer-generated performance data or they can provide the tools for employees to monitor their own behavior.

Management's values and expectations ultimately determine how computer-based control systems are used, a fact illustrated by another aspect of the same reengineering project at the telephone company just described:

> The new computer system that was installed in the telephone company's repair centers provided detailed performance measures. The computer tracked the time spent on each call, the number of calls handled each hour, and the accuracy of the "trouble" reports that were sent to the repair-dispatch center. Reports could be generated that detailed the performance of each person, each group of subordinates, or the repair center as a whole. In early planning discussions, the repair centers' managers had talked about empowering the employees by having them monitor their own performance on the basis of the performance information they received. Management had intended to teach the employees how to obtain their daily individual performance results and planned on having supervisors review group and repair-center performance results with the employees in order to stimulate employees' ideas and actions for improved performance.

> Once the center became operational, however, management shifted its focus to achieving cost goals by minimizing the time spent on each call. Employees were never taught how to pull their performance results from the computer system. Instead, supervisors collected the data on each person's average time spent on each call and "counseled" those employees who spent too long. Repair-center performance data were posted on bulletin boards, but no time was spent discussing with employees what could be done to improve performance. Managers viewed any time off the phones as an unnecessary expense and were reluctant to schedule any employee meetings. The control-oriented culture of the telephone company, and the very real performance pressures it faced, drove out the early intention of empowering the workforce.

The message from this case is clear: information technology makes work more abstract and flexible. It expands the options for work design. Work can be designed to empower employees or to control them. The result is determined by the values, culture, expectations, and imagination of the designers rather than by the technology or by the raw materials on which it operates.

Tacit Knowledge Versus Intellective Skills

As work becomes more abstract, something is lost. Zuboff (1984) argues that computerization often means replacing the immediacy of the sensory experience of work—the sound of a machine, or the feel of a product coming off a production line—with a "data interface" that conveys the same information via a very different medium: "It's as if one's job had vanished," she notes, "into a two-dimensional space of abstractions, where digital symbols replace a concrete reality" (p. 63). Predictably, this transformation is often accompanied by feelings of vulnerability, frustration, and loss of control. These feelings were voiced by those new maintenance administrators in the telephone company who had previously worked as maintenance technicians (rather than as customer service representatives):

> Before reengineering, the maintenance technicians had tested telephone lines and determined whether repair crews needed to be dispatched so that problems could be fixed at customers' sites. They responded to job orders from customer service representatives and did not speak directly to customers. Computer support was limited, and the maintenance technicians had to understand how the phone lines worked. They had extensive technical training and could troubleshoot most problems.
>
> With the new expert system, maintenance administrators could test the telephone lines while talking directly to customers. The former maintenance technicians no longer needed to draw so much on their technical knowledge because the expert system did any necessary analysis. They voiced frustration that the computer analysis seemed distant from physical reality: many still ran the old backup tests to check electronic patterns. As a result, their performance suffered as they spent too much time on each customer call.

The computerization of work can result in the loss of *tacit knowledge,* the kind of knowledge that comes from using human senses to experience work and take action. Tacit knowledge is holistic. It cannot be broken down into segmented parts. For example, playing the piano is more than learning the order in which one's fingers need to strike the keys. Neisser (1983), a cognitive psychologist, describes tacit knowledge in the following way: "The skilled carpenter knows just how a given variety of wood must be handled, or what type of joint will best serve his purpose at a particular edge. To say that he 'knows' these things is not to claim that he could put his knowledge into words. That is never entirely possible. . . . The practitioner's knowledge of a medium is tacit. It is essential to skilled practice: the carpenter uses what he knows with every stroke of his tool." (p. 3). As work becomes more abstract, employees may lose their tacit knowledge about certain aspects of their work, as well as the satisfaction that derives from the intimacy and sentience of this knowledge.

This is not an inevitable outcome, however. The abstract distance of "informated" work can also be an opportunity for reflection, for thinking analytically about one's work, using explicit scientific knowledge rather than relying exclusively on implicit understandings and intuition. A new set of competencies is required—"intellective skills," Zuboff (1984) calls them—before one can take advantage of the information and the opportunity offered by our new technologies. The development of intellective skills builds on a foundation of tacit knowledge. Seeing patterns and creating meaning from data requires inductive and deductive reasoning, as well as the ability to apply a conceptual framework to the information at hand. In effect, the development of intellective skills requires tacit knowledge of data and information. Just as a carpenter can know the properties of a piece of wood by its look and feel, the new intellective technicians will be able to intuit the properties of their own work materials via the abstract data sets generated by the technology of their work. This kind of intuiting can be at least as satisfying as the explicit requirements of physical work.

New multimedia technologies can help by creating virtual realities that stimulate the senses and help transform abstract data into technology-based tacit knowledge. Users will put on head-mounted displays that provide images and sound; they will wear gloves that provide tactile stimulation, and they will be able to manipulate their environments by using joysticks and control gloves (Van der Spiegel, 1995). Physicians will be able to practice heart surgery, pilots to fly airplanes, and emergency crews to rescue earthquake victims—all from the safety of their offices. New computer systems, by helping people develop both tacit and explicit knowledge, can augment human capability and performance.

Intellective abilities can also be developed through opportunities for collaboration (Mohrman and Cohen, 1995). Studies of service technicians (Orr, 1990) and insurance-claims processors (Wenger, 1991) have shown that learning and innovation emerge from interacting with others in "communities of practice." Innovation often results when people from different backgrounds combine their perspectives in novel ways to develop solutions to problems (Kanter, 1985; Pinchot, 1985). The use of information technology expands these opportunities for collaboration and innovation by enabling people to work together regardless of where they are. Virtual-reality technologies enable groups of people to share the same experiences and environments, even though they are miles and even continents apart (Van der Spiegel, 1995). Shared experiences can help people transcend their differences and strengthen the basis for collaboration. Electronic collaboration creates the potential for people to become smarter and more innovative.

In short, computer-based work can be designed to augment the capabilities of users and help them develop intellective skills. Information systems can be designed to enable self-management and help users develop and maintain tacit knowledge. Of course, individuals will vary in their intellective capabilities and in the satisfaction they derive from self-management and upgraded skills. Some will not be able to adjust to the new intellective demands and will find that their skills are no longer needed. Others who excel at these new abstract tasks will find many opportunities available to them.

This change in the nature of work creates new winners and new losers, but the future is promising for those who can adapt to the new realities, feel empowered by the new technologies, and understand their work. Organizations will increasingly value and reward employees who can make fast, customer-oriented, point-of-action decisions. These people will provide their own controls and will focus on creating positive performance results. For them, at least, work will be designed to increase individual potential. For their organizations, the result will be more effective tackling of the competitive challenges accompanying the transition to the twenty-first century (Lawler, 1996).

Telecommuting and Its Downside

Information technology reduces constraints on where, when, and how we work. Telecommuting is possibly the most visible demonstration of the inherent flexibility of knowledge-based work. With the new communication technologies, employees and independent contractors alike can work at home or in neighborhood satellite work centers. They can communicate with others in real time, as necessary, or they can do so asynchronously by responding to e-mail messages, downloading reports and analyses, and writing memos as the need arises. Their schedules are set by due dates and milestones, not by the availability of team members.

The images are now commonplace: working at home, sometimes at great distances from the office and co-workers; sending and receiving messages at any hour of the day or night via fax or e-mail. The potential benefits associated with the lowering of time- and space-related barriers to work are many. Workers can go at their own pace. They can adapt their work schedules to fit their lives, rather than the other way around. They can save money on clothes and commuting (and we all gain from reduced traffic and auto emissions). Workers' increased productivity contributes to the company's bottom line. Evidence on the ultimate economic impact of time- and space-independent work is still emerging, but the potential impact on our lives, as well as the flexibility and options that such freedom offers, are unmistakable (Nilles, 1994).

Technology can support telecommuting by helping to create collaborative environments across time and space. A collaborative environment consists of shared space—places for many people to express ideas, draw sketches and models, and manipulate data: "It takes shared space to create shared understandings" (Schrage, 1995, p. 94), and this is the essence of collaboration. The whiteboard filled with employees' suggestions for next month's meeting agenda is a shared space. The blackboard covered with mathematical proofs developed by a professor and revised by his graduate student is a shared space. Technology enables shared space to be created for people who are not co-located (Schrage, 1995). A note faxed back and forth, capturing the design changes of two engineers, allows them to collaborate. More advanced and higher-bandwidth technologies add richness and simultaneity to this technology-enabled collaboration. Videoconferencing, combined with shared computer access, is the next best thing to being there. There is no substitute for the immediacy and richness of interaction in face-to-face meetings, but these tools do enable collaboration without the need for physical co-location.

In recent years many companies have turned to telecommuting, among them DuPont, Hewlett-Packard, Pacific Bell, and the thousands of companies that continued the telecommuting programs they had begun when the 1994 Northridge earthquake devastated critical segments of southern California's freeway system. After the quake, Pacific Bell offered free installation of telecommuting services to businesses and residents facing months of traffic delays because of damaged freeways and streets. Seven months later, after many of the freeways had been repaired, the company surveyed 660 of the customers who had accepted the earlier offer and found that 93 percent were still telecommuting (Dodd-Thomas, 1994).

A few companies, taking the idea a step farther, have eliminated office space for many of their employees. For example, Tandem Computer in Sunnyvale, California, gives employees access to small cubicles and offices when they need them. Employees sign up and reserve these spaces through a "hotel manager." Much of the space in Tandem's facility is reserved for meeting rooms, where people can get together to exchange information and work on common projects. The company provides support in the form of laptop computers, cellular phones, and technical advice to employees so that they can work independently—from their homes and on the road. Tandem has done this as a way of reducing costs, but the arrangement also enhances employees' flexibility (Lawler, 1996).

Of course, telecommuting has its downside. For example, some employees stop telecommuting because they feel too isolated and lonely. If forced to telecommute, they may experience anxiety. Others reduce their connections and commitment to their work groups and companies. Still others complain that work too easily creeps into home life when the office is just down the hall. Families of telecommuters may resent the intrusion of work into their personal lives, as well as the resulting difficulty of balancing the demands of family and work life (Davis, 1995). Employees with young children may find it impossible to work at home, and others—distracted by the dishes that need to be washed, the lawn that needs to be mowed, the afternoon soap opera or sporting event waiting to be watched, or the snacks in the kitchen calling out to be eaten—may have trouble disciplining themselves to work at home.

Neighborhood work centers may provide an alternative to the isolation and demands of working at home and the long commutes to the company's office. Working side by side with others from the same neighborhood may build a sense of community. Networks across organizations may develop through the use of shared office space. For example, scientists from one firm can be co-located in shared laboratories with scientists from another firm, and both firms can benefit from the shared intellectual stimulation and investment in laboratory facilities as long as proprietary rights and intellectual capital can be protected. Companies can decide to rent neighborhood work space together with their suppliers and customers, building relationships that increase their competitiveness. Organizational designers can intentionally use this commuting alternative to create interorganizational networks. Furthermore, it may be less costly for companies to obtain space in neighborhood work centers than to provide company space for all their employees.

Another problem associated with telecommuting is that managers may experience difficulty giving up the control that comes from seeing subordinates each day. Managers need to manage the performance of telecommuters by monitoring goal accomplishment instead of moment-by-moment behaviors. They need to involve employees in running the business. Involved employees will exercise self-control whether or not they work in the same offices as their managers. They will care about satisfying customers and competing in the marketplace. For example, Hitachi Data Systems has several field service offices that are remote from their managers. In one particularly successful remote location we studied, the service technicians spoke proudly of always doing what was right for customers. They were dedicated to fixing any problem, day or night, and, on the basis of this goal, managed their own schedules in order to do so.

Finally, organizations need to be flexible in their use of telecommuting arrangements. One approach does not fit all circumstances. For example, a manager in a high-technology firm found it very frustrating to adhere to her company's policy allowing all employees the opportunity to telecommute. One of her people who had chosen to telecommute really needed to be on site to do his work, and so she was in the unusual bind of trying to go along with her company's policy while still getting her department's work done. Clearly, managers need to be able to require employees to be on site when the employees' presence is necessary. Telecommuting also does not mean that people never meet face to face. Face-to-face meetings should be judiciously planned when projects need to be formulated, sensitive deliberations need to be made, and critical decisions need to be reached that require commitment to a course of action (Sproull and Kiesler, 1991).

From Individual Jobs to Teams of Many Types

Teams provide the potential for producing products and delivering services faster than the competition does, at lower cost and with higher quality. Therefore, it is no surprise that companies have dramatically increased their use of teams. According to Gordon (1982), 82 percent of companies with one hundred or more employees reported using teams; and, according to Lawler, Mohrman, and Ledford (1995), 68 percent of Fortune 1000 companies reported using self-managing work teams in 1993, with only 28 percent using them in 1987, and 91 percent of Fortune 1000 companies reported using employee participation groups in 1993, with only 70 percent using them in 1987. Capelli and Rogovsky (1994), examining data on fifty-six thousand U.S. production workers, have found that the skill most commonly required by the new work practices is the ability to work in teams.

If teamwork is the key to high performance, information is the key to effective teamwork. In a practical sense, information *is* the work. It is raw material to be manipulated and transformed, and it is the basis for the process by which team-based actions occur. Information is what is exchanged by team members as they analyze and deliberate. Ultimately, teams' results—the solutions they develop, the decisions they make, and the knowledge they generate—are information-based. This is not just the case for work that has always been knowledge-based, such as market research, new-product development, and financial services; rather, *all* work is becoming more knowledge-based, even the work of production teams. Therefore, team members need "tools" to help them gain access to information, to manage and analyze it, to share it among themselves, to communicate it to others, and to stay connected with customers. These tools come in the form of new information technology. IT is what will enable teams to function effectively within the rich matrix of information that, from the executive suite to the shop floor and the retail outlet, now comprises the very essence of modern work.

Types of Teams

"A team is a team is a team," Gertrude Stein might say if she were reincarnated today as a manager or an organizational consultant. Like most other people, she would probably assume that all teams are pretty much the same. This view is widely held, but it is inaccurate and tends to overlook important differences in the various ways people have of working together. There are five major types of teams in organizations today:

- Work teams
- Project and development teams
- Management teams
- Parallel teams
- Ad hoc networks

The use of information technology can transform all five types into high-performing teams.

Work teams are continuing work units responsible for producing goods or providing services (Cohen, 1993). The self-managing work team, a form of work team growing in popularity, involves employees in making decisions that were formerly the province of supervisors, managers, and support staff. Self-managing work teams reduce the need for supervisors and unnecessary staff support, thereby reducing costs. IT can help reduce costs even further while enhancing team performance. For example, an insurance company that we studied installed a new information system and reorganized its back-office support from a functional to a geographical basis. In the functional organization, a customer with questions about multiple policies had been referred to as many as twenty employees, each having knowledge of just one function and product line. After the reorganization, in which self-managing work teams of employees were assigned responsibility for all the policies in a given geographical area, a customer's question could be answered with one or (at the most) two telephone calls. Each customer service representative could access the necessary information just by looking at a computer screen. As a result, the employees were able to focus directly on meeting customers' requirements. Not surprisingly, customer satisfaction improved dramatically, and the costs of providing service decreased.

Project and development teams produce one-time outputs, such as a new product or a new information system. They frequently draw their members from different disciplines and functional units so that specialized expertise can be applied to the project at hand. In the petrochemicals industry, for example, integrated development teams of geology, geophysics, and engineering staff are dedicated to specific oil-exploration projects. They are supported by technical experts in offices around the world. Supercomputers, networks, and advances in three-dimensional seismic acquisition and processing have drawn these disciplines closer together and enabled expertise to be provided worldwide for solving any problem any time of the day or night (Neff and Thrasher, 1993). Another advantage of project teams is that they can handle multiple activities simultaneously, thereby saving time. Consequently, companies are expanding the use of project teams as a response to time-based competition (Stalk and Hout, 1990). For example, Boeing used 230 teams around the world to develop each component of its 777 aircraft. These teams were composed not only of representatives from different functions but also of customers so that Boeing could be sure that customers' wishes were considered in the plane's design. Boeing connected the 230 teams into a vast three-dimensional IT-based design network. The network allowed people working on different parts of the aircraft to coordinate their actions and shift data among themselves. The technology, the team approach, and the design process eliminated problems before they reached the manufacturing stage, reducing manufacturing rework by 90 percent and cutting the normal development time in half (Taninecz, 1996).

Management teams coordinate and provide direction to the subunits under their jurisdiction, laterally integrating interdependent subunits across key business processes (Mohrman, Cohen, and Mohrman, 1995). Faced with the complexity and turbulence of the global business environment, a top management team can help a company achieve competitive advantage by applying collective expertise, integrating disparate efforts, and sharing responsibility for the success of the firm. AT&T, for example, has a self-governing operating committee of senior executives who report to the chairman of the board; this committee rotates its leadership every six months. The global corporation of the future could conceivably have an office of the CEO with members in different locations linked electronically. This virtual team could have members in Asia, Europe, and the United States, providing twenty-four-hour global coverage (Lawler, 1996).

Parallel teams are used for problem solving and for improvement-oriented activities. They pull people together from different work units to perform functions that the regular organization cannot perform well (Stein and Kanter, 1980). Because of the widespread interest in employee involvement and total quality management, almost all companies use parallel teams. For example, a computer company needed to improve the way in which its sales and service personnel used its new technology platform. It established a virtual team whereby representatives from different units identified problem areas and worked together (via predominantly electronic means) to develop tools for using the new platform.

Ad hoc networks consist of individuals and groups from the same organization, or from different organizations, who connect with one another on the basis of shared interests. These networks may be intentionally designed, or they may emerge spontaneously as work-related tasks bring people into unplanned contact. Organizations can support the formation and operation of ad hoc networks through the use of new communication networks that link people and groups regardless of locations or schedules. For example, Hewlett-Packard created a dispersed-learning network to disseminate information about innovative practices, provide an antidote to the "not invented here" mentality, and foster peer consulting as a mechanism for learning and support. Between face-to-face network meetings, Hewlett-Packard people stay in touch via the company's intranet. Ad hoc networks offer easy, flexible, spontaneous access to knowledge. Teams can be formed rapidly in response to changing needs, and everyone can share the pooled knowledge and experience of the entire organization.

The use of these five types of teams can result in the development of a team-based organization, one in which teams are the basic units of performance and serve as a way of achieving integration and coordination through lateral processes (Mohrman, Cohen, and Mohrman, 1995). Team-based organizations are flexible, and an individual who works in one can perform different roles on different teams (for example, being a technical contributor for one team and being the team leader for another). They are dynamic organizations in which changing configurations of teams can be used to accomplish strategic objectives. They are organizations in which the logic of how people relate to one another and get work done has fundamentally changed.

Authority, Power, and Influence

New designs for teams and technology change the political dynamics of the workplace and of the organization. Teams often decentralize authority and distribute power, and the new technologies, by increasing access to information, have similar effects. The consequences are most easily seen in the case of networked designs, both technological and social. Instead of the static, one-directional, hierarchical relationships of more traditional work structures, network relationships tend to be dynamic, diffuse, and lateral. Technical expertise, access to information, and the ability to apply these to the tasks at hand supplant formal roles and job titles as the primary sources of power.

The net result can be quite profound. For example, new power relationships can change how work gets done and who does it. In traditional hierarchical organizations, formal organizational charts and process-flow diagrams indicate—in theory, at least—the pathways to be followed and the individuals to be contacted in accomplishing certain tasks. One moves the forms, pursues the inquiries, and so forth, in a readily discernible series of straight lines from point A to point Z. In practice, of course, there are frequent end runs around the formal organization via unofficial networks of people and unwritten rules that do not show up on charts or in policy manuals. In addition, the results often run counter to the company's overall goals and objectives.

Teams and new information technologies can help close the gap between the formal and the informal organization and align the goals of the formal organization with the outcomes of the informal organization. In team-based organizations, pathways are designed as webs rather than straight lines. Because power is diffuse and collective, approaching one individual or pursuing one particular path may not be enough to get things done; a more appropriate metaphor is "working the room"—moving around, making contact with many individuals and groups, and pursuing several alternative pathways, never sure that this is the right path or contact but hoping that one will pay off. This kind of uncertainty may be unsettling, but the potential gains—higher levels of knowledge throughout the organization, better solutions to problems, broader commitment to actions pursued, and more effective implementation of change—are well worth the uncertainty.

The team-based organization also defines the legitimacy of authority in new ways. Authority is no longer based solely on one's rank or on one's position in the organizational chart. Instead, authority can derive legitimately from expertise and from the power to get things done. Those with power are the ones who have the interpersonal skills to effectively "work the room" and the expertise to contribute to solutions. The ability to enhance knowledge and skill by collaborating with new colleagues and using new technologies becomes critical. For those who are accustomed to traversing the traditional corridors of power, the new terrain of work may be quite unsettling, and even more so for those who are well placed within these corridors. These people have a lot to lose with the advent of the team-based, technology-supported organization, but they have also a lot to gain if they can learn to collaborate and use the new information tools that have been literally placed at their collective fingertips.

Dependence on Co-Workers

In a team-based organization, individuals are held accountable for collective results. Whether an individual is a member of a permanent work team, of several work teams, of several parallel improvement-oriented teams, or of ad hoc networks, results are still achieved collectively. An individual's success or failure is inextricably linked to that of his or her co-workers. This dependence on co-workers is uncomfortable for most of us. We are afraid of being dragged down by poorly performing colleagues and of not being judged on our own individual merits. Our culture also socializes us to value individual responsibility and achievement, and to resist reliance on others; we value individual autonomy (Mohrman and Cohen, 1995).

Nevertheless, business success *is* collective success. It is no longer sufficient just to do one's individual piece of work unless it contributes to the team's and the business unit's success. It is the responsibility of all performers, especially the good performers, to make sure that their own work is integrated with that of others and that others' poor performance is addressed. Good working relationships are crucial to the support of those transactions that are necessarily involved in providing a service, developing a product, or managing a process. Although we fear the loss of our individual autonomy, contributing to a successful team effort is rewarding. People derive meaning from contributing to something greater than themselves. In addition, working closely with others can build fulfilling relationships. Members of high-performing teams develop commitment to the purposes of their teams, as well as dedication and commitment to one another (Katzenbach and Smith, 1993). Personal meaning is derived from the engagement with a task and from successful interpersonal relationships with co-workers (Kahn, 1990). Productive collaborative relationships are inherently satisfying.

Dealing with Conflict

Conflict and tension inevitably arise when people work together. Diverse viewpoints, positions, and goals need to be reconciled, and compromises and trade-offs need to be made. Compromise means that nobody gets everything she wants, and that everyone needs to give up something she values. Conflict is uncomfortable for most of us, but it cannot be avoided when we have to work directly with others who are different from us.

Conflicts among co-workers are more likely to occur in team-based organizations because people from different functions, disciplines, departments, and personal backgrounds view their worlds in dissimilar ways. Dougherty (1992) has documented the distinct "thought worlds" of employees from research and development, sales, manufacturing, and marketing in new-product development efforts. People from dissimilar functions viewed uncertainty, critical issues, and key values in fundamentally different ways. In addition, changing demographic patterns mean that people now collaborate with others of different ages, races, ethnicities, nationalities, and genders, and the interpersonal styles and behaviors of those from different demographic groups may clash. These demographically and functionally based differences can produce conflict and interpersonal distance that may get in the way of collaboration. The good news, however, is that dealing with differences openly can help resolve conflicts and, in the process, produce innovation and improve business performance (Mohrman and Cohen, 1995).

Spanning Functions, Departments, and Organizations

The relatively impenetrable boundaries of department and function have become less formidable in recent years. In many organizations they now serve primarily as indicators of position, role, and level of expertise rather than as barriers to collaboration. Innovation, adaptability, time to market—whatever the issue, it is the rare manager these days who does not recognize that rigid intraorganizational boundaries can threaten a firm's long-term viability.

It is no coincidence that this awareness comes as new boundary-spanning technologies proliferate. Information technology breaks down barriers. As it becomes easier for people in different work units to communicate, it also becomes easier for them to collaborate. Teams form and spread, reinforcing the perception that intraorganizational boundaries can be easily crossed, and in time these formal distinctions will act even less as barriers to collaboration than as facilitators. They will provide convenient indicators of useful expertise, which can be drawn on as it is needed, rather than as barriers that keep people with diverse kinds of expertise from working together on issues of mutual concern and benefit.

Essentially the same information technologies can be used to cross boundaries that separate one organization from another. What better indicator of the growing importance of technology-based interorganizational communications than the business card? Not long ago, addresses and telephone numbers were enough. Then fax numbers were added, and now Internet e-mail addresses are almost as ubiquitous. Individuals need to communicate easily and rapidly, not just with co-workers in their own companies but also with customers, suppliers, strategic partners, and colleagues in other organizations. Moreover, Internet addresses and cross-organizational kinds of collaboration are just the early indicators of an organizational change that is of potentially far greater significance.

The same business imperatives that led to the deconstruction of so many organizations in recent years are now driving the formation of alliances, strategic partnerships, and joint ventures. In effect, the slimmed-down, reengineered organizations of the 1980s and 1990s are now being combined and reconstructed into metaorganizations for the twenty-first century (Nadler, Gerstein, Shaw, and Associates, 1992; see also Chapter Three of this book, where Galbraith discusses the design of these metaorganizations, or *networked organizations*). Nike, for example, controls the design of its athletic shoes and clothing, but it contracts with a wide range of suppliers for its manufacturing, distribution, shipping, and selling. Movie production is carried out by metaorganizations made up of independent contractors (actors, writers, directors, producers), equipment suppliers, postproduction houses, and so on. Construction projects involve general contractors and their networks of subcontractors. The shape of the organization of the future can be seen in these networked companies today. Large, vertically integrated companies that do everything from market research and new-product development to distribution and sales, and everything in between, are sinking in the tar pits of turbulent change, much as the dinosaurs did in their day. Slimmed-down, flexible organizations that can quickly find partners to form adaptable metaorganizations are the ones that will thrive in a business environment where opportunities emerge with little warning and fade just as quickly (Mankin, Cohen, and Bikson, 1997).

Dealing with Constant Change

As people gain experience with the new organizational structures and processes, they will learn—about their organizations, their work, and themselves, as well as about using their knowledge to "work smarter." They will then be able to modify and adapt the very structures and processes that led to this learning. Abilities want to be used. Just as well-developed athletic skill contributes to a motivation to use it, an ability to create change will increase the pressure for change.

In the face of continual and often dramatic change, however, employees also need some constancy, a safe harbor where they can withdraw from the turmoil around them. They need a work space that they can call their own, a place where they can leave work on their desktops, knowing that when they return it will still be there, in the same orderly (or chaotic) state in which they left it. Most people want to identify with some entity—if not with the organization then at least with the team members with whom they work on projects. Projects and team members may change far too often for most people's tastes, however, just as everything else also seems to do.

The goal is flexible organizations, not chaotic ones. Organizations that change, not for change's sake, but to meet competitive demands, are the ones positioned for success. Organizations need to provide some structure to help employees find their way, but organizations should also enable employees to participate in the design of that structure: the limits that we set on our own individual behavior, as members of work teams, are more useful than the limits imposed on us by others.

In an organizational world of constant change, what is secure? Companies can no longer promise lifetime employment. Jobs change. Projects end. Companies merge, and then they outsource people and whole departments. The only security for employees resides in their skills, knowledge, and willingness to learn. Individuals are responsible for developing and maintaining the skills and competencies that will keep them marketable, and maintaining marketable skills will help people continue providing value to their current employers and position them for future opportunities (see Chapter Five).

In essence, we are all self-employed. Whether we work for a large corporation or do temporary contract work, we are all in a situation of temporary skill-based employment. Being "career self-reliant" means that we have the skills and attitudes to take advantage of the wide variety of available work options, from working as an independent contractor to developing a virtual corporation to obtaining positions through a temporary agency to working as an employee for a large company. Of course, some of us will be able to adapt to this new work environment better than others will, and to thrive on opportunities for continually improving our skills. Those who cannot adapt will be the victims of the new economy, losing their jobs and not being able to obtain new ones to maintain their standard of living. Given the disruption involved in the evolution of the new economy, our society will need to determine what kinds of safety nets should be provided to ease the transition from the old economy (Lawler, 1996).

The dynamic nature of *work* is antithetical to the traditional concept of a *job*. Organizations need people who can regularly change what they do and develop the knowledge and skills necessary to contribute to successful business performance. Job descriptions are constraining. If an employee says, "It's not in my job description" when asked to take on additional responsibilities, the organization may not be able to respond quickly to the challenges it faces. The organization must view its employees as human resources who continually develop the capabilities required for addressing competitive challenges. The transformation from jobs to competencies requires fundamental shifts in human resources systems and practices (see Chapters Eight and Nine).

When co-workers and projects constantly change, staying connected becomes paramount. When physical communities no longer exist, virtual communities can be built. The new collaborative technologies enable us to stay in touch. Interest groups and bulletin boards provide opportunities for dialogue with people who share our interests. Professional networks bring those in the same specialties together and help them keep abreast of professional developments and job opportunities. The relationships we develop can outlast the teams and projects we work on, and even the companies we work for.

Summary and Conclusion

The demands brought about by global competitive pressure, in addition to the powerful capabilities of the new information technologies, have fundamentally changed the nature of work. These changes are summarized in Table 6.1. In the area of technology, for example, we have moved from mainframe computing to personal and networked computing on a global basis. Work has become

Table 6.1. Changes in the Nature of Work.

Theme	Old	New
Technology	Mainframe computing	Personal computing
		Multimedia
		Portable systems
		Networked computing
		Global communications
		Virtual reality
Work design/tasks	Rigid	Flexible
	Narrow and routine	Broad and varied
	Physical	Abstract and symbolic
	Materials-based	Information-based
	Manufacturing-based	Services-based
	Independent	Interdependent
	Static	Dynamic
Physical location	Office or factory	Flexible arrangements (telecommuting from home or neighborhood work centers)
	Separate work space	Collaborative environments
Performers	Individuals	Teams of many types
Knowledge and skills	Focus on job requirements	Focus on competencies and marketable skills
	Tacit, sentient knowledge	Intellective skills
	Relative fixity	Continuous development
Organization	Bureaucracy	Reduced boundaries
	Functional or departmental "silos"	Networked or adhocratic arrangements
	Hierarchical	Lateral
	Roles and positions	Team-based
Authority	Position-based	Expertise-based
	Top-down	Diffuse and collective
	Management-based	Self-control–based

flexible, abstract, interdependent, and dynamic. People are more likely to process information and provide services than to handle materials and make products. As the traditional concept of the job disappears, the foundation of a successful career will be intellective skills, competencies, and the willingness to engage in continuous learning. Work can be performed at any time and at any place and is more likely to be performed by teams than by individual contributors. Teams will be increasingly cross-functional and even cross-organizational. More and more organizations will become team-based. Authority will be diffuse and collective, and it will be based on expertise rather than on position and hierarchical control. These changes in the nature of work are dramatic. In the past, work was predictable, routine, structured, explicit, and individual. In the present and in the emerging future, work is and will be ambiguous, abstract, collaborative, subject to constant change, and sometimes even chaotic.

The organizational challenge is to manage this new world of work and ensure that this effort is aligned with and focused on business objectives. Many of the organizational systems and practices described throughout this book are mechanisms for addressing the challenge of maintaining alignment in this dynamic environment. The diamond and star models, which are depicted in Figures 2 and 3, respectively, in the Introduction, both highlight the importance of business strategy. All the employees throughout an organization should understand not only the corporate business strategy but also how their own goals and objectives, as well as the goals and objectives of the business units in which they participate, are related to the corporate business strategy. This knowledge is crucial to employees' ability to make day-to-day decisions that are aligned with strategic objectives.

Systems for performance management and rewards should recognize and pay for collective success. Team members should be held accountable and recognized for accomplishing collective objectives. Performance appraisal that focuses solely on the individual needs to be redesigned to encourage goal setting, development, performance feedback, and rewards at the team and business-unit levels. Base pay should be person-based, not job-based. People should be paid for their intellective skills, competencies, and labor-market value. Lateral career moves should be supported and encouraged. Training should be provided to help individuals deal with change and to help them resolve the conflicts that inevitably emerge from working closely with many different kinds of people. These are just a few of the corporate systems that will have to be modified in organizations.

For organizations that make these transitions, the benefits will be great. They will be able to compete more effectively in the global economy. They will be able to develop agility in responding to changing competitive demands. They will continuously create new competitive advantages, satisfy their customers, and, as Galbraith and Lawler note in the Introduction, create market disruptions for their competitors. They will be able to use the new information technologies and innovative work designs to achieve success in the marketplace.

Benefits for employees may also be significant. They will have the opportunity to learn and develop new skills. They will be able to experience the challenge of working on multiple projects and know that they are contributing to business success. Employees can be stimulated and challenged by their interactions with the new information technologies, and they can be deepened by expanded opportunities for collaboration. They will be able to have flexible, challenging careers that take advantage of the variety of work options available today.

Nevertheless, the transition can be rough. Employees are now far more dependent on one another for their success; even the rugged individualist needs to be able to collaborate effectively. Employees need to resolve conflicts directly in organizations where the old rules about authority no longer apply. They now face the insecurity of constant change. Those who are unable to learn and develop marketable skills will not succeed. They will become the victims of the new ways of working and will not be able to maintain their standard of living.

Organizations that are flexible, that encourage participation and learning, and that value people will create the foundation for the adaptability that is needed today and that will continue to be needed in the future. The future is bright for people who can accept change, improve their knowledge and skills, and derive meaning from collaboration. They are the ones who even now are successfully adapting to the changing nature of work.

Chapter Seven

Employee Involvement, Reengineering, and TQM

Focusing on Capability Development

Edward E. Lawler III
Susan Albers Mohrman

Since its inception, the field of management has been character-ized by differing views of how organizations can be most effectively managed. Until the 1980s, much of the debate took place in aca-demic journals and inside corporations; as a result, it was not a highly visible public activity. During the 1980s the situation changed dramatically. Perhaps the key defining event of this change oc-curred in 1982, when Peters and Waterman published their best-seller *In Search of Excellence.* Suddenly the debate concerning the best way to manage complex organizations became front page news in the *Wall Street Journal, Business Week,* the *New York Times,* and virtually every other newspaper and magazine in the country. Since the publication of *In Search of Excellence,* management has main-tained its prominence. Indeed, it has become a major business, with consulting firms billing companies millions of dollars a year for organizational improvement programs and a proliferation of tapes, books, and seminars, all of which claim to have found the key to effective management.

Why is there an overwhelming concern with the effectiveness of different management approaches? The answer, we believe, is iden-tified in the Introduction of this book: the growing consensus that an effective approach to management is a powerful competitive advantage for a corporation. Before the 1980s, there was agreement that being a well-managed corporation was a possible source of competitive advantage, but building an effective organization was not a major focus of most corporations, and there was little discussion of ideas about how major corporations should be managed. Instead of competing on the basis of managerial innovations, companies competed on the basis of their ability to execute traditional management practices. Most organizations adopted the traditional, bureaucratic, hierarchical organizational model and simply varied in how well they executed it.

Mass acceptance of the traditional paradigm began to break down in the 1980s. Since that time, there has been a search for its replacement. Three approaches have received the most attention: employee involvement, total quality management, and business-process reengineering. All three of these have been very popular at one time or another and have been accused of being nothing more than fads.

There is some truth to the view that at times all three of these approaches have had a fadlike character: each has often been implemented as a "quick-fix program" with little thought and little understanding on the part of the implementing companies. Each has also been adopted, to at least a limited degree, by a wide range of major U.S. and international corporations (Lawler, Mohrman, and Ledford, 1995). But saying that they have been fads does not answer the basic question of whether these approaches and the concepts they embody are part of or truly represent a new managerial paradigm that can and should replace the traditional bureaucratic one. Are these approaches a type of fool's gold that seduce companies into spending millions of dollars but produce no tangible results? Or do they represent part or all of a valid new paradigm of management that can produce significant competitive advantages for companies that accept it? In this chapter, we will review these three approaches with an eye to assessing both how they have unfolded and their long-term implications for the field of management.

Employee Involvement

There is no single authoritative source or theory to define employee involvement as a management approach. It has a long history, dating back to early research on democratic leadership in work organizations. It includes writings on job design, organizational design, pay systems, and organizational change. The research on democratic leadership started in the 1930s and emphasized the consequences of employee involvement in decision making. It showed that under certain conditions employees are more committed to decisions, and that better decisions are made if they are involved (Lawler, 1986).

Another important part of the work on employee involvement concerns work design and its impact on intrinsic motivation and job satisfaction. The work on individual job enrichment stresses the creation of jobs that are significant, have variety, give an individual responsibility for performing a whole task, provide meaningful feedback so that the individual can self-correct and experience a sense of accomplishment, and enable autonomy (Hackman and Oldham, 1980). The work on self-managing work teams and sociotechnical work systems takes the notion of motivating work and extends it into team settings. It forms a critical part of all the separate pieces of historical thinking that have combined to develop employee involvement as a management approach. Creating teams is seen as a way to make a group of people collectively responsible for carrying out a work process that delivers a product or a service (Hackman, 1987). A core principle of sociotechnical design is that the team should include all the capabilities and authority required for controlling variance in the work process—that is, those places where the work process can go out of control and yield poor results (Pasmore, 1988). Individuals who are working on teams designed in this manner, and who are given meaningful tasks and provided with, direction, feedback, and autonomy, experience intrinsic satisfaction and motivation and are able to manage their own technical work processes.

Perhaps the most important overall emphasis in the work on employee involvement concerns locating decisions at the lowest level in the organization (Lawler, 1986). A bottom-up approach to management is consistently advocated. It is argued that individuals or teams should be given the power, information, and knowledge that they need to work autonomously or independently of day-to-day managerial control and direction. The job of management is seen as one of preparing individuals or teams to function autonomously. Management is an enabler, a culture setter, and a supporter. It sets the broad direction and goals of the business rather than directing employees' actions.

The logical evolution of employee involvement is toward a flattening of the organization and, in many cases, the elimination of substantial amounts of staff and support work (Lawler, 1996). This work is often seen as either moving out of the organization or being done at lower and lower levels within the organization. Enriched jobs and/or self-managing teams often include tasks (such as quality assurance, scheduling, and equipment maintenance) previously performed by specialized support groups. Employee involvement stresses that substantial amounts of the work done by managers is unnecessary because it simply supports a command-and-control approach to management, which is not needed when employees are involved in their work and are capable of self-management.

Some writings on employee involvement place a strong emphasis on reward systems (Lawler, 1990). They advocate combining participatory decision making and democratic supervision with rewards for skill acquisition and for organizational performance. Gainsharing, profit sharing, and employee ownership are important reward practices that are associated with employee involvement. Skill- or competency-based pay provides an incentive for and reinforces the acquisition of skills that enable an individual to become more highly involved and contribute more to organizational success.

Organizational change is given a considerable amount of attention in the literature on employee involvement (Mohrman and Cummings, 1989). The transition to employee involvement is viewed as involving a challenge to deeply held assumptions about how best to control organizational performance, about the appropriate role of managers, and about the most efficient way to design and organize work. A combination of bottom-up and top-down change is stressed: from the top comes the establishment and reinforcement of the overall philosophical direction and the broad parameters of the organization's values and strategy; at the bottom there is broad participation in the determination of the organization's operating principles and the design of its new work systems and roles. In many respects, the argument for employee involvement is not so much an argument for continuous improvement as for discontinuous change. It talks of substantial gains in organizational effectiveness as a result of the move to completely new work structures and new ways of organizing work.

A key finding in the research is that to be successful, the transition to employee involvement must involve a systemic change—

changes must be made in the distribution of information, knowledge and skills, power, and rewards throughout the organization (Lawler, 1992). These changes can be accomplished only through changes in work design, management structure and style, human resources practices, and information systems. Companies that implement mutually supportive changes in all these areas experience greater positive impacts on organizational performance and employee outcomes than those that implement single thrusts toward change, such as participation groups or changes in rewards (Lawler, Mohrman, and Ledford, 1995).

Some of the most complete embodiments of high-involvement approaches have been achieved in start-up settings (so-called greenfield organizations), particularly in the manufacturing sector (Lawler, 1978; Walton, 1985). New settings tend to be unencumbered by past practices. From the outset they are able to establish consistent sets of mutually supportive structures, roles, and processes. At the outset of the movement to employee involvement, the primary outcomes of interest were operational effectiveness and employee commitment, but the intensified competitive pressures of the late 1980s extended the focus to measures of effectiveness that more directly reflect competitive performance and profitability. Involving employees more fully in business performance by adding a focus on financial-sharing pay systems, on contact with customers and suppliers, and on the new information technology (IT) was a natural extension of this paradigm (Lawler, 1992). The hotly competitive environment also created more interest in taking concepts that previously had been embodied primarily in greenfield organizations and incorporating them into the ongoing and more established parts of companies. As a result, many major corporations began efforts to transform their cultures and existing facilities so as to incorporate the high-involvement philosophy and approaches (Lawler, Mohrman, and Ledford, 1995).

Total Quality Management

At approximately the same time that interest in employee involvement was expanding, U.S. companies became aware of another approach to performance improvement that had burgeoned in Japan and was being brought to the United States by various consultants: total quality management, or TQM. This approach focused directly on what was emerging as a potential Achilles' heel of American industry, one that made it vulnerable to competition: the quality of American products and services. Many organizations seeking ways to improve their performance grabbed onto TQM as a way of focusing employees on quality improvement.

The roots of TQM are in quality engineering. TQM focuses on the improvement of the organization's work processes as a way of having an impact on product quality and costs. As is true of employee involvement, there is no single theoretical formulation of the TQM approach, nor is there any definitive "short list" of practices associated with it (see Hill and Wilkinson, 1995). The TQM approach is primarily the product of the work of such American quality experts as Deming, Juran, and Crosby and of an important Japanese expert, Ishikawa. Their writings, as well as the application of their ideas to many Japanese companies and some American companies, allow us to identify the characteristics that are most typical of TQM programs (Deming, 1982; Juran, 1989).

TQM is best viewed as a management philosophy that combines Deming's and Juran's teachings on statistical process control and group problem-solving processes with Japanese values concerned with quality and continuous improvement. The movement started to become popular in Japan during the 1950s as that country tried to recover from World War II. During the 1980s the movement became increasingly popular in the United States and Europe, in great part as a result of the success of Japanese firms in a number of global markets (Womack, Jones, and Roos, 1990).

The movement started with quality circles: groups of employees were placed on teams to identify and solve the problems that were leading to poor quality. The major emphasis was on teaching teams about group process and problem solving. The adoption of quality circles assumed faddish proportions; many programs came and went very quickly (Lawler and Mohrman, 1985), in large part because companies saw quality circles as a low-cost approach to getting employees involved in improving the business. These companies often failed to understand the depth of the changes in philosophy and managerial practice that are required to sustain true participative process improvement. Some companies—Xerox and Motorola are prime examples—persevered, however. With considerable leadership from the top they painstakingly built quality-oriented cultures and organizations. In the process, they implemented a much more complete version of TQM, one that emphasized statistical tools, planning methods for linking quality-related activities and strategy with the company's business strategy, sophisticated quality-measurement systems, cost-of-quality analysis, and an intense focus on relationships with customers and suppliers.

A major focus of TQM is on creating a new understanding of quality and what it is. With TQM the emphasis shifts from auditing and detecting defects to finding the root causes of poor quality. Process problems are identified to prevent future defects. The emphasis also shifts from internal to external assessments of quality. Customers' reactions are regarded as the most important measure of quality. Customers are seen as either internal (that is, within the organization) or external, and quality is seen as a means of gaining a competitive advantage. It is argued that if quality is improved, rework will be reduced, costs will drop, and organizations will respond more quickly and effectively to customers' requests. One indication of how important it is for companies to develop a quality capability is the recent trend for many organizations to avoid doing business with suppliers who are unable to demonstrate that they have effective quality programs in place.

TQM emphasizes the importance of top management's acting as the main driver of TQM activities because TQM is viewed as a culture, not just as a program, and as such it has to be built into the organization. It is a culture in the sense that it tries to change the values of the organization and its employees, as well as their behavior in multiple areas. Top management's support is thought to be necessary so that the right priorities will be set (quality activities are linked to the business strategy) and so that commitment to the principles of TQM will exist throughout the organization as major changes are introduced into organizational processes.

According to TQM advocates like Deming, most quality-related problems are caused by managers and the systems that managers create and operate. By contrast, the proportion of quality-related problems that is estimated to be traceable to the performance of nonmanagerial workers ranges from 25 percent to less than 10 percent (Deming, 1982). Dysfunctional relationships within and between organizations and work units are a common managerial failing. For example, because work processes often cut across different functionally delineated organizational units, and because members of the respective functions do not always relate properly to one another, quality is poor because things fall through the cracks. For this reason, quality-improvement projects and teams are often composed of members from multiple functions. In addition, suppliers are seen as a major factor in the creation of quality products and services; thus companies are urged to create dedicated relationships with those suppliers who demonstrate that they can deliver components and raw material of superior quality.

Another area in which the TQM approach requires a new definition of relationships is the interface between managers and employees. Employees are seen as having good ideas for improving quality and as wanting to do a good job, but organizational measurements often stress throughput, irrespective of quality, and production targets are often held over people's heads. Among the fourteen action points that Deming advocates as embodying the management principles that should guide a quality-oriented organization are "driving fear out of the organization," eliminating numerical quotas and goals, removing barriers that rob people of pride in their work, and substituting leadership for supervision (Deming, 1982).

The technologies used to support both quality measurement and quality improvement are very visible elements of many TQM programs. A typical program includes methods that aid in identifying issues and solving problems: statistical process control, measurement of nonconformance, measurement of the cost of quality, cause-and-effect analysis, root-cause analysis, and various kinds of group-based decision making. These methods typically focus on creating and using accurate information about production and quality and on precisely measuring and quantifying problems. Most employees are trained in the use of these methods and have the opportunity to become involved in quality-improvement activities.

Great emphasis is placed on including all employees in the TQM culture and in the continuous improvement of organizational performance. This is where employee empowerment (TQM talks of empowerment, not involvement) comes into play. In two important respects, employees are expected to take responsibility for quality: they are expected to call attention to quality-related problems as they go about doing their normal work, and, perhaps more important, they are expected to accept the culture of continuous improvement and to look for ways in which they can do their work better and in which the overall operation of the organization can be improved. To meet these expectations, of course, they need skills and information, as well as vehicles for producing change.

Quality circles and quality-improvement groups are the major vehicles that employees can use in making suggestions and changing work processes. Often they work on problems of lateral coordination, and sometimes they make suggestions for improving managerial systems, work methods, and work procedures. Employees are also encouraged to meet in their natural work groups and to look for improved approaches and new work methods. Emphasis is usually placed on simplifying and codifying work processes. The objective is to create a simple work flow that carefully specifies the activities that can reliably be carried out.

There is typically a substantial amount of quality-related information given to employees in TQM programs. A TQM program often marks the first time employees receive training in quality-related matters and valid information about quality. The program may also be the employees' first chance to influence the work methods and work procedures that influence quality. The program almost always marks employees' first chance to monitor their own quality and make decisions about its adequacy. Employees may also be gaining their first exposure to internal and external customers and to suppliers.

Business-Process Reengineering

The term *business-process reengineering,* and the ideas associated with it, burst upon the management scene in the early 1990s. Thanks to several articles in the *Harvard Business Review* (for example, Hammer, 1990) and a spate of books (for example, Hammer and Champy, 1993; Davenport, 1993) about the advantages of reengineering, the concept gained in popularity. Indeed, few if any management trends have ever enjoyed the almost instant popularity associated with reengineering, a popularity driven primarily by a group of consulting firms that offered reengineering programs to major corporations. The names most closely associated with the reengineering movement are those of consultants Michael Hammer and James Champy. Perhaps the most visible academic associated with the reengineering movement is Thomas Davenport, whose background is in information technology, where reengineering has its strongest roots (although it is not firmly rooted in any particular discipline).

When reengineering was introduced, many companies were trying to discover why their huge investments in IT were not paying off in productivity gains. Considering that many of reengineering's change activities are directed toward improving the use of computer systems in large organizations, the seemingly sudden interest in reengineering is understandable. Companies like Toyota were heralded as proving that the well-conceived use of IT, combined with a rethinking of how business processes are executed, can indeed constitute a competitive advantage. Reengineering offered an approach to determining how a company should be organized to take advantage of expensive IT resources. During the 1990s a number of consulting firms (notably Gemini, Index, and Anderson Consulting) signed multimillion-dollar reengineering contracts with major corporations. For a while it appeared that virtually every large U.S. corporation had a major reengineering project going on.

In many ways, reengineering builds on TQM's focus on processes and customers. For example, reengineering focuses on the key organizational processes that take various inputs and deliver outputs of value to customers (Hammer and Champy, 1993). TQM programs, however, often run into problems designing and implementing process improvements when they encounter a political reality: namely, that in a functional organization different parts of a major work process are carried out in different organizational units. Barriers also appear when process improvements impinge on the autonomy and local logic of different units because significant changes require buy-in from the managers of all the units involved in the improvements.

An even greater threat to the status quo is the reality that for a significant change to be effective and lasting, activities have to be realigned so that all aspects of a process are addressed and connected. This point is similar to the sociotechnical-systems principle stating that process variance is best controlled when a single organizational unit or department controls an entire process and has the capability and the authority to make decisions about that process. Advocates of reengineering argue that internal forces specific to each unit tend to pull things back to their original state, and so it is not sufficient to establish a cross-functional team that pulls people from various units and has responsibility for making process improvements, or for ensuring that a process stays under control. The reengineering solution is to ensure that all the subprocesses of a major process are managed in the same organizational unit so that they are not optimized independently of one another.

The first step in business-process reengineering is to reconceptualize the whole organization in terms of its key processes and the technology available to carry them out. Reengineering then introduces changes in how the processes are carried out, and in how the organization is managed and structured, so that these processes deliver optimal value to customers. The change process is almost always run from the top down, in part because it entails a significant redistribution of power and authority and a significant investment in information technology and because it may also entail a restructuring of business units and work groups so that there are fewer levels of management and fewer employees. Participative reengineering teams are generally established, but, given the scope and the focus of business-process reengineering, their membership is often quite top-heavy.

Particular emphasis is placed on taking advantage of information technology and simplified processes to reduce the costs and cycle time involved in many routine transactions. For example, perhaps the most commonly reengineered area of an organization is order administration. Information technology can be used to integrate the often slow and labor-intensive production-line process that orders travel through in order to be executed. After a reengineering effort in this area, individuals or small groups with access to interactive on-line databases are typically able to execute orders quickly and to give customers intelligent responses when questions arise about the progress of orders. They may also be able to integrate this kind of information with data about the state of a customer's account and credit.

Similarities Among Employee Involvement, TQM, and Reengineering

There is some obvious overlap among the management principles and practices associated with employee involvement, TQM, and business-process reengineering. This overlap leads us to see these three approaches as different manifestations of an emerging new paradigm of management and organization. All three see employees taking on additional responsibility, being better skilled, and getting more and better information. All three focus on the need for improvement and change in organizational systems, as well as on the need for managers to change their behavior and roles dramatically. All three emphasize the importance of systems thinking, stressing that organizations are better viewed as complex interrelated systems than as combinations of independent pieces. All three also emphasize the advantages of lateral processes and their ability to make levels of management unnecessary and reduce the need for traditional control-oriented supervision.

The complementarity and compatibility of employee involvement and TQM are particularly striking. By 1993, approximately two of every three Fortune 1000 companies had substantial employee involvement programs in place, and three out of four had TQM programs; most of the companies that had one kind of program also had the other (Lawler, Mohrman and Ledford, 1995).

TQM, despite its emphasis on top-down initiation and leadership, does stress substantial employee involvement. Whereas the original framework for employee involvement emphasized employees' involvement in work, TQM emphasizes their involvement in improving organizational performance. Employee involvement emphasizes a multiskilled, highly trained workforce; TQM particularly stresses training in process-improvement techniques. Employee involvement emphasizes shifting responsibility for quality, maintenance, and other aspects of work into the work unit; TQM expands this emphasis to include the work unit's representation and involvement in process improvements that cut across teams and business units. In various ways, both approaches have introduced elements that focus employees on the broader business picture. TQM does this by stressing the cost of quality and by focusing employees on customers and suppliers; employee involvement uses various reward systems that give employees a stake in business performance.

There are also some key differences. Employee involvement places much greater stress on work designs that optimize motivation. This emphasis reflects employee involvement's roots in managerial and organizational psychology. TQM places greater stress on creating and simplifying reliable work processes, an emphasis that reflects TQM's roots in industrial engineering. Employee involvement envisions superior, high-performing work designs; the concept of continuous improvement is central to TQM, a difference that may reflect the nature of the competitive environment at the time when each approach made its appearance. Recent articulations of involvement-oriented high-performing systems, in this era of intense global competition and more stringent standards for costs, cycle times, and responsiveness to customers, include continuous improvement and learning as key systemic attributes (Lawler, 1996). The evolution in employee involvement's focus, which now encompasses a more expansive involvement in the business, reflects the recognition that employees can be appropriately involved not just in the operations of their own particular units but also in the factors that lead to overall high performance and competitiveness.

Our research indicates that a combination of employee involvement and TQM has a greater positive impact on business, productivity, and employee outcomes (Lawler, Mohrman and Ledford, 1995) than either approach used alone. This result fits with other research, which finds that approaches like gainsharing (often viewed as an involvement-oriented reward system) have a greater impact on performance when they are combined with meaningful participation mechanisms like quality-improvement groups where employees can generate improvements and influence the larger organization. Therefore, it appears that the combination of an involvement-oriented management philosophy and work design, on the one hand, and an improvement-oriented set of tools, structures, measurements, and philosophies, on the other, constitutes the underpinnings of an emerging new organizational paradigm. This paradigm focuses on creating units that are not only highly effective in carrying out their tasks but also able to learn and improve over time.

There are clear connections between the reengineering models of Hammer and Champy (1993) and Davenport (1993), on the one hand, and the model of employee involvement, on the other. Both models advocate the automation of routine work, but both also advocate the use of information technology to bring workers more (and more easily integrated) information so that a worker can carry out a process more fully and in a much more informed manner. Both models address the empowerment of the workforce, the shifting of decisions to the point of contact with customers, and organizational redesign that gets management out of the day-to-day loop. The results of many employee involvement programs, particularly those that use self-managing teams, point to the advantages of organizing for lateral activities, and to the improvements in coordination that are possible when lateral relationships are established. Research also points out that teams can be self-managing and that fewer layers of management are needed as a result (Lawler, 1996). There are excellent examples of reengineering that has established a true high-involvement culture (see Mohrman, Tenkasi, and Mohrman, 1997), but there have also been many instances in which this did not happen, and in which a business-process reengineering effort was reduced to a short-term cost-cutting exercise.

Differences Among Employee Involvement, TQM, and Reengineering

The major differences among employee involvement, TQM, and business-process reengineering are summarized in Table 7.1. The three approaches differ in terms of age and disciplinary base. Employee involvement has been around for a long time, is based on a long tradition of research on organizational behavior, and has slowly grown in popularity. TQM, which is based on a set of quality-engineering approaches, is newer and enjoyed a dramatic spurt in popularity during the 1980s, but its growth was slow by comparison with the almost overnight popularity, during the 1990s, of business-process reengineering. We argued earlier that the rapid growth of reengineering occurred in part because of a confluence of dramatic competitive pressure, on the one hand, and, on the other, greater sophistication of information technology and a stronger corporate desire to reap the benefits of its use.

Table 7.1. Major Differences Among Employee Involvement, TQM, and Business-Process Reengineering.

	Employee Involvement	TQM	Business-Process Reengineering
Age	Young adult	Adolescent	Infant
Teams	Self-managing teams	Problem-solving work cells	Business-process teams
Feedback	Business-unit performance	Customer feedback, quality levels	Process performance
Disciplinary base	Social science	Quality engineering	Information technology
Implementation process	Bottom-up	Top-down	Top-down
Preferred work design	Enriched	Simplified, standardized	Mixed
Unique contributions	Group processes, motivational alignment, employee well-being	Quality emphasis, worker tools	Downsizing, process focus, technological change

Note: Based on work by G. E. Ledford Jr.

All three approaches stress the importance of teams, but employee involvement is distinct here. Much of its early history was based on the development and use of self-managing work teams. Inherent in the idea of a self-managing work team is the concept of lateral process management, which was later to become the cornerstone of the process-reengineering approach. Historically, employee involvement–driven change efforts often looked at small processes (such as parts of a production process), whereas TQM focused on quality-improvement teams to improve processes that in many cases cut across work teams and work groups (thus emphasizing the internal-customer perspective). Business-process reengineering has defined processes much more broadly, as well as much more ambitiously in terms of entire sets of activities that deliver value to customers. In fact, it has talked about eliminating some functions entirely (such as marketing and sales) and simply building an organization around processes. This step has been taken in some companies, such as Harley-Davidson, which says that it now has only two processes—business development and order fulfillment.

There are different foci for organizational design in employee involvement, TQM, and reengineering, leading to measurement and feedback about different kinds of performance. Employee involvement tends to favor small, self-contained teams and larger units that are, in effect, somewhat autonomous minibusinesses. The minibusiness approach is a natural extension of the concept of self-managing teams. Feedback is about how well the team or the minibusiness is doing on a comprehensive set of business measures. TQM, by contrast, focuses heavily on groups that have clearly established customers, and in which quality levels can be established. These groups may be self-contained business units, but in many cases they are highly interdependent with other parts of a business. Feedback tends to come from customers and to be about the level of quality that the unit attains in meeting internal or external customer requirements. Reengineering tends to focus more broadly on the major processes that cut across an organization and ultimately deliver value to customers and on how a total corporation can be organized around these processes. Therefore, reengineering is more likely to focus on feedback concerned with cycle times for an entire process and with external customers' satisfaction.

One of the places where TQM and reengineering differ most from employee involvement concerns the change or implementation process. Advocates of employee involvement have argued consistently that the process used to introduce employee involvement should match the ultimate desired culture and operating state; therefore, they believe that the change process itself should be participative (Lawler, 1986). High-level steering teams may initiate the transition, but employees are put on teams to redesign their work areas, design gainsharing plans, and so forth.

Both TQM and reengineering have been installed in a much more top-down manner. In the case of TQM, this top-down flavor reflects the emphasis on changing the management culture and systems, the heavy investment in training and development that provides employees with uniform tools and language, and the fact that processes cut across units. TQM is believed to be best implemented within a uniform corporate context established through a process that builds support from all managers. The top-down implementation of reengineering reflects not only the scope of the endeavor—what is at stake is the overall power and operating structure of the organization—but also the massive IT investment that is required. The IT underpinnings also push reengineering toward top-down implementation. Part of reengineering's appeal is that it promises to integrate the many incompatible information systems that historically have been decentralized and controlled by functional units. Reaping the benefits of information technology requires the creation of an integrated IT infrastructure that enables information to be distributed throughout the company.

Lest we overstate the case that the implementation of TQM and reengineering has been top-down, we should point out that both recommend participative design teams (albeit largely involving management-level participants), and both envision the organization operating through participative teams and/or units. In practice, however, and by contrast with employee involvement, both TQM and reengineering usually have the feel of top-level direction and of being "rolled out." Furthermore, in both TQM and reengineering, outside experts or consultants have tended to bring formulae and, in some cases, have simply told organizations how work should be reorganized, have installed new computer and information systems, and have trained employees in how to operate within the new organizational structure. This approach contrasts with the style of most employee involvement–based consultants, who have a much greater tendency to work with employees in generating new work designs.

More than TQM and reengineering, employee involvement has focused on creating rich, challenging, motivating work. Originally, much of this emphasis focused on creating individually enriched jobs. An extensive literature was developed on what makes a job motivating and on how to enrich jobs (see, for example, Hackman and Oldham, 1980). Although individual job enrichment is still popular, self-managing teams are increasingly preferred in employee involvement–oriented designs (Lawler, Mohrman, and Ledford, 1995). There are a number of reasons why this is true. They include the fact that teams are more likely to make supervision unnecessary and can manage lateral relationships in ways that make layers of management unnecessary.

Both TQM and reengineering are less clear than employee involvement with respect to preferred work designs. TQM advocates simplified, standardized work processes that make statistical process control possible. TQM also stresses that individuals should be responsible for their own quality, an emphasis that moves more power into the hands of employees. Sometimes TQM (except for its expectation that employees will do some of the monitoring of their own performance) seems to be almost a throwback to the days of scientific management, with its emphasis on standardization and simplification. TQM has often been implemented without major revisions in work designs and without the transition to a generally high-involvement culture, despite the finding that TQM's impact is strengthened if these other elements are also in place (Lawler, Mohrman, and Ledford, 1995).

In many respects, reengineering is similar to TQM in matters of work design. Reengineering's major emphasis is on integrating lateral processes through the use of information technology. The promise held out in the reengineering literature is that making information available to the lowest levels of the organization will enable much greater work enrichment and autonomy. Some of reengineering's advocates also argue that the benefits of process redesign depend on the empowerment of front-line employees to operate processes and respond to customers (Davenport, 1993).

Nevertheless, in many reengineering change efforts, little attention is actually paid to whether and how individuals will be motivated to do the work that results from the intensive use of information technology. Various analyses show that the success of reengineering depends on management's ability to actually change the power structure and establish work-design and human resources practices that enable the system to perform in the intended manner (Thach and Woodman, 1994; Schonberger, 1994).

As Table 7.1 shows, employee involvement, TQM, and reengineering have all developed important new technologies and concepts. Given their very different disciplinary bases, it is hardly surprising that their contributions have been somewhat different. The social science–based focus of employee involvement, for example, has led it to place particular emphasis on organizational approaches that lead to the development and motivation of employees. TQM, by contrast, has focused more on tools that improve the reliability of work processes and the quality of products. Reengineering has been particularly powerful in stimulating organizational designs that fit well with modern information technology and with a process view of the organization.

Impact of Change Programs

It is not too early to evaluate the major outcomes that are produced by employee involvement, TQM, and business-process reengineering change efforts, particularly where employee involvement and TQM are concerned, because here we have years of experience, as well as a considerable amount of academic research. Reengineering is much newer and has been the subject of much less rigorous academic research; still there is a considerable amount of experience with it, and so some conclusions can also be reached about its impact on organizations. Table 7.2 summarizes the major outcomes that are associated with the three approaches.

When it comes to costs, there seems to be little question that reengineering, particularly when it is applied to a large bureaucratic organization, produces the biggest short-term gains. Reengineering is the most direct route to examining the process problems that exist in highly segmented top-down organizations that have a proliferation of overhead and operating staff. Reengineering sets out

Table 7.2. Major Outcomes of Employee Involvement, TQM, and Business-Process Reengineering.

	Employee Involvement	TQM	Business-Process Reengineering
Cost	Mixed results; possible impact on productivity	Savings from improved quality	Reductions due to downsizing; overall possible positive impact
Quality	Increased quality motivation	Positive impact	Possible positive impact
Speed	Mixed results	Possible positive impact	Process focus improves cycle time
Employees	Increased satisfaction	Some positive impact	Negative impact on job security and satisfaction

to build a macrostructure that enables more connection across whole processes, using information technology to integrate work, eliminate steps that do not add value, and establish a more direct line to customers. Nevertheless, many companies have quickly distorted it into a primarily cost-cutting endeavor, with downsizing justified on the basis of what consultants claim should be the productivity gains of the reengineered processes. The one qualification to be noted here concerns the amount of money that the organization may have to spend in order to reduce its costs: if reducing layers of management and a large number of employees requires the purchase of information technology, as well as payments to the displaced employees, then a significant up-front cost may be the price of the savings from downsizing.

In the 1950s, articles began to announce that middle management was soon to become obsolete because of computers' ability to link people and make them more self-managing. In virtually every decade since the 1950s that prediction was restated, but there was little reality associated with it. Suddenly, in the 1990s, the argument took on a new sense of urgency and reality when reengineering programs showed how information technology could in fact substitute for a substantial number of management layers and managers. By linking employees directly with one another and providing them with information and expertise, IT could eliminate staff-support specialists in areas like quality control, human resources management, and order administration and scheduling. It could also eliminate middle managers, whose major role is to coordinate the work of individuals in microscopic jobs or functional "silos."

It is hard to argue against the need for downsizing in many large corporations: during the 1980s, many of them were bloated bureaucracies with too many levels of management and too many managers, particularly middle managers. However, downsizing by itself is not enough to allow companies to carry out complex processes with fewer managers and other employees. Reconfiguring work and the organizational structure, upgrading systems, and transferring power are all necessary if gains in productivity are to be realized (Bashein, Markus, and Riley, 1994).

The gains realized from TQM and employee involvement programs stem in part from the creation of an organization able to do more with less, but the downsizing occurs more indirectly in these two approaches; they are not normally associated with dramatic up-front downsizing or with the elimination of layers of management. Instead, these approaches are based on the argument that fewer managers are needed over time as employee involvement takes hold and as units become more capable of self-management. With employee involvement, the typical approach is to reduce management gradually through attrition rather than through immediate and highly directive action on the part of senior executives. To some extent, we are talking here about a matter of degree: the hard reality is that the implementation of high-involvement management practices is often stalled as long as there is a full cadre of managers who are willing and able to control and direct, and many companies have found that they do not reap the full benefit of high-involvement approaches until they reduce their layers of management (Lawler, Mohrman, and Ledford, 1992).

Advocates of TQM often argue that as TQM is adopted, the role of management changes and that many people who were previously involved in supervision now become involved in managing process improvements. They also point out, however, that with good process controls in place, quality can be dramatically improved so that extensive quality-control functions and levels of management become much less necessary and overhead costs are greatly reduced. Thus even though all three approaches are advocated in large part because they increase both the effectiveness and the efficiency of a system, reengineering alone has tended to be implemented in a manner that associates it dramatically and immediately with reductions in the number of employees.

TQM can also reduce costs, but here the reductions come from an emphasis on doing things right the first time and on employees' being responsible for the quality of their work, both of which lead to reductions in rework and warranty costs (Lawler, Mohrman, and Ledford, 1995). The evidence is mixed with respect to employee involvement's ability to increase productivity and reduce costs. There is an extensive literature on this topic, and some of it clearly does show that the gains in motivation produced by effective programs of employee involvement can lead to higher productivity and lower labor costs (Lawler, 1992). It is important to emphasize, however, that cost reductions are not guaranteed, particularly if only a single practice of employee involvement is implemented (for example, democratic decision making, or job enrichment). What employee involvement often requires before it can demonstrate significant cost reductions is a combination of new approaches to supervision, work design, and the organization's reward system.

There is little question that the TQM approach is the one most likely to produce improvements in quality. This is hardly surprising: TQM's methods are particularly focused on measuring and enhancing quality, whether quality concerns manufacturing or customer satisfaction.

There is a considerable amount of evidence that employee involvement's changes in work design often lead to higher quality. The evidence suggests that when employees are doing interesting and challenging work, they care more about doing high-quality work (Hackman and Lawler, 1971). They may also produce gains in productivity, but their greatest focus seems to be on quality because it is high quality that employees associate with doing the job correctly and well. Thus the additional motivation that comes from self-managing work teams and enriched work tends to get funneled into doing a high-quality job. In the service sector, this trend often shows up as improved service to customers and better rapport with them.

Reengineering is often focused on improving the speed of decision making and on shortening cycle times. With improved lateral processes and the use of IT to move information quickly from one individual to another, dramatic improvements in processing time can sometimes be achieved. Analysis of an administrative process can often eliminate unnecessary steps and dramatically cut the time (often from weeks to days) for orders to be processed, for example, or for insurance claims to be reviewed. Still, reengineering may have oversold its promise to make major corporations both more cost-effective and faster in response to customers and to the rapidly changing competitive environment. Early reports on the impact of reengineering that mentioned improvements of up to "100 times" (Davidson, 1993) in some performance dimensions appear to have been overstated.

TQM can also improve speed because of the type of process analysis that it calls for. It focuses on eliminating unnecessary steps—and, of course, it places major emphasis on doing things correctly so that they will not have to be done over again. As used in some designs, employee involvement can also have a major impact on speed—for example, in the area of customer service when employees are empowered to resolve disputes immediately or to make certain decisions with respect to customers and their needs (Schneider and Bowen, 1995).

One major criticism of employee involvement has been that it may slow the decision process when decisions are made democratically. This criticism can certainly be valid because group decision making often takes longer than decision making by a single person. Three points should be raised here, however. First, employee involvement does not necessarily call for group decision making; it may simply involve allocating decision-making power to somebody at a much lower level in the organization than the level that traditionally has been involved in making decisions. Second, sometimes groups are slower than individuals to make decisions, but there is considerable evidence to show that once a decision has been made by a group, the decision is implemented more quickly than when it is made unilaterally by a single manager in the hierarchical structure. The manager often has to take the time to inform others of the decision and gain their agreement. Third, and perhaps most important, organizations making use of teams and group decision making can establish systematic processes for decision making and develop group decision-making skills that speed decision making (Mohrman, Cohen, and Mohrman, 1995).

There is overwhelming evidence that employee involvement leads to significant increases in employees' satisfaction and well-being (Lawler, 1986). A great deal of the research on employee involvement is focused on how employee involvement affects a variety of employee-related outcomes, ranging from absenteeism and turnover to mental health and physical well-being. Virtually all these studies have shown the positive effects of employee involvement: it gives employees more autonomy, more self-control, more skills, higher self-esteem, and, in general, creates a more satisfying work environment for them.

The evidence with respect to TQM and employee outcomes is also generally positive (Lawler, Mohrman, and Ledford, 1995). Employees enjoy learning the additional skills that are involved in

TQM, and they tend to like participating in problem-solving groups and quality circles. The changes that TQM introduces may also make the work environment itself more satisfying and rewarding (or at least less frustrating) because of the satisfaction that employees may feel as a result of doing high-quality work. Employees also end up with more skills and may ultimately earn higher pay.

Without question, the major criticism of the reengineering approach has been its treatment of people. The problems begin when the change process is implemented by consultants in a rather autocratic manner that gives employees little chance to influence what their new work and organization will be like. The individuals who most obviously suffer as a result of reengineering programs are those who lose their jobs. In many cases they are relatively highly paid individuals who have had long careers in the corporation. Often, however, they are not the only losers in a reengineering effort; even the survivors may suffer—first, from considerable anxiety over whether they will be retained and, second, from what may be a very different career situation for them once the reengineering effort has been completed. Often the jobs that survivors had aspired to are eliminated, and the survivors now have to dramatically alter their concept of what career success looks like. Undeniably, the primary reason why reengineering has been so heavily criticized—and, in many cases, resisted—is the layoffs it causes.

It is important to note that sometimes reengineering can improve the situation of individuals who are able to retain their jobs. They often end up with more responsible jobs, less direct supervision, and the opportunity to do more as a result of the increased use of information technology. Overall, there is the possibility that the survivors' career prospects will be enhanced by the reduction of control and the opportunity to broaden their understanding of the business and be involved with modern information technology.

Most research on organizational improvement efforts finds that a sustainable positive impact on organizational effectiveness depends on a multifaceted set of changes. A combination of approaches is needed to create lasting changes in operational capability, financial and market performance, and employee outcomes. In other words, although employee involvement may bring positive changes to all three of these outcome areas as a result of its approach to sharing information, power, knowledge, and rewards, its impact will be enhanced if they are accompanied by the implementation of the TQM approach, with its own tools and philosophy (Lawler, Mohrman, and Ledford, 1995). Employee involvement creates a management system in which employees are motivated to perform effectively; TQM brings a focus on the customer and on ways to improve the work processes of the organization. The two reinforce each other.

There is evidence that the successful implementation of reengineering also depends on multisystemic changes entailing organizational structure, philosophy, information systems, roles, and ongoing process improvement (Mohrman, Tenkasi, and Mohrman, 1997). The real power of information technology lies in its ability to connect and inform. Taking advantage of it requires the establishment of an organization that is able to shift power so that people within the organization can operate laterally, using information to make decisions and effectively carry out work processes for meeting customers' needs. The reengineering framework, by directly tackling the integration of powerful new information technologies into new organizational models, and by making salient the need to organize in a way that allows an integrated focus on major organizational processes, has brought a wider focus to the quest for high performance in organizations. Without attention to employee involvement and continuous quality improvement, however, reengineering cannot be optimally applied.

Employee Involvement, TQM, Business-Process Reengineering, and the Future

There is no question that employee involvement, TQM, and reengineering have all contributed to reshaping the practice of management in large, complex organizations. Each of the three approaches emphasizes important aspects of how complex organizations can be made more effective, and many key aspects of each approach have become accepted wisdom with respect to how large corporations should be managed. But what does the future hold for employee involvement, TQM, and reengineering?

Given the relative longevity of employee involvement, as well as the breadth of the issues it has dealt with, it is hardly surprising that employee involvement has produced practices and thinking that have become accepted dogma. For example, teams are increasingly used to manage complex processes, and in many cases the use of teams is seen less as employee involvement than as simply the right way to organize. Reward systems involving profit sharing, stock options, and gainsharing are also increasingly popular; likewise, they are not necessarily seen as part of an employee involvement effort but rather as simply an aspect of the right way to run a complex business. It is likely that in the future, fewer and fewer organizations will consciously embark on an "employee involvement program"; rather, they will institute many of the principles and practices developed as part of employee involvement simply because they are regarded as the best way to organize. In essence, employee involvement as a separate program or approach is likely to disappear, the victim of its own success.

A good guess is that TQM's fate will be very similar to employee involvement's. TQM also introduced a number of new management practices that are now generally accepted. Quality-improvement teams, statistical process control, quality measurement and goals, and ideas concerning customer focus are all rapidly becoming recognized simply as good management practice. As a result, it is becoming less and less necessary for companies to have separate TQM programs or initiatives. Instead, organizations will increasingly recognize that a quality capability is crucial to success in almost any business and will simply adopt those practices that are necessary for developing that capability. Thus TQM's practices will continue to be used, but they will be incorporated into the body of what constitutes good management and will no longer need to be championed or installed as part of TQM programs.

The fate of reengineering as a change program is likely to be quite different from the fate of employee involvement and total quality management. Recent reports, supported with viewpoints expressed by the founders of the reengineering movement, claim that more than 70 percent of reengineering efforts have failed to achieve their purposes (Bashein, Markus, and Riley, 1994; Hammer and Champy, 1993; Hammer, 1996a, 1996b). This outcome is blamed on a number of factors, including the failure of many top managers to recognize that reengineering is not just an exercise in downsizing, but that it entails considerable investments in the people, structures, and systems of the organization, as well as the transfer of power and profound changes in the organizational culture. If the popular literature on management is already full of books and articles (some by the founders of the movement) that emphasize going beyond reengineering and countering the negative effects of earlier reengineering efforts, clearly there is a backlash. Thus, reengineering is not likely to become a movement that is historically revered. With its extreme reductions in employees and its often top-down, autocratic implementation, it is much more likely to be seen as a fad with significant negative consequences for many individuals and some corporations that came and went rather quickly.

The perception of reengineering's high rate of failure is also likely to be balanced by the perception that reengineering did help solve some of the problems that large, bureaucratic, corporate dinosaurs had in the 1980s and 1990s. Even if the word *reengineering* disappears, there is no question that it is correct in arguing that integrating information technology into a company often requires significant changes in how the work of individuals is organized and how corporations are structured. Therefore, organizations will continue to deal with the basic tasks conceptualized by the creators of the reengineering movement: the development of integrated information systems to support new ways of doing work, and the development of an organization that can take competitive advantage of its vastly increased ability to distribute information.

With its emphasis on lateral, IT-mediated relationships among individuals, the process focus of reengineering is particularly important and will continue to be a major driver of how organizations are designed in the future (Galbraith, 1995). It is also clear that to be effective, organizations require conscious design and implementation of the interface between information technology and structure (see Chapter Twelve). Moreover, top management must continue to make hard choices that bring down empires, reduce layers and hierarchical control, and redistribute power.

It is ironic that another feature identified with the reengineering movement—the elimination of layers of management—is likely to survive as good practice even while the whole idea of reengineering is more and more frequently vilified and rejected. The elimination of managerial layers is often, on balance, positive, even though it may result in layoffs of many long-term employees (Lawler, Mohrman, and Ledford, 1995). The simple fact is that many corporations had and still have too many managers and too many layers of supervision; as a result, neither employee involvement nor TQM programs can be used effectively.

Employee involvement, TQM, and business-process reengineering have all contributed important and generally accepted ideas to the literature on how complex organizations should be managed. Each approach envisions an organization whose operations are significantly different from those of the traditional, hierarchical, functional organization. The challenge for the future is to develop a complete system of management that integrates and goes beyond what is offered by any one of them. None of the approaches discussed here offers a complete system of management; each of them offers the promise of performance improvements that can be fully experienced only in the presence of systemic change in how organizations are managed.

Part Three

Managing People in the Competitive Organization

The New Human Resources Management

Creating the Strategic Business Partnership

Susan Albers Mohrman
Edward E. Lawler III

Lifetime employment is dead. Jobs are being replaced by ever-changing work assignments. Careers are becoming portfolios of activities. People increasingly have multiple careers. Companies have core employees and peripheral employees. More and more companies are flexible and self-designing—reinventing themselves frequently as their environments change rapidly. Companies are becoming networks—systems of alliances and relationships. Organizational competitiveness depends increasingly on organizational capability—the ability to configure people and design organizations for optimal execution of strategy. As a result, the future effectiveness of most organizations increasingly depends on the very human resources who feel that the company is no longer committed to them and who do not know what the future holds. Herein lies the rationale for the complete and total transformation of the human resources function.

Human resources professionals have created and administered the systems—compensation, career, training and development, performance appraisal—that define key parameters of the field on which employees have played out their careers. The human resources function has had a well-deserved reputation as the bastion of the status quo. In the future, however, it can deliver immense value to the corporation by helping it navigate the uncharted waters of the new era. The key, we believe, is dealing with the paradox that just as employees can expect less loyalty from companies, companies are more than ever dependent on high-level performance and commitment from employees. To deal with this paradox, we believe the human resources function will have to reshape itself, populate itself differently, and blur its mental and organizational boundaries. This chapter deals with the development of the new human resources function. It argues that the human resources function not only must become a true business partner but also must be a microcosm of the organizations in which it is embedded.

Design Trends in Organizations

The emergence of the global economy, overcapacity in almost every industry, monumental strides in the power of computer and telecommunications tools, and the emergence of the knowledge economy are among the forces mentioned in the Introduction that have resulted in fundamental change in the design of organizations. Rapid environmental change, which places a premium on the ability of organizations to adapt quickly, and stringent competition, which results in the demise of organizations that do not adapt, have conspired to alter the logic of organizational design (Galbraith, Lawler, and Associates, 1993).

A whole constellation of organizational features—vertical integration, managerial control, stability, and two-way loyalty between organization and employee—that fit the old world of growth in a benevolent environment are giving way to new organizational designs for competitiveness, flexibility, continuous improvement, and self-management. The importance of organizational design and the attention being given to it have grown significantly. An argument can be made that organization is the most lasting competitive advantage (Lawler, 1992). Organizational design shapes competencies and yields capabilities that enable the organization to enact its strategy effectively.

A number of trends in design are noticeable as organizations seek to be more flexible and competitive. The overarching trend involves the notion that the essential criterion for all organizational design decisions is whether the design contributes maximum value to the accomplishment of the organizational strategy (Galbraith, 1993). This trend has led to the reexamination of design at the level of the corporation, the business unit, the work unit, and the work processes that cut across the organization. Whatever does not add value is eliminated—units, levels, signature requirements, services, and so forth.

The traditional framework for corporate design has been taken apart and put back together again in many companies, and new organizational "architectures" have resulted (Nadler, Gerstein, Shaw, and Associates, 1992). In that process, a variety of new organizational forms has emerged. For example, the vertically integrated company is being transformed by outsourcing and networking (see Chapter Three). Companies are determining which competencies need to be kept inside because they are critical to the ability to achieve organizational strategies, and which ones are best purchased externally because someone else can provide them better or less expensively. Staff groups, once shared across the business units of the corporation or placed in each unit, are being broken apart, with some elements being placed in business units, others being kept central and leveraged across the units, and yet others being outsourced. For all functions, decisions are made about whether to create flexibility and variation through redundancy, by distributing the functions in each business unit, or whether to create efficiency, by sharing them and leveraging approaches.

Within the same organization, different units are being constructed with very different logics, and the value that each unit adds is being optimized through the tailoring of its design features to the work that the unit does. This internal variety allows the organization to respond effectively to the requirements of many subenvironments and different work processes. A manufacturing unit, for example, may be constructed around manufacturing processes in a flat manner, with self-managing teams and very few managers. The new-product development unit may be organized around product families, with cross-functional teams and a more traditional management structure. The sales and service organization may be organized around customer sets, as is the case in front-back organizations, with individual contributors selling and serving customers within a traditional hierarchical structure.

Because the environment continues to change and competition continues to escalate, the redesign process in most organizations needs to continue through multiple, often more complex iterations. Organizations increasingly find it is not enough to optimize one dimension (product, geography, or functional performance) of the business; rather, they have to jointly optimize multiple dimensions in order to compete effectively (Galbraith, 1994). They must find ways to make complex trade-offs between the needs of multiple product families, customer sets, geographical areas, and technical arenas. This leads to an increase in complexity, so that traditional hierarchical mechanisms for control and direction break down—general managers cannot know enough and respond quickly enough to the myriad of trade-off decisions.

Organizations are finding that in order to staff many of the new organizational forms, they need a shifting array of workforces, including a core workforce, contractors, and contingent part-time or temporary workers (Handy, 1990; Rousseau and Wade-Benzoni, 1995; Hall and Mirvis, 1995). Even the core workforce increasingly operates through a series of dynamic structures—work teams, task teams, and projects—so that the concept of the "job" is becoming increasingly elusive (Mohrman and Cohen, 1995). As the orderly, uniform, stable landscape of the hierarchical organization gives way to variety, dynamic change, and idiosyncrasy, and as the vertically integrated structure of the organization breaks apart, an organization emerges in which the human resources management practices of the past no longer fit.

For the human resources function, these massive organizational upheavals pose challenges and opportunities. The first challenge is to design human resources practices that fit with the new way of organizing and the new business requirements—in other words, practices that fit into a dynamic, unpredictable corporation with a myriad of approaches to getting work done. The second challenge is to help organizations find their way through this upheaval—in other words, to become integrally involved in thinking through organizational design and human resources issues in a systemic way. The third challenge is for the human resources function to find its place in the new organization—in other words, to redesign itself with an eye to adding maximum value to the corporation. This situation provides an incredible opportunity for the human resources function. Organizations are faced with a situation that cries out for solutions to the thorny challenges of integrating business- and people-related needs. If it can rise to the occasion, the human resources function is in an excellent position to become a true member of the business team and to add value far above what this function has contributed in the past.

People-Management Challenges

A key component of every organizational system is its human resources. In service organizations they can represent 70 to 80 percent of the total cost of doing business (Lawler, 1995). Even where capital equipment and raw materials account for a large percentage of the cost of doing business, the human resources add the value that drives revenue and profit. Although reducing the cost of human resources may be a worthy and important goal at some stages in an organization's life, surely the most important long-term goal should be to ensure the availability of highly motivated and qualified human resources who are organized to effectively carry out the core tasks of the organization. This is no trivial task. It extends well beyond providing training for people so that they have the needed competencies.

A number of key and interrelated issues are paramount, each of which requires a true blending of business- and human resources–related concerns. In the paragraphs that follow, we identify and discuss five such issues, all of them systemic, which is to say that they all involve the strategy, design, work systems, and human resources of the organization. None is a purely human resources–based issue; they do not fall cleanly into the domain of the human resources function. They can be addressed only if the organization is dealt with as a system and if systemic solutions are generated.

Organizing for High Performance

Often forgotten in organizational restructurings is that this process should have as its ultimate outcome the most effective application of human resources to accomplish the mission of the organization. Fashionable changes—creating small, flexible, cross-functional units; aligning people around value-adding tasks rather than "overhead" tasks; outsourcing; partnering; configuring work around core processes; creating customer focus—will be successful only if the human resources of the organization are supportive of them. Legitimate concerns exist about the condition of the workforce that is left in place after rounds of downsizing, takeaways, and restructuring. Sustained high performance will result only if new organizational forms result from a design process that is truly sociotechnical—one that takes into account the nature of the task and the nature of people (Trist, 1981; Pasmore, 1988). This demands deep knowledge not only of strategy and design but also of the principles of motivation. It will demand new and more varied approaches to goal setting and rewards, approaches that give people a meaningful stake in business performance.

Deploying People

The infrastructure that supported people deployment in the traditional organization has disappeared, and at a time when matching tasks with the right people is more important than ever. Gone are the days of people's orderly progression through a series of jobs in a functional hierarchy, where functional managers could observe the performance of their subordinates and, on the basis of functional capabilities, determine who got hired, promoted, and assigned. In the new organization, people are as likely to move through series of projects and rotational moves as through an orderly progression of jobs. Functional managers, if they exist at all, may have very little ability to observe the work of functional contributors. People are likely to report to a project head who has little understanding of their particular knowledge bases. Much work will be done by "virtual" organizations—assembled from across the company, often informally, and possibly linked only electronically to complete their tasks (Savage, 1990). Boundaries will not be respected: people may have co-workers from other departments, business units, and countries or from partner companies, suppliers, and customers.

In such organizations, the challenge of deploying people with the right talents to different work opportunities is a daunting one, especially when it is combined with the need to develop people.

Much of the development that takes place in an organization will occur through work or task assignments (Hall and Mirvis, 1995). In fact, a person's career will increasingly consist of the creation of a portfolio of experiences; people will be competing for work assignments rather than for promotions up a hierarchy. Issues of affirmative action and equal opportunity are increasingly likely to be seen in this context (Mohrman and Cohen, 1995).

The "workforce" to be deployed is likely to include core workers, contractors, and temporary or part-time workers. The company will have to become proficient at determining when it is appropriate to use employees from these different pools—in other words, proficient at managing a network of human resources. A completely new infrastructure will be required to make possible the tracking and deploying of the human resources available to the company, as well as the efficient and effective movement of people between assignments.

Managing Core Competencies and Organizational Capabilities

In the knowledge economy, the management of the competencies of the human resources of the organization is an urgent task with survival implications. Knowledge and information are increasing exponentially, requiring the nurturing of the deep knowledge bases central to the task of the organization, as well as the development of enhanced analytical capabilities to exploit knowledge at a faster rate than competitors can. New strategies and designs require new competencies: cross-functional knowledge is becoming increasingly important to the success of new approaches to increasing speed, improving processes, and solving important organizational problems. In flat organizations, front-line employees must develop a broad understanding of the business issues being faced by their firms. They must also develop self-management capabilities, once the purview of individuals holding higher-level management jobs (Lawler, 1996). They must engage in more complex information processing (Mohrman, Cohen, and Mohrman, 1995).

Dynamic environments, strategies, designs, and technologies mean that the need for competencies and capabilities changes, with some becoming obsolete, noncritical, or irrelevant while the new organization requires different and, often, a more advanced group of competencies and capabilities. Organizations need strategies for growing and maintaining a deep understanding of their own current and long-term strategic interests in the midst of a core workforce that grows and evolves with the company (Rousseau and Wade-Benzoni, 1995). They also need to secure talent in emerging areas and to ensure that they do not find themselves burdened with large numbers of obsolete skills. Changes in approaches to training and development, as discussed in Chapter Ten, are important, but they are only one piece of the puzzle: the strategic make-buy-partner decision applies as much to human resources talent as to decisions about products and services.

Managing Organizational Learning

An issue closely related to the management of competencies is the management of organizational knowledge and learning. In the traditional organization, company-specific and deep disciplinary knowledge were carried in people's heads and shared through the interaction of people in discipline-based departments and workgroups. Different groups often "recreated the wheel" if they were not privy to the fact that elsewhere in the organization problems had been solved, designs created, code written, or information and analyses compiled.

Organizations can no longer function competitively with informal approaches to knowledge and learning. People come in temporarily, needing a quick way to gather information and get on board, and they leave, taking with them years of acquired knowledge. Finding ways to embed knowledge in organizational processes and documents, to distribute information and know-how in readily accessible forms, and to disseminate knowledge and accelerate learning are key challenges facing organizations. Designing the infrastructure for learning, defining accountabilities to include ongoing learning, devising easy ways for key learnings to be diffused throughout the organization and pass from experienced to inexperienced workers—these are all focuses that can greatly enhance the productivity of the organization and its human resources.

Defining the New Psychological Contract

The psychological contract reflects the individual's understanding of the employment relationship's terms, as well as the normative beliefs about what organizational members owe and are owed in return (Rousseau and Wade-Benzoni, 1995). It includes such things as duration of the relationship, performance requirements, and equitable outcomes. Recent changes in organizational strategies and designs have resulted in major disruptions of the prevailing psychological contract, and a new one has yet to be established in most organizations. Although this expectation is changing, most employees working in large organizations did not enter with the expectation that their employment would be temporary, or that it could be terminated in spite of their satisfactory performance. Many entered with the expectation of a career—the expectation that the company would give them a chance to grow, develop, and advance hierarchically. They expected their wages to increase with time, experience, and performance. They did not expect their salaries to be at risk; they expected a fair wage for the work they did. They saw the company, not themselves, as responsible for providing opportunities for growth, development, and careers. In return, they expected to be loyal and to do what the company needed to have done.

Clearly, the rash of downsizing, restructuring, outsourcing, and hollowing has put an end to the old psychological contract, and new contracts are emerging in reaction to the new situation. A major question is whether the new contracts, which often take shape amid fear and disillusionment, can create the conditions for high performance. We appear to be entering an era of highly differentiated psychological contracts. The contracts established with different groups of employees—core workers, contract workers, and temporary and part-time workers—will have to acknowledge the needs and motivations of each particular group of employees. Organizations will have to formulate approaches to each type of group and each type of contract. Some companies are carefully crafting new sets of mutual expectations with their employees. It seems clear that if new norms and expectations are not purposefully set, and if new ways of contracting for work are not devised, behavior in the new organization may not meet the new organization's performance needs. It also seems clear that if the new contracts do not give employees a stake in the performance of the organization, the organization is unlikely to obtain anything like the depth of commitment found in the old era of two-way loyalty.

The Value-Adding Human Resources Function

All too often, the personnel function adds value primarily through the performance of administrative activities (Lawler, 1995; Evans, 1994). It is the keeper of the formal systems through which people are selected, developed, reviewed, and rewarded in the hierarchical organization. It establishes policies, negotiates and monitors labor contracts, and serves as the auditing and policing function to make sure that the organization does not break the law. Toward this end, it also serves as an employee advocate, ensuring that people are not treated unfairly, and that they have recourse if they are. It is not expected to play a strategic role or a role in improving the performance of the organization; rather, it is expected to take care of "people" issues in order to free up the line to deal with the performance of the organization.

In some organizations, the personnel function has transformed itself into the human resources function (Lawler, 1995; Evans, 1994). As such, it operates in a functionally specialized hierarchical organization with such subfunctions as human resources planning, compensation, selection, and training and development. Each of these subfunctions relates to its own professional community and spends time updating company practices to reflect current best practice. In some organizations, human resources executives sit at the general management table. In the most progressive organizations, the human resources function is perceived as offering services of strategic import and is viewed as contributing value by controlling labor costs and providing the human resources planning, performance management, training and development, and change management capabilities that ensure a ready supply of competent employees who can carry out the changing business strategies and organizational initiatives. The human resources function, although it is achieving more centrality in the organizational system, is still clearly seen as playing a supportive, "staff" role.

The future of the human resources function involves being an integral part of the management team—helping to build strategy, improve organizational performance, and develop such organizational capabilities as the ability to get new products to markets quickly and the ability to build quality into products and processes (Lawler, 1996; Evans, 1994). Such capabilities are integral to the successful enactment of strategies. Once acquired, these capabilities can provide an ongoing strategic advantage as the organization refines them and builds on them. These capabilities are difficult for other organizations to copy because they reside in multiple systems and multiple parts of the organization. In essence, the organization's design, which includes its human resources systems, underpins organizational capabilities.

Competitive advantage is attained through the way in which a company organizes, not merely through the acquisition and development of superior human resources (Galbraith, Lawler, and Associates, 1993). Human resources practices are an integral part of the larger organizational system. For human resources to contribute optimally to organizational performance, they must be optimally organized, and the various aspects of the organizational system must be aligned with each other. Human resources practices must fit with each other and with the strategy and design of the organization. In order for the members of the human resources function to have an impact on performance, they must be knowledgeable about, have influence on, and be closely connected to the other parts of the organization.

The argument that organization, not simply competent individuals, creates competitive advantage through the creation of organizational capabilities means that the human resources function must be able to operate at multiple levels—at the level of the individual, the work group, and the business unit, as well as at the organizational and cross-organizational levels. It must stop working exclusively at the level of the individual performer and deal with the factors of design that influence larger performing units. It must contribute to the development and performance management of teams, product lines, divisions, joint ventures, and so forth.

The human resources function is just one of many staff functions that needs to be redesigned. Staff organizations in general have been under fire in organizations because they are frequently perceived as controlling rather than adding value. The need to move out of a controlling role reflects the transition in the larger organization from a hierarchical-control orientation to a performance-focused, involvement orientation (Lawler, 1992).

Our view of the expanded value that the human resources function can add argues for its having a full partnership role in each of the following four key business processes:

1. *Developing strategy.* The human resources function can contribute to business strategy on the basis of its knowledge about the organization's competencies and capabilities, its understanding of the organizational changes that will be required to support different strategic directions, and its knowledge about the network of human resources available to the company and about the opportunities or constraints inherent in that network.

2. *Designing the organization.* The human resources function can be the repository of organizational design expertise, and it can play the role of internal consultant in the ongoing design and redesign that will characterize organizations and their subunits as they continually modify themselves to achieve shifting strategies, new capabilities, and higher levels of performance. It can help address the need to design simultaneously for high levels of performance, for the development of particular organizational capabilities (such as innovation, quality, and organizational learning), for the development and maintenance of needed competencies, and for high levels of motivation.

3. *Implementing change.* The human resources function can help the organization develop the capability to weather the changes that will continue to be part of the organizational landscape. It can help with the ongoing learning processes required to assess the impact of change and enable the organization to make corrections and enhancements to the changes (Mohrman and Cummings, 1989). It can help the organization develop a new psychological contract and ways to give employees a stake in the changes that are occurring and in the performance of the organization.

4. *Integrating performance-management practices.* The human resources function can work with line managers to make sure that the performance-management practices of the organization (goal setting, performance appraisal, development practices, and rewards) are integrated with one another and with the business-management practices of the organization, and that they fit with the nature of the work. If human resources management practices are not to be seen as separate from the running of the business, then they must be integrated as completely as possible with the business processes (Mohrman and Mohrman, 1995). For example, goal-setting processes for individuals and teams should be nested within goal-setting processes for business units, and business accountability must be reflected and reinforced through performance-management systems and pay systems. These processes must give individuals a stake in the performance of the business, and they must measure and reward performance that supports the business strategy.

We have been arguing that the human resources function needs to shed its administrative and auditing functions, as well as its routine servicing tasks, and move into a more central role in helping the organization determine and achieve its strategic direction. Interestingly, in the performance-management arena, the change that human resources has to make is to turn responsibility over to the line and serve as the line's consultant and partner in developing these practices; the human resources function should not be seen as the "owner" of the human resources practices. Moreover, in the first three arenas—developing strategy, designing the organization, and implementing change—the human resources function has to become involved in activities traditionally carried out by the line.

Studies support the perception that a major shift in the human resources function is occurring, albeit slowly. Table 8.1 illustrates the increased time that the human resources function is spending as a strategic business partner and as a developer of human resources systems. These increases suggest that the human resources function is being blended more and more into the business management of the organization, as a full partner bringing expertise

Table 8.1. Percentage Share of
Time Allocated to Human Resources Roles.

Role	5–7 Years Ago	Now	Difference[a]
Maintaining Records Collecting, tracking, and maintaining data on employees	23.0	15.4	Significant decrease
Auditing/Controlling Ensuring compliance with internal operations, regulations, legal, and union requirements	19.5	12.2	Significant decrease
Providing Human Resources Services Assisting with implementation and administration of human resources practices	34.3	31.3	Significant decrease
Developing human resources systems and practices	14.3	18.6	Significant increase
Being a strategic business partner Member of the management team; being involved with strategic human resources planning, organizational design, and strategic change	10.3	22.0	Significant increase

[a]The change was significant in 130 companies, the total sample. The percentage of change was significantly higher in companies with several groups or sectors of businesses.

Source: Adapted from Mohrman, Lawler, and McMahan, 1996, p. 26. Used by permission of the Center for Effective Organizations.

and a specialized perspective to the process of running a business and improving its performance.

The new human resources role requires deep expert knowledge, broad business knowledge, and change-mastery skills (Ulrich, Brockbank, and Yeung, 1989; Mohrman, Lawler, and McMahan, 1996). Human resources professionals will also need the ability to work at multiple levels of analysis and to take a systemic view of the organization. Currently, many human resources professionals are not prepared for this new role. Our research shows that the majority of companies believe that at least 40 percent of their human resources professionals do not have the requisite skills to play the role of business partner (Mohrman, Lawler, and McMahan, 1996). Clearly, this new role also requires a reconfiguration of the human resources function.

The Design of the Human Resources Function

We began with the argument that organizations are redesigning themselves in line with the idea that each part of the organization should contribute more fully to the ability of the whole organization to achieve its strategy. We then argued that this kind of redesign raises very significant issues for the human resources function, which can contribute to the organization the key value of helping to address these issues. This contribution in turn requires the human resources function to take on a new role: that of full partner in the management of the business.

A major trend in organizational design is toward cross-functional or process management. This trend is being manifested in a myriad of ways: in the number of lateral mechanisms for moving strategic and operational decision making lower into multifunctional forums; in the establishment of multiple self-contained business units at many levels (divisions, subunits, teams, and projects); and in the large number of cross-functional teams that conduct special and ongoing work for the organization. An underlying premise of these cross-functional approaches is that people will no longer work within functional "silos"; rather, they will work as teammates or partners, building on each other's expertise in conducting one integrated chunk of the organization's business. A second underlying premise is that general management decisions will be moved into these units, which will have significant say over how they are organized and over the parameters within which they operate and do their work. This will lead to an increased variety of structures and processes in the organization.

Because all organizational units face human resources–related issues as they organize to do their work, it is imperative to have human resources expertise in all units or to make such expertise available to them. This imperative drives several key design decisions for the human resources function and for other staff groups that traditionally have been centralized. We will consider the most important of these decisions as we offer specific suggestions for (and predictions about) the kinds of principles that should guide the redesign of the future human resources function.

Allocation of Expertise and Functions

What kinds of expertise and functions will be placed within decentralized business units? What kinds of functions will be performed centrally and/or provided from a central service group on a service-contract basis?

Because it is unlikely that each business unit will need the continuous presence of deep subdisciplinary knowledge (about compensation, labor, and so forth), the trend will be to place only human resources generalists in the various business units. These generalists will provide or assemble the resources for imparting the expertise needed in fashioning human resources approaches to the units' particular business issues and work processes.

Deep functional experts will be available from a central pool. They will provide systemwide capabilities through the development of tools or templates, or through the offering of their services to business units on an as-needed basis. Deep functional expertise may also be acquired from contractors.

Allocation of Responsibilities

Which human resources responsibilities can be made part of the jobs of general business managers within business units, and which need to be carried out by human resources professionals?

A basic tenet is to move ownership for human resources–related issues into business units. Therefore, key design questions in the staffing of decentralized, cross-functional business units are which specialists will be needed and when contributors can be cross-trained. In some cases, especially when there are recurring human resources–related tasks, business managers will need to learn how to apply a great deal of general knowledge about the human resources function, without the presence of human resources staff members. In the cross-functional organization, many tasks currently performed within the human resources organization (planning, competency development, compensation decisions, conflict resolution) will have to become the purview of others (in engineering, marketing, and so forth) who are cross-trained in human resources. The human resources function may play an overall coordinating and consultation role across the corporation, as well as playing an enabling role by providing software programs and tools for analysis and planning. Indeed, systems and tools are being developed to enable business managers and operational discipline experts to perform many of the ongoing tasks concerned with the management of human resources, tasks that used to be performed by human resources professionals.

Cross-Skilling and Rotation

How much cross-skilling should be provided, and what kinds of rotational mechanisms should be established to provide human resources professionals with the knowledge and experience to think and contribute more systemically?

Cross-functional management in general works best if there are individuals who have worked in a number of areas and can translate among various members of a team (Galbraith, 1994). In order to provide generalist human resources support as members of business teams, human resources professionals have to be knowledgeable about business issues and work processes as well as about the different subdisciplines of human resources. They have to have such basic business skills as strategy formulation, business planning, and financial management. Line managers who are now expected to do more of their own human resources management can also benefit from cross-training in human resources processes. There will also be an increase in the amount of planned rotation within human resources, and into and out of human resources from other parts of the organization.

Core Tasks and Cost Effectiveness

What are the core human resources tasks that add value to the business? What is the most cost-effective manner of effectively delivering human resources services?

The other major design imperatives facing the business, and human resources as part of the business, are the need to drive non-value-adding costs out of the processes and the need to reengineer processes, taking advantage of information technology to reduce labor-intensive tasks. Companies are disaggregating themselves by reaching make-or-buy decisions about all tasks that are not of core strategic import. Company human resources functions may get out of the business of administering and even developing such systems as those for performance appraisal. Instead, they may act as experts, buying and tailoring state-of-the-art systems provided by vendors.

The human resources function is reengineering processes to eliminate non-value-adding steps and to provide routine transactional services through information systems, so that organizational members can serve themselves. Routine processing tasks are being contracted out or being performed through central processing pools that, as suppliers to business units, are managed with service contracts that ensure efficiency and responsiveness to customers. To maintain flexibility and deal with the dynamic nature of the business, as well as to reduce costs, the human resources network will increasingly include contributors with a broad array of employment relationships. A core set of employees will be retained and developed to play the key business-partner roles that require both business-specific knowledge and broad, generalist human resources capability. We will also see a proliferation of part-time or temporary employees performing noncore tasks, as well as contractors and consultants providing specialized services on an as-needed basis.

A number of the human resources issues faced by organizations will be hard to resolve within the bounds of one company. Examples of issues needing transorganizational solutions are the provision of efficient and cost-effective ways to help people move from one company to another, or the creation of mechanisms whereby benefits can be made portable and/or extended to part-time and temporary employees. Therefore, the human resources function will increasingly manage a service-delivery network that extends beyond company boundaries.

Increasingly, human resources professionals will work outside the traditional corporate walls—in alliances and other cooperative or community-based relationships, or in specialty firms—to pro-

vide services once offered by internal human resources departments. Where will the future human resources generalists learn
their trade? How will specialists be developed? As in other profes-
sions, we will increasingly see careers that move across different
employment settings. In the future we may see human resources
professionals start their careers in consulting or services firms,
much as accountants do now, and move into corporations after
having acquired a foundation of experience and expertise. A human resources business partner may be required to have an M.B.A.
and experience in line management, strategic planning, financial
management, people management, and change management that
can be carried into the human resources function.

The Future Is Here

Major change is already occurring in the ways in which many organizations are designing and staffing their human resources functions, particularly in companies that are undergoing a great deal
of strategic change (Mohrman, Lawler, and McMahan, 1996). The
changes in the human resources function are being driven by and
are microcosms of the major changes in the business. The role of
business partner is emerging in large part because the issues of organizational performance and human resources management are
inextricably intertwined.

So far, our studies indicate that the human resources function
is taking on the role of business partner more rapidly and willingly
than it is shedding its old service roles (Mohrman, Lawler, and
McMahan, 1996). The human resources function appears slow to
blur the boundary between itself and the rest of the organization
by moving human resources–related responsibilities to the line. Although processes are being automated, in most companies there
has not yet been a major reinvention of the way in which the human resources department functions. Outsourcing is on the increase, but it still accounts for a minority of services in this area. The
human resources function does seem to be stepping up to the challenge of a strategic business partnership, but for the most part it has
not yet addressed the formidable internal challenge of reconstitut-
ing and reshaping its own workforce so that its competencies fit the
new roles and make truly high-performance designs possible.

As the human resources function changes in the direction of a strategic business partnership, human resources professionals increasingly will have careers that reflect the careers of the workforce in general. In other words, they will have multiple careers that they will have to build for themselves. They will have to worry about their own employability. People who choose to make their careers as human resources professionals may find themselves working in a variety of settings and creating portfolios of experiences that prepare them for a variety of higher-level jobs as business partners, expert consultants, managers in human resources consulting firms, and human resources network managers. In other words, they will seek and benefit from exposure to other kinds of roles, which will increase their value as partners in dealing with systemic change as it unfolds in the new workplace and in the new workforce.

We believe that the human resources function ultimately will be redesigned and will perform radically differently from the way in which it has performed in the past. It will be a true partner in managing the business. Responsibility for human resources will be owned across the organization. The core human resources professionals in the organization will be fewer, but their skills and knowledge will be broader, and their value to the company will be much greater. The company will receive human resources services through a broad array of mechanisms, and human resources problems will be solved through mechanisms that blur traditional organizational boundaries. In many ways, changes in the human resources function will be a microcosm of the changes that are fundamentally transforming the landscape of organizations.

Chapter Nine

The New Learning Partnership

Sharing Responsibility for Building Competence

David Finegold

The contradiction is becoming so common that we hardly notice it. In IBM's 1994 annual report, the CEO writes, "I want to emphasize just how much of an asset we have in our people." Two years later, the newspapers report, "IBM has just announced its third major restructuring in three years, bringing the total number of layoffs to 70,000."

On the one hand, many of the world's largest and historically most successful companies—household names like AT&T and Nissan—have ended their commitment to employment security and have announced major cuts in their workforces. On the other hand, corporations and the leading management strategists who advise them are stressing the need to develop the core competencies of organizations and the individuals within them in order to sustain competitive advantage (Hamel and Prahalad, 1994).

Human resources (HR) professionals bear the brunt of this contradiction. At a time when many HR departments are shrinking in proportion to the size of their firms, they are facing unprecedented new demands to develop individuals' capabilities. And they must strive to develop these competencies in an environment far from conducive to traditional corporate approaches to training. Traditional job descriptions are rapidly becoming obsolete. Employees are reacting to ongoing layoffs by displaying lower commitment to their organizations. And many of the individuals on whom a company depends for competitive success may not even be that company's employees.

Before managers can devise strategies for meeting the particular skill-development challenges facing their firms, they need a broader framework for understanding the changes that are already under way, changes that are increasing the demand for skills while making it more difficult to meet that demand. This new framework will start from an understanding of how major changes in the global marketplace and in organizations have undermined the old psychological contract between employer and employee. What is needed now is a new bargain—the learning contract—centered on the concept of shared responsibility for ongoing development (see, for example, Hall, 1996). To fulfill their side of this bargain, companies must shift from the old training paradigm to a new learning paradigm for building competencies. This chapter, after describing the main elements of this new paradigm, reviews the steps that firms can take to identify a clear set of priorities for development and to evaluate the make-or-buy decision regarding training. The chapter concludes with an example, based on research from the banking sector, of how the new learning contract might operate.

Increase in the Demand for Skills

A recent survey of a nationally representative sample of U.S. firms with more than twenty employees found that 57 percent had experienced an increase in the need for skills over the past three years, whereas only 5 percent had experienced a decrease and 39 percent reported no change (National Center on the Educational Quality of the Workforce, 1995). Similar trends toward growing needs, and a consequent rise in rates of returning to education, are apparent across the developed countries, where more than half of gross domestic product is now accounted for by knowledge-intensive industries (Paye, 1996). A combination of globalization and deregulation and an accompanying growth in competition have raised both the pressure and the level of uncertainty for companies and the individuals who work in them (Reich, 1991). At the same time, the ongoing rapid pace of technological innovation has made it possible to automate or outsource many routine tasks. The workers who are left must keep pace with technology and master higher-level skills.

In response to these trends, companies have adopted a variety of restructuring strategies intended to make their organizations more flexible and competitive. These restructuring strategies come with a variety of different labels—"reengineering," "downsizing," "lean production"—but the efforts typically have a similar effect on organizations: they reduce the layers of management and the number of people available to do the work (London, 1996; Lawler, Mohrman, and Ledford, 1995). Economists project that as many as one in three Americans will lose their jobs in the next four years as a result of restructuring (Birch, 1997). The demands on the employees who remain are increasing. They are being asked to perform a broader array of tasks, to take responsibility for their own quality control, and, in some cases, to contribute to self-managed teams. All these tasks require new sets of skills (for example, scheduling, statistical process control, or people management).

The factors that are driving the increase in the demand for skills are, ironically, the same ones that have made it more difficult for companies to develop individuals' capabilities. In the new, flatter organizations many of the traditional paths to skill development have been closed or at least narrowed:

- There are fewer job levels, and so individuals can no longer learn jobs incrementally by advancing slowly through the hierarchy.
- There are fewer mentoring relationships because senior people now have greater responsibilities and spans of control and therefore less time for developing others' skills.
- There are fewer internal personnel dedicated to training and development as firms cut back on HR staff and push additional responsibilities onto line managers.
- There is less incentive for individuals to invest in company-specific competencies because people are less certain of employment tenure.
- There is less time off to participate in training as pressure intensifies to meet performance targets.

The Learning Contract

In an environment characterized by major external and organizational changes and by increasingly unstable employment relationships, a central challenge facing companies is to find ways of developing workers' competencies and of encouraging workers to use their competencies effectively (see Figure 9.1). This challenge has led to calls for a new employment bargain, or psychological contract, suited to the realities of today's more turbulent business climate (Rousseau, 1995; Nicholson, 1996).

One possible basis for an alternative bargain between employer and employee is a mutual commitment to ongoing competency development, or a learning contract (see Table 9.1). The organization, although not able to offer employment security, pledges to increase the employability of its workers and managers by investing in their continuous skill development and by providing them with opportunities (including lateral career paths) and rewards for using these skills (Waterman, Waterman, and Collard, 1994). If the organization's focus changes, or if demand slackens and it no longer needs a particular individual's set of competencies, then the

Table 9.1.　The New Learning Contract.

Employer	Employee
Provide ongoing opportunities and support for education and training	Invest in own development of competencies
Structure daily work and career paths to use existing competencies and build new individual capabilities	Use competencies to help achieve organizational objectives
Encourage and reward individuals who use capabilities effectively	Help build competencies of co-workers
Help individuals find new work opportunities, either internal or external, if demand for existing competencies decreases	Contribute to organizational learning

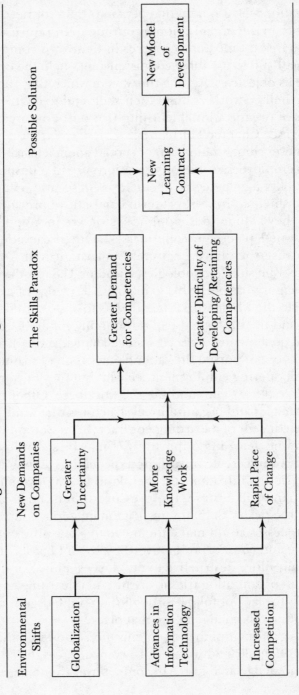

Figure 9.1. Drivers of Change in Skill Development.

Environmental Shifts

New Demands on Companies

The Skills Paradox

Possible Solution

Globalization

Advances in Information Technology

Increased Competition

Greater Uncertainty

More Knowledge Work

Rapid Pace of Change

Greater Demand for Competencies

Greater Difficulty of Developing/Retaining Competencies

New Learning Contract

New Model of Development

organization will also help that person retrain for new opportunities either in the organization or outside it. In return, individuals agree to invest time and resources in their own competency development and to use these competencies to help the organization achieve its objectives. Among the ways in which they can do so are to help their co-workers build their skills and to contribute to the process of organizational learning (for more on organizational learning, see Chapter Thirteen).

Not every organization can or should adopt a learning contract with its employees. Some organizations are in a position to continue to offer a high degree of employment security, either because they are shielded from short-term competitive pressures (for example, they belong to the public sector, are monopolies, or are family-owned, paternalistic businesses). Others can offer job security because they have been able to sustain high growth (for example, Kingston Technologies, a leading U.S. producer of computer memory, has been able to maintain its pledge of employment security to the whole workforce, thanks to consistent double-digit growth and the strategic use of outsourcing for all but its core design and quality-control processes; see Flanigan, 1996). Such firms could choose to pursue the other elements of a learning contract while still offering employment security, but they need not do this in order to attract and motivate the workforce. Other companies have strategies and organizational structures that would fit poorly with the concept of a learning contract. In a fast-food restaurant, for example, learning opportunities may be so limited that the company would create unrealistic expectations among its employees if it tried to introduce this new kind of employment bargain. In companies like these, the pressure to minimize labor costs and/or the desire to maintain strict managerial control over all work processes could make the move to a learning contract unattractive and counterproductive (Bowen and Lawler, 1992). It is potentially more destructive to employees' morale and commitment if an organization tries to create a new learning contract and then fails for lack of follow-through than if the organization does not institute this change in the first place.

For a growing number of organizations, however, the learning contract offers clear advantages. If a company sees the creation and use of knowledge as a source of competitive advantage, and if it requires skills that cannot easily be hired from outside, then that company needs a new way of fostering the development of both individual and organizational competencies. This need is likely to intensify in the future: the United States is projected to have unprecedentedly low rates of growth in the labor force, even when immigration is taken into account (Birch, 1997), and this trend will compel companies that want to attract and retain knowledge workers to create a work environment that knowledge workers will find appealing. The learning contract offers a new basis for the employment relationship from which both sides can benefit. For individuals, it provides opportunities for ongoing development that will enhance their market value if they leave their organizations. For firms, it can serve as a spur for innovation because companies, to uphold their end of the bargain, must continuously find new ways to challenge their employees.

A New Approach to Development

Organizations need to radically rethink their traditional approaches to skill development if they are to deliver a new learning contract. This means revisiting the basic questions that underlie the old model of training (see Table 9.2): Who is to be developed? What do people need to learn? Where does learning occur most effectively? When in people's careers should learning occur? Why

Table 9.2. New Approach to Development.

	Old Model	New Model
Employees Trained	Select employees	All contributors
Training Content	Technical and managerial skills	Cross-functional capabilities
Setting for Training	Classroom	Learning organization
Timing of Training	Beginning of employment	Throughout employment
Reason for Training	Effective job performance	Creation of competitive advantage

invest in development? The ways in which leading companies are answering these questions suggest that a shift is under way from the focus on "training and development" to a focus on "development and learning" (Ulrich and Greenfield, 1995; Mohrman and Mohrman, 1993).

Developing All Contributors

Until recently, U.S. companies concentrated their training dollars on the segment of the workforce that was already the best educated—managers and professionals (Lillard and Tan, 1986). These white-collar workers still receive proportionally more training than other employees, but there is now growing pressure to raise the skill levels of the majority of the workforce. In the United States, recent estimates suggest that up to 20 percent of the workforce lacks the literacy and numerical skills needed to function in the modern workplace (Finegold and Mason, 1996; National Center on the Educational Quality of the Workforce, 1995). As companies establish product- or service-delivery and quality-control systems that place greater responsibilities on front-line employees, they are finding that they must raise the basic skills of the workforce before the initiatives can succeed.

The restructuring of the workplace is also increasingly shifting the focus of development from the individual to the group as teams are used to accomplish more work and solve more problems in organizations (Mohrman, Cohen, and Mohrman, 1995). Teams become both a new source of demands for development (so that their members can function effectively as a group) and a means of developing capabilities (as individuals learn new skills by working with experts from other disciplines or by rotating through different tasks; see Fletcher, 1996).

Growth in the demand for skills is not confined to the people inside a company. Large corporations are increasingly recognizing the need to build the capabilities of their suppliers and customers. The impetus to invest in the training of suppliers has been the growth in strategic alliances and in networked organizations (see Chapter Three). As firms seek to move from adversarial, market-based supplier relationships to partnerships with a smaller number of preferred suppliers, they also increase their dependence on their suppliers to deliver high-quality goods or services on time. To strengthen these partnerships and address any problems that may arise, many leading corporations (for example, Toyota, Chrysler, and Motorola) are offering their suppliers extensive training programs, which the smaller companies lack the resources to develop (MacDuffie and Krafcik, 1992).

The emphasis on developing customers' capabilities is not new. Vendor training that accompanies the purchase of a new piece of equipment, for example, has been a traditional and primary source of skill development for many firms (National Center on the Educational Quality of the Workforce, 1995). But the TQM movement's focus on "delighting the customer," as well as the push by many firms to increase the value of customer relationships by becoming full-service providers, has increased the emphasis on customer training.

Linking Individual and Organizational Competencies

Until recently, development has focused almost exclusively on enhancing individual capabilities. Under the new development model, however, organizations are seeking to link individual competencies far more closely to desired organizational capabilities (see Chapter Five). It is important to recognize, however, that these two versions of competency come from very different roots. One version, as identified by leading business strategists (Hamel and Prahalad, 1994), focuses on identifying the "core competencies" that can generate a lasting competitive advantage for an organization (miniaturization at Sony, for example, or logistics at Wal-Mart). The other version originated in the HR community; it seeks to identify those competencies that individuals require in order to succeed in environments where rapid organizational change and the move toward team-based development and delivery of products and services have made traditional job definitions increasingly obsolete.

If these two competency movements are to succeed, it is vital that they become more closely intertwined. A core competency is unlikely to be sustainable if it is not aligned with the HR policies that are designed to select, develop, and retain the individuals who are responsible for creating and enhancing this organizational competency. Likewise, although individuals will continue to require a large set of general competencies in order to perform their jobs effectively, only the subset of individual competencies that are derived from an organization's specific strategy and requirements are likely to help a company build a distinct and sustainable competitive advantage (Galbraith, Lawler, and Associates, 1993). One way in which companies are seeking to ensure a closer link between individual and organizational competencies is by moving away from general courses and toward customized training whose content is based on current business issues facing the company.

The particular set of competencies that individuals require will vary according to the stages of their career development and their places in the organization. A product-development engineer, for example, will require a very different set of skills, attributes, and technical knowledge than will a sales representative, even though there may be some corporate-specific competencies that they share. Therefore, the crucial task for HR departments is to define competency requirements so as to generate the desired overall mix of capabilities and align different individuals' development plans with the overall needs of the organization.

The Learning Organization

Traditionally, development has often been equated with "training" (Ulrich and Greenfield, 1995). In the new paradigm, formal training remains important, but it is only one of many ways that organizations seek to enhance individual capabilities. Greater emphasis is placed on designing the work process so that opportunities to learn are built into individuals' day-to-day routines. Through such mechanisms as the use of workplace mentors, planned job rotation, and the use of expert networks, individuals are encouraged to learn on the job, not just in the classroom (Mohrman and Mohrman, 1993; McCall, 1997).

There are a number of factors that have contributed to this shift. It is now well recognized that people learn more effectively by doing than by listening (Hall, 1996). Likewise, the shift from the classroom to the workplace as the main location for learning helps ensure that what is being taught is more closely linked to the demands of the workplace, and that it keeps up with the rapid pace of change. Moreover, as time demands on workers become more onerous, workplace learning becomes a way to develop individuals' capabilities without releasing them from the job (inability to release employees from their jobs is one of the most common reasons that organizations cite for not training; see Finegold and others, 1996). As individuals are being asked to do more, and as the time set aside for instruction is less clearly demarcated, however, there is a risk that "action learning" will become a euphemism for a situation in which less development is actually taking place. Therefore, true learning organizations need to ensure that a supportive infrastructure and incentives encourage individuals at all levels to focus on development. This means, for example, performance management systems that balance the need for short-term results with long-term building of capabilities by rewarding managers for developing their own and fellow employees' skills and for investing in the ongoing improvement of the organization's processes.

Continuous Learning on Demand

Training in organizations has tended to be heavily front-loaded. Individuals would go through orientation and then take a series of courses to equip them with the skills they needed to perform their jobs. This has been particularly true of management development programs in large companies, which often feature traineeships of one or two years for new recruits; the traineeships are intended to familiarize the new employees with the different parts of the organization and help them decide on their desired career paths. Training for more senior employees has often been provided only after a promotion, or as a reward for good performance.

The new approach to development replaces the emphasis on initial training with a concentration on continuous learning. It is hard for organizations to recoup the investment in long, unproductive initial training programs when there is no certainty that the individuals who have been trained will remain with the organization. Indeed, the heavy investment in human capital may make recent graduates of such programs more attractive to competitors. Instead, companies are seeking to hire individuals who are better prepared for their initial tasks by more clearly specifying and evaluating the required competencies. They then spread the investment in individuals' development more evenly over their careers, by providing initial training and then more frequent, individually tailored learning opportunities. This approach has two advantages: it enables an organization to target resources at those employees who have demonstrated superior performance and loyalty, and it allows the organization to avoid the losses associated with front-loading all the training content (much of which will be forgotten before the new employees can put it to use).

Creating and Retaining Competitive Advantage

Underlying all the other changes in companies' new approach to skill development is a shift in the rationale for this investment. Development is no longer just a way of equipping individuals to do their jobs, or of rewarding top performers. Instead, the ongoing development of individual and organizational capabilities is seen as an essential part of the company's strategy. As one commentator puts it, "Firms are using education to meet specific strategic goals or transform corporate culture; organizational transformation is replacing a focus on personal development" (Finegold and Schechter, 1995).

An example of how the different elements of this new approach to development can help dramatically improve an organization is provided by our research with the Allfast Corporation, a manufacturer of airline fasteners:

Allfast faced a crisis in the early 1990s when its key customer, Boeing, threatened to drop all suppliers that could not meet its demanding new quality standard. Allfast, recognizing that it did not have the internal capability to create the new quality system and retrain its workforce, sought the assistance of Glendale Community College. The college put together a twenty-week program for individuals who were purposely selected to represent a cross-section of all the major business functions and levels in the organization. The trainees included the head of accounting, a middle-level operations professional, and a marketing manager, as well as supervisors and machinists from the shop floor. Half of the training was devoted to general concepts, which were illustrated with examples taken from the firm's experience. The other half consisted of a supervised team project designed to tackle the redesign of a key process in order to improve quality. The firm's development did not end when the formal training program ended. The college helped institute a process of ongoing learning so that trainees could implement what they had learned and could build new teams that would continue to improve the organization. The results were savings of $1.5 million in costs for scrap metal costs, increased profits (which allowed bonuses for all the workers and their first raise in three years), a lucrative "preferred provider" contract with Boeing, and enthusiastic support from the employees, who now actively participate in weekly trouble-shooting team meetings.

I use the acronym SPORT to describe this model of individual and company development because it combines *s*kill building, *p*roblem solving, *o*rganizational *r*estructuring, and *t*eam building and because the process of transformation, with individuals combining their different talents to reach a common objective, is analogous to the activity of a well-functioning athletic team. The SPORT model exemplifies the changes inherent in the movement from the old to the new model of development. HR strategy, instead of being seen as distinct from and subordinate to business strategy, now becomes an essential component of setting and meeting corporate objectives. The unit of development is not the individual; it is the team. The focus of the effort is on company-specific problems rather than on more general training. And the results of this investment are not judged by improvements in skills but rather by progress in meeting desired performance targets. The features of this model and the way in which it differs from traditional company approaches to management development are shown in Figure 9.2.

Doing More with Less: Implementing the New Approach to Development

Setting Priorities for Training

Formal training is accorded relatively less importance under the new skill-development model, but it remains a vital component of any development strategy. As the HR department, faced with growing skill demands and fewer staff, seeks to make the transition to its new role as business partner, it will need to think strategically about what training the company requires and who should provide

Figure 9.2. The SPORT Model of Development.

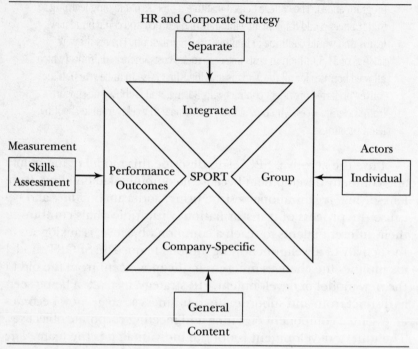

Note: SPORT = skill building, problem solving, organizational restructuring, and team building.

it. In setting priorities for the use of scarce development resources it is useful to examine each skill requirement along two dimensions: Is the competency generic or specific to the organization? Is it in an area where the capacity for developing the competence internally is high or low? Mapping these two dimensions against each other yields four distinct approaches to the make-or-buy decision on training (see Figure 9.3):

1. Developing competencies internally
2. Treating training as a revenue generator
3. Giving individuals primary responsibility for competency development
4. Developing strategic HR partnerships and customized training

Figure 9.3. The Make-or-Buy Decision on Training.

Type of Competency

	Company-Specific Core Competencies ←——————→ Generic Competencies	
High	Development of competencies internally	Training as revenue generator
Low	Strategic HR partnerships and customized training	Individual responsibility for training

Training Capabilities

Developing Competencies Internally

Individual competencies that are closely related to an organization's strategic priorities, and in which a company has clear development expertise, are the areas where a company should focus its internal training and other skill-development efforts. For example, Toyota has become the world's most efficient and flexible automobile manufacturer by developing a system of "lean production." Although this system has been heavily studied both in Japan and abroad (Womack, Jones, and Roos, 1990), most companies have had difficulty making the full system work because they lack the capabilities that Toyota has developed gradually over the last thirty years. Through extensive investment in continuous improvement and organizational learning, reinforced through intensive training programs for the entire workforce, Toyota has become a pioneer in the development of zero-defect production techniques and in the building and managing of partnerships with key suppliers (Fruin and Nishiguchi, 1990). The difficulty of replicating these core organizational and individual competencies has helped Toyota and its suppliers sustain their competitive success despite the threat to exports posed by the dramatic rise in the value of the yen.

As companies target more of their HR resources at competencies that are closely related to business objectives, the line between development activities and operations can become increasingly blurred. The goal is to build development directly into the work process rather than treating it as a separate activity. For example, it is increasingly common for firms to have an organizational development expert working as a full member of a product-development team, addressing group-process issues and at the same time helping improve the capabilities of individuals to work in a team environment. Likewise, companies are blurring the distinctions among traditional business functions and are enhancing cross-functional skills through job rotation (for example, by having an electrical engineer spend six months working under a mentor in manufacturing engineering so that he will be better prepared to perform on an interdisciplinary project). These forms of planned on-the-job learning can more effectively develop both individual and organizational capabilities than traditional training classes can (see Chapter Thirteen).

If the in-house capacity for developing key competencies does not already exist, the organization may deem them sufficiently important to make the creation of an internal development capacity in these areas a clear priority. For instance, a multinational company seeking to make the leap from multiple, relatively independent subsidiaries to a more integrated global operation is unlikely to have the internal expertise needed to facilitate this change. It can hire external consultants or trainers to help bring about the organizational restructuring, but if it is truly to implement the change and get individuals to adopt a global perspective when making decisions, then it may need to invest in a more ongoing, companywide effort to develop global capabilities.

A small but growing number of firms view competency development as so central to their business objectives that they have established their own company schools or universities to support this effort (Finegold and Schechter, 1995). Firms such as Motorola, General Electric, Fiat, and Xerox have established autonomous business units whose primary function is to meet the continuous education and training needs of the firm and its strategic partners. Because of the level of resources required to sustain these activities, such units are limited to very large companies. Such corporate universities can play a vital role in building corporate culture and facilitating organizational change efforts, but there is a danger that they can become large bureaucracies that are too distant from the requirements of the business.

Motorola University (MU), one of the best-known examples of this model, seeks to avoid this problem by acting more as a planner and contractor than as a training provider. The mission of MU is simple: to provide Motorola's 120,000 employees worldwide with opportunities to continuously upgrade their skills. To deliver this mission, MU has units at various corporate locations, sometimes forming partnerships with local colleges or private providers to deliver courses. Motorola's in-house research suggests that the benefits provided by MU far outweigh the annual cost of over $100 million. One advantage of the MU courses is that they strongly reinforce the firm's key strategic objectives (such as quality improvement, cycle-time reduction, and technology leadership) aimed at achieving total customer satisfaction. MU can also respond to changing objectives much more quickly and cohesively than external providers because of its intimate knowledge of Motorola's business.

Treating Training as a Revenue Generator

If a company has become a leader in developing an area of competency that is commonly required across many organizations, then there is an opportunity to market this training capability to other firms. This external marketing of training can take a variety of forms. One is to treat training as a revenue generator, with outsiders charged for each person sent to a course. This would be typical of equipment manufacturers, which will often include a training package with each new machine they sell. Likewise, some of the larger transit agencies are making the technical training courses they develop available to smaller transit properties in their regions that have no training departments of their own and can find few colleges or private training organizations with the expertise and equipment needed to train in bus maintenance.

A second approach is for companies to trade training programs, thereby avoiding reinvention of the wheel and reducing the costs of development. Even such giant corporations as Ford and Motorola have strengthened their business relationship by striking such a deal, with Motorola providing training materials to Ford that accompany Motorola's quality program, and with Ford in turn sharing with Motorola its TOPS program for problem solving.

A third approach is to offer training at little or no cost to outside suppliers or customers. As noted earlier, many companies are providing training of this type as part of efforts to upgrade the quality of their supplier base, or as a marketing tool to attract and retain customers.

There are many additional advantages to providing training externally. Within the organization, it can help training be perceived less as a cost center than as a potential source of revenue and a more integral part of the business. It can also help defray some of the costs of development and delivery by mixing students from outside with in-house trainees in a single session and expanding the overall customer base for a given course. And it can help keep the training at a world-class standard by testing its competitiveness in the marketplace and obtaining additional feedback through delivery of the course in different organizational contexts.

There are dangers associated with externally providing training, however. At a time when HR departments are already being asked to do more with less, delivering courses externally may be perceived by internal customers as a diversion that is preventing development experts from focusing on the organization's needs. Moreover, although a course might initially appear generic, it often requires tailoring, and therefore additional investment, if it is to be effective in outside organizations. And in the absence of a good system of activity-based costing for training, some organizations are not charging rates that fully cover the costs of delivery (Finegold and others, 1996).

Giving Individuals Primary Responsibility for Competency Development

Long before the growth of strategic human resource management and the current emphasis on outsourcing the delivery of basic functions (like payroll services) that are not related to corporate objectives (Mohrman, Lawler, and McMahan, 1996), most companies had recognized that it made sense to go to outside experts, such as universities or private training providers, for the development of general competencies rather than trying to develop them in-house. According to human capital theory, individuals rather than firms should pay the full costs of developing these general skills because by definition general skills can easily be transferred to other companies, and so a firm cannot be certain of capturing the benefits (Becker, 1962); the rewards associated with general skills (higher wages, improved career prospects) should compensate the individual for the costs of the investment. In contradiction to human capital theory, however, much of the more than $30 billion that U.S. companies spend annually on education and training goes for individuals to develop general skills (Hollenbeck, 1996; Bishop, 1996). Among the reasons given for why firms should make this kind of investment in development of general skills are the following (Bishop, 1996):

- Imperfectly functioning labor markets, which enable firms to capture some of the benefits of training through greater productivity
- Capital constraints, which limit individuals' ability to finance an optimum level of general training
- Positive externalities—for example, skills (such as the ability to operate an e-mail system) that a high percentage of individuals must use in order for there to be clear benefits

As the competition for firms' human resources–related investments intensifies, firms have begun to question the value of general-skills development to the bottom line: "While it may pay off for the individual participant, there is little evidence of how such education has increased the value of the business corporations" (Finegold and Schechter, 1995). As a result, companies are pursuing a number of strategies that encourage individuals to take greater responsibility for their own general-skills development.

One approach is to use the firm's competency requirements as a more effective screening mechanism in hiring decisions. An electronics company seeking to expand its operations in China, for example, recognized the need to add individuals with a good understanding of Chinese culture and language as well as world-class technical and managerial skills. This firm has found it far more cost-effective to hire Chinese nationals, who already possess some of the cultural skills and who may have acquired the technical expertise at U.S. universities, than to try to develop these skills itself by sending employees to China on expatriate assignments.

A second approach is for firms to specify the competencies that individuals require for promotion without providing all the training needed to develop these competencies. One leading company in the telecommunications industry, for example, faced with growing competition and major restructuring, has opted to eliminate most of its general development courses while using performance reviews to identify the competencies that managers must develop if they wish to retain their jobs or advance within the rapidly changing company.

A third approach is to make greater use of often neglected tuition-reimbursement programs. Pratt & Whitney, for example, has made a generous new tuition-reimbursement program the focal point of its efforts to create a new bargain with its employees, paying all course costs and providing three hours per week of paid time off for each employee enrolled in an outside course. Employees who complete their degrees receive a stock grant valued between six and seven thousand dollars. Individuals are thus encouraged to take more responsibility for their own career development, and the company provides opportunities and resources for career development to occur. Programs like this one still entail the company's paying some of the costs of general-skills courses, but tuition reimbursement has a number of advantages over company-provided general training:

1. It eliminates the need to pay employees for time spent in courses, because individuals typically take courses on their own time. Moreover, when courses are provided by community colleges or public universities, as is often the case, course fees are heavily subsidized by the state.

2. Individuals who are making the effort and the initial cash outlays to attend courses are demonstrating a motivation to learn that is not always present when an organization sends people to take courses during normal work hours.

3. The company can specify the attainment level or other conditions that an employee must satisfy (for example, a B average or better) in order to be fully reimbursed. When the company is pay-

ing all the costs of a degree (say, an M.B.A. earned through part-time study), the employee may be required to sign an agreement specifying that the company will be paid back if the employee leaves for another firm within two to three years after the degree has been earned.

Developing Customized Training and Strategic HR Partnerships

The greatest challenge for the company putting together a strategy for skill development is to address those areas in which it has identified a clear business need to build competencies but in which it also lacks the internal capability to develop the competencies effectively. The preferred solution to this problem is the development of a strategic training partnership. Just as firms are building partnerships with material suppliers, to provide the design and production of key components, they are also now constructing alliances with experts in education and training, to develop programs tailored to their own needs. The education providers, chosen for their expertise in particular areas, work with the company to customize general courses so that the courses will include company-specific examples and current business problems.

This move toward the customization of educational content is a worldwide trend, but the United States appears to be a leader in this movement (Finegold and Schechter, 1995). At the American Management Association (AMA), the largest private U.S. provider of management training, customized courses are the fastest-growing area of service. The AMA competes with a vast array of small firms that have carved out specialized niches by combining consulting with educational services, to solve firms' specific business problems rather than just meet their training needs. Customized courses are also the major growth area in U.S. business schools. UCLA's Anderson School of Management, for example, is typical of this trend: in just three years, the school's customized courses grew from 10 percent of the executive education division's revenue to 40 percent, and this growth is expected to continue. UCLA's customized courses use real problems faced by actual firms, and course attendees are selected and teamed up in such a way that when a course is over the skills acquired can be utilized on the job and shared with co-workers.

Many companies, particularly smaller firms, do not have the resources to interest business schools or consultants in developing customized solutions for their problems. For these firms, the contract training centers of local community or technical colleges can provide an affordable alternative. The states of North Carolina and South Carolina, for example, have become leaders in attracting foreign direct investment to create high-skilled jobs by offering companies subsidized training to prepare their new workforces at local technical colleges.

The strength of customized training is that it allows firms to target their investments in professional development, and it often results in direct performance payoffs. The danger of customized training is that it can lead to insularity: If a firm's employees are the only people taking a course, who will provide fresh ideas and external opinions? Moreover, customized training is typically more expensive than an off-the-shelf course. For the individual, customized training may be less generally useful than a broader education that provides certified skills for a variety of domains and applications. Therefore, many firms use customized courses to supplement rather than replace more individually directed programs in management development.

Putting the New Learning Contract into Practice

An example of what the new employment bargain may look like in practice is provided by recent research on changes under way in the banking industry (Keltner and Finegold, 1996). No single bank has put a full learning contract into place, but many banks are now adopting a new approach to the development and retention of employees, an approach that does move them in the direction of a new learning contract.

The banking industry has some distinctive characteristics (such as a legacy of government regulation) that distinguish it from the service sectors. Nevertheless, many of the strategic issues that banks face are commonly found in other industries as well. These issues include the need to find ways of developing and motivating employees at a time when many organizations are downsizing and flattening their hierarchies and, in the process, cutting off traditional routes to on-the-job training and promotion. Banks used to offer some of the most secure jobs in the private sector, but deregulation, fierce competition, and the accompanying waves of consolidation and downsizing have put an end to "jobs for life" in the banking industry. As banks face nonbank competitors who have lower costs in a market where product innovations can be copied rapidly, many are recognizing that an exclusive focus on cutting costs and increasing transaction volumes may not be the best way to achieve competitive advantage. Instead, banks are seeking to capitalize on their traditional strengths by building close relationships with individual and business customers and becoming their full-service financial providers (Schlesinger and Heskett, 1991). Yet if banks are to succeed at a relationship-driven strategy, they must restructure their human resources policies, with attention to such labor-market constraints as high employee turnover (Schneider and Bowen, 1995).

Some banks are experimenting with a new bargain between employer and employee, offering individuals continuous opportunities to develop and use new competencies in lieu of employment security. With layoffs spreading throughout the industry, those banks that offer this new bargain become relatively more attractive employers. In our interviews with bank managers, one human resources executive expressed the new contract between employee and employer as follows: "We can't promise lifetime employment, but we can give employees the resources they need to take control of their own careers." This new bargain has four elements: competency-based career ladders for entry-level employees, modular training for high-skill positions, higher levels of internal promotion for all positions, and increased pay for skills and performance.

Competency-Based Career Ladders

A first step toward a new learning contract is to broaden responsibilities and improve opportunities and incentives for skill investment among all employees, not just managers and technical experts. Many banks, taking as a given both high turnover and the constraints of hiring low-skilled recruits from the U.S. educational system, have sought to build service strategies around narrow jobs filled by interchangeable employees.

In contrast, a few banks (ranging from Citibank to First Federal, a California-based retail bank) have sought to align their HR practices with a strategy focused on building customer relationships. They have constructed competence-based reward and promotion systems to broaden the skills of branch employees and lower staff turnover. As in other banks, entry-level recruits receive a short introductory training designed only to prepare them for their immediate job tasks. But in the case of these two banks, motivated employees have the opportunity to enroll in ongoing training modules to prepare themselves for advancement. The decision about whether to participate in ongoing training classes is left to individual employees, but the banks try to make clear how the completion of training courses is linked to opportunities for advancement into different branch positions. As one Citibank executive told us, "It's up to the employees to take the initiative in developing these skills, but the bank has an interest in helping employees make more informed choices."

Modular Training for High-Skill Positions

Another part of the new human resources strategy is the shift toward modularized training for high-skill positions. If the problem for the lower-level bank employee has been too little training and career development, the reverse has been the case in training programs for the new graduate or M.B.A. These programs often involve a heavy up-front investment and long periods of unproductive time spent in the classroom. In a labor market with high levels of poaching, this type of training program is generally not cost-effective. A long period of initial training leaves new recruits with very marketable skills before they have developed a strong attachment to the training firm, making them easy prey for competitors that have not invested in training programs.

An alternative way of meeting training needs for high-skill positions is to take an iterative approach by alternating skill development with work experience. Both Citibank and California Federal Bank, as they have moved to bring investment and insurance products into their branch offices, have adopted modularized training for high-skill branch employees. Instead of spending several months in the classroom, Citibank's all-around banking officers have a few weeks of introductory training on products and services. This period of introductory training is followed by enrollment on an as-needed basis in training courses that cover investment and consumer credit products. Personal banking officers at California Federal Bank can enroll in a succession of courses, interspersed with work experience, to earn the licenses needed to sell progressively more sophisticated investment products. After completing courses on money market funds and life and disability insurance, personal bankers spend several months working before they return to take classes on mutual funds and annuities. They then have another period of work experience before returning to take the course they need to become certified brokers.

The modularized training programs in each of these banks are geared implicitly to individuals with longer employment tenures. Employees pick up more skills the longer they work for the firm. This approach to training has two advantages for banks: first, employees do not spend unproductive time in classes learning skills that they will not need right away; and, second, modularized training also mitigates poaching because employees are increasing their skills while developing a stronger attachment to their employer.

Internal Promotion

Another essential element of the new employment bargain is the shift toward more internal promotion. Too strong an emphasis on promoting from within can stifle innovation by reducing the flow of new ideas and talent into an organization. Many banks, however, as a natural response to the difficulty of retaining their own trainees, have erred too far in the other direction, relying heavily on external recruiting for high-skill positions. External recruiting is an imperfect solution. It leads a bank's existing employees to see their own chances for upward mobility blocked and encourages them to look to the external labor market for opportunities. Meanwhile, those employees who have been poached from competitors have little reason to feel loyalty to their new employer and are likely to leave as soon as a better opportunity presents itself.

A different approach to recruitment and promotion can be found in innovative banks like California Federal, Chicago's Harris Bank, Citibank, and First Federal. As an extension of their commitment to stronger career paths, all four banks rely more heavily than their counterparts in the banking industry do on internal recruitment for high-skill positions. They do not promise their employees job security, but they have made a commitment to meeting their skill needs internally, looking to the external labor market only when there are no qualified individuals within the organization. For example, Harris Bank fills its commercial lender positions almost exclusively from its own pool of credit analysts rather than recruiting from the M.B.A. pool or from the pool of competitors' lending officers. To allow its credit analysts to build their knowledge of business and market dynamics, it will send these individuals back to school to earn an M.B.A. while they continue to work for the bank.

A strong internal labor market supports the shift to a higher-quality service strategy in two ways: first, it means that employees in high-skill positions know the bank, its products, and its customers; and, second, a strong internal labor market helps reduce turnover (Schneider and Bowen, 1995). The belief that there are clear opportunities for upward mobility encourages employees, even those in part-time, branch-level positions, to stay with their present employers. Internal placement also means that banks are promoting individuals who have demonstrated a commitment to their present employers. The creation of a strong internal labor market has helped First Federal and Harris Bank reduce employee turnover to less than 10 percent annually (that is, to less than one-third of the industry average). This reduction in turn has yielded major reductions in recruiting costs, as well as improved productivity from more experienced workers.

Pay for Skills and Performance

As banks, like most other U.S. corporations, seek to flatten their hierarchies by eliminating layers of middle management, opportunities are more limited for rewarding high performers with promotions. To retain and motivate these individuals, many banks are moving toward greater use of pay-for-performance strategies that enable top performers to earn even more than they might have earned by moving into the managerial ranks. In the past, bonuses were often a relatively small part of compensation and were only loosely tied to individual performance, but more and more banks are now putting 20 to 30 percent or more of compensation at risk and attempting to tie it more explicitly to the attainment of business targets for each office and its staff. The introduction of pay for performance has helped banks pursue a relationship-focused strategy because pay for performance enables them to maintain continuity in customer relationships by rewarding people who stay in their jobs. For example, a large California bank has recently reorganized its commercial operations to provide much greater segmentation. More junior managers of customer relationships start with smaller clients and will stay with those clients as the clients grow and as their banking needs expand. In this way, these employees move up in responsibility without changing positions.

Few banks, however, have taken the additional step that is now being experimented with in other sectors: paying for skills as well as for performance (American Compensation Association, 1996), a trend in which companies ranging from Frito-Lay to Monsanto seek to define the competencies that individuals require for success and then use those competencies instead of traditional job descriptions as the basis for managing individuals' careers and defining individuals' compensation levels within a broad band (Ledford, 1995; Jagmin, 1995; Schopp, 1995). First Federal Bank has enabled tellers to increase their pay by demonstrating additional skills, but few other banks have systematically defined the competencies required for competitive success and linked those competencies to rewards.

Future Issues in Development

The ongoing pressures posed by global competition and the pace of technological change are likely to maintain or accelerate the demands on companies to enhance the capabilities of their employees and strategic partners. There is no simple formula to enable organizations, often with reduced human resources staff, to cope with these new demands. The framework presented here suggests elements of a strategy that companies can adopt to cope with the skill-development challenge, with a first step of reexamining basic assumptions about individual and corporate responsibilities for development. The new approach to development focuses on building learning into the organization and developing the competencies that the company and the individuals within it require for competitive success. This set of competency requirements, combined with an analysis of internal development capabilities, can then be used to identify development priorities. This section briefly outlines some of the key development issues that corporations, individuals, and the society as a whole are likely to face as we enter the next century.

Making the Learning Contract a Reality

As noted in the examples from the banking industry, most organizations have only begun the process of implementing a new learning contract with their workers, whereby ongoing opportunities for individuals to develop competencies and use them effectively become the focal point of the employment relationship. Leading companies are transforming their development experts from trainers into business partners who can work closely with the line organization to build the capabilities needed for competitive success. A far more difficult transition, however, is selling the existing workforce, often grown cynical after repeated restructurings, on the merits of the new learning contract. New employees, who grew up without the expectation of employment security, seem willing to accept the new bargain, but it is unlikely to succeed unless companies can convince the majority of managers and workers that the basis for the employment relationship has to change, and that the learning contract offers the best alternative for both the company and individuals.

Developing Global Capabilities

Globalization is widely cited as one of the main forces shaping the future competitive success of large corporations and the skill requirements of current and potential executives (Adler, 1997). Many leading U.S. manufacturers and high-technology companies already obtain the majority of their revenue and expect most of their future growth from foreign markets, whereas firms in the service sector, previously shielded from international competition, are increasingly global in their scope.

Despite the growing interest in and importance attached to globalization, there remain significant stumbling blocks to the creation of effective global organizations. Research on fifty leading global corporations (Adler and Bartholomew, 1992) found that companies' organizational structures and processes, in particular the human resources function, have failed to keep pace with the growing internationalization of business. As companies seek to operate in a more integrated and effective manner across national boundaries and cultures, they will need to devote substantial resources to building global capabilities, ranging from the use of transnational teams (Snow and others, 1996) to the selection and development of potential executives with the skills needed to lead an international business(Spreitzer, McCall, and Mahoney, 1994).

Making Good Use of New Training Technologies

There is a plethora of new information technologies with great potential for supporting the new model of development in organizations. Computer-based training packages, interactive CD-ROM programs, distance-learning courses delivered through videoconferences, and expert networks on the Internet are just some of the recent applications of advances in information technology that are already spreading through the corporate world. The capacity of these technologies to deliver self-paced instruction when and where it is needed can greatly facilitate individuals' taking ownership of their own development. Research into the introduction of new technologies (such as computer networks and videocassette recorders) suggests that the development potential of these new technologies is unlikely to be realized unless they are accompanied by major organizational changes, as well as by changes in the way these technologies are delivered, changes that include early consultations with end users (Mankin, Cohen, and Bikson, 1996; Attewell, 1994).

Measuring Training Effectiveness

As the pressure intensifies for all parts of the corporation to demonstrate their contributions to the bottom line, there will be increased demands to quantify the benefits of training. Measuring the relationship (if there is one) between innovations in skill development and performance enables HR managers to do several things:

- Justify the investment in training to top management
- Build continuous improvement into the training process
- Identify factors outside trainers' control that may be hindering the effective use of skills
- Eliminate or redesign programs that do not show payoffs

Nevertheless, most organizations make very little effort to show the connection between training programs and the performance that these programs are meant to enhance. Recent studies (U.S. Bureau of Labor Statistics, 1996; Bassi and Cheney, 1996) found that only a minority of companies had formal training budgets, and even fewer firms made rigorous assessments of the effects of training (Mason and Finegold, 1995). Those organizations that did adopt indicators of training effectiveness often used only one or two measures, which may have unintended consequences by encouraging individuals to maximize one factor (for example, productivity) while neglecting others (such as quality; see Finegold and others, 1996).

It is often difficult to isolate the impact of improved skills from other factors that affect performance, particularly as the development of capabilities is integrated more closely into day-to-day operations, but some leading companies have made this effort. Texaco and Motorola have sought not only to measure changes in individual attitudes, skills, and behaviors that result from training but also to establish the link with performance. They have done this by seeking opportunities for natural experiments, comparing the results of pilot training programs in some groups or facilities against results in control groups and their own past performance (Schaffer, 1995). Pacific Bell has attempted the even more difficult evaluation task of showing the payoffs of its tuition-reimbursement program. Employees are asked to specify their objectives for a course before attending and then to document what they have learned, how they are applying it to their jobs, and what performance improvements (if any) have resulted. This is far from an exact science, but the very act of seeking to quantify the return on this training investment has forced individuals and the company to focus more clearly on the relationship between training and business objectives. For individuals, and for the society more generally, the next century is likely to pose a parallel set of development challenges:

1. Leading organizations will require major investments to build new global capabilities. Likewise, individuals who wish to succeed in the new economy will be willing to invest in enhancing their own global capabilities. The United States is in many respects well positioned to take advantage of the emerging global economy: English is the worldwide business language, and the United States has the world's most ethnically and culturally diverse society, one that is continually being replenished with talent from around the globe. In educational terms, however, the vast majority of Americans are ill prepared to operate effectively in the global marketplace. Fewer than 10 percent of native English speakers are fluent in another language, only a small percentage of Americans travel outside the United States, and the average U.S. student lacks even a rudimentary understanding of world geography. Individuals will need these basic tools to thrive in the international economy. More important, they will need to develop a global mind-set, that is, the ability to step outside their own country's deeply rooted assumptions and to see problems and business opportunities from the perspective of other cultures. This in turn requires an ability to learn from experience, one of the characteristics closely associated with successful international executives (Spreitzer, McCall, and Mahoney, 1994).

2. At a time when uncertainty in the labor market has created an unprecedented need for good career education and guidance, most U.S. schools and colleges have been forced to cut back on their career specialists because of budget constraints. There is a growing industry of private career consultants, but these are beyond the means of most individuals. A few corporations, such as Raychem and the Big Three automakers, have made a major investment in career centers to help employees, particularly those who have been displaced, plan new careers. But these firms are still the exception. The major burden of planning career paths and the accompanying development requirements will fall on individuals themselves. One

young woman we interviewed at Pratt & Whitney, who made the transition from clerk to manager while getting a degree at night, put it this way: "You need to learn how to become your own career counselor because no one else is going to do it for you."

3. One of the most significant economic phenomena of the last fifteen years has been the widening gap between the earnings of college graduates or holders of advanced degrees and the rest of the population (Bishop, 1996). With the ongoing internationalization of the economy and continuing improvements in technology, this trend is likely to accelerate. The best educated, who are also the most likely to receive additional training, will generally be able to increase their salaries by keeping their skill sets current with the rapid pace of change. At the same time, those without at least some college education are likely to see an additional decline in their standard of living and to experience greater difficulty finding stable employment: good careers that once were open to high school graduates (in the aerospace industry, for example) are increasingly closed because the jobs are being eliminated or moved offshore, or because hiring requirements have been raised to reflect the new skill demands and the larger supply of college graduates. How long this trend can continue without causing major societal unrest is likely to be one of the most pressing issues facing policymakers in the future.

4. If the new learning contracts are to become a reality, fundamental changes will be required in the relationships of government, employers, and individuals. Government has begun to tinker with the existing benefits system—for example, by creating more portable pensions and health care benefits—but the system continues to be premised on employers' rather than individuals' responsibility for careers. As individuals move more frequently between organizations, and an increasing proportion of work is performed by part-time, temporary, and self-employed workers, more radical policy changes are likely to be considered. The possibilities include an unemployment system designed to assist individuals more proactively in transitions between jobs instead of serving as a safety net for those who have been laid off. Another possibility is a lifelong learning account whereby the individual, his or her successive employers, and the government share the costs of ongoing human capital investment.

Dealing with this complex set of issues will be a major task for companies, their employees, and public policymakers as we enter the next century. The United States suffers by comparison with its main competitors on many educational dimensions, but one of this country's greatest and often neglected strengths is the widespread acceptance of education as an investment that will benefit individuals throughout their working lives, by contrast with the perception that education is a privilege available only to a select few. As the need for lifelong development becomes more pressing, the government and firms will need to build the right kinds of organizations and incentives to help individuals make this investment.

Chapter Ten

Executive Education

A Critical Lever for Organizational Change

Jay A. Conger
Katherine R. Xin

Over the past decade, executive education has been undergoing a gradual but radical transformation. Programs operating today are far more innovative, learner-centered, and relevant to immediate company needs than ever before. In some corporations, such as General Electric, Levi Strauss, and Motorola, executive education has risen in stature, becoming an essential lever to facilitate strategic transitions. No longer just a reward for high-potential executives or a chance to renew an individual's knowledge base, programs are being used as opportunities to recast the worldviews of executive teams and to align organizations with new directions. Through educational forums, CEOs are discovering that they are often better positioned to communicate and implement corporate strategy, to build strategic unity throughout the company, and to create a cadre of change agents (Bolt, 1993; Ready, 1995). Executive education has, in essence, become a strategic tool.

In this chapter, we will look at the forces that have been reshaping executive education and causing a radical transformation not only in its delivery but also in its purpose. We will highlight certain fundamental trends that we believe are here to stay—trends that will continue to increase the stature and role of executive education. We will also discuss important dilemmas that the future of executive education must face as it seeks to play a more strategic and enduring role. Finally, we will look toward the twenty-first century and describe what executive education will become.

The Changing Complexion of Executive Education

Twenty years ago, education for executives consisted primarily of either university-based programs or seminars offered by specialized training organizations. Participants learned the latest theory and techniques for effective management, largely by studying cases and listening to classroom lectures by notable academics. The content of the training was decided by university faculty, who offered courses on strategy and such functional skills as finance or marketing. Many programs were essentially abridged M.B.A. programs. For the attending executive, the experience itself was seen as both a reward and as a preparation for promotion to senior levels. It was an honor to attend a management course at an Ivy League school for three months and then to return with more of a general manager's perspective.

Beginning in the early 1980s, however, a fundamental shift began to occur in executive education, a transformation that was the product of new competitive challenges (see the Introduction). Simultaneously, there was a growing realization that education could actually be turned into a strategic intervention capable of building key organizational competencies. As a result, programs moved from being university-based and standardized to being in-company and customized, from having a focus on functional knowledge to having a focus on subjects like strategy implementation and organizational change, from being teacher-centered to being learner-centered, and from dealing with general case studies to dealing with the real-life problems facing the company.

In a handful of leading-edge companies today, education is no longer targeted to the individual as the key learner but rather to the organization as the key learner. Because organizational transformation demands the support and attention of a company's senior management, a new focus is emerging on bringing top managers together as a working group to map out and implement change initiatives. As a result, executive education has been increasingly guided by four new objectives:

1. Facilitating large-scale organizational change
2. Ensuring immediate application of useful knowledge
3. Building depth of leadership talent
4. Meeting the "bottom line"

The first objective—an emphasis on organizational change—is driving the other three. The focus on change efforts has increased the need for knowledge to be more immediately useful and relevant to the change initiatives at hand. As a result, subject matter is now tailored to a company's specific, at-the-moment needs. If brand management, for example, is a weak competence but a necessity for today's competitive environment, it takes a central place in the educational experience. If strategy implementation is currently of paramount importance, skills in that area become a centerpiece of the learning experience. This drive for useful, applied knowledge not only has influenced the selection of subject matter but also has shaped the formats in which learning takes place. Thus, for example, we are witnessing a dramatic rise in action learning for executives.

In a world where the successful companies are the ones that continuously change and develop new capabilities, there has been a realization that leadership skills are especially critical. Looking inward, however, many companies in the 1990s discovered that their managers tended to be stronger in management skills than in leadership skills. For example, they were often better at planning and budgeting than at strategic vision. They were effective at day-to-day problem solving and were able to provide policies and create systems for monitoring performance, but they were weak in communicating, motivating, and inspiring. In addition, today's faster-paced environment demands more strategic and tactical decision making on the part of leaders beyond the CEO. Therefore, the need for distributed leadership is paramount. As a result, more and more executive programs today focus on leadership development.

Competitive pressures have also heightened budgetary concerns. As corporate cost cutting has become standard throughout industries, budgets for education have also received greater scrutiny, a trend that in turn has heightened the attractiveness of in-house, customized training programs. It is usually much less expensive to use five university professors or consultants to design and teach an in-company program to fifty managers than it is to send each of those fifty managers off for individual training.

To promote an understanding of the impact produced by the new objectives that are driving executive education, we will use the framework shown in Figure 10.1, which depicts the major components of an educational initiative. At the outset, such environmental issues as strategic shifts and organizational design issues determine the learning objectives, and these in turn shape the four critical components of any educational initiative.

First, the learning objectives influence who the owners or *sponsors* of the undertaking will be. These are, in essence, the individuals or groups in the organization who not only see the need for an educational initiative but also undertake its actual coordination and usually its funding. They play a powerful role in determining the "who," "what," and "why" questions associated with any initiative. The learning objectives also determine the *learning content* and

Figure 10.1. Components of an Executive Educational Initiative.

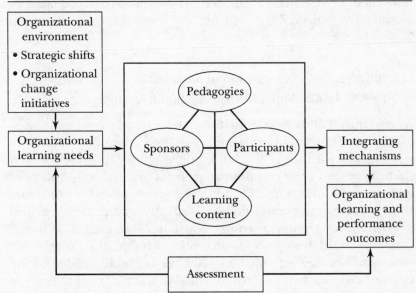

types of learning materials, as well as the instructional *pedagogies* that are most appropriate. Finally, the learning objectives influence the selection of the *participants*: Do we involve specific executives, or do we involve the entire senior management team and operating units as well? For example, a companywide initiative must involve a broader set of participants than a change initiative affecting simply one or two line functions. There also have to be mechanisms for transferring or integrating learnings back into the organization. These may take the form of task forces and special projects, new reward and appraisal systems, and so on.

Both at the front end and at the back end of any program, assessment must play a role. At the front end, assessment plays a pivotal role in identifying specific learning needs, program content, pedagogies, participants, and integrating activities. At the back end of a program, assessment helps in measuring the effectiveness of the undertaking and its longer-term impact and in determining whether further initiatives may be needed.

If we look at all these components in terms of the objectives that are driving executive education today, we see changes in most of them. Assessment and sponsorship are the two components that have yet to be significantly affected. As we will discuss a bit later, assessment remains quite simplistic, and sponsorship is still driven largely by corporate headquarters.

Learning Needs: From Functional Knowledge to Strategic Leadership and Organizational Change

As executive educational initiatives have shifted from being mini-M.B.A. programs to being strategic change initiatives, we are witnessing a major shift in the knowledge focus of programs. Given that the name of the competitive game is finding new sources of advantage and then quickly adapting an organization to them, there is now a far greater emphasis on strategy, leadership, and organizational change as course content. Nevertheless, as noted earlier, certain areas of specialized knowledge must receive attention in keeping with the competencies being demanded by the current competitive environment of the organization. For example, in retailing today, information technologies play a pivotal role as a competitive advantage. Therefore, an educational initiative at a mass-merchandising chain would most likely contain some emphasis on this area. Finally, knowledge itself is moving away from the more theoretical to the more applied, and this movement is being driven by demands for immediate and practical application.

Learning Content: Toward Greater Customization

In the last decade, there has been a significant shift toward customizing learning materials to fit the situations of individual companies and industries. For example, if case studies are used, they will often be about the company itself and its industry. Action learning is built around company issues, in stark contrast to the executive education of a decade or two ago, when participants studied examples of companies and industries far from their own.

This shift has had a profound impact on the offerings of university-based executive educational operations and their delivery. For example, universities and their business schools continue to be heavily involved as providers of executive education, but growth in their public, open-enrollment programs is stagnant with the exception of certain specialized programs. Growth is occurring in programs that are customized for individual companies. Indeed, this growth has been so strong that over 75 percent of all dollars spent on executive education in the United States now go for customized programs (Fulmer and Vicere, 1995).

Public programs are playing this smaller role in executive education for three reasons. First, public enrollment limits the ability of business schools to tailor their course materials to the concerns of a single company. By necessity, public programs must offer material on a wide range of industries and companies. This practice creates the perception on the client side that the company's executives may not be acquiring knowledge that is immediately applicable to their own organization and industry. Second, as mentioned earlier, customized, company-specific programs typically are more economical for the sponsoring companies. Third, in-house programs ensure that a critical mass of the senior managers in an organization will be having the same experience.

Pedagogy: Toward Action-Learning Pedagogies

The general trend in executive educational pedagogy is toward greater learner involvement, especially in action-learning programs. The term *action learning* denotes a variety of approaches in which managers use issues from their own companies as the basis for learning. These programs are best exemplified by the designs used at General Electric's educational facility at Crotonville, New York. They typically involve team-based experiential exercises that aim to solve real-life problems of immediate relevance to the company (Noel and Charan, 1988). For example, a company division might be contemplating new markets in Malaysia or leasing its products rather than selling them. These decisions become the learning initiatives. Action-learning teams conduct market research, test ideas and implementation issues, and present recommendations for action.

The appeal of action-learning formats is threefold. First, in the quest for greater relevance, these learning experiences based on actual and current company challenges have enormous appeal and utility. Second, action-learning projects can serve as vehicles for exploring possible strategic initiatives that will further the company's change agenda. Third, we know from research in adult learning that individuals generally are more motivated to learn when they are actively involved in the learning process and when they can deal with issues of relevance to their lives and careers, and action-learning formats address both the dimension of involvement and the dimension of relevance.

Participants: Toward Learning in Executive Cohorts

As we move from the hierarchical to the lateral organization, there is a far greater need for coordination across the organization. Further, change efforts often demand broad-based change for an effective fit to be maintained between a rapidly changing environment and an organization's capabilities, competencies, and strategy. Both factors—the need for coordination, and the broadness of the need for change—demand that educational experiences involve entire executive teams as participants, if only to ensure broad buy-in and coordination of efforts. Thus, for the implementation of a new strategy to succeed, there must be widespread agreement and commitment to the initiatives, as well as integration across multiple functional fronts, so that strategy, structure, people, processes, and rewards are all aligned. Such an outcome will not be achieved if one or two executives are sent off to a university program on organizational change, where they alone might craft a multifunctional change effort without the input or commitment of their peers.

Integrating Mechanisms: Toward the Cascading of Learning Experiences

Strategic and organizational initiatives brainstormed by the senior team are of little value if the senior managers are unable to garner support for them and commitment from all levels of the organization. Instead, as we learned from experiments at various companies in the 1980s—for example, at General Electric, with its Workout program (see Fulmer and Vicere, 1995; Tichy and Sherman, 1993)—that educational events linked to change efforts succeed by cascading downward throughout the entire organization. An effective cascading process facilitates the translation of "big picture" initiatives developed at the executive level into actionable initiatives at the levels where they are being implemented. As a result, more and more companies are focusing on educational formats that cascade their outcomes from the top to the bottom.

One example of effective cascading has been the effort conducted by the electronics giant Philips Corporation of the Netherlands. With the aim of rejuvenating itself in the face of intense competition, Philips undertook a series of executive educational strategy forums (called Centurion sessions) in the early 1990s. The aim was to conduct a candid assessment of where Philips stood vis-à-vis industry competitors and to benchmark more successful organizations. These sessions also involved action planning and goal setting for new strategic initiatives intended to turn the company around. The cascade process began with an initial session of the company's top 120 managers. Then individual sessions were held, with a mix of levels and functions, at each product division and for the majority of the national or regional organizations. In total, some thirty thousand people have been involved in Centurion sessions. Beyond these middle and senior levels, "town meetings" were held with groups of up to four hundred people at lower levels, with operators and senior management together, in facilitated sessions lasting several hours. Philips also employed interactive satellite links to survey the reactions of over 120,000 employees to improving customer satisfaction—one of the Centurion action-planning issues. In addition, twenty-two corporate-level task forces were initiated to tackle major problems identified by the Centurion sessions, as well as more than six hundred change projects at other levels. This type of broad-reach initiative will increasingly characterize the more successful executive educational undertakings aimed at large-scale change in the future.

Challenges and Dilemmas for the Future of Executive Education

The changing complexion of executive education is clearly enhancing its impact and its relevance. At the same time, however, certain components of our model of effective executive education (such as assessment) continue to be overlooked, and in the other components important tradeoffs are still being made (Cairns-Lee, 1996; Fulmer and Vicere, 1995; Ready, 1995). Table 10.1 provides an overview of the changes that we foresee for the future of executive education in each of the components, and the following discussion describes the major changes that we believe must occur if executive education is to be successful as it moves into the next century.

Learning Needs: From Industry Strategy to Ecosystem Strategy

Leading organizational change will continue to be a central theme for the vast majority of executive educational initiatives through the first decade of the twenty-first century. We say this simply because competitive pressures will continue to heighten in most industries. They will be driven by the continued acceleration in the pace of technological change, the more rapid commodification of products, and the nonstop ascendancy of important Asian competitors like China, Korea, and Taiwan. To be effective, however, training in strategy must increasingly shift toward industry-ecosystem skills in strategy formulation. (An *industry ecosystem* is a competitive environment that includes not only present competitors but also potential future competitors who currently reside outside today's markets but may possess certain competencies and technologies that will allow them to capitalize on upcoming changes in industries from which they are currently absent.)

A recent example of an ecosystem shift is Microsoft's rise to dominance in the encyclopedia industry with its *Encarta* CD. In this case, technological changes in both software and compact disks allowed an outside company to enter the encyclopedia industry and then command it in less than a decade. Future markets will increasingly be characterized by such shifts, and strategy-skill development in executive education will shift toward greater emphasis on anticipating as well as proactively causing these types of industry changes. In addition to content changes, delivery of these programs will most likely be affected. For example, experts in technology will increasingly be called on to play a role in programs where they will work with company participants to determine future technological trends that may prove disruptive to the company's current competitive state. We may also see a return to scenario-based planning techniques in which participants plot out a range of possible futures for their industries and then plan strategic responses.

Sponsors: From Corporate Headquarters to Line Management

Many of today's executive educational initiatives are driven by corporate staff rather than line operations. In part this can be explained, first, by the fact that these initiatives are frequently initiated by a CEO or a corporate human relations executive and, second, by the fact that the corporate level often possesses the resources to drive expensive initiatives, whereas line operations tend to reserve their training dollars for skill development at the lower and middle levels of the organization.

The principal advantage of corporate-driven educational initiatives is that coordination and commitment can be achieved across the company. The dilemma, however, is that there are often fewer opportunities for the line organizations as entities to address their specific needs. Since many of the corporate-driven initiatives focus on only the executive levels, the middle and junior levels of

Table 10.1. Time Line Changes in Executive Education.

	1960s–1980s	1990s	2010
Learning needs	• Strategic/functional/mini-M.B.A. • Theory-based • Broad multiindustry focus	• Strategic/organizational change • Highly applicable knowledge • Single-industry focus	• Ecosystem industry focus • Leadership in lateral organizations/change in hypercompetitive environments • Applied and novel learning
Pedagogies	Case studies and lectures	Action learning Single case Company-based	Action learning Multiple sessions on a specific topic Ecosystem industry–based Parallel industry cases Scenario planning
Participants	Individuals	Executive cohorts	Executive cohorts Line operating managers Alliance partners Suppliers/customers Consortium members

Sponsors	Corporate	Corporate	Line operations Corporate headquarters as resource provider and clearinghouse
Integrating mechanisms	None	Task forces	Task forces, follow-up sessions, reward and performance-measurement changes, structural changes
Assessment	Simple postsession evaluation by participants	Simple postsession evaluation by participants	Individual and organizational assessments tied to actual learning and performance outcomes as measured by participants and their peers, bosses, and subordinates; assessments conducted also at follow-up sessions; tracking systems to measure longer-term outcomes of action-learning projects through company intranets

operating divisions are usually excluded. In addition, an initiative may be set around a corporate agenda that conflicts with the priorities of the business units and thereby negates some of the hoped-for educational outcomes.

Another troubling aspect of many a corporate-driven initiative is that it may be a one-time event; another five or ten more years may pass before a similar initiative is held. As a result, momentum and follow-up tend to be nonexistent, and the initiative eventually dies out.

As organizations begin to realize that line involvement is critical to the transfer of learnings from these initiatives, several important changes must occur in today's approaches. More and more programs must shift from being corporate-driven and corporate-designed to being cooperative ventures with extensive up-front design involvement on the part of line operations. Operating units need to have far greater say in designing and implementing executive educational efforts. This will allow business units to own and drive the initiatives that best fit their needs and market conditions. Corporate headquarters must see its role as providing *resources* for education rather than education itself. In addition to serving as a funding source, corporate headquarters can serve as a clearinghouse for educational "best practices" across the company.

Pedagogy: Multiple Learning Sessions As the Norm

Without a doubt, action learning will continue to play a central role as the pedagogy of choice well into the next century because of its learner-centered emphasis. We must realize, however, that there are certain limitations with current designs, and these should cause us to rethink how we can best use action learning.

At the heart of the problem is that most action-learning programs involve learning from a single case study (focusing on one company's problem). This limited exposure to an issue does not, in most cases, facilitate deep learning (Clark, 1992). The dilemma resides in the complex knowledge that action learning is attempting to teach. In contrast to more formula-based knowledge, such as knowledge about financial ratios or accounting procedures, action learning's aim is to tackle rich, complex topics (devising a strategic initiative, developing a new product, managing complex change), and these require learners to develop sophisticated sets of concepts and principles that can then be used later, when learners undertake their own projects. We know from the field of adult learning that at the heart of this type of complex learning is the ability to create and use analogies connecting several domains of knowledge (Clark, 1992). The more frequently individuals can successfully link seemingly unrelated yet actually similar events to new problems that they are addressing, the more likely they will be to produce effective solutions. But this process requires learners to be exposed to multiple case experiences (Clark, 1992). With its focus on a singular problem, much of today's action learning is failing to develop the knowledge that action-learning programs are promising.

In the next decade, action learning must shift to include multiple sessions in which similar learning objectives are spread across several action-learning projects for an individual participant. For example, if the goal is to teach new-product introduction into foreign countries, the learner will be exposed to three or four action-learning projects, each one involving an actual new-product introduction into a different country. Thus the learner will be allowed to build a useful repertoire of principles. In addition, projects need to involve longer time spans and to provide implementation opportunities. These characteristics will ensure both that participants are able to understand issues more deeply and that they have greater opportunities to learn from the trials and tribulations of implementing proposed solutions.

There is an additional dilemma with certain action-learning formats. Since action-learning problems are usually addressed by participants from the same corporation, the possibility is heightened that a shared mind-set may impede divergent and creative thinking, which in turn could facilitate longer-term organizational adaptation. As a result, these factors may reinforce a focus on finding ways to sustain current competitive advantages—and, as D'Aveni (1994) argues, doing so can actually be counterproductive in a hyper-competitive industry, particularly when company insiders play coaching and facilitating roles and when company executives are involved in implementing actual learnings and are the audience for participants' presentations on their learnings. To overcome this dilemma, greater reliance on outsiders to conduct action-learning programs is critical. In addition, consortia of companies should be undertaking joint action-learning projects so that participants themselves represent a mix of worldviews and are in a better position to more easily challenge one another's perspectives.

Learning Content: Going "Outside the Box"

The move toward greater customization of learning materials has increased the relevance of executive educational experiences, but these changes may also be lessening the ability of organizations to think "outside the box." Given that the winners in the new competitive world are those who change the rules of the game, educational materials are needed that challenge company and industry paradigms. The best way to achieve this outcome is to look to outside industries, but ones that offer situations analogous to the future of our industries.

This argument is based on recent research from the field of cognitive psychology, which indicates that one major obstacle to an individual's learning is the principle of *automaticity* (Weiss, 1992). In essence, the research shows that a person's work expertise and performance tend over time to become highly automatic and unconscious. The more we repeat a performance, the more it becomes automatic for us. This is true even of creative and complex problem-solving activities, such as those involved in structural engineering or open-heart surgery, and it is true despite the fact that seemingly similar problems may have different underlying causes and will therefore require different activities in terms of solutions. Nevertheless, this automatic approach is efficient because it lessens demands on our brains to handle many things at once. There is a major drawback, of course: once we learn a set of decision rules about an activity, any future mistakes are not self-correcting; the unique nature of a problem is missed simply because of an automated approach. As a result, most people at any organizational level, even when facing highly novel situations, continue to implement familiar strategies despite the fact that these strategies do not produce the best outcomes. This is one of the greatest challenges facing any adult learner, whether that person is a CEO or a front-line manager.

The most effective way to break this established pattern of problem solving is through novelty (Weiss, 1992), but it must be intensive, and the learner must be conscious of the novelty. The novelty must also challenge the learner's existing routines. For instance, novelty in the form of mistakes is a powerful source of learning. Mistakes cause reflection on one's existing routines, and then relearning. Once a disjunction like this has occurred, skills in critical thinking and knowledge acquisition may be enhanced.

The novelty principle is applicable to executive education. Program content for action-learning practices and executive retreats are frequently designed around issues that the participants face in their daily lives (for example, a brand-management project for a packaged-foods company). Even though these issues represent problems, the problems are often routine or familiar. In addition, the problem-solving approaches that the participants may be encouraged to use in their sessions may be the familiar ones that they use in their everyday activities (such as analyzing the results of the company's market research). Therefore, neither the content nor the approach of these programs is sufficiently novel to generate deeper learning; relying on extensions of existing company practices and worldviews may not introduce sufficient novelty to cause relearning.

In essence, as executive education has moved dramatically to meet executives' needs for increasing relevance, it may have swung too far. The move toward greater relevance is diluting a significant earlier advantage of the university-based public programs: broader experiences, multiple case experiences, and the possibility for greater novelty. This suggests that in the future there will need to be a return to educational content that includes material from outside industries, but with an edge of greater sophistication. This time the learning materials need to be carefully tailored to parallel situations occurring in other industries.

Participants: More from the Outside

In attempts to rectify the problems just described—shared mind-sets, and solutions from "inside the box"—it is important that the mix of participants be expanded. As alliances continue to become more and more commonplace, alliance partners need to join in on educational initiatives. To better grasp concerns and trends among suppliers and customers, these two groups must at times become "educators" in programs—providing their perspectives on the organization and its products and services, and responding to action-learning lessons. As mentioned earlier, educational consortia composed of different companies sharing similar learning concerns are an additional means to ensure multiple perspectives. Diversity of individuals is more likely to encourage creative examination of markets and organizational design issues, as well as healthy challenges to each company's paradigms of strategy and design. To ensure greater possibilities for the cascading of learning, the next generation of executive educational programs must also have creative tie-ins to middle-level line managers. These tie-ins might take the form of action-learning projects with a mix of levels in each one (although with all participants coming from the same operating unit).

Assessment: From Simple to Sophisticated

Assessment encompasses evaluation of executive learners' needs, evaluation of the organization's needs, and evaluation of training results. Executive education has traditionally paid little attention to any of these areas of assessment. In the 1970s, businesses and executive educational programs frequently used off-the-shelf psychological tests to determine learners' needs and characteristics. The subsequent movement toward action learning in teams and organizational learning, however, has lessened the importance of and interest in these individually oriented tests. For example, one study of more than six hundred American companies with more than a thousand employees each showed that most companies do not conduct extensive evaluations: 42 percent of the companies using executive M.B.A. programs for their managers conducted no evaluation, and although 92 percent did conduct postprogram evaluation of their in-company courses, that evaluation consisted largely of a simple form completed by participants, or a discussion session with the participants (Saari, Johnson, McLaughlin, and Zimmerle, 1988). After surveying 120 international companies, Cairns-Lee (1996) similarly found that even though most did conduct postprogram assessments, they were based either on simple surveys or on brief feedback sessions.

In general, few companies do an effective job of evaluating the outcomes of training initiatives. At the close of a training session, participants may be asked to write a few lines describing how much they have learned and how satisfied they are with the program, but no one can accurately and objectively assess a program's effectiveness and usefulness right away. Time is required for learnings to be assimilated, and for their usefulness to be tested against day-to-day demands.

A further problem arises with both the practice of using off-the-shelf tests and the practice of asking participants to write descriptive evaluations of educational programs (whether immediately afterward or later on). Participants who enjoyed the experience may give generally high evaluations of an educational session, not necessarily because the experience was valuable and effective but because they enjoyed it. A smart test-taker may be able to write a beautiful paragraph about empowerment or innovative strategic thinking and then return to work with the same closed mind as before. Assessment often measures what people *know,* which is quite different from what they *do.* In this regard, the perspectives that bosses, peers, and subordinates bring to an individual's implementation of new learning are crucial and likely to be somewhat more objective.

Learning outcomes from executive-level programs that seek to impart complex knowledge are very difficult to assess until the executive faces situations in which the new knowledge can be tested (Conger and Xin, 1996). Given the new emphasis on strategic change, executive educational programs and their graduates need to be evaluated in terms of contributions to the firm's strategic goals, and yet practically no organization assesses its educational efforts against this standard.

Ultimately, to be effective, assessment must play several roles throughout the learning process of executives. First, the needs and motivations of both the learner and the organization must be assessed. Second, the educational methods that most effectively satisfy those needs must be assessed and selected. Third, the outcomes of educational interventions for the learner, for the learner's operating unit, and for the learner's organization must be assessed.

Unfortunately, our tools today are largely underdeveloped and simplistic in all three assessment areas, even though it is clear that the general lack of thoroughgoing prior assessment is a major impediment to effective executive education.

In the future, two important changes will need to occur in assessment. First, company intranets need to be used for easy follow-up and for pre- and postprogram assessment. For example, months after a program has ended, an e-mail questionnaire could track participants' perceptions of the longer-term effectiveness of a learning initiative. A questionnaire could also conceivably be posted on a quarterly basis to the bosses, peers, and subordinates of the participants, to provide 360-degree assessment of the behavioral changes and performance outcomes that are linked to a learning program's objectives. Second, indicators of intellectual capital will be developed to provide better measurements of learning. We are still relatively unsophisticated in this area, but some interesting experiments are taking place. For example, Skandia, a Swedish-based financial organization, has developed the "Balanced Scorecard" system, which includes intellectual capital as one key element (Cairns-Lee, 1996). As a business, intellectual capital is critical to Skandia: it has few tangible assets and is built instead around customer relationships, the organization's capacity for learning and renewal, and the organization's databases and processes. Skandia expects its individual business units to develop indicators of performance success in four areas—finances, customers, processes, and renewal and development. Assessment in the last of these areas essentially requires the creation of specific indicators for demonstrating the impact of management development programs.

Integrating Mechanisms: Building True Links

From our research with companies, it is clear that many educational initiatives are seen as stand-alone events. In other words, there is little recognition of the need to link the outcomes of the educational experience more powerfully with other design elements of the organization. As a result, we have seen, time and time again, how existing systems for rewards and performance measurement can easily undo newly learned competencies or initiatives generated by an educational program. For example, in one recent company program, the educational content focused on building greater teamwork and collaboration across the organization. A few months after this educational initiative, which involved the firm's top five hundred managers, little cross-company collaboration had materialized. In follow-up interviews to detect the sources of the problem, managers responded that the current reward system militated against any change. The reward system, which historically had emphasized business-unit competition and individual performance, had not been changed to reinforce teamwork. Thus, although executive education had become more tightly linked to strategy on the front end, it continued to be poorly backed up by organizational design.

One of the few exceptions to the rule of education lacking organizational design support is Levi Strauss. In 1987, after an expensive leveraged buyout, the company sought to revisit its fundamental mission and corporate values. This led to a major initiative called the Aspirations, whose goal was to define the shared values that would guide both management and the workforce into the future. Early on it became clear that simply reformulating and endorsing a mission statement produced few if any results. Starting at the very top and cascading down the organization, a series of educational sessions (titled Leadership Weeks) drew attention to the leadership behaviors necessary to make the Aspirations a reality. Shorter versions of the program were created for the more junior levels. In 1989, a survey showed that although employees now understood and supported the company's new values, they did not believe the values were being acted on. Levi Strauss then instituted a communications program through newsletters, established a series of initiative-oriented task forces, and began offering consultation services to operating units through in-house organizational development experts. More important, company performance appraisals and rewards were changed completely to recognize and encourage greater leadership within the firm. Components of salary were redesigned to link pay with demonstration of specific leadership and teamwork behaviors, as outlined in the company's mission. This type of comprehensive package of changes must accompany executive educational initiatives of the future. In addition, initiatives need to run in parallel with design changes in the organization, not only as a means of education but also as a source of reinforcement.

Conclusion

Given the pace and intensity of today's competitive environment and the likely competitive environment of the future, executive education's role in company change efforts will probably continue to grow in significance. The challenge will be for practitioners to become far more sophisticated in their understanding of education's use as an intervention. As the situation stands today, we are relatively naïve: one could say that we are in the Stone Age of our understanding of executive education.

Our prescription for success begins with the notion that organizations must think more comprehensively about their educational initiatives. Many companies today employ educational interventions as one-time events rather than as ongoing processes to facilitate change. In addition, when programs are implemented there is little consideration of their integration with organizational design factors. As a result, learning from these experiences tends to be short-lived at best, with little transfer of learning back into the organization. If this situation is to change, we must take the important steps outlined in this chapter. A brief summary of the essential ones follows.

To begin, we must increasingly focus learning needs on the demands of a hypercompetitive marketplace. This means that as we train for strategic skills we must shift from an industry focus to an ecoindustry focus. Just as important, we must train for the core competencies of the next generation of whatever our industry is, not just for today's competencies (for example, a decade ago the encyclopedia industry needed to be training its managers in understanding software and CD-ROM technology).

Next, sponsorship must increasingly move toward joint ventures with line units in which the units shape the learning objectives and program content. The reasons are obvious. First, this type of shared involvement ensures greater ownership and commitment. Second, implementation of change occurs in the operating units, not at corporate headquarters.

We must also come to recognize the current limits of action learning. It has allowed learning to become more applied, but most experiences are built around a single case study. Research in adult learning tells us that this is a flawed approach. We learn best through multiple case experiences. In addition, most learning experiences involve a homogeneous group of participants in the sense that they are generally all from the same organization. As a result, the odds of divergent perspectives, which could challenge a company on the paradigms of its strategy and its organizational design, are minimized.

Participant mixes also must expand. Customers, suppliers, alliance partners, and new-technology experts increasingly must be involved in the learning process. We also recommend a return to case studies outside one's own industry, such as are found in open-enrollment university programs, but their selection will need to be far more thoughtful, and examples will need to be chosen for their close parallels to future industry trends. Through the novelty of examples outside the norm, we can ensure potentially deeper learning and more divergent thinking.

Our current assessment practices must change radically. Company intranets can provide a highly accessible medium for conducting far more comprehensive and longer-term pre- and postassessments. Moreover, feedback must no longer be gathered only from participants; rather, it should also come from the learners' bosses, peers, and subordinates, who are best able to observe learning outcomes. Our metrics must also be improved to measure as accurately as possible whether learnings are implemented at both the individual and the organizational level.

Finally, we believe strongly that educational initiatives must be better coordinated with other ongoing change initiatives within a company. An educational initiative's timing, its participant mix (especially the mix of levels in the hierarchy), and its links to organizational design changes are now poorly coordinated. For example, changes in rewards and performance measurement need to closely track educational interventions so that they reinforce messages and learnings from those interventions. Greater use of task forces, multiple education sessions, and cascaded events is also essential to keeping momentum alive.

If we can begin to implement a number of these changes, executive education's role as a critical lever in facilitating organizational transformation will be significantly enhanced. Executive education may ultimately prove to be one of our most powerful interventions both for accelerating the pace of change and for making change itself more profound.

Chapter Eleven

Strategic Pay System Design

Edward E. Lawler III

Strategic pay system design is not about a set of new practices; rather, it is a way of thinking about the role of pay systems in complex organizations that is becoming increasingly important because it represents a way to position pay as a significant value-added system. It argues for designing pay systems to fit business strategies and organizational structures. This means beginning the design of the pay system with a focus on business strategy and organizational design rather than on what other organizations are doing. It also argues against assuming certain best practices that must be incorporated into an organization's approach to pay.

The major pay system strategic design principle is drawn from the star model (see Figure 2 in the Introduction): to be effective, organizations must have congruence among their various operating systems. The pay system is a critical part of any organization's design. How well it fits with the strategy and the rest of the systems in an organization has an important impact on how effective the organization is and on the quality of life that people experience in the organization. Particular pay practices are neither good nor bad in the abstract. They must be evaluated in the context of the other systems in an organization and in the context of the organization's business strategy (Lawler and Jenkins, 1992).

Note: This chapter is based in part on Lawler (1995). Reprinted by permission of the publisher, from COMPENSATION & BENEFITS REVIEW JUL/AUG 1995 © 1995. American Management Association, New York. All rights reserved.

The business strategy indicates what the organization is supposed to accomplish and how it is supposed to behave. It specifies the kinds of performance and the performance levels that the organization needs to demonstrate in order to be effective. It identifies the core competencies and organizational capabilities that an organization needs in order to enact its strategy. The reward system, in combination with other features of the organization's design, drives the performance of the organization because it influences critical individual and organizational behaviors. Therefore, it must be designed to support the needed organizational behaviors.

Over the past decade, some new pay practices (for example, team- and skill-based pay) have become popular means of aligning pay systems with the important changes that are occurring in the way organizations are designed and managed (Lawler, 1990; Schuster and Zingheim, 1992; Lawler, Mohrman, and Ledford, 1995). This is a natural and logical outcome of a greater focus on strategic organizational design. In the future, not only are these practices likely to become more popular, other new pay practices are likely to be invented and become popular.

Figure 11.1 depicts the design process that an organization should use in creating a pay system and testing its effectiveness. It

Figure 11.1. Design of a Pay System.

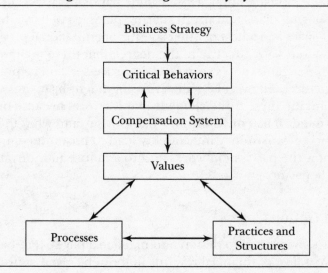

shows that business strategy should be the foundation for identifying the critical behaviors that the organization needs to demonstrate. The need for these behaviors in turn is shown as driving the compensation system. The challenge here is to correctly identify those features of a reward system that will produce the behaviors needed to make the business strategy come alive in terms of individual and organizational behavior.

Three critical elements of the compensation system are identified in this figure. The first is the core reward values that the organization holds. These core values may be stated or simply implicit in the way the organization operates. Regardless of whether they are stated, they are a part of all reward systems. Examples of core values are a belief in pay for performance, a belief in secrecy about pay, and other fundamental, relatively long-term commitments that organizations make in the area of reward systems. The compensation system also is shown to be made up of processes, which include such things as communication policies and decision-making practices. These are critical not only because they reflect the overall management style of the organization but also because they influence how well the compensation system's practices will be accepted and understood, and how much commitment there will be to them. Finally, the compensation system also includes actual practices and structures. These are the features of a reward system that get the most attention. They include pay-delivery systems, such as gainsharing plans and profit-sharing plans, as well as administrative policies and a host of other specific organizational programs.

Pay systems are effective to the degree that there is alignment among the organization's core vales, its processes, and its practices and structures. Figure 11.1 shows this alignment by means of the arrows linking these three elements. Fit is critical because organizations need to be consistent in what they say and what they do; violations of consistency inevitability lead to misunderstandings about how the pay system works and to a failure to motivate the proper behavior.

Design Options

There are many ways to design and manage a pay system because there are a host of financial rewards that can be given, as well as a large number of ways in which they can be distributed. A useful dichotomy in thinking about options in the design of reward systems is the already-mentioned process/structure one. Both process and structure need to be aligned with the business strategy in order for the pay system to be strategically correct. Because it is beyond the scope of this chapter to consider all the design options that are available, consideration will be given here to those options that are of the greatest strategic importance.

Paying the Job or Paying the Person

Pay is often based on the types of jobs that people do. Indeed, with the exception of performance bonuses and merit-based salary increases, the standard policy in most organizations is to evaluate the job, not the person, and then to set the reward level. This approach is based on the assumption that job worth can be determined, and that the person doing the job is worth only as much to the organization as the job itself is worth (Lawler, 1990). This assumption is valid in many instances because through such techniques as job evaluation programs it is possible to determine how much other organizations are paying people for performing the same or similar jobs. Among the advantages of this system is that it ensures an organization that its compensation costs are not dramatically out of line with those of its competitors, and it gives a somewhat objective basis to compensation levels.

An alternative to job-based pay is skill-based pay, which has recently been tried by a number of organizations (Lawler, Mohrman, and Ledford, 1995). Perhaps the most important changes introduced by this approach occur in the kinds of culture and motivation it produces in an organization. Instead of people being rewarded for moving up the hierarchy, people are rewarded for increasing their skills and developing themselves. This practice can create a culture of concern for personal growth and development, as well as a highly talented workforce. In factories where this system has been used, it typically has meant that many people in the organization can perform multiple tasks, which means that the workforce is highly knowledgeable and flexible (Jenkins, Ledford, Gupta, and Doty, 1992).

Paying for Performance

Perhaps the key strategic decisions that need to be made in the design of any reward system concern whether pay will be based on performance and, if so, how the performance-based pay system will be structured. Once these decisions are made, a number of the other features of the reward system tend to fall into place. One alternative to basing pay on performance is to base it on seniority. Many government agencies, for example, base their pay rates on the jobs that people do and on how long people have been in their jobs. In Japan, individual pay is also based on seniority, although individuals often receive bonuses on the basis of their corporation's performance.

Most business organizations in the United States say that they reward individual performance, and they call this kind of pay system a *merit system*. An effective merit pay system is often easier to describe than to implement, however; it can be difficult to specify what kind of performance is desired and to determine whether it has been demonstrated (Heneman, 1992). Indeed, it has been observed that many organizations would be better off if they did not try to relate pay and promotion to performance and relied instead on other ways of motivating performance (Kerr, 1975).

There are numerous ways to relate pay to performance, and pay can take a number of forms, including stock, stock options, salary increases, and cash bonuses. Further, the frequency with which rewards for performance are given can vary tremendously, from every few minutes to every few years. Performance can be measured at the individual level, so that each individual gets a reward on the basis of his or her performance. Rewards also can be based on the performance of groups and on the performance of the total organization (Blinder, 1990). Moreover, many different kinds of performance can be rewarded. For example, managers can be rewarded for sales increases, productivity volume, their ability to develop their subordinates, their cost-reduction ideas, and so on.

Market Position

The reward structure of an organization influences behavior partially as a function of how the organization's rewards compare with those of other organizations, and organizations frequently have well-developed policies concerning this point. For example, some companies deliberately set their pay rates at higher levels, whereas other companies are much less concerned about being in a leadership position with respect to pay and so set their pay levels at or below market rates.

Centralized and Decentralized Reward Strategies

Organizations that adopt a centralized pay strategy typically assign a corporate staff group responsibility for seeing that pay practices are similar throughout the organization. They typically develop standard pay grades and ranges, standardized job evaluation systems, and, perhaps, standardized promotion systems. In decentralized organizations, the design and administration of pay systems are left to local entities. Sometimes a decentralized organization has broad guidelines or principles that it regards as part of its core values, but the day-to-day administration and design of the reward system are determined locally.

Degree of Hierarchy

Closely related to the issue of job-based versus person-based pay is the degree to which the reward system is hierarchical. Hierarchical systems usually pay more and give more perquisites and symbols of office as people move up in the organization. The effect of this approach is to strongly reinforce traditional hierarchical power relationships in the organization and to create a climate of different status and power levels. There are usually more levels in a steeply hierarchical reward system than there are in the formal organization chart, and so even more differences in status are created. Often no formal decision is ever made to use a hierarchical approach rather than an egalitarian one; the hierarchical approach simply comes into being because it is so consistent with the general way in which the organization is structured.

The alternative to a hierarchical system is one that dramatically downplays differences in rewards and perquisites that are based only on hierarchical level. For example, in a large corporation that adopts an egalitarian stance, the pay system may contain just a few broad pay bands; things like private parking spaces, executive restrooms, and special entrances are eliminated. This less hierarchical approach tends to encourage decision making on the basis of expertise rather than on the basis of hierarchical position, and it is supportive of teamwork and lateral integration (Lawler, 1990).

Communication Policy

Organizations differ widely in how much information they communicate about their reward systems. Some organizations are extremely secretive, particularly in the area of pay. They forbid employees to talk about their pay, they give individuals minimal information about how reward decisions are reached, and they have no publicly disseminated policies or information about such things as the market position of pay, how market data are gathered, and budgets for pay increases. At the other extreme, some organizations are so open that everyone's pay is a matter of public record. In these organizations, all promotions are subject to open job postings, and in some instances peer groups also assess people's eligibility for promotion.

Decision-Making Practices

Closely related to the issue of communication is the issue of decision making. Open communication makes possible the involvement of a wide range of people in decision-making processes that are related to pay. In order for individuals to be actively involved in decisions about the reward system, they need to have information about policies and practices.

In discussing the types of decision-making processes that organizations use in allocating rewards, it is important to distinguish between decisions that involve the design of a reward system and decisions that involve the ongoing administration of a reward system. It is possible to have a different decision-making style in each of these two areas.

Objectives of the Reward System

The research on reward systems suggests that they potentially influence six factors, which in turn have an impact on strategy implementation and organizational effectiveness. We will discuss these and then consider how key pay system design decisions can affect organizational performance.

Attraction and Retention

Research on job choice, career choice, and turnover clearly shows that the kinds and levels of rewards that an organization offers influences who is attracted to work for the organization and who will continue to work for it (Lawler, 1990). Overall, organizations that give the most rewards tend to attract and retain the most people.

The types of rewards offered are also critical in determining who is attracted and retained by an organization's pay system. For example, high levels of risk compensation attract different types of people than do pay systems that emphasize security and extensive benefits.

The objective should be to design a pay system that is effective at attracting and retaining those employees who are strategically the most important ones because of their skills and competencies. To do so, the system must distribute rewards in a way that will lead people to feel satisfied when they compare their rewards with those received by individuals performing similar work in other organizations. The emphasis here is on external comparisons because attraction and turnover involve comparisons to situations in other organizations.

Motivation of Performance

When certain specifiable conditions exist, reward systems have been demonstrated to motivate performance (Gerhart and Milkovich, 1992; Lawler, 1971, 1990; Vroom 1964). What are those conditions? Valued rewards must be perceived as being tied to effective performance and as being distributed in a timely fashion. People have needs that determine the value of rewards. They also have mental maps of what the world is like, and they use these maps to choose behavior that will lead to outcomes that are likely to satisfy their needs. Therefore, organizations get the behavior that leads to the rewards their employees value.

Employees are not inherently motivated or unmotivated to perform effectively; their motivation depends on the situation, on how it is perceived, and on their needs. In general, an individual's motivation to perform effectively is greatest when the individual (1) believes that effective performance will lead to outcomes, (2) feels that these outcomes are attractive, and (3) believes that effective performance is possible. The implication for a pay system are clear: in order to be motivational, the pay system must create a line of sight between employees' behavior and their ability to receive valued rewards.

Skills and Knowledge

Just as a pay system can motivate performance, it can also motivate learning and development. The same motivational principles apply. Individuals are motivated to learn those skills that are rewarded. Skill-based pay has been developed to capitalize on just this point. It allows organizations to strategically target the learning that it wants employees to engage in, by contrast to many job-based pay systems, which indirectly affect learning by tying pay and perquisite levels to job level or scope.

Culture

An organization's reward system, as well as how it is developed, administered, and managed, has a strong impact on the organization's overall culture. For example, the reward system can influence the degree to which the organization is seen as having a human resources–oriented culture, an entrepreneurial culture, an innovative culture, a competence-based culture, a fair culture, a participative culture, and so forth. The reward system has the ability to shape culture precisely because of its important influence on skill development, motivation, satisfaction, and organizational membership. The behaviors that it motivates become the dominant patterns of behavior in the organization and lead to perceptions and beliefs about what the organization stands for, believes in, and values.

Reinforcement and Definition of Structure

The pay system of an organization can reinforce and define the organization's structure (Lawler, 1990). Often, however, this structural impact is not considered in the design of a pay system. As a result, the pay system's impact on the structure of the organization is unintentional, but this does not necessarily mean that its impact on the organizational structure is minimal. The pay system can have a strong impact on how integrated and how differentiated an organizational structure is because the pay system can create "seams" or act as a filler of seams (Lawrence and Lorsch, 1967). When people are rewarded in the same way, they tend to be united, and when they are rewarded in different ways, they are divided. The pay system can also help define the status hierarchy, and it can strongly influence the kinds of decision structures that exist.

Costs

The reward system is often a significant cost factor. Indeed, pay alone may represent over 50 percent of an organization's operating costs. Therefore, in strategically designing a reward system, it is important to focus on how high its costs should be and on how they will vary as a function of the organization's ability to pay. For example, a reasonable outcome of a well-designed pay system might be an increase in pay-related costs when the organization has the money to spend, and a decrease in these costs when the organization does not have the money. An additional objective might be to have lower overall costs for the reward system than business competitors do.

Pay and Organizational Effectiveness

The combined impact of the pay system on the six factors just reviewed can affect organizational performance in two primary ways: it can motivate strategically key *performance,* and it can support the creation of strategically important *capabilities.* Focusing on the desired effects is the key to choosing among the many design options that are possible for a pay system. Figure 11.2 shows that the key to motivation is pay for performance, whereas capability is influenced by base pay, market position, and degree of hierarchy. Thus in deciding how to pay for performance, it is crucial to focus on motivation, whereas a focus on capabilities should be used to determine

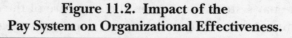

**Figure 11.2. Impact of the
Pay System on Organizational Effectiveness.**

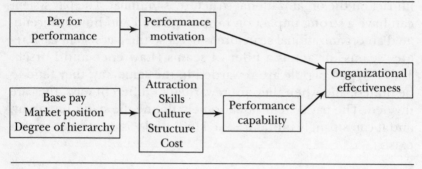

what to pay the person, what market position to take, and how hierarchical the pay system should be.

Pay for Performance

Rewarding some kinds of behavior and not others has clear implications for performance because rewarded behavior tends to be more frequent, and unrewarded behavior tends to disappear. Therefore, decisions about what is to be rewarded need to be made carefully and with attention to the overall strategic plan of the business. Once the strategic plan has been developed to the point where key performance objectives have been defined, the reward system needs to be designed to motivate the appropriate performance. Decisions about such issues as whether to use stock options, for example, should be made only after careful consideration of which pay-for-performance practices will best support the kinds of behavior that are desired.

Consideration needs to be given to issues involving what is measured—short-term versus long-term performance, risk taking versus risk aversion, divisional performance versus total corporate performance, maximization of return on investment versus growth in sales, and so on. In addition to focusing on what is measured, it is important to consider the amount of reward that is tied to each measure. This decision has the power to signal what is important and to determine just how motivated individuals will be to perform in particular ways.

It is beyond the scope of this chapter to go into any great detail about the pros and cons of the many approaches to relating pay to performance. A few general points do need to be made, however. First, bonus plans are generally better motivators than pay-raise and salary-increase plans because a bonus plan can substantially vary an individual's pay from time to time. This is very difficult to do with a salary-increase plan because past raises become an entitlement or annuity.

Second, approaches that use objective measures of performance are better motivators than those that use subjective measures. In general, objective measures enjoy higher credibility—that is, employees will often accept the validity of an objective measure (such as sales volume or units produced), whereas they will not accept a boss's rating. Therefore, when pay is tied to objective measures, the perception is usually clearer that pay is determined by performance. Objective measures are also often public. Thus when pay is tied to them, the relationship between performance and pay can be much more visible than when pay is tied to a subjective, nonverifiable measure, such as a supervisor's rating.

Third, group-based and organizationwide bonus plans are generally best at producing integration and teamwork. Under such plans, it is generally to everyone's advantage for any one individual to work effectively because everyone shares in the financial results of higher performance. As a result, good performance is likely to be supported and encouraged by others; this is not true under an individual bonus plan, which tends to produce differentiation and competition.

Fourth, group-based and organizationwide plans are often the easiest ones to relate to strategic objectives because they are the easiest to tie to performance measures of business success. Most business plans focus on measures that are applicable only to groups or to the whole business. Therefore, although it is difficult to measure and reward individuals strategically, it is often relatively straightforward to measure and reward business units and companies for strategic results. The group approach has one key drawback, however: the line of sight is usually weak. Therefore, if this approach is to be effective, individuals need to be told how they can influence the organization's strategic results, and they need to be given the power and skills to do so.

Performance Capability

Paying individuals for their skills and competencies can have a direct impact on the competencies and capabilities of the organization. As was discussed in Chapter Five, the key here is to develop a link between the competencies and capabilities that the organization needs to develop, on the one hand, and, on the other, the specific competencies and capabilities that are rewarded at the individual level. This is not an easy objective to accomplish. In addition to the measurement problems associated with rewarding competencies at the individual level, it may be difficult to determine exactly what the pattern of competencies and capabilities is that individuals need. In a complex organization, developing organizational competencies is usually a matter of developing the right pattern of competencies and capabilities among different individuals; it is unrealistic to expect every individual to have all the competencies and capabilities that the organization needs. Therefore, it is important to determine how many individuals need to have the skills and knowledge that will generate particular capabilities and competencies, and to develop reward systems that motivate individuals to develop the needed mix of individual skills and knowledge so that, together, they constitute an effective organizational capability or competency.

This means that the organization should pay for skills and competencies only when it can identify the specific skills and knowledge that individuals need to have and only when it has the measurement and support systems that are necessary for rewarding those individuals who develop the needed skills and knowledge. This is difficult, but the strategic leverage here is potentially enormous. It can move an organization away from a situation in which there is essentially no connection between the pay system and the development of strategically important individual competencies and capabilities, toward a situation in which the reward system and the business strategy are integrated and mutually supportive.

Paying for skills and competencies can also help an organization be more nimble in its strategic orientation. The pay system can be used to reward individuals for learning new capabilities as changes in technological factors and organizational needs occur. The pay system can also aid the organization in its development of such capabilities as quality and low-cost operations. In the absence of a nimble reward system that pays for the development of new competencies, there is a very great danger that the organization will be unable to change its performance as the environment or the strategy demands new kinds of behavior (Ledford, 1995a).

In most cases where skill-based pay has been tried, it has tended to produce somewhat higher pay levels for individuals, but the higher pay is usually offset by greater workforce flexibility and performance (Jenkins, Ledford, Gupta, and Doty, 1992). Flexibility often leads to lower staffing levels, fewer problems when absenteeism or turnover occur, and, indeed, to lower absenteeism and turnover because people like the opportunity to utilize and be paid for a wide range of skills. Nevertheless, skill-based pay can be a challenge to administer because it is not clear how one goes to the outside marketplace to determine how much a skill is worth. A number of well-developed systems exist for evaluating jobs and gathering salary survey data, but none does this with respect to the skills an individual has. Skill assessment is often difficult and may require that tests be developed.

In general, skill-based pay seems to fit those organizations that want to have a flexible, relatively permanent workforce oriented toward learning, growth, and development. Skill-based pay has been used frequently in plant start-ups and in plants that are moving toward high-involvement management approaches (Lawler, Mohrman, and Ledford, 1992, 1995). It is beginning to be used more with knowledge workers and with managers (Ledford, 1995b). It is also being used more in situations where the organization's strategy calls for one stop-service and a high level of customer satisfaction.

The market position of pay is a critical design factor because it strongly influences the kinds of people who are attracted and retained by an organization. It also influences the turnover rate and the selection ratio. As a result, it directly influences the competencies and capabilities of the organization.

If many of the jobs in an organization are low-skill positions, and if the labor market has people who are readily available to occupy them, then a strategy of high pay may not be appropriate. It will increase labor costs and produce a minimum number of benefits. Of course, an organization does not have to be a high payer for all jobs. Indeed, an organization can identify certain key skills that it needs and adopt the stance of being a high payer for those skills and an average or below-average payer for other skills. This approach has some obvious business advantages in terms of allowing the organization to attract the critical skills it needs for success while controlling costs.

The kind of market position that a company adopts with respect to its reward level can also have a noticeable impact on organizational culture. For example, a policy that calls for above-average market pay can contribute to the feeling in the organization that it is elite, that people must be competent to be there, and that they are indeed fortunate to be there. By contrast, a policy that puts certain skill groups into high-pay positions and leaves the rest of the organization at a lower level can contribute to a spirit of elite groups within the organization and cause decisive social tensions.

It is interesting to note that some organizations try to be above-average in nonfinancial compensation as a way of competing for the talent they need. They stress working conditions as well as interesting and challenging work. This stance is potentially a very effective one because it can give the organization a competitive edge in attracting people who value nonfinancial rewards.

As always when strategic choices about a reward system are concerned, there is no right or wrong answer to the question of how hierarchical the system should be. In general, a steeply hierarchical system makes the most sense when an organization needs relatively rigid bureaucratic behavior, strong top-down authority, and a strong motivation for people to move up the organizational ladder. This kind of system creates hierarchical seams in the organization, which reinforce top-down authority while discouraging cross-level teamwork and communication. A more egalitarian approach fits with a more participative management style, and with the desire to retain technical specialists and experts in nonmanagement or lower-level management roles. Therefore, it is not surprising that many of the organizations that emphasize egalitarian perquisites are in high-technology and knowledge-based industries. In these organizations it is important to develop knowledge-based core competencies, and decision-making power needs to go where the knowledge is instead of following hierarchical lines.

The Pay System's Operating Effectiveness

It is not enough to have a reward system that measures and rewards the right things and is properly structured. As Figure 11.3 shows, an effective pay system must be positioned to operate correctly with respect to the organizational structure, and it has to have appropriate communication policies and decision-making processes.

Communication: Openness Versus Secrecy

The amount of communication about how a pay system operates is an important determinant of how and how much it influences behavior. Unless there is at least minimal communication and understanding, it is impossible for the pay system to be an effective motivator. The motivation of performance and skill development depends on individuals' knowing what is rewarded. The cultural difference between an open communication policy and a closed one is enormous in the area of rewards. As is true with respect to all the other choices that must be made in structuring a reward system, there is no clearly right or wrong approach to the degree of openness. Rather, the issue is to choose a position between openness and secrecy that is supportive of the overall culture and of the types of behavior needed for organizational effectiveness. An open system tends to encourage people to ask questions, share data, and, ultimately, be involved in decisions; a secretive system tends to put people in a more dependent position, to keep power concentrated at the top, and to let the organization keep its options open. Negative side effects of a secretive system include considerable misunderstanding about the actual rewards that people get, as well as

Figure 11.3. Operational Effectiveness of the Pay System.

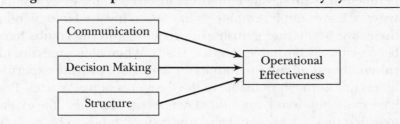

a low-trust environment in which people have trouble understanding the relationship between pay and performance. Therefore, with secrecy, even a structurally sound pay system may end up being ineffective because it is misperceived.

An open system puts considerable pressure on an organization to do an effective job of administering rewards. Therefore, if such difficult-to-defend policies as merit pay are to be implemented, considerable time and effort need to be invested in pay administration. If a merit-pay policy is poorly administered, strong pressure usually develops to eliminate the policy and pay everyone the same. Ironically, if an organization wants to spend little time on the administration of its reward system but still wants to base pay on performance, then secrecy may be the best policy, although secrecy in turn may limit the effectiveness of pay for performance.

Decision Making:
Hierarchical Control Versus Participation

Reward systems typically are designed by top management, with the aid of staff support, and administered through strict reliance on the chain of command. The assumption is that this arrangement provides proper checks and balances and locates decision making where the expertise resides. In many cases this assumption is valid, and this sort of arrangement certainly fits well with a management style that emphasizes hierarchy, bureaucracy, and control through the use of extrinsic rewards. It does not fit, however, with an organization that believes in more open communication, higher levels of employee involvement, and control through individual commitment to policies. It also does not fit when expertise is broadly spread throughout the organization.

There have been a number of reports about organizations experimenting with having employees involved in the design of pay systems. For example, employees have been involved in designing their own bonus and gainsharing systems, and the results have been generally favorable (Lawler, 1990). When employees are involved, they tend to raise important issues and provide expertise that is not normally available to the designers of pay systems. Perhaps more important, once these systems are designed, the extent to which they are accepted and understood tends to be greater, and this often means that they can start up rapidly and that employees are committed to seeing them survive and work well. Not surprisingly, employee commitment has been found to be an important factor in the success of skill-based pay systems.

There also has been some experimentation with having peer groups and lower-level supervisors handle day-to-day decisions about who should receive pay increases and how jobs should be evaluated and placed within pay structures. The most visible examples of this kind of experimentation have been in team-based plants that use skill-based pay. Typically, the work group reviews the performance of the individual and decides whether he or she has acquired the new skills. What evidence there is suggests that this process usually goes well, and in many respects this finding is not surprising: peers often have the best information about performance and are therefore in a good position to make performance assessments.

Structure: Centralization Versus Decentralization

The strategic advantages of a centralized reward structure rest primarily on the expertise in pay administration that can be developed and on the degree of homogeneity that can be produced in the organization. A sense of homogeneity can in turn lead to a clear image of the corporate culture, to feelings of internal equity, to the belief that the organization stands for something, and to a sense of organizationwide integration that may make career moves easier and that can support cooperation. Homogeneity also eases the job of communicating and understanding what is going on in different parts of the organization. A decentralized structure allows for local innovation, and for practices that fit with particular businesses and strategies.

Here, as in the other critical choices bearing on the design of a pay system, there is no one right approach. Overall, a decentralized pay system tends to make the most sense when an organization is involved in various businesses that are facing different markets, need different competencies and capabilities, and are at different points in their maturity. A decentralized pay system allows unique practices to surface that can give a competitive advantage to one part of the business but could prove to be a real hindrance or handicap to another. For example, such perquisites as company cars often represent standard operating procedure in one business but not in another. Similarly, extensive bonuses and stock options may be needed to attract and motivate individuals in a start-up business but may make little sense in a more mature business.

Integration, Fit, and Organizational Effectiveness

Our discussion has focused on designing the elements of a pay system so that they fit with the business strategy. This is a critical first step in creating a strategic pay system, but it is not the last step. Once a clear picture has been developed of the pay practices that are appropriate for an organization, it is important to look at these practices as an integrated whole in order to determine whether they are in alignment with each other. It is also important to see how they fit with the overall management style of the organization, as well as with its basic processes for communicating and making decisions. Ultimately, the alignment of all these features is what will determine the effectiveness of the organization and its ability to implement its strategy effectively.

Conclusion

The design of a strategically effective pay system is as much about business strategy and organizational design as it is about the pay system itself. If an organization is unclear about the competencies and capabilities it needs in order to be effective and implement its strategy, then there is no way for it to know what kind of pay system it needs or to determine how the pay system should be administered. In these circumstances, it is not an understatement to say that any pay system will do—any pay system that does not cost too much, that is. Any pay system will do because there are no criteria by which to assess its effectiveness. It is possible to determine whether a pay system is producing the correct behavior and the desired level of performance only when there is a well-thought-out strategy.

Once a well-thought-out strategy is in hand, the design of a strategically effective pay system can be carried out in a somewhat lockstep fashion. The design of the pay system needs to start with the identification of the necessary organizational behaviors. These then need to be translated into measures that can be used as the basis of a pay-for-performance system. The design of the system also has to focus on the kinds of organizational core competencies and capabilities that are needed. Translating these into individual skills and knowledge and into organizational systems is a crucial step in the development of the pay system. This is a crucial and necessary step because it focuses the organization on rewarding the right kinds of learning. It also allows the organization to support key processes concerned with change, communication, and decision making and to support the development of the right capabilities.

Finally, there is the issue of using an effective design process to create a pay system that is understood and on target. Particularly in a participative environment, the prescription here is clear: use employee involvement and open communication. This is the best way to ensure both an understanding of the new pay system and a positive response to it when it is rolled out to the organization.

A strategically designed pay system is one of the critical foundations of an effective organization. It is neither more nor less important than the other foundations on which organizational effectiveness rests. An organization that fails to design its pay systems strategically will not be able to avoid the problem of having people behave in strategically inappropriate ways that are rewarded by the pay system. The organization that focuses too much on the pay system, failing to recognize the importance of work design, information processes, and other features, will often be disappointed: its pay system will not perform well, and the organization itself will not perform well, either.

The challenge for organizations is to integrate their pay systems with business strategy and with overall organizational design. This challenge must be met if organizations are to compete effectively in rapidly changing global markets.

Part Four

Transforming
the Organization

Teams and Technology
Extending the Power of Collaboration

Don Mankin
Susan G. Cohen
Tora K. Bikson

Teams and information technology (IT) are two of the most important developments in organizations today. Year after year, organizations increase their investment in new information systems (Stewart, 1995) and use teams to do more and more of their work (Lawler, Mohrman, and Ledford, 1995). They devote vast amounts of time, money, and energy to teams and new technology with the expectation that their impact on the bottom line will eventually justify their costs. But many organizations are disappointed in the results. Few are getting the bang from the many bucks they spend each year to create teams (Dumaine, 1994) and develop new information systems (Attewell, 1994). The challenge facing organizations is how to fulfill the potential of these two promising and complex developments.

One assumption underlying the current interest in teams and technology is the belief that they can contribute to the most important strategic resource of the postindustrial era—knowledge. Whether solving production problems on the shop floor, creating new products in the laboratory, or mapping strategy in the executive suite, organizations need access to knowledge that is at the same time both interdisciplinary and highly specialized. That is why organizations are now so intensely interested in teams and IT. IT provides access to diverse sources of specialized information and enhances our ability to analyze, manage, and apply this information to our work. Teams bring together different individuals who know and can do different things. They are a means of pooling and using the diverse knowledge and skills of their members to accomplish mutual goals (Drucker, 1994).

Separately, teams and technology will have only minimal impact. Each can help take full advantage of the possibilities created by the other—that is, IT can make teams more effective, and teams can help fulfill the promise of the new technology. When they are integrated, their joint contribution to knowledge and organizational performance is greater than the sum of their parts (see Figure 12.1).

It is easy to see how technology can catalyze team performance. As was pointed out in Chapter Six, information is the very foundation of teamwork. Regardless of purpose or setting, all teams are becoming more information- and knowledge-dependent. Therefore, team members need tools to help them gain access to information, manage and analyze it, share it among themselves, and communicate it to others.

What is less obvious but just as significant, teams can make information technology more effective. In recent years, organizations have come to realize that the payoffs from huge investments in technology have more to do with the reengineering of work

Figure 12.1. Synergy Between Information Technology and Teams.

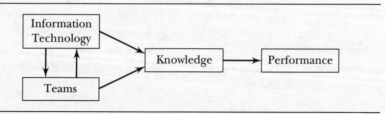

processes and structures around the new technology than with the specific features of the technology itself. Sociotechnical change strategies are now helping more and more organizations fulfill the potential of their new IT. Specifically, organizations are using their new technologies to integrate some of the very functions dismantled by the division of labor. With IT, they are lowering functional boundaries so that pooled knowledge can be brought to bear on complex, time-critical issues. Everyone involved in the work process can have access to the same information; as a result, everyone can work together more effectively to serve customers' needs. Thus the technology creates the potential, and teams help the technology fulfill that potential.

Although integrating teams and technology is an important step toward high performance, it is not enough. The growing use of teams and IT has significant implications for organizations. The nature of the organization itself—its structures, policies, practices, and technology platforms—must change to support the teams and their technologies as they operate within, and increasingly across, its boundaries. The development of new technologies and team designs should be embedded within a broader change effort if their full potential is to be truly unleashed. Team-based, technology-enabled organizations need to create high-level structures, policies, and systems to support individual teams and the information tools they use. This macrostructure must be able to integrate teams and their technology to help create the new organization. This chapter describes the change processes needed to create the new organization.

Mutual Design and Implementation (MDI) Process

High levels of performance require the integrated development of teams, technology, and organizations. We call this integrated development process *mutual design and implementation,* or MDI. Our use of the concept of mutuality reflects two connotations in everyday use: the correlations, connectedness, and reciprocal influence among things, events and ideas; and the common interests and relationships among people. The first connotation involves the focus of the MDI process—teams (we will hereafter refer to these teams as *user teams*), the information tools they will use, and the organizational context for their use. Mutuality characterizes the interdependence of all three, as shown in Figure 12.2. This figure forms a triangle, which is also the Greek letter delta, the symbol for change. Since a change in one corner of the triangle will necessarily influence the other two corners, all three should be addressed so that changes in one corner will complement and reinforce changes in the others. The second connotation reflects our emphasis on the many diverse people and constituencies that need to collaborate in the design of teams, technology, and organizations. Integrated development of all three is a difficult task that involves complex decisions and multidimensional designs. Trade-offs and compromises have to be made, and, ultimately, designs have to be linked and integrated. This process requires diverse, high-level skills and knowledge, and many people will be profoundly affected by the decisions that are made. Therefore, a number of people with different kinds of expertise and interests need to collaborate throughout this change process.

The collaboration should include those people whose work will be most affected by the changes, whose knowledge and skills are needed in the change effort, and whose commitment to the changes will play an important role in their success. These people are the stakeholders in the development process; they have a stake in the outcomes and are critical to its success. Many stakeholder voices, expressing diverse interests and concerns, need to be heard during the MDI process. They all contribute to the rich symphony of knowledge that is essential for broad, complex change.

Figure 12.2. Mutual Design and Implementation Process.

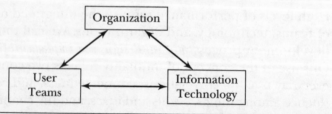

Some of the most important voices belong to those most affected by the changes—the user teams. They will use the new IT and work together in new ways within a redesigned organizational context. They know the most about the work to be modified, redesigned, or transformed. They possess essential knowledge about the intimate, hands-on, day-to-day details of the work, knowledge that cannot be provided by any other means. They comprise the key collaborative relationships needed to fulfill their increasingly complex and multifaceted mission. They also need to own the changes being made. In other words, they should help shape the changes and commit themselves to making them work. The best way to create this commitment is to build a system that meets their needs, and the best way to meet their needs is to incorporate their knowledge by involving them in the process through which design decisions and implementation plans are made.

IT experts also need to participate in the MDI process. Their role is critical: to provide the technical expertise for translating users' needs into new information systems, to support the systems once they are implemented, and to integrate the systems into the organization's IT infrastructure. Since they need to work closely with the user teams they serve, the quality of their collaboration is one of the best predictors of a system's ultimate success (Klein and Ralls, 1995).

Others are also affected by team, technology, and organizational change or possess critical knowledge or skills relevant to these changes. These others include the following groups:

- Managers and supervisors to whom individuals and teams report
- Human resources (HR) staff who can help facilitate the MDI team, develop training programs, and advise senior management on the changes in HR practice and policy that will be needed to support team-based work
- Customers and suppliers, both internal and external, who work closely with the team and use the same systems
- Senior managers who can use their authority to support and sponsor the project, and who also will be responsible for implementing new policies concerned with the overall organizational change that emerges from the MDI process

These are all stakeholders; they literally have a stake in what happens and need to feel a sense of ownership over the outcomes. Their commitment, skills, and authority are needed to create new work forms, technologies, and organizations. They all need to collaborate in the design and implementation of these changes. Of course, not all the individuals in these groups can directly participate in this process; there are just too many of them. Therefore, a team made up of representatives of these stakeholder groups must be formed to take primary responsibility for the MDI effort. This MDI project team (hereafter referred to as the *MDI team*) is the primary agent of the change effort. The members will work together to design the technology and the user teams, put them in place, and recommend the organizational changes needed to support them. Not all MDI team members need to participate in the same way. For example, the role of senior managers is to legitimate, support, and oversee the project, via a steering committee, rather than be involved in the detailed tasks of design and implementation.

The composition of the MDI team, like that of any other project team, needs to be quite fluid to reflect the changing dynamics and agenda of the MDI process. As the MDI team moves from issue to issue, new representatives may be added and others may drop out. Some may rejoin as earlier issues are revisited and decisions are reconsidered. Frequently, the project will have to be partitioned into component tasks, with separate MDI teams created to focus specifically on each subtask. Therefore, when we refer to the MDI team, we mean to refer in a broad, dynamic sense to the steering committee, the multiple-task teams, and the changing composition of the team as the project evolves.

New Approaches to Change

The context for MDI is highly dynamic and complex. New technologies come on the market almost every day, business conditions are in constant flux, and opportunities emerge without warning and fade just as quickly. Therefore, the processes of change, whether or not they involve teams and technology, must be able to deal with the ever-shifting conditions and circumstances buffeting all organizations today. The MDI process should be as dynamic as the environment in which it unfolds.

The problem is that the scope and the approach of most organizational and IT change projects in recent years have embodied the very antithesis of the flexibility and agility needed in these increasingly turbulent times. One of the problems, according to a recent study by the National Academy of Sciences, is that these projects are often too large and cumbersome to be implemented effectively. These "bet the company" IT projects, according to this study, are likely to be "overly complex, over budget, delayed, and mismatched to customer needs by the time they are implemented."

> For many years, IT vendors and popular journals overemphasized the importance of large-scale "system solutions." Managers too often responded by seeking to install mega-projects with high visibility. Such projects generally have multiple objectives that must be reconciled and integrated across several divisions. Mega-projects tend to be very complex. And they often take inordinate amounts of time, investment risk, and political compromises to bring into being. As a result, even companies with well-established track records for innovative uses of IT have experienced difficulties with large-scale projects [National Research Council, 1994, p. 171].

A related problem is the manner in which these projects are usually carried out. Technology guru Patricia Seybold (1994) uses the metaphor of the waterfall to describe the traditional approach to systems development. The "waterfall method of application development," as she describes it, is characterized by a roughly linear sequence of steps (see Figure 12.3). The process flows downstream, one waterfall spilling over to another in a one-way series of sequential steps. And therein lies part of the problem: the development process does not move from one step to the next until the prior step is complete, and so none of the earlier steps can benefit from the knowledge gained in the performance of the later ones (Kantor, 1994). This approach also requires a great deal of up-front planning and is relatively inflexible. Since the design is more or less set in stone early on in the project, it is difficult to take advantage of new technologies and unexpected opportunities or to respond to changing conditions. Furthermore, approximations of the final system are usually not available for users' reactions and feedback until it is too late in the process for them to have much impact.

Figure 12.3. Waterfall Model of Systems Development.

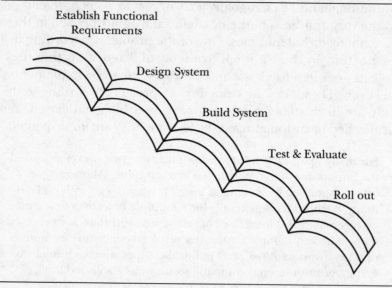

Establish Functional
Requirements

Design System

Build System

Test & Evaluate

Roll out

Yet another problem is that these projects are typically developed and implemented from the top down. In them, as Davenport (1995) notes in his critique of top-down reengineering, a small group of people designs work processes for a much larger group—and, we would add, ongoing links and interactions between the designers (the smaller group) and the larger group of users are often minimal at best. Therefore, "there is little participation in the design process by those who will actually do the work" (Davenport, 1995, p. 25). As a consequence, designs rarely reflect the implicit, intuitive knowledge about the hands-on details that can come only from doing the work day after day, nor do they take into consideration the often subtle collaborations that are so critical to team-based work.

By now the outcome of these top-down, overengineered megaprojects is all too familiar: systems and workplace designs that are costly, behind schedule, and obsolete by the time they are implemented. Horror stories about such projects abound. It is no wonder that organizations are desperately seeking alternatives to these outmoded change processes. Fortunately, the outlines of these alternative processes can be seen in new approaches to organizational change, systems development, and technology implementation. The MDI framework falls squarely within this emerging paradigm.

The Action-Learning Approach

The first step toward successful change is to adopt new ways of thinking about change itself. Effective organizations are open to change and committed to innovation. Instead of trying to minimize or resist change, these organizations encourage and nurture change and learn how to manage it so that they can take advantage of the opportunities it presents. Therefore, all change efforts should be viewed as ongoing and continuous experiments that can produce learnings useful for the design and implementation of further change.

Mohrman and Cummings (1989, p. 107) characterize the process as "action learning"—that is, as "a process where organizational members try out new behaviors, processes, and structures; assess them; and make necessary modifications." In essence, the action-learning approach treats the change process as an experiment in which ideas, theories, hypotheses, and informed guesses are tested in the real world of organizational life. Therefore, organizational change should be implemented in a way that enables implementers to learn from the consequences of their actions. The results of these action-learning experiments are examined. If they diverge significantly from what was expected or desired, actions and plans can be modified on the basis of what was learned from these analyses, and the actions and plans can be tried again. When they are finally successful, the learnings can be applied to subsequent steps, which may increase in complexity and scope. This process continues until all the changes are implemented successfully.

The process does not progress in linear fashion from a well-defined beginning to an equally well-defined end, particularly when a change involves teams and technology. Because technology and organizational environments are constantly changing, the process is never really complete. It continues indefinitely as the organization strives for a competitive technological advantage and adapts to or tries to shape an increasingly turbulent environment. Throughout the project, things change—the business strategy, the environment, the technology, the work design—and the project team may need to pause, step back or sideways, or even go off in an entirely different direction. The team may eventually end up with an outcome quite different from what was originally intended.

It is not difficult to find examples of organizational change projects that have used an action-learning approach. A consumer foods company used this approach in designing new greenfield manufacturing plants and transforming many of its existing plants into high-performance work systems. After the initial vision was developed, employee task forces in the plants designed key elements of the new work systems and used the feedback from periodic assessments to refine their designs (Ledford and Mohrman, 1993). An oil and gas company used an action-learning approach to revise its performance-management system. After the new system was implemented, the company collected internal assessment data and external benchmark data to refine its design and improve its alignment with other human resources systems.

The implications of this action-learning process go well beyond the boundaries of particular projects. The experience of one project conducted in this manner will make it easier for the next project, and so on. Eventually, the organization will develop the ability to implement increasingly complex innovations with less disruption and greater success. The end result, therefore, is not only better designs and interventions resulting from specific projects but also enhanced knowledge about and skills for implementing change in general, regardless of the particular change being implemented.

Emerging Approaches to Systems Development

New and emerging approaches to systems development illustrate these new change processes well. Rapid application development (RAD) is the general rubric under which these various approaches, methods, models, and techniques fall. They go by such names as *spiral work flow, iterative prototyping,* and *joint application development* (JAD), to mention just a few of the most widely used. The following description of the spiral work flow model captures the critical elements of this new approach to systems development (see Figure 12.4):

> You combine process definition, functional design, interface design, and application development into a series of overlapping spirals, each one including the involvement and sign-off of the application's end-users. You cycle through each spiral in overlapping parallel, rather than in serial, steps. And you don't iterate once: you run through the process at least three or four times. The resulting applications are designed faster [and] deployed sooner, map directly to the business process, deliver immediate business benefits, and are simpler to improve and less costly to maintain [Seybold, 1994, p. 2].

Figure 12.4. Spiral Work-Flow Model of System Development.

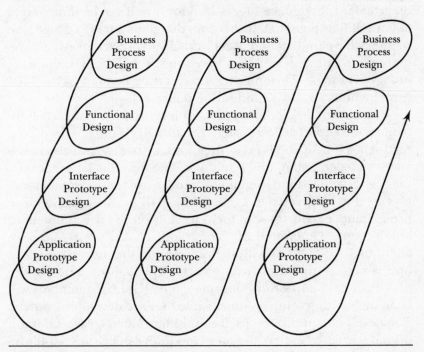

Source: Adapted from Seybold, 1994, p. 2.

Iterative prototyping is critical to this entire process; it is the common element in almost all the new approaches to systems development. Prototypes provide potential users with an opportunity to actually experience the work in progress—that is, to "see, feel, and touch" aspects of the systems and tools they will eventually use in their work (Carey and Currey, 1989, p. 30). This is especially important when the purpose of the system is not just to automate what the users are already doing but also to enable them to do new things. The possibilities offered by new systems will be little more than abstractions to users in the early stages of a project. What better way to get a handle on just what the new system has to offer than to try out a preliminary version and see what it can do—and what users can do with it when they apply it to their work?

Prototypes can help users expand their horizons beyond immediate needs and existing technologies. In effect, prototypes make the abstract concrete. A prototype provides users with the opportunity to explore the system's potential, give feedback based on actual use, and make suggestions for how it can be modified to better fulfill its potential. It also gives designers a way to gauge how well they have understood users' verbally expressed needs and requirements and how well they have interpreted them in the technology prototype. This information can then be used by the MDI team members to revise and refine their work.

Concurrent development of modules is another critical feature of most RAD approaches. Systems can usually be broken down into relatively self-contained sets of functions, or *modules,* which are relatively independent of other modules. The individual modules can then be developed independently and concurrently. Not all modules need to be developed at once. The MDI team—using iterative prototyping, of course—can focus initially on the development of only a couple. Other modules can be added as the project takes on additional staff, and as both the project and the user teams move up the new-technology learning curve. Throughout much of the middle to later portions of this stage, the MDI team members will be implementing some modules while they are developing others. The development process itself should be guided by agreed-upon overall standards so that all system modules can be successfully integrated over time and remain open-ended for future modifications and extensions.

The following example, based on a project in a large international nonprofit organization, illustrates this new, more flexible approach to systems development.

The project involved the development of a new, integrated system for acquiring, processing, and disseminating data on economic and social conditions in various regions of the world. The new system was planned as a modular, user-driven system that would enable users to choose the applications and tools that best suited their tasks, to modify the way these applications and tools functioned, and to integrate compatible external products (existing and future) into their work.

The development strategy involved two converging tracks, referred to by the development team as the "technology" track and the "substantive" track. The technology track included all those activities concerned chiefly with the development of the system's core components. These activities were independent of specific end-user applications, which were the main focus of the activities in the substantive track. User representatives were to be only minimally involved in the activities of the technology track, but they were to be intensively involved in the substantive track, working closely with systems experts to develop application prototypes for exploring various design options and their potential uses.

Each track involved three stages. In general, the first two stages in each track would proceed independently, although high-level decision making and consultation would be conducted across tracks throughout the entire effort, particularly during the first stage. The teams and the products of the two tracks would be merged in the third stage, to produce a prototype of the complete system for pilot testing. After pilot testing, the prototype would be modified, implemented, and tested again. This process would be repeated until the development team felt that the system was ready for rollout to the rest of the organization.

In this example we can see all the critical elements of the RAD approach. The system is divided into separate core and application modules, which are then developed concurrently. Users are intensively involved in the process, especially in application development. And, perhaps most important, prototypes are used throughout to test designs, elicit user feedback, and generate new ideas and uses for the system.

Organizations adopting rapid application development—including GTE, CIGNA, UPS, General Motors, American Airlines, and Andersen Consulting, among others—are discovering its many benefits. As the name implies, one benefit is speed. Another is cost. Redesign of a system in the final stages of development is far more costly and time-consuming than having a prototype reveal problems early on. User feedback based on experience with prototypes produces another benefit—systems that more closely match users' needs. Finally, the iterative nature of the process means that technological innovations and changing business conditions can more easily be incorporated into designs and plans as they emerge.

Creating a Culture of Change

This iterative, adaptive, learning approach can be applied to all new design processes in organizations. For example, Takeuchi and Nonaka apply this model to new-product development, urging organizations to "stop running the relay race and take up rugby," the metaphor they use to compare traditional sequential approaches to newer, iterative ones (Takeuchi and Nonaka, 1986, p. 137). As in systems development, the benefits of these team-based, cross-functional processes are speed, cost, and innovation—in other words, getting to market faster with competitive products.

Organizations may be understandably resistant to adopting these new change processes. Most large-scale change efforts require significant commitments of energy and time, as well as large sums of money. As a result, there are enormous pressures to get it right the first time. But "right" may well end up being far less than what could have been achieved, and not enough to justify the costs of the effort. Furthermore, for there to be any learning from change efforts, their effectiveness should be evaluated frequently so that designs and implementation plans can be modified as necessary. The problem is that most people, work units, and organizations feel threatened by the prospect of having their work evaluated. Often they are afraid that they will appear incompetent and be punished for their apparent inadequacies. To overcome these fears, they need to feel secure that they will be given the time, resources, and opportunity to learn how to do better.

To be successful, the organization needs to create a culture that supports risk taking, tolerates occasional failures, and enables all the individuals and units involved in change efforts to learn from experience. The organization's senior management needs to instill this culture by creating systems for ongoing assessment and evaluation, by rewarding innovative behavior and not just successful outcomes, and by disseminating information about successful projects throughout the organization so that others can learn from these efforts.

User Reinvention

A central element of almost all the emerging approaches to change is the ongoing involvement of those who will be most affected by the changes and who are the most knowledgeable about its likely day-to-day impacts. This element has already come up in our discussions of user team representatives on the MDI team and the use of prototypes.

There is yet a third, especially powerful form of user involvement, one that often gets overlooked because it is an unplanned result of enlightened hands-off management rather than an intentional outcome of hands-on design. Researchers, managers, and others have often observed that workers may change or reinvent their work when new technologies are introduced into the workplace. The technology presents an opportunity—in some cases an imperative—to develop new processes, identify new tasks and responsibilities, and even modify the technology itself (see, for example, Rice and Rogers, 1980; Bikson and Eveland, 1986; Leonard-Barton, 1988; Von Hippel, 1988). Reinvention can take several forms, including modification of the technology, of the task, of the job, and of the tasks, structure, and mission of the team. As we will see in what follows, the end result of this serendipitous process can often be surprisingly productive.

Tool, Task, and Job Reinvention

Tool reinvention usually happens as users gain experience with a new technology, begin to recognize its implications, and discover what it can and cannot do in its existing form. As Tyre and Orlikowski note

(1994, p. 98), "New technologies are almost never perfect upon initial introduction. Instead, users' efforts to apply technologies reveal problems and contingencies that were not apparent before introduction. . . . These problems, in turn, require adaptation of the technologies already in use." Tool reinvention often goes hand in hand with task or job reinvention; one can lead to the other, which in turn can then reinforce the first. And, given the close interrelationship between knowledge-based tasks and information technologies, the distinction is often hard to make.

Often when new technologies are introduced into the workplace, certain individuals unintentionally reinvent their tasks, and even their jobs, by becoming de facto IT experts and trainers for their co-workers. They are the individuals who seem to be particularly interested in and facile with their new information tools. They are the ones who come to work early or stay late to "play" with the new system. They master the basic operations of the system before anyone else does, and then they move on to more advanced functions and applications. These local experts or "gurus" often think of new ways to use the system and modify it to do new things. Their co-workers increasingly turn to them for help in learning how to get the most out of their new technology. In time the local experts will be the first to recognize the limits of the existing system and lead the way in developing upgrades, or even new systems, to meet the evolving needs of their units. As experts in both the technology and in their teams' tasks and responsibilities, they can provide a previously unavailable but now indispensable service to their teammates.

In what may be the most familiar example of job reinvention, the secretaries of the 1970s and before have evolved into information assistants, coordinators, and managers. In the early 1980s, computers and word processors enabled managers and professionals to type their own letters, reports, and documents, and voice mail in the 1990s has enabled them to take their own messages. In response to these technological developments, innovative and resourceful secretaries have reinvented their jobs. Instead of typing and taking messages, they control documents, organize databases, service printers and copiers, and teach others (including the managers and professionals for whom they used to type) how to use the new technology. What was reinvention by a few in the 1980s has become a formal job description for almost all in the 1990s (Johnson and Rice, 1986).

Team Reinvention

If team members are highly interdependent, reinventions by one member can lead to reciprocal and complementary reinventions by others. Eventually these individual reinventions may reach a critical mass. At that point the team can decide to redefine and reallocate tasks among its members and then redesign its structure to better accommodate and support these new tasks. In other words, the team can reinvent itself. Such was the case at XYZ, Inc. (a fictitious name for an actual company), when new information tools enabled several work groups to take on new tasks and responsibilities and even widen or redefine their missions:

> The Industrial Engineering department has redefined its mission to take in work "where the rubber meets the road." That is, making use of technical skills within its own staff, it is helping other work groups adapt information systems in unique ways to address specific business objectives, filling a serious gap that could not have otherwise been closed by existing information support services. The corporate IT department was unwilling to devote their resources to address such specific, short-term needs, so team members from Industrial Engineering stepped in to provide technical assistance. Nobody foresaw this need in the early stages of the project, and it would otherwise have gone unfulfilled if Industrial Engineering had not reinvented their mission and if management had not permitted this reinvention to occur.
>
> The sales department also used the opportunities presented by new information tools to redefine its mission. By using portable computers, it was able to turn sales visits to customers, usually supermarkets, into data-based consultations. The sales representative would use the computers to download data about a range of relevant products (XYZ's and their competitors') from commercial data bases to help customers analyze the potential profitability of different allocations of shelf space for various products. Instead of just selling a product, they now saw themselves as "information teams," providing their customers with useful knowledge and reinforcing XYZ's ties to their customers in the process [Bikson, Stasz, and Mankin, 1985, p. 47].

The Reinvention Dilemma and What Organizations Can Do

Reinvention has its downside. Users can get so absorbed in exploring the potential of the technology and testing the boundaries of their jobs that they neglect their formal job responsibilities. Not surprisingly, many organizations, managers, and technologists try to discourage reinvention because they fear that it will compromise the efficiency of the technology and the work process.

Others recognize the vitality and potential of reinvention and try to find ways to encourage and channel it into productive directions. Organizational theorist Claudio Ciborra, for example, urges organizations to encourage and support the reinvention process (he calls it *bricolage*, French for "tinkering") so that "new ideas from the bottom of the organization [can] bubble up" (Ciborra, 1991, p. 189). And "the more volatile the markets and the technologies, the more likely it is that effective solutions will be embedded in everyday experience and local knowledge. This is the petri dish for tinkering; here creative applications that have strategic impact will be invented, engineered, and tried out" (p. 288).

What should organizations do? The first thing they can do is recognize what many elementary school and kindergarten teachers have long known: that the most successful learning often takes place in the context of play rather than work. Translating this insight to the world of work means that people learn best how to use a new technology when they have the opportunity to explore its capabilities and potential—in other words, to play with it.

If given the chance, users will experiment with their new technology to see what new people they can communicate with, what databases they can access, and what functions and operations it offers. As a result, they will be able to apply these new features to their work—to do it better, easier, and faster. One of the consequences of this process is a more effective integration of people with their tools. With the familiarity and the sense of mastery that accompany play, the separation between users and their tools begin to blur. The tool becomes an intrinsic extension of the users' capabilities and enables them, depending on the nature of their tools, to exert more force, see better, work more precisely, and so on.

The same merging process can also happen with new tools for information and communication. Users play with them, gaining mastery and familiarity as they do so. The web of their collaboration spreads, the information that informs their work becomes richer, and their analytical capabilities both broaden and deepen. As they adapt their tasks to their tools, and vice versa, processes and interactions flow more naturally. In effect, the users have psychologically merged with their tools, which have become an intrinsic extension of the users' cognitive and intellectual capabilities. The end result is not only smarter, more efficient work but also new kinds of work that can transform businesses and create entire new industries. One need only look to the rapidly expanding multimedia and Internet service industries to witness the transformative power of play.

Unfortunately, users cannot play with their new technology and use it to reinvent their tasks, teams, jobs, and tools if they are under pressure to get work out. Therefore, whenever possible, organizations and managers should build some slack time into daily schedules and change efforts in order to give users the psychological space they need to explore and experiment with their new ways of working. The problem is that this runs counter to the culture of downsizing, where less is more and where being lean is as important to corporations as it is to movie stars. But the performance results from downsizing have been disappointing (Cascio, 1995), and innovative companies are beginning to take a different approach (Lawler, 1996). They are focusing on building the capabilities of their most important resource—people. One of the best ways to do that is to encourage users to experiment with their new tools and work designs, to explore the possibilities they offer, and to learn how to use them for doing things they have not been able to do before.

Eventually, encouragement should be supplemented by more tangible rewards. This may be especially important for local experts, who rightly see their particular form of job reinvention as critical to the long-term effectiveness of their work units. Therefore, organizations should consider implementing competency-based pay systems, for example, that reward local experts with bonuses or pay raises for acquiring new IT skills. Opportunities for learning and professional development can also be rewarding for local experts. For example, liaison and dotted-line relationships with the corporate IT function can enhance local experts' access to technical seminars and colleagues. Temporary assignments and job rotation into the IT department can further develop their skills and their networks of contacts.

Those organizations with the foresight and flexibility to support the boundary-busting initiative and creativity of their more inventive employees will reap significant benefits. Cost-savings and quality improvements are the most obvious benefits; new products and services that emerge as users tinker with the technology and push the envelopes of their jobs are the most dramatic. The problem is that nurturing play and reinvention may go against the grain in many companies, but for those that can align their cultures, programs, structures, and policies in support of these activities, the potential payoffs will be well worth the effort.

Conclusions

Many of the chapters in this book have argued that the future belongs to those organizations that can learn how to harness the power of technology-enabled collaboration. Designing more effective teams, developing more useful information tools, creating organizational contexts that support teamwork and innovation, and, most important, merging all three activities into high-performance work systems—these are the keys to competitive advantage in the twenty-first century. In this chapter we have argued that getting there will require a new way of thinking about change, as well as new approaches to the processes that make change happen. It will also require developing new kinds of skills, attitudes, and behaviors in the people who will work for and with these new organizations.

The boundary-spanning nature of the technology puts a premium on people who can work effectively with others of different backgrounds, different work experiences, different knowledge bases, and different skills. They also need to be facilitators, not resisters, of change. Flexible, tolerant of uncertainty and ambiguity, able to communicate and collaborate across functional boundaries, willing to take risks, and able to learn from the risks that do not pan out—these are the kinds of people who can create success in organizations today, as well as in the twenty-first century.

Many organizations will devote much effort and considerable resources to finding new people who have these skills and attitudes, but a better approach may be to explore ways of developing these capabilities in all employees. An obvious place to begin is with training programs that develop common languages. With new information technology spreading into just about every corner of almost every organization, the basic concepts of IT are as universal a language as can be found in organizations today. In developing cross-functional skills it is also important to teach individuals about dealing with conflict and functional diversity (as well as with ethnic and racial diversity) and to sensitize them to interpersonal and group dynamics.

Competency-based pay systems can be used to motivate employees to take advantage of these training opportunities. In addition, creating lateral career paths that enable people to move from one project team or business unit to another would periodically expose them to new people, functions, and perspectives. An especially relevant example of lateral career paths is offered by technology guru Peter Keen (1991). To cultivate the kinds of people who can bridge the cultural gap between the IT department and the business units it serves, Keen recommends that individuals from IT departments be selected and assigned to business departments or teams for periods ranging from six months to two years. Eventually they will return to their original departments with broadened perspectives, knowledge, and skills. Perhaps most important, they will have developed a more collaborative and client-focused approach to their work, and this new focus can lead in turn, as Markus and Robey note (1995, p. 607), to "a more thorough understanding by both parties of the problem being addressed and the solution being designed." Lateral moves to IT departments on the part of local experts would also help develop cross-functional capabilities and more effective, business-focused information systems.

These are just a few of the ways in which organizations can change their practices, programs, and policies to help create a culture of change. Others are described in other chapters throughout this book. This culture of change—of continuous improvement—provides a foundation for high performance and competitive advantage. The organization that successfully creates a culture of change will be the one most likely to survive and thrive in the emerging information-and knowledge-based economy of the twenty-first century.

Chapter Thirteen

Accelerating Organizational Learning During Transition

Ramkrishnan V. Tenkasi
Susan Albers Mohrman
Allan M. Mohrman Jr.

In this world of constant change, the only sustainable competitive advantage is an organization's capacity to learn (Senge, 1990). Organizations are changing to become dramatically more responsive to customers, efficient, fast, and flexible. Critical core competencies such as lean manufacturing, process improvement, customer focus, concurrent engineering, and integrated process management underpin the ability of the organization to deliver products and services quickly, efficiently, and responsively. Competencies such as networking, partnering, lateral management, and organizational self-design underpin the flexibility required in the dynamic environment. In order to grow in increasingly competitive markets, organizations must generate and respond to unanticipated competitive directions. To do this, they must be able to reconfigure themselves as needed: to apply resources where they are needed, shift arrays of projects and activities, establish temporary and lasting partnerships, and maintain relationships with a variety of customers who prefer to do business in different ways.

All this requires new organizational architectures: "Those companies that are creative in designing new organizational architectures will be those that gain significant competitive advantage in this new era of change" (Nadler, 1992, p. 8). Transformation has become a major organizational activity as organizations try to adapt to their new environmental realities. A major leadership challenge has been to guide organizations through the transition process (Bennis and Nanus, 1985; Tichy and Devanna, 1986).

In transforming themselves, organizations are faced with two dilemmas. First, we know that organizational transformation is a long, involved process, and yet the environment is demanding flexibility and speed. Second, organizational learning is often an accumulation of many small, incremental changes that spring up as units design and redesign themselves (Weick and Westley, 1996; Levitt and March, 1988), and yet dramatic impacts on the overall capability of the organization depend on the simultaneous accomplishment of change in many of the aspects of the way the organization functions (Ledford, Mohrman, Mohrman, and Lawler, 1989). For example, the establishment of a team-based organization requires far more than the creation of teams; it also calls for changes in information systems, rewards, management positions and roles, and other aspects of the organizational context within which teams are performing units (Mohrman, Cohen, and Mohrman, 1995). In embarking on the transition to becoming team-based, organizations go through a gradual and profound learning process about how to bring the many aspects of organizational architecture into alignment with this new way of doing work. Even when these are company-initiated changes, teams learn to become effective at varying rates. The challenge facing organizations is twofold: to put core architectures in place that are themselves flexible and that promote the continuous and intense learning that will be required for an organization to succeed in today's environment, and to develop the internal capability for ongoing self-design and accelerated learning.

This chapter is based on close study of many organizations as they have gone through a fundamental transformation in their organizational model and of the factors that contribute to accelerated learning during such transitions. We begin by conceptualizing the learning challenges inherent in these transitions as changes in three related areas—strategic/market architecture, technical architecture, and social architecture—and by focusing on the cognitive, behavioral, and structural changes that are required. We then describe the dynamics that characterize organizational learning as organizations change their underlying architectures.

Architectural Change and Organizational Learning

Many organizations today are undergoing large-scale transitions in which they are purposefully introducing fundamental change into the way they are organized and the way they do business. This kind of change entails the establishment of new organizational architectures that shape and enable new ways of performing. Crafting and successfully implementing such change involves considerable organizational learning. In our experience of studying organizational change, we repeatedly hear people say, "We changed the organization, but behavior didn't change" or "We restructured the organization, but performance stayed the same." Thus the organization changed some of its formal attributes but did not succeed in changing the underlying patterns of behavior. Another recurring phenomenon in organizations undergoing large-scale change is that some units seem more able than others to learn how to operate effectively in the new directions. This phenomenon makes us very interested in how organizations learn to operate differently. It also leads us to believe that the phenomenon of organizational learning occurs at least in part within individual operating units, even when the stimulus for learning is a company-initiated change process.

There are many competing frameworks for understanding organizational learning. These frameworks include those that reduce organizational learning to the learning of individuals within the organization (see, for example, Argyris and Schön, 1978; Kolb, 1984; McGill, Slocum, and Lei, 1993). There are also frameworks that focus on particular activities, such as TQM and training (Ulrich, Von Glinow, and Jick, 1993), as well as frameworks that look at generic competencies like shared vision, team learning, and mental models (Senge, 1990). In trying to understand the learning that occurs during organizational transition, we choose to think of organizational learning as a collective phenomenon, one in which organizations put in place new approaches that enable them to perform more effectively and improve performance over time. This broad definition allows us to reconceive organizational transformation as a learning process and to search for the processes that allow the organization to establish new and better ways of functioning and achieving its objectives in a dynamic, complex environment.

Substantively, organizational transformations frequently aim at putting new organizational architectures in place. Organizational architecture is a metaphor and a concept that has been gaining prominence in the organizational design literature (Keidel, 1995; Nadler, Gerstein, Shaw, and Associates, 1992). The term *architecture,* as originated by the Greeks, referred to something higher than mere structure; it was intended to denote a superstructure (Keidel, 1995). Architecture can be thought of as creating a framework around one's life through the shaping of space and thereby creating opportunities for certain kinds of views, movements, and actions while constraining others (Rasmussen, 1991, p. 10). In the organizational literature, the term has been used to refer to a framework for the conduct of organizational life. Gerstein (1992) suggests that organizational architecture is the shaping of organizational space to meet human needs and aspirations. Nadler (1992) has presented a systemic view of organizational architecture as consisting of the various systems, structures, management processes, technologies, and strategies that make up the 'modus operandi' of the firm.

The concept of organizational architecture is connected to the concept of organizational design, which is the process of "bringing about a coherence between the goals or purposes for which the organization exists, the patterns of division of labor and interunit coordination and the people who will do the work" (Galbraith, 1977, p. 5). In keeping with Galbraith's use of the term, we use *design* to refer to the process of determining how the organization will be configured. The word *architecture* we use to refer to the configurations and processes that result.

Applying the notion of design to organizations raises to consciousness the fact that organizational architectures are purposeful artifacts that "embody goal-oriented operational principles specified for them by the person or persons who contrived them. The specification of the purposes and operational principles of artifacts is essentially a human activity, and it is this activity that sets out the criteria for success or failure of that artifact" (Turner, 1992, p. 369). Galbraith (1977) argues that organization designs that explicitly relate strategy and purpose to decisions about their architecture outperform organizations where patterns of activity simply emerge as a result of personal interactions. Designers have certain intentions that are related to the strategy of the organization and the kind of performance that needs to be delivered, and they generate architectures that embody a logic, or chain of reasoning, concerned with how particular architectures will yield intended patterns of behavior.

Today's organizational transformations are simultaneously having an impact on almost all aspects of the organization's architecture. To understand the richness of the changes that are going on, we have identified three coexisting and intersecting architectures:

1. *Strategic/market architecture* is the organization's patterns and practices for relating to its business and market environment. This architecture includes the elements of the organization's market strategy, its customer and supplier relationships, and its financial model. There are some commonly used elements of emerging strategic/market architectures:

- Establishing partnerships with customers and suppliers
- Outsourcing nonstrategic functions
- Using product strategies that rely on rapid generation of new products, which essentially cannibalize old offerings
- Offering families of related products and services rather than stand-alone products
- Taking work to the customer's location

In the case of partnering with customers, an underlying logic may be that growth in the organization's business depends on growth in its customer's business, and so the likelihood of growth in the organization's business can be increased if the organization partners with its customer to deliver greater overall value to end customers.

2. *Technical architecture* encompasses the choices that the organization makes with respect to accomplishing the technical transformation processes that deliver value to its customers. This architecture includes technical know-how, tools, methods, processes, routines, problem-solving strategies and steps, and related technical artifacts that underlie the core transformation process. Various computer-based systems, such as application software, groupware, networks, and shared databases, are often components of an organization's technical architecture. Advanced manufacturing technologies—flexible manufacturing systems, concurrent

engineering, and computer-aided design, manufacturing, and engineering—represent emerging directions of technical architecture. An underlying logic of concurrent engineering is that if tasks that used to be done sequentially (for example, product marketing followed by design and development of the product followed by development of a manufacturing process) can be done concurrently, then these activities can inform one another in real time, which will prevent rework and enable much faster cycle time.

3. *Social architecture* embodies those organizational design choices that structure and provide the context for interactions and behavior in the organization. This architecture includes the designation of such organizing features as units, levels, coordinating mechanisms, authority structures, and performance-management practices (which include reward systems). Flat organizations, multi-functional units, team accountability, business performance–based rewards, distributed information and authority, and lateral coordinating mechanisms represent emerging directions of social architecture. An underlying logic of the flat, cross-functional business-unit structure is that a business unit with all the skills for carrying out a piece of the business can be given authority, act quickly in meeting immediate needs, and be held accountable for its performance.

An important component of all three facets of organizational architecture is the norms and values that underpin them. For example, a strong value and behavioral norm of collaboration and cooperation must underpin a market architecture that emphasizes partnerships with customers. A value of market success for the product and norms of cross-functional collaboration must underpin concurrent engineering. The value of employee involvement and development and norms of power sharing must underlie a social architecture that creates flat, empowered business units. Herein lies part of the reason why the learning that accompanies transformation is so difficult: the organization is learning not just to put a new architecture in place but also to make the new architecture work effectively. In this effort, the design artifacts are not the only important element (although they do in fact set a context that makes certain kinds of behavior more likely and enables new norms to develop); organizational learning also occurs when elements of deep culture (language, behavioral routines, and values) change. These deep-culture elements are often embedded and automatic and have come to possess an aura of naturalness. Therefore, they are taken for granted and seen as immutable givens when in fact they constitute the background conditions for all organizational interpretation, action, and behavior; thus they are less susceptible to direct intervention and alteration (Ciborra and Schneider, 1992; Sandelands and Stablein, 1987; Drazin and Sandelands, 1992).

Successfully implementing new organizational architectures requires the establishment of new *webs of shared meaning* that shape the interpretation of organizational situations, inform action and behavior, and underpin ongoing design decisions. The logics underpinning choice in architectural features are not always immediately self-evident to the people in an organization, and failure to understand or accept the meanings embedded in organizational changes often correlates with faulty implementation.

As Figure 13.1 shows, particular architectures are enacted through changes in cognitions, behaviors, and local structuring that occur throughout the organization (Drazin and Sandelands, 1992). The term *cognitions* refers to mental models consisting of concepts and beliefs connected with action-outcome relationships, mental models that actors use to identify relevant issues, frame problems, and understand situations, other actors, and the envi-

Figure 13.1. Learning Domains of Organizational Transition.

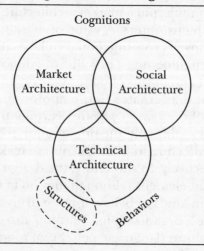

Cognitions

Market Architecture

Social Architecture

Technical Architecture

Structures

Behaviors

ronment. The term *behaviors* refers to how actors conduct themselves alone and with one another to get work done. *Local structuring* refers to arrangements and patterns of practice that a unit establishes to do its work. These may or may not conform to any formal, prescribed structure, and they may include local adaptations and extensions of a prescribed structure. Thus, for example, an architecture that calls for partnering with customers requires members of local partnering units to develop cognitive understanding of how partnering can lead to benefits for both organizations. It requires collaborative behaviors (such as information sharing and joint problem solving) and the establishment of active social structures (such as teams, information connections, and/or linking roles) at the local level.

There are both prescribed and emergent aspects of organizational architectures. Both are critical to the success of large-scale change, and both are integral to organizational learning. During times of turbulence demanding fundamental organizational change, large organizational units, such as corporations or the businesses within them, are having to radically change the way they function as macrostructures. Ironically, this kind of change may include the creation of a corporate architecture that permits great amounts of local autonomy, as well as variation in the architectures of the corporation's different business units—and, for an organization making the transition from a centralized, uniform architecture, even the architecture to permit diversity will need to be designed. Furthermore, even networked organizations manage some key strategic assets centrally (assets like knowledge, management skills, financial systems, and so forth). Therefore, the relation of the whole to the parts calls for the crafting of some organizationwide architectural features.

Successful transition also depends on the ability of many units of the organization to take up the new directions, establish local practices that will make the new directions a reality, and continue achieving and improving performance outcomes over time. For example, Brown and Duguid (1991) in their study of Xerox repair technicians, found that these technicians, on the basis of "learning by doing" (or what these authors call "situated invention and innovation"), developed new repair procedures different from those prescribed in repair manuals, invented new ways of working with each other and with customers, and found unique modes of sharing knowledge with one another. Indeed, the purpose embedded in many organizational changes is to create architectures that make it more likely for this kind of local learning to occur.

Weick (1993) has criticized the use of the architectural metaphor because he sees it as leading to a rather limited conceptualization of the design process as a bounded activity occurring at one point in time and focusing primarily on structure. This critique evidently stems from the vernacular use of the term *architecture* in reference to buildings (which literally are set in concrete and stone). Nevertheless, Weick also argues for the creation of organizational designs that make it more likely for local learning to occur. Our experience has been that many organizations going through fundamental transitions do go through major redesign efforts that include structural reconfiguration, but architectures also undergo continuous minor shifts as local units learn and engage in self-design. Moreover, local units operating within a broader large-scale transformation frequently generate novel approaches that ultimately may be disseminated throughout the organization. Therefore, we find the architectural metaphor useful because it enables a simultaneous focus on the overall configuration of the organization and on the forms that emerge in different units. This view even has currency in connection with the actual architecture of buildings, which have been observed to "learn" in much the same way as we have seen organizations learn (Brand, 1994).

Learning Challenges: An Illustration

Many companies are currently making the transition from an integrated, functionally organized architecture to an architecture that consists of multiple cross-functional business units, each of which has responsibility for delivering products or services to customers. We will discuss this kind of transition as a way of illustrating the nature of the organizational learning challenges inherent in large-scale transformations that involve the establishment of fundamentally different architectures. There are of course a number of different kinds of architectural changes going on today (see Chapters Three, Four, and Five, this volume, for more discussion of several of them). The choice of the transition to a business-unit structure will serve as our example here, but that choice does not in any way suggest this as the architecture of choice for any particular organization. Nevertheless, because the establishment of agile, flat, self-contained business units is occurring as part of many transitions today, that kind of architecture seems an appropriate focus for this illustration.

The nature of the transition to a business-unit organization is depicted in Figure 13.2. The business-unit organization might be a program, in the case of an aerospace or defense firm; a product unit, in the case of a consumer electronics firm; or a customer service team, in the case of a financial services firm. A business-unit style of social architecture might be put in place along with an integrated technical architecture linking the work of various disciplines through common databases and applications and making concurrent technical work possible. Simultaneously, a new market architecture might be designed, one that aims at achieving a new level of customer focus or even a partnership with customers. For example, it might include customers on program teams or new-product development teams, or it might establish key-account links or customer advisory boards in order to create more responsive links to customers.

Figure 13.2. Organizational Transition.

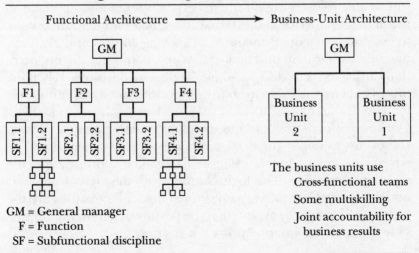

Functional Architecture → Business-Unit Architecture

GM = General manager
F = Function
SF = Subfunctional discipline

The business units use
Cross-functional teams
Some multiskilling
Joint accountability for
business results

This set of changes might be crafted by a design team responsible for generating an organizational design that can achieve a changeable business strategy relying on superior customer service and on local flexibility in meeting customers' needs. The design team may go through a learning process that entails exposure to what other companies are doing, internal diagnostic and input-generating activities, and exposure to organizational design or process-reengineering frameworks (Mohrman and Cummings, 1989). The team might generate an organizational "blueprint" as a product of learning processes enabling the creation of discontinuous change that truly embodies a new logic.

The logic underpinning the functional organization is a bureaucratic one: its form is justified by the need to maintain disciplinary expertise, to have people supervised by individuals with the same expertise, to create standard processes that enable efficiency and the orderly introduction of process improvements, and to have integration occur at higher levels in the organization, where people have visibility into the larger picture. The argument is that if these conditions are maintained, the organization will gain maximum efficiency and control over work processes, which in turn will lead to predictable organizational performance.

The business-unit organization embodies a different logic. The logic here is that if a single unit contains all the skills and knowledge to perform a whole piece of the organization's work, then that unit will be able to carry out all the necessary operations and make all the necessary internal and external adjustments for delivering value to customers in a timely manner. By moving control into performing units rather than into managerial and staff units, the organization can avoid costly delays and nonresponsive decisions. When the unit is held accountable for business performance and not simply for technical accomplishment of tasks, work decisions are more likely to take account of multiple and sometimes conflicting systemic outcomes (for example, financial, technical, and customer-related focuses), and any trade-offs are more likely to be appropriate to the situation in question. This logic contrasts with the logic of the functional organization: that organizational business measures are the purview of management, and that the performing units are responsible for their own internal process measures.

Our work with design teams indicates that they are often able to adopt this new logic and to envision an organization that works according to these different principles. There is often a period, however, in which design teams work according to both logics, and they may make decisions that reflect an inability to fully abandon the comfort of the old model. Moreover, political pressure from organizational incumbents may lead to design compromises that weaken the new model and result in an organizational plan that contains conflicting logics and elements of both architectures. Nevertheless, organizational leaders frequently agree on the image of a business-unit organization and set out to implement it, and this is the point where true organizational learning must occur; the organization will have learned only when it has established new approaches that allow it to perform more effectively against its own target aspirations. Until their implementation, the new architectures are abstractions and blueprints; the reality of putting them in place and establishing the new ways of operating is still ahead. The design team may have learned something, but the organization cannot be said to have learned until this learning becomes embodied in the organization.

Within the logic that underpins the new architecture, it is a relatively straightforward process for the design team to describe the new attributes of the system at a level of minimal specification. In fact, the ease with which this transition can be described masks the magnitude of the transition. The transition consists of putting in place many artifacts to support the new way of operating: new measurement systems, information systems, roles and positions, coordination devices, skills and understandings, and performance-management processes like goal setting and rewards, to name a few. Some of these may be envisioned by the design team at the outset; the need for other architectural elements may be discovered only as the organization proceeds through the processes of implementation and learning. Thus the specification of a "blueprint" for change simply begins the process of architectural design, and leads to a number of iterative design processes, each of which requires the development of new ways of thinking and the determination of new approaches and organizational artifacts. Consequently, each of these iterative design processes requires learning by design teams, and implementation requires organizational learning (Mohrman and Cummings, 1989).

The change from functional to business-unit organization strikes (as do most changes in organizational architecture) at the very heart of the existing culture of the organization—its language, organizational artifacts, membership, identity, and action routines. For the change to be successfully implemented, organizational members must learn to think differently about the organization, to behave differently within it, and to carry out new routines with different patterns of interaction. What has struck us in many of the sites we have studied is that the change in logic is so great that it is difficult for people who are not on the design team to accurately capture the reasoning behind the new organization, let alone determine its implications for their own behavior. In other words, they may have trouble with the cognitive and behavioral aspects of the transition. The implementation may also bog down when the local units have to "figure out" how to structure themselves to work effectively in the new architecture, a task made more difficult if the cognitive understanding and behavioral implications are poorly apprehended. Table 13.1 shows some of the cognitive, behavioral, and structural learning that is required for successfully implementation of a business-unit organization.

Cognitive Learning Challenges

People in the mode of accomplishing their technical tasks and interpreting the level of their performance only through the lens of technical effectiveness may have to learn what it means to deliver value to customers. The shift to understanding success from the viewpoint of the customer is truly a cognitive shift. Likewise, to people used to working in a functionally homogeneous setting, the notion of working cross-functionally may be limited to an image of meeting with others to share information. An understanding of cross-functional work as the application of information from multiple disciplinary bases, so as to gain fuller understanding and a better course of action through different work situations, represents cognitive learning. When one is used to thinking of management as something done hierarchically by others, one needs to learn what is meant by self-management. A typical cognitive error

**Table 13.1. Learning Challenges in the
Move from Functional to Business-Unit Organization.**

Areas for New Understanding

Delivering value to customers

Working cross-functionally

Self-management

Being accountable for business results

Areas for New Behavior

Holding team members accountable

Sharing leadership

Soliciting customers' input

Resolving conflicts cross-functionally

Areas for New Structures

Coordinating activities

Tracking and reviewing business performance

Soliciting customers' feedback

Making decisions cross-functionally

is to understand self-management as absence of management. There have also been many examples of business units that were set up and composed of people who had no experience of thinking about business results and who may not even understand what business results are or how they are influenced.

Behavioral Learning Challenges

In the functional organization, an employee is often in the situation of not holding and not expecting to hold co-workers accountable for their pieces of the work; that is the job of supervisors. The business-unit organization relies on lateral coordination and integration, which in turn requires the voicing of mutual expectations and feedback. It also requires the business unit to develop competency in cross-functional conflict resolution because operating across the "thought worlds" of multiple disciplines is fraught with the potential for conflict (Dougherty, 1992). In a cross-functional business unit, leadership tends to move among members according to the issue of concern and the members' various kinds of expertise. If the members of the business unit have had experience only with single-point leadership, then the behavior of sharing leadership flexibly will have to be learned. For example, customer service teams may never have had to solicit customers' input, and so they may not know the questions to ask or even whom to ask.

Structural Learning Challenges

This kind of learning involves finding and applying new ways to create new patterns of behavior (routines) for carrying out the work of the business unit. People who have been individual contributors in the functional organization may have had little experience coordinating their work with that of others, particularly when others perform quite different tasks. Creating flowcharts, setting mutual expectations, developing systems for keeping all the members of a business unit aware of real-time interdependencies, developing a system for soliciting customers' feedback—these are all structured approaches that may have to be learned before coordination can be supported. Moreover, many members of business units may have operated primarily within single functions for most of their lives, and so they will have little experience of making decisions that entail input from multiple knowledge bases. To be effective, they may eventually develop or adopt systematic processes for registering and taking account of others' perspectives and information.

All three of the learning challenges we have just described are true organizational challenges: individual education and training may provide some basic cognitive understanding or behavioral skills, but the cognitive, behavioral, and structural learning that is required in establishing an effective business unit is essentially *organizational* learning and cannot be reduced to the development of individual skills and knowledge. The incorporation of a new architecture changes the way a collective system operates; old routines are replaced by new routines, and this replacement is the essence of organizational learning (Levitt and March, 1988). The study of various units within organizations that are going through this kind of change makes it clear that *units* learn to be effective; no individual can learn effectiveness for a whole unit. The whole unit either "gets it" or does not. It either makes progress in establishing this new way of operating or does not. If the logic of the new architecture is sound, the whole unit either accomplishes performance improvement or does not.

A Model of Organizational Learning During Transition

We have argued that organizational transformations frequently involve the introduction of complex arrays of new architectures, which in turn entail changes in how the organization deals with the marketplace, carries out its technical tasks, and organizes its social architecture to do both. There are organizationwide aspects of this transition, and the organization, in pursuing a new strategy, embarks on some overarching changes, such as reconfiguring its basic building-block units or introducing new systems with the capacity to integrate and distribute information. Nevertheless, effective operation within an organizationwide architecture that is changing also requires each unit to learn. In essence, each unit must design its own local architecture if performance improvement is to result.

Organizational learning occurs at multiple levels: learning has to occur organizationwide as the whole system assumes a new architecture, as well as within and between units as they craft local approaches. Business units may be further composed of teams. These teams must also craft new approaches to doing work. Learning at all levels is needed. Organizationwide learning increases the capability for coordinated action across business units in implementing a strategy and leveraging and focusing the capabilities of the organization. Unit by unit and team by team, learning enables performing units to find new ways to operate in the changing organizational context but in response to local tasks, the local environment, and local opportunities.

Figure 13.3 depicts the cycle of the activities that constitute organizational learning during strategic transitions. It presupposes that the transition supports an organizational strategy and that the

Figure 13.3. Organizational Learning During Transition.

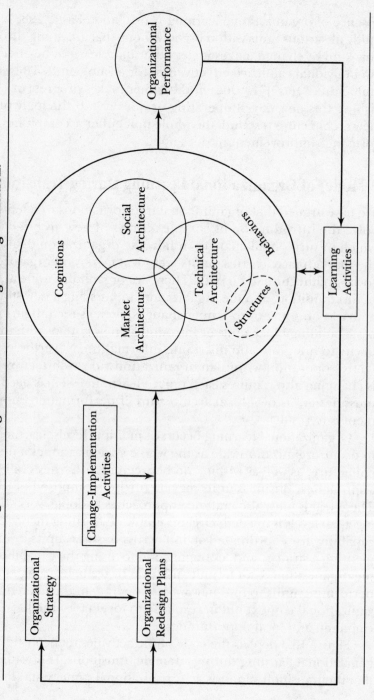

organization is embarking on purposeful changes in its architecture. In the typical strategic transition, there will be some array of organizationwide implementation activities; the essence of change leadership is the crafting of these. These activities focus organizational attention on the new approaches, provide a framework in which the organization can operate, and begin the process of interpretation that is key to the organization's developing shared understandings and letting them emerge. Common organizationwide implementation activities include the crafting and disseminating of a vision or mission statement; the establishment of design teams; the setting up of companywide cascading input, orientation, and education sessions; and the creation of training programs, design manuals, steering committees, and participative planning sessions. These are examples of change interventions that are intended to set up dynamics of learning in the organization.

Organizational Learning Is Iterative

In reality, learning activities are not neat and orderly in the sense of being cleanly masterminded in advance and then rolled out. Some organizations try to do things that way, but an organization rarely begins with a master blueprint; rather, it starts out by identifying key elements of the blueprint (flat structures, self-contained business units, partnerships with customers, integrated information systems) and then sets activities in motion through a series of interventions intended to direct attention and activities toward this high-level blueprint. Transitions occur in fits and starts, with strategic changes leading to organizational changes, and with experience of these changes leading to ongoing learning, which in turn leads to more changes. Organizational leaders and other members cannot fully predict what the organization will look like: "Events are set in motion, but the orderliness they will create remains to be discovered" (Weick, 1993, p. 350). Social designs are abstractions that have to be "made" in the realm of action (Perlmutter and Trist, 1986).

An organization may reconfigure itself as incorporating customer teams, and it may implement a new information system to support a new strategy of customer partnership. The organization may then embark on activities to share and achieve understanding of the new customer-oriented strategy, as well as to help employees develop the skills for operating effectively in teams and using the new information system. The organizational-change challenge is to stimulate the implementation of new market, technical, and social architectures throughout the organization. At the outset, these will exist only as high-level plans. Even putting people into teams does not ensure that they will operate as teams. Providing a new information system does not ensure that people will use it, let alone that they will use it to accomplish the performance gains made possible by greater access to information. The challenge, again, is to *stimulate* the learning that will be required for these architectures to take form and become the true modus operandi of the organization. All the implementation activities that we have enumerated here are intended to be learning activities and learning catalysts for helping organizational members develop new understandings, behave in new ways, and establish new practices.

Throughout the organization there are a multitude of units that are going through these "learning opportunities" with differing levels of interest and skepticism and different intentions. Some are waiting with the expectation that "this too will pass"; others take advantage of the opportunity for actively setting out to learn how to operate effectively in the changing organization and environment. At the local level, units embark on their own learning activities, which may result in their crafting their own local approaches to accomplishing their targets. In so doing, they frequently generate new architectures, which may be variations on a general theme created by the organization.

If organizationwide learning dynamics are in place, there will be good feedback loops so that what is being learned in different units can lead to midcourse corrections in the overall architecture and in the implementation processes that the organization is using. Furthermore, dissemination mechanisms can enable units to learn from each other—to build on each other's learning. Thus an effective learning system to support ongoing organizational transition in a changing environment would consist of ongoing learning processes taking place at multiple levels in the organization and in an iterative manner.

The Ultimate Criterion Is Organizational Performance

Performance is a result of the system's architecture and of behaviors within the organization and with its environment. Feedback about performance stimulates ongoing learning and leads, through a series of changes that represent often small and incremental improvements in the way the system operates, to continual enhancement of the system's capabilities. This feedback-guided learning occurs at the unit level and at the larger organizational level. Gradually, new business units will establish those elements of their local architectures—for example, new routines that take advantage of the information system, enable members to debate more effectively across their disciplinary viewpoints, and build customer feedback into ongoing interactions with customers—that will lead the organization to perform more effectively within its changing context. Gradually, the organization as a whole will establish those elements of an organizationwide architecture—for example, new relationships between central and distributed units, enhanced information systems, new policies that make customer-focused activity and rapid local response possible—that will provide the framework for integrating the organization and for allowing local self-management and self-design. Over time, as new architectures are put in place to enable and enhance performance, the organization will be learning. Ongoing learning is required as the conditions of the environment change and as new routines need to be developed.

If the learning system is working, changes in performance (taking the form of either negative divergences from targets or large improvements in the performance of some units) may gain organizationwide attention and lead to changes in strategy or in the overall architecture of the organization. Negative performance has the potential to generate conflict, which can stimulate dialogue and encourage members to devise solutions by reflecting on and experimenting with their own theories of action and their own behaviors, as well as with how they are organized to do work (Friedlander, 1984). This exploratory behavior may lead to novel architectural solutions. Jumps in performance results may propel further refinement and expansion of approaches that seem to be operating effectively. At the organizational level, attention may be drawn to units that are successful in implementing change and that have accomplished outstanding results. Other units may attempt to learn from them, or the organization may change organizationwide design features or provide support to help other units learn about and adopt successful practices. This has been observed, for example, in companies where units that were early adopters of lean manufacturing techniques achieved such obvious benefits in cost of product that the companies embarked on programs to help other units move in the same direction.

Dynamics of Organizational Learning

The preceding model of learning during transition is, in a sense, a normative one in that it describes how learning needs to happen. In actuality, many transitions abort before new approaches become established ways of doing business, and before it is even possible to determine whether these new approaches would have worked. In these cases, the organization has failed to establish an effective learning system and has not succeeded in establishing new organizational architectures or routines. However, a large number of organizations have persevered through some version of this learning cycle and have learned a new way of operating—in many cases very slowly and with great difficulty.

In today's world, where successful competition calls for rapid and relentless learning, a key question is whether this learning process can be accelerated. The ability to accelerate a process depends on an understanding of the process that one is trying to accelerate. Here we can describe the dynamics that are in place in units where accelerated learning occurs. We have found that a number of conditions distinguish units that quickly learn to establish new approaches and to perform effectively in organizations that are in the midst of strategic change.

Shared Meaning and Self-Design

At the beginning of a strategic transition, there is a great deal of uncertainty, not only about the rapidly changing environment but also about how the organization is trying to respond, as well as about the nature of the organizational transition. Orderly, predictable functioning was possible because, over time, the organization developed shared outcome preferences; now, common beliefs about what causes the organization to be effective have been disrupted. Therefore, shared understandings are what have guided decision making up to the point of the transition (Thompson and Tuden, 1959), and now those shared understandings need to be rebuilt. Even the purposes of the organization may have changed, in ways that will unfold as events take place. For example, an organization that once saw itself existing to deliver the highest-quality product at the lowest cost may not see itself existing to deliver solutions to customers, and what this new purpose means will not be fully apparent at the outset. Moreover, the new purpose itself may not be accepted by organizational members. How will the new purpose change those routines of the organization that will lead to effective performance? What does it mean to deliver solutions to customers? How will we best organize to do it? These questions will be come into play during the early stages of a transition.

The meanings of the old system were embedded in the culture of the organization—in its language, its action routines, and its material artifacts (Weick and Westley, 1996). Organizational learning requires that new meanings get embedded in altered language, routines, and artifacts. These are collectively held meanings, and organizational learning is a collective process. The understandings and meanings that people attach to the new purposes, and to the new architectures that the organization is striving to put in place, are as much a result of the activities that are unleashed by the introduction of change as they are of a predetermined set of meanings that the management team or design team intends. During times when agreement about purposes and about causes and effects falls apart, the organization needs to operate in a way that enables interpretation to take place. People need to engage in processes that allow a new shared agreement to emerge (Weick, 1993). Units that learn quickly do so because they engage in processes that enable members to affix meaning and to effectively design and establish new approaches that they continuously improve as they gain experience. Thus units learn through self-design.

Process Attributes of Accelerated Learning

There are six major attributes of the processes that characterize accelerated learning settings. These attributes are described briefly in the sections that follow and are illustrated by examples of the forms they take.

Dialogue

Accelerated learning units engage in rich *dialogue* that results in the assignment of collective meaning to the events that are taking place. Dialogue is conversation that brings in the multiple perspectives of the various members of the unit and is able to transcend individual views. The importance of dialogue as a key mechanism for continual generative learning has been underscored by Senge (1990), particularly for group or team learning. Senge, synthesizing the work of several scholars, suggests that dialogue enables the creation of a common pool of meaning that goes beyond any one individual's understanding. Through dialogue, individuals gain insights that cannot be achieved individually, and a new collective understanding comes into being that is based on the development of common meaning. In fast-learning units, we witnessed dialogues about purpose, goals, and priorities. These were recurring conversations that were triggered by such events as a request from a customer that fell outside the normal set of activities or a change in competitors' offerings. There was also dialogue about the meanings of the new words being used in the organization. What does it mean to be self-managing? What does customer focus really entail? When faced with decisions about where to focus or how to proceed, these units pulled together appropriate people to examine what course of action fit best with what they were trying to accomplish, and in so doing they established meaning about purpose and a new understanding of what actions would lead to desired outcomes. The meaning established through dialogue becomes part of the embedded meaning that provides a new set of shared expectations and new agreement to underpin action routines. Without this dialogue, a unit cannot establish new ways of operating. It may resort to old ways of doing work that are already known: "Even though we're in a team now, we'll just all do our usual tasks, and our leader will play the role our supervisor used to play." Alternatively, a unit may meet continuously and make decisions about particular aspects of the work but not put in place a shared meaning that will allow routines to take over. For this kind of group, the process of obtaining consensus becomes a never-ending drain on time and energy because no shared understanding is created.

Value Referencing

Fast-learning units engage in *value referencing*. They consciously focus on the valued outcomes they are trying to accomplish (their mission and goals) and on feedback about how well they are achieving them in their performance. Feedback is an important learning process because it reveals cause-and-effect relationships (Senge, 1990). Although slower-learning units may receive as much feedback about outcomes as faster-learning units, there is a marked difference in the attention they pay to it. Fast-learning units tend to discuss results and engage in problem-solving activities for improving them. They discuss an expanded set of values, including the social values having to do with teamwork and responsibility between members. They consciously articulate the norms required for operating effectively and realizing their values. By continually paying attention to these valued outcomes, they incorporate the outcomes into the culture. These outcomes then become objects of shared preferences.

Learning from Experience

The fast-learning units engage in more ways to *learn from experience*. There may be conscious experimentation whereby a unit tries out a new approach and assesses it before incorporating it into its routines. Successful or unsuccessful approaches may be shared between members, or some documentation of approaches may be developed and incorporated into the unit's practices. A unit may set aside time during regular meetings for sharing new discoveries or failures that people have learned from. Norms may develop to use e-mail or groupware to draw the group's attention to materials that have been developed or to methods that have been used for some activities and that may be applicable to other activities of the unit. These practices make it more likely that new routines will be introduced and become part of the way work gets done.

Systemic View

The fast-learning units take a more *systemic view* of themselves and of the larger organization, seeing it all as nested systems. They consider a balanced set of outcomes and costs, and they make decisions on the basis of how those outcomes and costs will affect performance overall. In designing a component, for example, a unit would consider cost, performance, the project timetable, maintainability, and future technology directions. Learning occurs in the nexus of these issues, where novel approaches are required for balancing and achieving multiple outcomes. These units do not talk in terms of narrow tasks—for example, soliciting new business—but rather in terms of soliciting new business that will enhance return on investment. They do not talk solely in terms of their own performance as systems but rather in terms of fitting themselves into the larger organization and contributing to systemic goals at the higher level. Taking a systemic view leads a group to pay attention to more aspects of the system and opens up a number of new avenues for improving performance. Systemic thinking enables appreciation of the whole rather than just of the parts. It creates a framework for seeing interrelationships rather than things, for recognizing patterns over time rather than static snapshots at one point in time (Senge, 1990).

Open-Loop Learning

Fast-learning units open themselves up to information from outside through *open-loop learning*. Information from customers, suppliers, other parts of the corporation, and technical and industry sources is infused into the deliberations of these units, providing external grounding and a perspective that prevents a group from engaging solely in self-referenced activity. Seeing service through the eyes of the customer or seeing the product through the eyes of repair personnel will enable a unit to develop novel approaches that are more directly linked to the environment. In some cases, this occurs when customers or suppliers are on a joint team with unit members. Other units have their members make regular visits to customers' or end users' facilities. Still others send members to conferences to gather "intelligence," or they appoint different members to keep track of developments in the environment and bring information back to the group. External focus leads to the exploration of novel approaches and avoids a primary focus on simply introducing incremental change (March, 1991).

Bridges

Fast-learning units have many structural *bridges* both within and across units that enable ongoing connectedness and prevent the compartmentalization of work. Internal bridges provide the foundation for learning processes by creating task-related connections and overlap among members. These connections may be facilitated in various ways:

- Cross-training that permits flexible transfer of tasks between members
- "Fuzzy" assignments that lead to overlapping responsibility and ongoing interaction
- The use of subteams with joint accountability for some piece of the work
- Liaison positions
- Overlapping memberships in the various teams that compose the unit

Between units, knowledge-sharing bridges are particularly important. These may include regular cross-unit reviews and sharing of lessons learned, to enable units to learn from each other's experience. They may also include networked information systems providing well-indexed sources of knowledge generated throughout the organization, or councils and interest groups for sharing best practices and infusing disciplinary or problem-centered knowledge. But there are also task-oriented bridges across units—for example, mechanisms for joint planning and review—that integrate teams whose members come from a number of units, and whose task is to integrate the interdependent work of the units with supplier-customer teams. By building in interactions that expand perspectives, provide ongoing feedback, and encourage new practices and shared meanings, such bridges make it less likely that groups will settle quickly into rigid patterns.

These processes that underpin rapid learning contribute to the ability of a unit to achieve shared meaning and design its own new performance routines. The six conditions are equally applicable to all levels of analysis. The organization is a set of nested systems: one division of a company might be composed of a number of business units or regions, each of which is composed of a number of teams or work groups. New shared meanings and new performance routines are equally applicable to, and equally necessary at, all levels. Shared meaning across business units is what enables a division to operate in an integrated way and apply its resources optimally to a number of environmental opportunities and requirements. The division must have established processes that enable it to self-design its divisionwide routines. At the level of the business unit and the subgroup, the same requirements exist for locally held shared meanings and ongoing self-design.

The learning processes described here clearly represent a resource commitment. It takes time and energy to reflect, engage in dialogue, build bridges, and learn from experience. Generally, organizations in a turbulent environment have a premium on cycle time, a shortage of resources in light of the tasks that need to be accomplished to deal with rapidly changing environmental resources, and a great deal of embedded knowledge about how to do things the *old* way. If this commitment of time and energy is not made, then the new units will slip into old routines. They will continue to work sequentially even though they have been organized into teams for concurrent engineering. They will continue to have people do narrow jobs even though everyone is given the same job title and is expected to develop generalist knowledge. They will continue to focus on product performance and schedules even though they are being given data indicating that customers are dissatisfied with product costs and with service. They may also become increasingly ineffective because their old routines have been disrupted but new routines are not yet in place. Their ineffectiveness may be masked for some time because the organization can still rely on its embedded knowledge and can count on people to do what they know how to do. Ultimately, however, the system will become underorganized for carrying out its mission if no self-designing occurs within the new architecture.

A striking pattern has emerged from our work—namely, fast-learning organizations and units have figured out how to embed learning in their day-to-day work. They review customer data as a regular part of their ongoing meetings. They solicit customers' input as they interact with customers to get their work done. They build reflection and action planning into project-review sessions. They include a review of lessons learned as the first step in a new project. Although they use special "offsites," design meetings, and improvement projects as effective tools when periods of intense focus on learning are required, even these are built into the new routines of the organization. For example, a self-design meeting is part of the start-up of every new project, or problem-solving meetings are automatically triggered by unanticipated quality problems in the field, and the documents generated to solve the problem are automatically shared with others who face similar situations. In this way, learning routines are built into the work-performance routines of the organization rather than being seen as extra. This is becoming increasingly important as accelerated learning and knowledge management become the basis on which an organization competes.

Future Challenges: Learning in the Reconfigurable Organization

Although the preceding discussion has been couched in terms of learning during transition, it is clear that in a turbulent environment transition never stops. Of necessity, organizational forms have to become fluid and transitory, continually shifting shapes. Structures will evolve into a myriad of constantly shifting teams, partnerships, interfirm alliances, and spin-off units (Nadler, Gerstein, Shaw, and Associates, 1992) and multiple forms will coexist in the same organization (Quinn, Anderson, and Finkelstein, 1996). Continuous improvement will be a necessity at the corporate level, the business-unit level, and the process level.

Organizations will have to build in the ongoing process capability to design and enact constantly adaptable architectures to meet changing performance demands. The routines and artifacts of the organization will have to include learning routines and artifacts. The metaphor of constantly adaptable architectures is well illustrated by the comparison of Western and Japanese architectures (Maruyama, 1994). Maruyama argues that Western architecture is based on principles of similarity, repetition, opposition, and stability. By contrast, Japanese patterns emphasize interaction, complementarity, continuity, and convertibility. This contrast is exemplified by traditional Japanese houses, in which internal horizontal boundaries and, to a more limited extent, external boundaries can be reshaped to fit various functions.

A similar notion is the "platform organization" (Ciborra and Schneider, 1992; Ciborra, 1996). The platform organization draws its name from the architecture of computer workstations, where a number of workstations act as computing platforms capable of being radically reconfigured for many different uses. Rather than having a stable architecture, the platform organization can be visualized as having the learning ability to reconfigure its resources and capabilities in fundamental ways, on the basis of changes in the environment.

Given this trend of continual architectural reconfiguration, the elements and processes of learning that were presented in the previous section will become increasingly important. Furthermore, organizations will need to develop institutional capabilities for ongoing learning. They will have to explicitly manage their learning processes by creating infrastructures and mechanisms to support purposeful learning. The model of organizational learning presented in this chapter, as well as that model's process dynamics, also suggest the nature of the market architecture and the social architecture that would specifically support a continuously learning organization. If the same learning attributes that facilitate learning during transition are built into the architecture of an organization, that organization can learn continuously.

What about the nature of the technical architecture that might support a continuously learning organization? New information technologies can play a key role in establishing these capabilities by creating new technical architectures to underpin the new social and market architectures. There are four domains in which information systems are evolving to the point where, as mechanisms, they can become an integrated part of the architecture of the learning organization:

1. *Thinking, reflection, and interpretation:* Experiential learning theory suggests that learning is a continual process of thinking, deciding, acting, and reflecting on the consequences of action for fu-

ture actions. This sequence is implicit in a number of the learning dynamics mentioned earlier. A problem organizations often run into is that cross-disciplinary groups of people often have trouble dealing with their different and potentially contradictory views of the same situation (for example, see Dougherty, 1992). Furthermore, individuals who have to work together on self-design tasks are sometimes in different locations. Groupware and other kinds of software applications are getting to the point of sophistication where they can be used to aid collective thinking (Malone, Lai, and Fry, 1992; Boland, Tenkasi, and Te'eni, 1994; Dykstra and Carasik, 1991). Many of these software applications use various tools and objects, such as cognitive maps or cause-and-effect diagrams, to help individuals uncover specific perspectives and unique understandings of a situation and engage in mutual dialogue to arrive at a shared interpretation.

2. *Capturing and distributing organizational knowledge:* In specific domains of human expertise, organizations are increasingly supporting or replacing knowledge-based routines with computer-based expert systems and distributing such expertise across the organization to increase efficiency and reduce processing errors. For example, Merrill Lynch captures and distributes the firm's knowledge base through software and leverages its professional intellect in very creative ways (Quinn, Anderson, and Finkelstein, 1996). Merrill Lynch's financial specialists create a scientific knowledge base for making investment decisions and create proprietary software systems that distribute the resulting investment recommendations to brokers at retail outlets, who create further value by customizing the central investment advice to meet the needs of clients. The knowledge system ensures that all brokers adhere to the current regulations, make no arithmetical or clerical errors, and provide customers with the latest market information. This system is an example of the types of systems that are emerging in many arenas and that robustly encode part of a firm's knowledge base, making the information widely available regardless of how the firm's architecture may change.

3. *Mechanisms for encoding organizational memory:* Organizational memory and knowledge are closely related concepts. As an organization changes its architectures, it must maintain the ability to be self-referencing: to learn from the system's historical memory

and embedded knowledge. Organizational stories and examples are an important medium for transmitting cultural and technical knowledge (Brown and Duguid, 1991). They can be stored in centralized databases, perhaps in the form of pictures and graphics that illustrate past quality defects or product solutions, as well as in the form of text that can be referred to if people want to learn from the past. Roth and Senge (1996) have suggested the creation of organizational learning histories that can capture and convey the complexity of real situations in participants' words by describing work issues and learning experiences from multiple and often contending perspectives.

4. *Experimentation:* Technical simulation programs have become standard tools for developing new products and making scientific breakthroughs. These programs embed and employ the latest algorithms and knowledge base of a field. In the future, it is possible that organizational design principles will be understood richly enough to enable the establishment of simulations that can aid the self-design process. One field-tested software package for organizational simulation is "HITOP" (Marjchzak and Gasser, 1992). With this package, groups can simulate the consequences of various organizational design options and use the predicted consequences to inform their ultimate design decisions. Such software packages provide an electronic "practice field" (Roth and Senge, 1996) for experiments in design. Likewise, computer-aided system-dynamics simulations could compress time and space and quickly allow group members to role-play in simulations of the new organization so that they could see the effects of different operating assumptions on desired objectives. These "practice fields" would be designed learning spaces where people could experiment, make mistakes, accelerate their learning, and test new behaviors.

As information systems become key elements of the technical architecture in the conduct of business within the firm, and as they become integral to work routines, organizations are working to make them instruments of learning. In distributed and dynamic organizations, sharing data sets and lessons learned, solving problems through electronic mediation, and moving knowledge wherever it is needed will become mainstays of an organization's ability to be flexible and yet maintain and increase the knowledge it applies to succeeding in today's environment. A near-term challenge is to determine how the technical architecture should be related to the social and market architectures so that the organization can learn through new people-machine interfaces and appropriate combinations of human and computer systems and processes.

Conclusion

We have argued that organizational transitions involve intertwined changes in the organization's market architecture, its technical architecture, and its social architecture. Strategic transition often involves the replacement of a well-understood architecture, one that has generated a complete culture, with a new architecture that is based on a different logic and requires cultural change. Transition also entails changes in cognitive understanding, behavioral patterns, and organizational structures. We believe that the transitional process is a form of organizational learning, and that learning dynamics need to be established in the organization. As an organization sets out to establish a new and broadly specified architecture, that architecture's form and meaning will evolve through the processes by which organizational members interpret and make sense of this change and institute new ways of doing work. The creation of new shared meanings and the self-design of ways of doing work are the essence of learning for transition.

Finally, we have argued that learning processes are fundamental organizational capabilities for the future, as organizations in a shifting environment take on a variety of forms over time. The capability of the organization to continually reconfigure itself is critical to its long-term survival. Much of this chapter has dealt with the collective processes that have to be established. We have also speculated that advanced information systems will play an increasingly critical role in learning within the reconfigurable, flexible organization of the future.

Chapter Fourteen

Catalyzing Organizational Change and Learning

The Role of Performance Management

Allan M. Mohrman Jr.
Susan Albers Mohrman

Performance management is the myriad of formal practices that organizations create to help their performers know what they are supposed to do, develop the wherewithal to do it, find out how well they are doing, and be rewarded (or otherwise experience consequences) for what they do. Managers are recognizing that these practices should be integrated into a system that influences people's performance in a manner that supports the strategy and contributes to the performance targets of the organization. In reality, many organizations have a variety of practices—involving business planning, goal setting, performance appraisal, compensation and rewards, training and development, and placement and career planning—that are managed as independent practices, often by functionally distinct expert groups.

Performance management is central to managing the business, defining the individual's relationship with the organization, and providing a mechanism for feedback and control. Because of its centrality, performance management can be either a deterrent to change (when it is consistent with traditional organizational paradigms) or an enabler of change (when it includes practices consistent with the new paradigm). Performance management can become more than simply a deterrent or enabler of change, however, when it becomes the engine that *drives* ongoing organizational learning and change.

As surprising as it may seem to anyone who has had personal experience with most performance-management practices, we have sometimes actually seen performance management act as an important agent of organizational learning and change. In fact, we believe that this is the emerging role of performance management. In this chapter, we describe some of our research and experience to show how and why this happens. This knowledge can be used to design performance-management practices that lead to organizational learning.

Performance Management and Large-Scale Organizational Change

Large-scale change of the kind discussed in this book is fundamental change in the character of an organization that results in lasting change in the performance of the organization (Ledford, Mohrman, Mohrman, and Lawler, 1989). It is pervasive change in that it ultimately entails most if not all elements of the organizational system. It is deep change in that it affects people's beliefs, values, and understandings.

It seems almost self-evident that changes in performance-management practices are required to facilitate large-scale change that is designed to alter the performance capabilities of the organization. Yet for many organizations these practices are among the last to change. During many organizational transitions, performance-management practices are seen as (and in fact function as forces for) the status quo. To some extent, the lasting power of traditional approaches is due to the fact that performance-management practices reflect deep-seated beliefs and values, and they embody employees' relationships to the organization.

Performance management is not just one of the many features of organizations that have to change as part of large-scale change. Rather, it is a pivotal system of practices that are never neutral in the change process. These practices can be forces for the preservation of the status quo, thus working against change, or they can be instruments of the learning and change that are required to effect large-scale change. Furthermore, the nature of the performance-management system will affect the organization's ongoing ability to learn and change.

We begin this chapter by making a case for the centrality of performance management to the organization and its members. We then examine the changes in performance management that are required to fit with networked organizations, team-based organizations, partnerships, process organizations, and high-involvement organizations, all organizational models that are emerging in response to environmental requirements for new kinds and levels of performance (Galbraith and Lawler, 1993). We use the concept of paradigm shift to help show how performance-management practices can play different roles in the transition to these new organizational forms. Finally, we make the case that the emerging performance-management models will be forces for ongoing organizational change and learning and, as such, will be keystones of the learning organization. Throughout the chapter, we refer to findings from studies of performance-management practices in organizations that are in the process of transition (Mohrman, Mohrman, and Lawler, 1992; Mohrman, Cohen, and Mohrman, 1995). Brief cases encountered in that research will be used to illustrate our points.

The Centrality of Performance Management

Many performance-management practices tend to be despised, feared, barely tolerated, and often ignored in organizations. Completing appraisals, holding salary discussions, distributing rewards, dealing with problem performers, making and carrying out developmental plans, and updating information bases for placement and assessment purposes often elicit no more than perfunctory attention from managers, who complain about the time-consuming and constraining nature of these practices and do not take advantage of the opportunities that they provide for meeting the performance needs of the organization. Managers often see these practices as separate from managing the business, and they see the time required to carry them out as distractions from their jobs. Data from our performance-management studies indicate that managers and their subordinates frequently think that their organizations do not require managers to do a good job of carrying out these practices, and they see managers as having inadequate time and sometimes insufficient skills to do so. Yet in these companies the same managers and employees report that they would like to see effective performance-management practices. Managers would like to have tools for more effective management of organizational performance. Employees would like to have tools that better clarify expectations and acknowledge performance.

Done well or poorly, performance management is central to organizational functioning for three reasons: its activities are elements of the management of business performance, it is integral to employees' understanding of their relationship to the organization, and it is a system for feedback and control.

Performance Management and Management of Business Performance

The practices that help organizational performers know what they are supposed to do, develop the wherewithal to do it, know how well they are doing, and be rewarded for what they do are the practices that link these performers to the business of the organization. These performance-management practices shape performance by giving information about appropriate content and direction of activities. Ideally, they also align the performances of the various performers in the organization so that their activities combine to deliver effective and efficient accomplishment of the overall organizational mission.

Figure 14.1 illustrates the nested performances of performers at various systemic levels of the organization. Individuals exist in larger groups (such as departments, projects, or teams), which in turn are parts of larger business units. The performance management of individuals will ideally be nested within the performance management of the larger units to which individuals belong so that the activities of individuals contribute to organizational performance at the business-unit level. From the perspective of the organization, individual performance delivers value to the extent that it ultimately contributes to the goals and strategy of the organization. This usually happens because individuals are performing

**Figure 14.1. Nested Performances at
Different Systemic Levels of the Organization.**

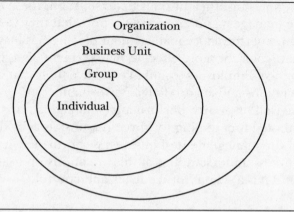

within organizational subunits that deliver value by carrying out an
organizational process or delivering a product or service.

Defining the Individual's Relationship
to and Understanding of the Organization

Performance-management practices, more than any other organizational practices, define the employee's relationship to the organization. Goal-setting practices, for example, might explicitly
connect the individual's performance goals with those of the group
and the business, or they might treat the individual's goals as if they
were unrelated to the business. Pay systems determine whether and
how the employee shares in the financial performance of the organization, or whether the employee is being paid for his or her
time, effort, and skills but not for business performance. Pay systems also establish expectations for equitable treatment; in fact,
they help define equity. Development systems reflect the organization's willingness to invest in its employees and whether employees have an opportunity for career growth and personal
development. Finally, performance-appraisal practices let employees know where they stand (with varying degrees of accuracy) and

are often the gatekeepers to other valued outcomes, such as career opportunities, development, and rewards. For this reason, even when employees see performance management as poorly done, arbitrary, and misleading, they are still reluctant to discard it completely. They look to their appraisals, the size of their merit increases, and their developmental opportunities as feedback that indicates where they stand and what kind of future in the organization they might expect.

Performance-management practices also have implications for the employee's self-concept and ability to derive satisfaction from work. Because of the evaluative nature of the performance appraisal and its reward consequences, performance-management practices can have implications for the employee's self-esteem and sense of accomplishment, and for whether the employee feels valued. Work can be defined in ways that give employees a sense of where they fit into the bigger picture. It can be defined in ways that make performance more meaningful, or it can be defined in isolated, focused ways that separate performance from the larger system into which it fits and therefore limit how meaningful performance can be.

Performance-management practices also shape an employee's understanding of critical aspects of the organization by communicating what aspects of performance are valued (rewarded) in the organization and what kinds of performance are required for getting ahead. When performance-management practices link the employee's activities to overall organizational direction, they shape the employee's understanding of the strategy and goals of the organization, his or her role within it, and the key drivers of organizational performance. When performance-management practices focus solely on the individual's performance, any understanding that the individual has about his or her performance is literally out of context.

Thus performance-management practices are a window to the larger organization, enabling a performer to understand where he or she fits and how he or she can make a difference. They are also a reflection from the larger organization, telling performers how they are perceived and where they stand. The visibility through the window and the clarity of the reflection will vary.

Performance Management as Feedback and Control

The feedback systems in the organization serve organizational control functions (Lundberg, 1980). They provide information intended to reinforce or alter behavior. Performance appraisal and performance feedback have often been characterized in the literature as control systems (for example, see Taylor, Fisher, and Ilgen, 1984). Combined with goals and performance criteria, performance feedback allows the performer to adjust his or her performance so that it adheres more closely to what is desired. Often when appraisals are used for human resources management, the focus is on other functions of performance appraisal, such as providing development information or ensuring that the distribution of rewards is fair. Whenever management orchestrates the feedback and criteria of appraisals, performance appraisal becomes a mechanism by which managers control performance. There are other sources of feedback for performers, but the official performance appraisal carries a lot of weight with the individual, in part because it is tied to such valued outcomes as rewards and career opportunities.

Implications for Large-Scale Change

We have been arguing that performance management is central to the management of business performance, that it is an organizational control system, and that it mediates the relationship of employees to the organization, as well as helps to form their understanding of the organization. Because of the centrality of performance management in the organizational system, it is also central to any organizational transition process. The large-scale changes that organizations are undergoing entail changes in the nature of the performances that are being managed, in the way control is exercised, in employees' relationship to the organization, and in employees' understanding of the organization. Large-scale changes also involve changes in performance-management practices. Just as important, as we shall see, changes in performance management can stimulate the other organizational changes that are required.

Changing Models of Organization and Performance Management

In this section we discuss the relationship between models of organization and performance-management practices. We first characterize traditional organizational models and performance management. Then we do the same for emerging models of organization and performance management.

Traditional Models

The traditional model of organization that still guides most organizational designs is based on dividing work into jobs performed by individuals. The basis of this division is often functions or specialties. Jobs are integrated into organizational wholes by the ways jobs are defined and by rules, goals, and hierarchical management (Galbraith, 1994). Each individual occupying a job is connected to a supervising manager by a hierarchical authority relationship. This model assumes relative stability: the jobs defined and the means of their integration remain constant enough that any changes over time can be managed.

The performance-management practices that have developed in traditional organizations reflect this underlying model (Murphy and Cleveland, 1991). Individuals are considered to be the performing units. Therefore, individuals are the targets of performance management. Because jobs are predefined, the definition of what performance is supposed to be is often a given. Because people are selected and initially trained for jobs, the ongoing development of performers to do their jobs is often not considered a major issue until jobs change or people change jobs. Consequently, performance management in traditional organizations has boiled down to the review of performance and the assignment of rewards (or other consequences) on the basis of reviews. For most traditional organizations, formal performance management has come to be thought of as performance appraisal and (often) pay for individual performance. In fact, performance appraisal is often thought of as existing only as a means for determining pay raises. Beyond this purpose, performance management is left to the informal practices and management styles of supervisors. Because individual performers are linked to the rest of the organization through their supervisors, performance appraisals are done and reward decisions made by supervising managers. The direction of the appraisals reflects the direction of exercised authority: downward.

The traditional organization model that we have just sketched out and the appraisal practices associated with it have shown themselves unable to cope with many of the issues of modern organizational life: frequent change, the uncertainty that makes it difficult to preprogram rules and completely specify jobs, a tendency for misalignment between individual performance and organizational needs, the inability of managers to cope with the frequent exceptions confronting them, the need for performers to work more with others (such as customers and co-workers), and the fact that supervisors are often distant from and out of touch with the performance of subordinates (Mohrman, Resnick-West, and Lawler, 1989). Consequently, there has been some evolution in the old, simple performance-appraisal practices. To help tie individual performance to business needs, many appraisal systems have been integrated with a business-planning process in which business goals are cascaded down the hierarchy. This process results in goals for individuals that are derived directly from business goals. Appraisal systems, whether or not they are connected to business goals, have tended to graft on goal-setting processes to help define what performers should be doing so that they do not rely just on job descriptions. Because of changes in job demands, appraisal processes have also begun to address the developmental needs of performers more seriously. More systems are providing for formal input from others in addition to supervising managers. Systems are becoming more participative, allowing performers to become partners in their own appraisal processes through such mechanisms as self-appraisal and a performance discussion held before the completion of the appraisal form. To cope with frequent change, appraisals are happening more frequently, often as interim reviews. As the focus of appraisal systems has expanded, they have become known as performance-management systems.

New Models

Even more change is occurring in the organizational contexts in which performance is managed. New models of organization are evolving because of the competitive realities of the new global environment and the rapid changes that are taking place (Galbraith and Lawler, 1993; Nadler, Gerstein, Shaw, and Associates, 1992). These new models emphasize the lateral or horizontal nature of an organization in terms of processes that cut across the organization (Davenport, 1993; Hammer and Champy, 1995), networks of technologies, business units, and people (Savage, 1990), new links with customers (Deming, 1986), or joint ventures. The lateral nature of organizations is necessitated by strong interdependencies that come into play among subsystems in the delivery of value to customers.

The performing units in organizations include individual people, but they are also collective systems and subsystems of people (teams, minibusinesses, business units). These performing units are related to one another as nested and overlapping systems (Mohrman, Cohen, and Mohrman, 1995). Therefore, it is better not to think any longer of a hierarchy as a set of reporting relationships; rather, it is a hierarchy of nested performing systems (for example, a cross-functional team performs with other teams in ways that contribute to a larger business unit, which in turn contributes to a larger corporate strategy). Each level in the hierarchy is a system whose mission and whose scope of responsibility is broader than the mission and scope of responsibility of any system contained within it.

To respond adequately to the demands of a quickly developing competitive environment, performing units must have authority to react to local developments in ways that are compatible with the needs of the larger system. In order to cope with the ever-changing environment and its constantly increasing competitiveness, new organizations must constantly learn (Senge, 1990) and improve themselves (Mohrman and Cummings, 1989).

Performance-management practices will support these organizational dimensions with their own set of matching characteristics (Mohrman, Cohen, and Mohrman, 1995). Because performance happens at every systemic level, performance-management practices will be multilevel in nature. The performance of a unit at any one level will need to be managed in the context of the performance of the larger unit in which it exists (see Figure 14.1). Because the larger system is made up of many interdependent subsystems, the performance of each subsystem will also have to be managed laterally so that it is coordinated with performance in the other subsystems. Finally, performance-management systems must themselves be self-designing and contribute to the learning capabilities of the organization.

Actual practices that fit these desired characteristics can vary, but some generalizations are possible:

- Rewards for performance can be based on performance at several systemic levels (individual, team, business, corporation).
- In settings where performing units can shift frequently, defining performance for a unit is a major need that can occur any time during a fiscal or calendar year. Performance-management processes will stress the defining of performance over the reviewing of performance.
- Continuous performance improvement requires continuous reorganization for improved performance. As performance is defined, reviewed, and redefined, organizational units must be developed and redeveloped, designed and redesigned, to perform as well as possible. These development processes will therefore become a major part of performance management.
- Review of performance will require multiple perspectives. For instance, the review of a team's performance can be done from the perspective of the larger business in which it is a part, from the perspective of other teams that are interdependent with it in the business, from the perspective of the external customers the team serves, or from the perspective of the individual members of the team. Each of these perspectives reflects a different stake in the performance of the team. The various perspectives cannot be expected always to be in agreement, but they are all important. Performance management will require practices that consider all stakeholders' perspectives.

Table 14.1 lists some of the key characteristics of traditional and emerging organizational forms and singles out features of performance-management practices in each form. If we view the organization as a system, we can predict that when each model is fully in operation, its organizational design features (including performance management) will fit with one another and yield a consistent logic of operating (Katz and Kahn, 1978). In an organization that is in transition from the traditional to the new logic, these features will be out of alignment, and the organization will gradually put the features of the new organization in place. Thus changed features become forces for further change as they create tension within the organization, and unaltered features hinder change as they perpetuate the old logic. The next section of this chapter examines this transition, employing the notion of large-scale change as a paradigm shift and illustrating how performance-management practices can either catalyze or hinder change and learning.

A Paradigmatic View of Organizational and Performance-Management Models

One way to view the transition from traditional to new organizational models is to see this change as a paradigm shift (Kuhn, 1970; Mohrman and Lawler, 1985). The concept of a paradigm also allows us to understand why organizational models and performance-management practices are so inextricably intertwined.

The term *paradigm* is overworked. It has been falling out of favor because of its almost faddish use over the last decade. Nevertheless, it is an important concept that helps us portray the relationship between the dimensions of depth and pervasiveness in large-scale organizational change. When we use the term *paradigm* in this chapter, we do not just mean a conceptual schema that a person might have. To us, a paradigm is a conceptual and physical *entirety* consisting of a worldview (Kuhn, 1970; Pfeffer, 1982), a way of doing things and the tools for doing them that are consistent with this worldview (Kuhn, 1970; Pfeffer, 1982), and the community of people who share this worldview and act according to its practices (Kuhn, 1970). The worldview (the *depth* dimension of large-scale organizational change is concerned with how strongly

Table 14.1. Characteristics of Traditional and Emerging Organizational Forms and Performance-Management Practices.

Traditional Models	New Models
Organization	Organization
Hierarchical: tall; individuals control individuals	Nested systems: individuals, teams, business units
Compartmentalized: jobs, specialties, functions	Lateral: flat, cross-functional, customer-oriented, process-oriented, networked
Stable: predefined jobs, rules, performance standards	Dynamic: learning, self-designing, self-improving
Performance Management	Performance Management
Downward control by managers	Multidirectional by multiple stakeholders
Individuals as targets	Multiple levels of performing units and performance management: individuals, teams, business units
Performance definition is a given (job description, performance standards)	Focus on dynamic definitions of performance
Emphasis on appraisal and rewards for individual performance	Rewards for individual, team, and business performance
Cursory attention to individual development	Emphasis on development and improvement of performing units at all levels

and deeply people hold a worldview) cannot be separated from the paradigm's way of doing things (the *pervasiveness* dimension of large-scale organizational change is concerned with the degree to which the paradigm permeates all organizational practices) or from the people who think and act according to the paradigm (the larger the relative size of the community, the stronger the paradigm). In this sense, organizational and performance-management models are components of a worldview, performance-management practices are components of how things are done, and the people in an organization constitute the community that shares the worldview and acts according to its practices.

When a paradigm shifts, several things take place (Kuhn, 1970; Mohrman and Lawler, 1985). Exceptions or anomalies begin to occur that the prevailing paradigm is not equipped to handle. For example, product and market forces change so quickly that the old hierarchical style of decision making is not fast enough to respond. The resultant change is a more lateral and flexible way of functioning. But this change taxes performance-management practices that are based on the old job descriptions. When organizations engage in elaborate efforts to update job descriptions, they often discover that the results of their efforts are already obsolete. The emerging lateral interdependencies among individuals tax managers' ability to coordinate, and managers frequently lack the perspective they would need in order to determine and weigh the contributions of the various contributors.

When anomalies—situations that cannot be handled with current approaches—develop, the dominant paradigm adjusts at first by adding on ideas and practices that are responsive to the anomalies. For example, as a way of dealing with changing performance needs, a performance-appraisal process might add on a goal-setting component, or an annual review of job descriptions. If change accelerates, appraisals may be held more frequently. To deal with increased coordination needs, managers might encourage individual performers to coordinate and set goals directly with others, which means that complete appraisal of the individual performer will probably require the addition of a mechanism (such as today's favorite, the 360-degree appraisal) for gathering input from co-workers.

As anomalies develop and practices adjust, people begin to develop different ways of viewing the world. A new but incomplete paradigm starts to form. New organizational design features and practices are put in place. For example, cross-functional product-strategy teams might be established to respond to rapid changes in competitors' products. Concurrent engineering approaches may be implemented. Some people begin to see the world differently and adopt new practices. As anomalies accrue and patchwork fixes are generated, they put the old paradigm under stress, and new views of the world gain ground. More people share new views and practices. The paradigm shift occurs in the presence of two factors: (1) the anomalies threatening the old paradigm reach such proportions that the old paradigm is no longer able to cope with them simply by adding on features; and (2) a new paradigm has been sufficiently developed, both conceptually and practically. At this point of crisis for the old paradigm, the shift takes place. A critical mass of people now shares the new way of behaving and understanding the world; most features and practices have been brought into alignment, and the new paradigm becomes dominant.

Not only is the new paradigm able to handle the developments that were seen as anomalies under the old paradigm, it also incorporates the old paradigm, although within a new worldview (Kuhn, 1970: Mohrman and Lawler, 1985). For instance, in the new organization, hierarchical authority is but one form of organizational control. Hierarchy remains, but it is now a hierarchy of nested systems. The level of the individual is just one of several systemic levels of units whose performance must be managed.

In a stable organization, definitions of the kind of performance that is needed are also stable, as are the competencies necessary to produce that kind of performance. Consequently, performance management will tend to stress processes that review and reward performance, and to do this as a way of controlling performance so as to create predictability and uniform treatment. In the new organization, flexibility is no longer the enemy of dependable performance, but organizations and their performing units must dependably adjust to the ever-changing demands of the marketplace. In this open-systems approach, performing units must first ascertain what the marketplace demands are and define their strategies. Then they must organize themselves and develop themselves accordingly, in order to achieve the level of performance that is needed. These defining and developing processes become the driving performance-management processes. It is still important to review and reward performance—not, however, in order to control performance in the direction of relatively stable performance needs, but in order to learn how well the chosen organizational and performance strategies are working and to provide incentives for their improvement.

The open- and nested-systems views of the organization also require a multiple-stakeholder view of performance management. Every performing unit, whether that unit is an individual or a group, must actively involve many stakeholders in the management of its performance. The manager (perhaps in the form of a management team) is still there as a stakeholder but is now seen as representing the larger system to which the unit contributes. Some stakeholders represent the other units with which a unit must work. Some stakeholders represent the unit's customers and the marketplace. The final stakeholder is the performing unit itself.

Viewing organizational change as a paradigm shift helps us see why performance management can be both a deterrent to change and an enabler of change. The cases we will describe in this chapter illustrate both possibilities.

Performance Management as a Deterrent to Change

Performance management can serve as a deterrent to change when it continues to reflect the old organizational logic and to focus attention on old values, thus tying the employee's self-image to the effectiveness of a kind of performance that no longer meets the needs of the organization. The case of Medco illustrates this situation.

> Medco creates and markets medications. It employs hundreds of skilled professionals, many with Ph.D. and M.D. degrees, who work with doctors to develop new medications. Recently Medco has been facing rapid change in its business environment. Global competition, reduced profit margins, and a changing health care market have necessitated a major redirection of corporate strategy and have increased internal performance demands. Medco has had difficulty getting its professional cadre to reorient and reconceive its work in light of the new business realities. For the research labs, the required reconceptualization is to see science as being oriented to market needs, not just to interesting research questions. This reconceptualization will also mean a redefinition of the concept of laboratory yields to focus on usable, *marketable* compounds, not just on new ones.

The formal performance-management practices used in the research labs are a performance-appraisal process and a merit-pay system. For performance appraisal, the individual professional compiles a file of his or her accomplishments for the year, which tend to consist of accomplishments in the laboratories, and submits it to his or her supervisor. Feedback from the supervisor about those accomplishments is uneven from one supervisor-employee pair to another, but the norm is for the supervisor to say, "You've done a good job this year. Keep it up." Because supervisors are scientists from the same discipline, what little feedback people do get tends to focus on the quality of the processes applied to the laboratory work and on yields obtained in the lab. Professionals in Medco tend to have a very academic view of their work. Laboratory results are considered important, and publications and patents are concrete affirmations of this view. People tend to talk in terms of "my science." Within the rather general disease categories they work in, people pursue their interests.

After the appraisal documentation is complete, supervisors get together and rank employees in similar job categories to determine merit raises. Because management is worried about legal issues, there is considerable pressure on supervisors to make performance-appraisal ratings match the merit-pay rankings. Therefore, even if they are told to keep up the good work, performers may receive low official ratings that reflect their status in the rankings. Many performers consider a pay raise to be the best indicator of how one is doing.

This performance-management process does not make the business needs of the corporation visible to the lab scientists. The scientists assume that laboratory yields and good science are the only performance criteria. Their concepts of their own value to the corporation are based primarily on their merit pay and on whether they "get ahead." As part of this worldview, in fact, the belief exists that some of the most valuable scientists may never be associated with a compound that gets to market. The academically oriented performance-management practices work against the corporate thrust toward market focus and responsiveness. Despite announced missions and strategies requiring this closer focus and the integration of laboratory performance with business needs, the academic worldview in the labs is self-reinforcing.

When an organization like Medco attempts to instill a new worldview, it is thwarted by its actual practices and the perspectives implicit in them. For Medco, the performance-appraisal process continues to celebrate the science of the individual, independent of the business. Furthermore, this process has an extremely strong impact on the viewpoints of the individual scientists because it represents the only formal feedback they get on their performance. It is seen as directly measuring the worth of these individuals and as reflecting the value that the organization places on them and expresses through pay decisions. Moreover, it reflects a deeply held belief from the old paradigm: that the best way to yield useful compounds is to yield lots of compounds.

One of the tensions within Medco stems from the fact that producing useful compounds is a multidisciplinary process that works best on the basis of collaboration, formal or informal. The scientists are highly interdependent with one another, and yet the performance-management process focuses on individuals within single disciplinary frameworks. Consequently, efforts to create cross-disciplinary teams have been slow to materialize because of the strong within-discipline orientation of all contributors. These performance-management practices are not questioned by the scientists who grew up with them. Traditional approaches to performance management can persevere even when they are detrimental to performance, largely because they have shaped employees' understanding not only of what is important but also of what is equitable. These approaches reinforce the view that it is fair to use a person's individual performance to determine his or her value to the organization. They also perpetuate the assumption that the management of individual performance is an appropriate way of managing collaborative behavior.

This issue of the appropriate systems levels at which to conduct performance management (individual, group, business unit, and so forth) is accentuated by our findings from research conducted in the late 1980s on the performance-management practices of the professional and managerial corps of two corporations (Mohrman, Mohrman, and Worley, 1990; Mohrman, Mohrman, and Lawler, 1992). The companies were in the defense and aerospace industries and were operating at the cutting edge of technology. They employed a large number of professionals, including engineers, scientists, and specialists from other functions of these organizations. Many of these knowledge workers were engaged in projects in which their performance was highly interdependent with that of others. Although performance pressures were growing and the companies were aware that they needed new approaches if they were going to be able to respond, these workers were still being organized and managed with traditional individual, discipline-based approaches. Our research was conducted because managers in each of these companies felt that they could not respond to the performance pressures with their current performance-management systems. At that point in time, they thought of their problem as needing to more effectively eliminate individual performance problems and motivate higher levels of individual performance.

Both companies practiced formal performance appraisal of individual employees and had merit-pay systems based on rankings of employees. We found that the performance-appraisal and merit-pay systems did foster planning, goal setting, and feedback between the employees and their supervisors but that none of these activities was related to the performance outcomes of individuals or of the projects they worked on. In one of the organizations, which particularly stressed the ranking process, we found that the individual pay-for-performance system had a negative impact on performance in projects—in other words, the formal, individually oriented performance-management practices mostly had no effect on either individual or collective performance and sometimes made collective performance worse.

We also found, however, that informal performance-management processes that were conducted in groups of co-workers did have a positive impact on both project performance and individual performance. These practices included collective planning, within-group feedback, goal-setting, and group self-assessment. Although none of these companies had formal team performance-management practices, these practices were being implemented informally because they were advocated by some managers and had a real impact on group performance.

In these organizations, pay for individual performance, as implemented through the merit-pay system, was considered fair. Furthermore, the issue of whether people believed that their pay was in some way related to their projects' or their teams' performance was not related to their sense of equity, which was determined by the issue of whether they as individuals were being paid at a level commensurate with their individual job performance. In summary, these two organizations had individually oriented, supervisor-

centered performance-management practices that did not contribute to the collective performance required for organizational
results but that were perceived as fair. Moreover, managers in these
two companies truly believed that corporate success depended on
individual "stars" and that they had systems in which the cream
would rise to the top. ("Rising to the top" was a major concern of
everyone in these tall hierarchical organizations.) This worldview
was strong, and it was not thought feasible to undertake significant
changes in these individually oriented performance-management
systems even though the data showed that the practices of these
systems were ineffective. There was a tendency to disbelieve or dis-
regard the findings; in fact, the only changes that were made were
undertaken to strengthen the existing paradigm of individual performance management by improving processes between individuals and their supervisors, changes that were more in concert with
the prevailing organizational paradigm. Several years later, each of
these two companies was struggling to create effective teams in a
culture that still appraised and rewarded individuals. The performance-management systems in both companies locked the existing paradigm in, largely because these systems were so closely
linked to people's deep beliefs and values.

Performance Management as an Enabler of Change

In this section, we will consider two companies in which performance-
management practices encouraged change. In the first company, a
minor change in performance management—the introduction of
peer input into appraisals—stimulated a particularly fundamental
change. In this case, individuals engaging with a changed work system found themselves beginning to internalize a new worldview. They
could understand the inappropriateness of the more traditional
performance-management practices, and they exerted pressure for
these practices to be changed and to conform to the new organizational paradigm. This kind of pressure becomes apparent as an organization moves from its traditional way of managing and organizing
to a new way that is more lateral and less hierarchical. A common
structural design element is to use teams as formal performing units.
This is what was done in the following case.

The research lab of a major food manufacturer had been using increasingly self-managing teams for about two years. The company had not changed its formal performance-management practices, which focused on the individual performer and on individual pay for performance and used a ranking process. At the end of the second year, however, as a newly initiated part of the annual performance-management cycle, all the teams were asked to help rank their members.

One particularly mature team, called the ChemTeam, had successfully adopted the new organizational logic. This team was made up of Ph.D.- and master's-level analytical chemists who supplied consulting services to various customers throughout the corporation. In practice, the delivery of the consulting services had moved from individually oriented project assignment to the forming and disbanding of temporary subteams composed of people with the necessary collection of expertise and experience to carry out particular projects. When the ChemTeam, to begin the ranking process, sat down and considered how each of its members had done as individual performers, the team eventually came to the conclusion that it was impossible to isolate any one person's individual performance because all the members were so interdependent that each depended on the others in order to perform at all.

As a result, the team members refused to continue the ranking process. They demanded that the performance-management process be changed or that, at the very least, all members of the ChemTeam be placed at the same level in the overall ranking, and that they all receive the same percentage of pay increase. Incidents like this one put pressure on management to reconsider the company's performance-management system.

The worldview of the ChemTeam members had begun to shift as they started to do their work in teams instead of as individual consultants. When the new practice of peer input was introduced into the individual performance-appraisal and merit-pay system, going through the new process made the team members aware of how inconsistent the established approach was with the way in which work was actually being done. They no longer saw individual merit pay as equitable.

This kind of shift in beliefs is a relatively deep change, one that comes only when people actually experience living in a new paradigm—in this case, a team-based organization. In the case of the ChemTeam, changes in the way work was done led to changes in perceptions of equity, and these changed perceptions were brought to the surface when peer appraisal was added to the company's performance-appraisal practices. A small performance-management change enabled and unleashed more fundamental change.

In the following case, changes in a company's performance-management system were introduced to spur changes in the organizational culture and in the organizing model.

In the late 1980s, Oilco, a petroleum and chemicals company, began to shift its corporate strategies and its organizational models in order to become more competitive in its fast-changing global environment. At that time the organizational change strategy was relatively uncoordinated, with pockets of different changes taking place throughout the company. There were some TQM efforts, some team-based reorganizations, some attempts at change in the organizational culture, and some projects aimed at organizational effectiveness. All were initiated at the local business-unit level.

At a retreat of the corporate management team, a new corporate mission and vision were drafted, and a new strategy for responding to environmental challenges was delineated. In order to put the vision and strategy into practice, a high-level team of line managers was appointed to design and introduce a new performance-management system (for pragmatic reasons, pay practices were omitted as an agenda item) and to lead, support, and catalyze change.

Oilco's existing performance-management system was a combination of management by objectives and performance appraisal for individuals. It also entailed a ranking process for the determination of salary raises. In many parts of the organization, ranking had come to be done before appraisals so that appraisal ratings could be made to conform with salary rankings.

The new system was designed to embody many of the cultural directions that the corporate leaders had identified in the new mission statement: increased employee involvement and participation in the business, increased teamwork, and increased customer focus, among other directions. Therefore, the new system included participative mechanisms by which supervisors and performers assumed a more equal role in the whole appraisal process, from goal setting to evaluation (the latter two processes were to be conducted jointly). An interim review could be initiated by either party, as appropriate, so that changing business conditions could be incorporated into the performance-management process.

Performance was appraised on the basis of several goals and criteria that were *not* summarized by one rating or score that could be easily compared to salary ranking. This helped curtail the old practice of forcing summary performance ratings to conform to salary rankings. It also forced consideration of and feedback about the many dimensions of performance during performance review. Moreover, the ranking process for salary-determination purposes was now to take place after the performance review. Employees would receive feedback about where they stood in the rankings and about the basis of the rankings (to promote the understanding of salary rankings as not being based on performance considerations alone, but also to put some pressure on corporate pay practices by opening them up to scrutiny).

Supervisors and employees jointly decided which others (such as co-workers, customers, and other managers) should have input into reviews. To place the individual performance-management practices more squarely into alignment with business performance management, the individual processes of goal setting and performance review were to take place only after the group in which the individual worked had met with its supervisor to set group goals and review group performance. Moreover, individual and team goals and performance reviews were explicitly linked to business plans and corporate goals.

The new performance-management system was carefully set out in documents supplied to all employees. More than six hundred managers were given instruction in how to be trainers in the new practices, and they in turn conducted at least two days of training for every remaining manager and professional in the organization (about twenty thousand people). Baseline data were collected before the design process began, and the data collection was repeated at two-year intervals after the new performance-management system was implemented. The results showed that the new practices were increasingly being followed, and that people saw a closer link between their own performance and business performance. Furthermore, they reported higher involvement and more lateral participative processes, a reflection of the culture and values set forth in the mission statement. Immediately after the rollout of the new system, several parts of the corporation that had begun organizing as teams adapted the new system for team-level performance management by using the entire process to manage the performance of the team as the performing unit. In other units, the team planning and review processes spurred increased use of formal teams. The corporate level of Oilco later decided to recommend a corporatewide team-oriented performance-management process. In addition, corporate pay practices were changed to include bonuses based on local business-unit performance as well as larger divisional performance.

Ranking processes metamorphosed into processes that placed employees into a few pay categories (usually three or five).

The Oilco performance-management practices were designed to reflect the worldview to which the organization wanted to shift. The new performance management was a set of practices, a way of doing things, that implied a different organizational model from the existing top-down model of hierarchical control, and there are three reasons why it was able to have an impact:

1. The new performance-management system was a set of practices that were central to how every employee related to the organization and gained a sense of worth.
2. Because the performance-management system was a set of practices that touched every employee, it was an extremely efficient means of building a community of shared views with respect to the new paradigm.
3. Other change efforts were going on in many other areas of the organization, and these efforts allowed people to see other examples of the new organizational logic at work, as well as to see them reinforced by the new performance-management system.

We have been arguing that the centrality of performance management can make it either a key lever for change or a stubborn barrier to change. Figure 14.2 illustrates the central role of performance-management practices, showing that they can so shape worldviews as to keep a company locked into the status quo even when the company is faced with data about the need to change. Medco, for example, was having difficulty establishing cross-functional teams and getting its scientists to gear their activities to market needs. Likewise, the aerospace and defense firms that we studied (Mohrman, Mohrman, and Worley, 1990; Mohrman, Mohrman, and Lawler, 1992), when they were faced with the information that their traditional individual approaches were dysfunctional, tried to improve them by making them better individual approaches, thus perpetuating the old paradigm—even though many of the "fixes" were intended to remedy anomalies within the old paradigm.

At Oilco, by contrast, new approaches to performance management were explicitly and successfully used to stimulate changes

Figure 14.2. Role of Performance Management in Traditional and New Organizations.

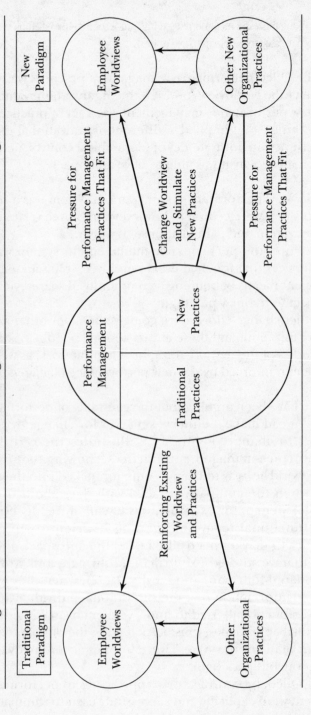

in worldview and further changes in organizational practice. The new performance-management practices deviated from the model of hierarchical control. They complemented some of the experimental lateral organizational work structures that were in place, and they stimulated the creation of others. These dynamics can redound in even further change in performance management. (Recall the ChemTeam, where changes in work design created a flatter organization, and where the use of teams, combined with a small change in performance management, created a push for more fundamental changes in the way performance was managed.) The key role of performance management appears to reside in its ability to stimulate *or prevent,* across the entire organization, the deep changes (that is, changes in worldview) that must accompany a pervasive change in practices.

An Open-Systems View of the New Performance Management and Organizational Learning

Some of the companies we have studied were well on their way to a flatter, team-based organizational model. Many features of that model were in place. In these companies, we were able to observe the ongoing central role of performance management. We have argued elsewhere that large-scale change is an iterative process of closer and closer approximation to the desired new organizational model, a process that entails continuous learning as the organization refines and evolves its design over time (Mohrman and Mohrman, 1997; Mohrman and Cummings, 1989). This argument is consistent with the notion that the new organizational paradigm includes the need for organizational learning. We saw performance-management practices play a key role in these ongoing learning processes and design iterations. To explain this phenomenon, we can look to the open-systems nature of the new organizational and performance-management paradigm.

Performance Management as an Open System

As mentioned earlier, the literature has often characterized performance appraisal and performance feedback as control systems (Taylor, Fisher, and Ilgen, 1984). In the traditional organizational paradigm, management provides feedback on performance as well as the criteria of appraisal, an arrangement that leaves employees to adjust their performance so that it adheres more closely to what their managers desire. When the criteria do not change, and when the appraisal device remains constant, this arrangement amounts to a thermostat model of performance management. It achieves a steady state of individual performance. Performance management in this sense is a closed system consisting of the manager, the performer, and the loop between them. Its overall effect is to preserve the status quo.

Under the new kind of performance-management system there is still the assumption that feedback is necessary for controlling performance, but individuals, teams, and businesses are seen as nested and *open* systems (Massarik, 1980). The openness of the systems is important: change is generated through each system's openness to feedback from all the stakeholders in its environment. Change is also due to the fact that performance management includes more than just appraisal and feedback. When performance management is considered to be only appraisal and feedback, performance can be adjusted only in terms of the criteria built into the appraisal. But when performance management includes processes for defining performance and developing the ability to perform, feedback can also be used, as necessary, to change the nature of performance and the way in which the performing unit organizes in order to perform. The experience of Techco illustrates both these sources of continuing organizational change.

Techco is a high-technology organization undergoing the change to a more customer-oriented, lateral way of functioning. Progress in this direction varies from location to location in the corporation. In the corporate headquarters, a cross-functional team-based organization was formed to develop and maintain various computer-based corporate human resources (HR) systems (including the system for compensation and benefits, the HR information system, and the system for affirmative action). Teams were organized around customers (that is, various HR departments) and consisted of HR systems analysts and corporate information systems (IS) personnel (analysts, programmers, and hardware people).

After the cross-functional teams had been in place for about a year, a task force was formed to develop a performance-management system that would be consistent with the new organization. The task force decided to take the performance-management task in stages. The first stage was to introduce a process by which each team could review its own performance as a team. To this end, each team was trained in a simple process of identifying people in the organization who had a stake in the team's performance. These stakeholders included managers, customers, and other teams. Each team then put together a basic survey consisting of open-ended questions, to determine how each of its stakeholders viewed its performance. Team members also answered the survey questions themselves.

After receiving the stakeholders' input, each team met to discuss all the evaluations (those of the stakeholders and those of the individual team members). The team then compiled a summary of the review and shared it with the organization's management team, which had itself gone through the same exercise. Next came a similar process, whereby the entire HR systems organization was reviewed on the basis of these and similar inputs. All of this preceded the traditional, individually oriented performance-appraisal process, which was to reflect the performance dimensions that had become important for individuals in the new team-based organization. Managers who filled out individual performance appraisals were asked also to take the performance of individuals' teams into account.

The result of the team evaluations was that team members embarked on an extended examination of their very organization as teams. For example, some teams came to realize that there was little internal interdependence among their own members and that they neither were nor needed to be functioning as teams: individuals were more interdependent with other teams than with each other. Other teams saw themselves perceived in very different ways by different stakeholders according to the function represented by the reviewer. These and other issues had surfaced informally from time to time, but the team-review process systematically highlighted their existence. The review started a process by which the entire organization began reorganizing itself into a more sensible team-based structure. This process was further spurred on when different team members received very different individual appraisals, apparently only because they reported to bosses representing different functions. For example, team members nominally employed by the IS function tended to be evaluated on the traditionally "hard," numbers-oriented criteria associated with the discipline of computer science, whereas team members nominally employed by the HR organization, but who belonged to the same team as the IS personnel, had the same backgrounds, and performed the same tasks, were evaluated on "soft," human relations–oriented criteria. This discrepancy uncovered the need for cross-functional management and for managers to agree on the purposes of the teams and the proper evaluation criteria for them. It also began a dialogue about the varying worldviews of the different disciplines, a variance that was leading to organizational changes that were not mutually congruent or supportive. In this organization, the introduction of a multistakeholder, team-based performance-management process initiated a significant redesign of the organization. It led to a change iteration that moved the various features and practices of the organization more into alignment with the model of a flat, team-based, customer-oriented organizational model.

When Techco went through the process of team-based performance review, the company ended up questioning both the very nature of the performance that was being delivered and the way in which the company was organized to deliver it. Techco learned about the factors that were impeding its effectiveness in applying the new team approaches. The result was further organizational change, but change that was still consistent with the new organizational paradigm to which the company was in the process of moving.

Our recent research on twenty-six team-based business units in the knowledge-work components of seven companies has found similar phenomena, as well as further evidence of the importance of the open-systems approach to performance management (Mohrman, Cohen, and Mohrman, 1995). In these various settings, performance-management practices ranged from very traditional, with only a nodding glance toward the team-based organization, to quite sophisticated. The sophisticated approaches employed practices that managed the performance of teams as well as that of the individual team members, using multiple sources outside the teams (sources that included managers, customers, and other teams) to determine both what the teams should be doing and to review how well the teams were doing those things.

Reward systems also varied in the degree to which they rewarded individual and team performance. This variance afforded us an opportunity to examine the impact of various aspects of the new performance-management paradigm. The practice of managers reviewing individual employees had a negative impact on team performance. In these cases, pay for individual performance was generally based on managers' review of individuals. Interviewees reported that when pay for individual performance exists, employees tend to focus on it to the exclusion of other forms of feedback, thus accentuating the closed loop.

Team performance was positively affected to the extent that both managers and customers reviewed teams' performance, and to the extent that the teams themselves were involved in defining what their performance should be. It was interesting to note that when a team reviewed its own performance, the self-review tended to be negatively correlated with the team's concurrent performance but resulted in the team's coming up with organizational and process improvements. These improvements also occurred to the extent that team members evaluated each other and the team jointly planned what its performance should be. We also noted that in these team-based settings, rewards for team performance tended to foster team performance planning and review by customers, managers, and the teams themselves—and, as we have just reported, team performance planning and review by customers, managers, and the teams themselves tend to be associated with team performance and/or team improvements.

In short, in team-based settings the performance-management practices that have the strongest impacts on team performance and process improvements are formal team-based practices and practices that bring in multiple stakeholders' perspectives. Performance-management processes within a team tend to focus on improvements in methods and processes; external stakeholders' inputs focus on performance. The only positive form of individual-level performance management was embodied in individual reviews by co-workers, which tended to lead to process improvements in the team. In other words, the review of an individual by co-workers does not stop with evaluation of the individual's performance but tends to progress to an examination of how the individual's performance is affected by the way the team does things, and this kind of review often results in the team's making improvements that help the individual perform. Finally, in these organizations both individual- and team-based pay for performance were perceived as fair by team members, who had expanded the notion of equity to include team and business-unit pay for performance.

In at least two organizations, team performance management was tied to organizational learning, not just to learning within the team. In both cases, the management team gave itself the task of guiding the ongoing change process. Management took advantage of team assessments to systematically solicit from the teams what organizational factors were impeding or facilitating their effectiveness. On the basis of this information, management planned further changes in the organization to strengthen the new model. In this way, more and more pieces of the new paradigm were put into place. This process was similar to what happened in Techco as changes resulted from team performance management.

If performance-management practices create an open system, they contribute to ongoing change and learning in the organization, not just in the performing units that are reviewed but also in the larger system encompassing many performing units. An open system can be created only if information comes from many sources and is shared in many directions, a development that fundamentally changes the nature of control in an organization. Similarly, an open system requires that the redefinition of work and the development of capabilities be included in the performance-management model. The traditional supervisor-subordinate individual performance-management system that focuses on appraisal and rewards is a closed system that impedes organizational learning. A characteristic of the new organizational paradigm is that the open-systems nature of the organization and its performance-management processes leads to continuous change by promoting organizational learning and improvement.

Conclusion

We have argued from examples and conceptual models that performance management plays a central role in large-scale organizational change and learning. It can be a force for the status quo, a force for change, and, most important, a force for continued organizational learning and change. Many of our points could be applied to any set of organizational processes and practices, but there are at least three reasons why performance management deserves special emphasis. First, performance management is a set of practices central to the very nature of the individual's relationship with the organization. Performance management is one of the principal means by which the individual knows his or her place, role, and worth in the organization. Therefore, performance management's unique role in the organization is to make a direct connection with the community of individuals and instill the desired organizational paradigm. Second, performance-management practices can nest the various performing units within the larger system's performance needs and relate the various units to one another. Third, performance management constitutes a feedback mechanism on the central concern in organizations: performance. It is a feedback loop that can be either open to or closed to the organizational environment. According to how performance management is conceived and practiced, the organization can be a relatively static, hierarchically managed entity or an evolving, learning, and continuously improving one.

Facing the Challenges of the Future

Susan Albers Mohrman
Edward E. Lawler III

A vast set of challenges lies ahead in the era of cyberspace and the information highway, the global village, hypercompetition, the high-energy organization, virtual teams, networked organizations, nimble rewards, the new employment bargain, and organizations that learn. These intriguing developments can engage our imaginations, challenge our creative juices, and serve as organizing concepts for understanding and surviving in the turbulence of a fundamental worldwide reordering of organizations and economies, or they can lead to activity that tears apart the very fabric of societies. This book has taken a positive view, a view underpinned by the fundamental belief that as organizations redesign, they will recognize the reality that they are composed of people, that organizational strength depends on meeting the needs of the human beings who constitute our diverse global societies, and that employee commitment is a key outcome that cannot be ignored if organizations are to prosper through time.

This book contains chapters that describe fundamental change in organizational forms as organizations reconfigure themselves in order to be competitive. It also contains chapters that describe frameworks and approaches for ensuring that people are beneficiaries of the new order. Achieving competitiveness through organizations that are also good for people is a tall order, full of tensions, contradictions, and thorny trade-offs, but it is the most important agenda item for the future. There is no question that the extensive change in organizational forms that has been discussed throughout this book has wrought and will continue to wreak havoc with the traditional relationship of employee to work and to employer. Lest we bend to the temptation (because of the dislocation we have experienced) of saying that we should retreat to the old relationship and the old forms, we should keep in mind that the old relationship was not without its problems.

The era of supposed company loyalty and lifelong careers produced an extensive literature and many change interventions seeking ways to humanize the workplace and involve the employee in decision making. It yielded institutions of collective bargaining that sought to increase the power of workers. It was dominated by bloated, control-oriented, top-heavy corporations whose dismantling and reconfiguring in response to competitive pressures have created a major dislocation and a brutal reminder that the relationship of employee to employer cannot be taken for granted. Today's era of turbulent change and the emergence of new organizational forms may in fact give rise to a new organizational era that offers a different but greater stake and opportunity for the members of organizations, as well as for their customers.

The Design Challenge

The overarching message of this book is that building the competitive organization is a complex, never-ending design task that must take into account the nature of the environment and its pressures and opportunities and the nature of the human beings who populate organizations and carry out organizations' work. The design task is to create organizations that are flexible enough to adapt to rapid change in the competitive environment, that are agile, creative, and daring enough to continuously abandon the old and create the new, and yet that are robust enough to build, nurture, and develop their competencies, their stock of knowledge, and their performance capabilities.

There is no question that the era of the vertically integrated bureaucratic form is over, and that the era of the flexible, dynamic, customized organizational form is here. Chapters Two, Three, and Four have argued that the winners will be organizations that stay one step ahead strategically, charting courses that cannibalize their own strengths and creating an ever-higher moving target for competitors to chase. Organizational forms will emerge and metamorphose as organizations seek ways to be world-class in all aspects, creating a unique configuration of internal activities, alliances, and outsourcing to deliver value to the customer. Global organizations will create a network of relationships and units that will enable them to achieve worldwide revenue from their considerable investments in the acquisition and application of knowledge that creates a steady stream of new products, processes, and services.

Organizations need to be reconfigured and redeployed as their performance requirements and tasks change. In order to be reconfigurable, organizations need to array their resources in many temporary, cross-functional structures, such as project teams, product teams, alliances, and venture units of various kinds.

In high-wage countries, organizations increasingly depend on their knowledge assets for survival: on acquiring, growing, and creating these assets to support strategy, and on being able to assemble the appropriate knowledge and skills to take advantage of opportunities and carry out strategy. The design challenge is to create systems that capture, preserve, and leverage knowledge. Organizations must attract, retain, and develop workforces with the necessary skills and competencies to learn and employ an ever-increasing stock of knowledge. They must craft and continually improve work processes in which rapidly developing knowledge is embedded. The knowledge-management challenge goes far beyond the individual competency-development challenge to include knowledge-management approaches built into the way the organization carries out its work.

The competencies that individuals need in order to succeed in today's environment are multifaceted. They include deep functional and disciplinary knowledge, broad cross-disciplinary and business knowledge, project- and people-management skills, global understanding, computer skills, system-development and process-improvement skills, and marketing and planning skills. We are in an era in which the value of an employee to a company does not lie in the succession of functional jobs and levels through which that individual has progressed. It lies in the total set of competencies possessed by the individual that can contribute to the dynamic array of activities that must be carried out to enact the organizational strategy. The premium is not on slow and gradual learning but rather on continuous, relentless, accelerated learning. The competency of ongoing, self-guided learning may be the single most important one for individuals in organizations who continually face new performance challenges.

Individual competencies need to be combined to produce organizational capabilities, which depend on individual skills and knowledge but, more important, require integrated activity. These capabilities are manifested through patterns of collective activity, such as process improvement, customer service, alliance formation, change management, systems development and implementation, lean manufacturing, and new-product development. Knowledge in these areas cannot be possessed solely by individuals. It has to be embedded in organizational routines, guidelines, norms, processes, and systems. It has to be shared and accessible. For the reconfigurable organization, perhaps the most important competency is organizational design and redesign.

Computer and telecommunications technology are critical enablers of organizational flexibility and learning. They provide the foundation for accessible distributed information and for connections among the diverse and dynamic parts of the network. Information systems are the locus for storage of software that enables many of the routines of the company and of databases that contain vast stores of information and knowledge. These systems enable work to be done and integrated anywhere in the world. Taking advantage of this technology, as Chapter Twelve points out, requires a simultaneous effort in organization design and technology design in which all stakeholders have active involvement. The power of the new technologies to change the very nature of work is daunting and intriguing. They can be used as agents of either empowerment or control (Zuboff, 1984). How they are used will in large part determine whether new work systems will result in meaningful work for employees, and whether the organization is able to tap the energies and knowledge of its employees to support high performance and ongoing learning.

The design challenge includes several key areas:

- Configuring the corporate structure and its units, networks, internal markets, global structures, and teams
- Creating the information, decision-making, and planning processes that will support the business strategy
- Creating the human resources development approaches that will support the business strategy
- Building into the organizational configuration the basic processes for developing and growing capabilities for organizational performance
- Developing the work-design and human resources practices for motivating people and involving them in business success
- Building in approaches to ongoing organizational improvement
- Developing approaches to knowledge management

Intertwined with these key areas and processes is the development of the technological infrastructure to support them. As Chapter Seven points out, approaches to organizational improvement have evolved to the point where they address the work-design and motivational aspects of the firm, the process-improvement approaches, and the identification and design of laterally integrated processes that deliver value to the customer. Design efforts to align information technology (IT) with the design of the enterprise and its key processes and work design are underpinning current attempts to more fully integrate and take advantage of the rapidly evolving technological frontier.

The Changing Nature of Work

The fundamental changes in organizational design that are occurring entail changes in the nature of work. Individuals no longer are hired into well-defined jobs with job descriptions that clearly define and neatly delineate ongoing roles in organizations. Work is fluid, and jobs are defined by what needs to be done to complete tasks. As organizations become characterized by networks and by dynamic series of cross-functional units, work content becomes increasingly dynamic and cross-functional. Organizations are dependent on team performance rather than on the aggregation of individual performances.

In the process-oriented organization, all individuals need to be cognizant of the whole process, of how their work and the team's work fits in, and of what adds value to the customer and to business and financial performance. Integrated information systems enable work teams and service deliverers access to all relevant information without requiring them to request reports or await communications through a chain of command. People are, in a sense, able to make decisions that are informed by the same data that used to be a source of the power of higher-level managers and staff groups. Through the use of automated systems, including artificial intelligence, people are able to make their own trade-offs, perform their own trouble-shooting, respond to requests about any aspect of their work, and easily perform tasks that used to be mediated by supervisors or staff specialists. As Chapters Six and Twelve point out, information technology not only changes the nature of work but also allows work to be done in any place where a computer and a modem can be found. IT truly enables the distributed, virtual organization.

In the lateral organization, individuals get direction from many sources—team members, internal and external customers, key process documents, and access to a stream of information about strategy and operations. Some individuals report to teams and do not have supervisors. Others may have supervisors in different states or countries. These supervisors may have responsibility for hundreds of people but no real insight into those employees' work. People working at home may have supervisors who make sure they are delivering their work but who are certainly not directing and supervising in the day-to-day sense. People working in a networked organization must be able to influence others and resolve issues laterally, without the intervention and mediation of the chain of command.

In this environment, management works by results, not through the assignment of supervisors who can keep an eye on the work of employees and make sure they are working consistently and carrying out their jobs effectively from a disciplinary perspective. Autonomy has increased, but so have individual responsibility and accountability. There is a premium on the ability of employees to manage themselves, of teams to manage themselves, and of both to take the initiative, solve problems, and build the network that is necessary for getting crucial information and collaborators to accomplish tasks. Individuals and teams are responsible for their own development—for becoming aware of new approaches and investing in self-development. There is no supervisor with enough visibility to closely monitor development activities. The role of functions and disciplines changes radically, away from day-to-day directing and top-down commands, auditing, and mentoring, and toward the creation of a context in which people have access to knowledge, information, and opportunities for skill development. The functional group, if it exists at all, is not staffed in such a way that it can worry about the skills and knowledge of each person; at most, it can make opportunities for development available, create policies and systems that enable and encourage people to take advantage of them, and assume that motivated and capable employees will take the initiative. In this era of rapid growth in knowledge and of the increasing importance of competing on the basis of superior knowledge management, organizational resources need to be diverted from chain-of-command supervision to creation of a knowledge infrastructure and to ongoing improvement in organizational performance capabilities. Individuals who prosper in this environment will do so because they orient themselves to learning.

Work increasingly needs to be performed across boundaries—across functions, business units, companies, and continents. It demands integration of worldviews with diverse goals and motivations, different knowledge orientations, and different cultures. Contractors work with full-time employees, and exempt employees work with nonexempt employees. Managers may serve on teams that are led by their subordinates. A person may manage or lead one activity and simultaneously be an individual contributor to another. The traditional functional organization was built to minimize diversity and maximize control. It created units of people similarly trained and performing similar tasks. In the new organization, work needs to be done across boundaries and cross-functional groupings among diverse groups of contributors. Success in this environment requires the ability to influence without formal power, to resolve conflict, to interact effectively with people of fundamentally different styles, cultures, and preferences, to bring differences to the surface and resolve them, and to create integrated frameworks for planning and tasks.

The People Challenge

The changing nature of organizations demands new competencies from employees, and it establishes a new relationship between employees and organizations. There has been much discussion of this new relationship, sometimes called the new employment contract or bargain, or the changing psychological contract. The psychological contract refers to "individual beliefs, shaped by the organization, regarding terms of an exchange agreement between individuals and their organization" (Rousseau, 1995, p. 9). As originally used, the term implied a balance struck between what the company expected of the employee and what the employee could expect in return (Barnard, 1938). Achieving a balance that is acceptable to both sides is critical to the ongoing commitment of effort by employees.

New organizational designs have changed the balance for all employees. Nonexempt workers can no longer narrowly define their boundaries and the limits of their effort and expect their organizations to be successful. Technical workers can no longer simply do their technical work and leave concerns about costs, customers, and schedules to managers. Staff groups increasingly find that they need to sell their services to the organization and become knowledgeable about the business. Managers are finding that there are fewer positions and management levels, that they need to have cross-functional capabilities, and that their old positions of authority and tools of command and control are disappearing, and so they have to use new approaches to managing and influencing. All employees are discovering that the downsizing and delayering of the past decade have changed the expectation that working hard and doing a good job will be rewarded by movement upward in the organization and a job for life. Even the CEO and other top executives are at risk: their jobs are more and more contingent on their performing well in a shifting and complex environment.

The shifting psychological contract has an interesting twist. Historically, the bargain has revolved around "hygiene" factors: wages and benefits, working conditions, security, and, in some cases, opportunities for career growth and greater status and income. Only recently have movements like employee involvement started to stress growth factors, such as learning and developing, being able to contribute more and experience the motivational impact of accomplishing a whole task, and having more say over one's own work. It was an uphill struggle to get organizations to worry about the growth and development of employees and develop a belief that the performance of the organization would improve if the organizational design were changed to promote involvement.

We now seem to be in the middle of an astounding reversal in the terms of the psychological contract. The Center for Effective Organizations has conducted studies of companies in the midst of fundamental transitions in organizational form, and these studies have found that the new forms are greatly increasing growth outcomes and, in many cases, diminishing availability of "hygiene" factors (see Table 1). As organizations have downsized, removed hierarchical positions (and consequently traditional career slots), frozen wages, made a greater percentage of pay variable, and introduced more self-management and significantly higher performance expectations, individuals report that they are experiencing more opportunities to learn and develop, greater ability to accomplish and contribute more, and more say over their work. The new organizations are geared to people with a high growth orientation. Nevertheless, individuals feel that their companies are benefiting from this situation more than they are themselves. Furthermore, the increase in growth opportunities is not necessarily experienced as an improvement in the quality of worklife; in the minds of many employees, quality of worklife is still associated primarily with the traditional "hygiene" factors.

The psychological contract appears in many cases to be changing by default rather than through planning. New organizational designs and new work designs are offering and demanding a higher level of learning and development, contribution, and accountability. These new organizational forms cannot function effectively if people do not rise to the occasion, and yet this shift is occurring at the same time that the historical underpinnings of the employment relationship are being destroyed. People are being asked to work harder, contribute more, learn more, and take more responsibility in order to keep their jobs as long as they are

Table 1. Perceptions of the Impact of Large-Scale Change in Nine Companies.

The changes have allowed me . . .	Nine-site average	Sites								
		1	2	3	4	5	6	7	8	9
• An opportunity to learn new things	3.83	3.7	4.2	4.0	3.8	4.0	3.1	3.9	3.9	3.9
• To accomplish more than before	3.42	3.3	3.8	3.5	3.3	3.7	2.7	3.9	3.2	3.4
• To have more say in my work	3.28	3.4	3.5	3.6	3.1	3.5	2.4	3.6	3.1	3.3
• A better quality of worklife	3.02	2.9	3.4	3.3	2.8	3.6	2.3	3.4	2.4	3.1
• An opportunity for career growth	2.90	2.7	2.7	2.6	3.1	3.5	2.8	3.0	2.8	2.9
• Job security	2.56	2.0	2.6	2.5	3.0	3.1	2.1	2.4	2.3	3.0
• An opportunity to make more money	2.50	2.3	3.0	2.2	2.4	3.1	2.1	2.2	2.4	2.8

Response code: 1 = strongly disagree, 2 = disagree, 3 = neither agree nor disagree, 4 = agree, 5 = strongly agree

Source: Mohrman and Tenkasi, 1997. Used by permission of the Center for Effective Organizations.

needed. As Chapter Eight points out, a compelling challenge to the human resources function of the organization is to help develop practices that give the employee a true stake in the organization. The crafting of new human resources approaches to support the changing organizational terrain is a critical design imperative.

One foundation that has been suggested for the new employment bargain is for the company to promise the employee opportunities to develop the skills needed for employability (Waterman, Waterman, and Collard, 1994). As Chapter Nine points out, developing a learning contract demands sophistication in planning and delivering development opportunities so that they meet business requirements, fit with the design of work and organizations, and create an environment where people feel they can grow. It requires the establishment of an organizational landscape in which individuals can seek out work assignments that create a portfolio of experiences where they can demonstrate and develop broad and deep skills. Indeed, the organization will have to develop a whole new shared understanding of career growth and development because all of this must occur in a flat organization. Companies will have to find new ways to value and acknowledge lateral movement and development.

Compensation approaches will also have to change to acknowledge that the organization is establishing a more market-mediated relationship with its employees—hiring the competencies it needs, and keeping them as long as it needs them. Chapter Eleven discusses the challenge. Reward systems must be nimble enough to meet the changing requirements and realities of the business environment and to motivate the kinds of performance that are required for success while building and retaining the key competencies of the firm. In this shifting employment situation, a key challenge is to find ways to give the employee a stake in business performance while not promising security or providing a sense of growth through regular raises and advancement along a vertical career path. The old response was to proliferate levels and grades (and consequently overhead and total labor expense) to give people a sense of movement and growth. In the future, other approaches must be found.

The current interest in competency management reflects the urgency of this challenge. While needing to preserve workforce flexibility, organizations also need to ensure that they have the needed competencies for effective organizational performance. They can hire, grow, develop, and partner with individuals and organizations that have the needed competencies. No matter which approaches are employed, the competitiveness of the organization depends not only on having the right organizational model but also on having a highly committed workforce with the competencies needed for performance. Organizational capability depends on having individuals and team members who possess or can easily secure the knowledge and skills to attend to the many performance pressures and requirements in today's complex environment.

The fact that we are in a knowledge-intensive era—that competitive advantage is derived from the organization's pool of knowledge and the way it is deployed, diffused, and embedded in work processes—makes the issue of competency management even more critical. It also elevates the task of creating an employee stake in performance to a critical priority. Giving the employee a piece of the action is no longer a radical humanist idea. It may become a key differentiator between high- and low-performing organizations. Finding new ways to value contributions (other than by using rank and authority, crafting new images of careers, and finding ways to give employees an upside earnings potential) is a compelling requirement.

Another key requirement is learning how to manage the many different workforces that are emerging. These include the "permanent" core employees who carry the organizational memory, serve as an ongoing pool of talent, and manage and orchestrate the shifting relationships and structures that constitute the organization. There are also the contractors and temporary employees, who bring in task-specific capabilities, and outsourcers, who carry out the work of the organization from a different organizational base, sometimes sitting side by side with the core employees of the organization. In this era of blurring boundaries, there are also partners who are intermeshed in joint work structures and who are working collaboratively with organizational employees (Rousseau and Wade-Benzoni, 1995). These different workforces have different relationships (often preferred by the individuals) to the company and different psychological contracts. There are differences not only in what they expect from the company but also in what they expect to contribute. Creating a work setting where these different workforces can work together productively is a key challenge.

The Challenge of Transition

The new organizational order described in this book is rapidly being put into place in large and small organizations throughout the world. Many small, entrepreneurial firms start up with these new approaches. Employees join knowing the nature of the organization. They focus on what they can learn from the firm to help them with their careers (defined more broadly). Many large organizations are in the midst of the transition. These companies have changed the rules of the game for a large number of existing employees who have critical knowledge and experience. They are discovering that reshaping an organization entails fundamental relearning.

A common theme in the literature of transformation is that large-scale organizational change is systemic in nature. Chapter Thirteen discusses the learning-process issues required for accelerated organizational transition. The authors argue that today's organizational transitions generally entail changes in three interwoven architectures: the market architecture of the firm, its social architecture, and its technical architecture. In order for organizations to become flexible, reconfigurable learning entities, learning must occur in all three of these arenas, and this learning must be ongoing as the organization continuously improves its performance and charts new strategic directions. Transitional learning entails shifts in people's cognitive understanding of how the organization operates, as well as in individual and collective behavior patterns. Both transitional learning and ongoing learning are process-intensive endeavors, entailing a change in what is seen as productive work to include the processes by which shared meanings are established and evolved.

Chapter Twelve explores a major aspect of the learning that is required in today's environment: learning how to design and integrate information systems and the work systems of the organization. The authors draw the conclusion that using information technology requires systemic design and learning that is best accomplished through collaboration by the many diverse stakeholders in the new technology. New information technologies are changing how organizations relate to one another, how organizations are configured, and how technical tasks are performed.

A critical facilitator of transition can be aligning employee self-interest with the adoption of the new approaches and the development of the new competencies required to carry out the organization's strategy. Employees define their interests to a great degree in terms of the outcomes they experience as a result of their performance in the organization. Performance-management practices are central to the establishment of a new psychological contract, for they define what is expected from employees, what competencies are required, and how performance is assessed, recognized and reviewed, as well as what kinds of rewards are distributed. As is pointed out in Chapter Fourteen, performance-management approaches can help unleash change or they can be agents of the status quo. Other aspects beyond rewards need to be nimble: just-in-time training and development, multiple and multidirectional reviews, frequent feedback, the building and rebuilding of teams, and dynamic definition of goals and priorities are all required in the dynamic, reconfigurable organization. Performance management needs to be carried out at multiple levels and must include teams and business units. Performance-management systems can be agents of learning if they are open and flexible, but they can operate against changing strategies and designs if they remain based on deep-seated assumptions from the past about the role of the hierarchy and about the primacy of individual performance.

Most important, transition will become the status quo of the future. New strategies, new organizations, new systems, and changing processes are becoming a way of life as organizations pursue a competitive course with great agility. Change management and organization design are bedrock competencies of an organization.

Societal Challenges

Resources, activities, and jobs move around the world as organizations increasingly compete on a global terrain. The dislocation that has been part and parcel of this transformation is familiar to us all as it appears relentlessly on the airwaves and in our lives. Companies struggle with the desires of their communities for a stable employment base and the desires of their stockholders for ever-growing markets, revenues, and profits. Sometimes these can be best achieved through moving activities where they are done most inexpensively, moving operations into new markets and different host countries, and meeting the insatiable requirement for doing more with less. One manifestation of the complexity and broader impact of these trade-offs, and of the need to keep an eye on the balancing role that management must play, is increased attention to the role of the board of directors, as Chapter One discusses. That chapter argues that management is too important to be left unaudited to managers, and that the principles of effective organization should be applied to the organization and functioning of the board of directors as it carries out its stewardship role.

The last half of the twentieth century has seen major competition between two economic and political ideologies: capitalism and communism. Capitalism won this contest for a number of reasons, but perhaps the major one is that it was more successful at producing wealth than communism was. That, combined with the degree of personal freedom that it allowed, convinced people around the world that it is a superior economic system. As a result of the triumph of capitalism, enormous new markets have been opened to global corporations, and over a billion people have entered the capitalist labor market. The potential is enormous where worldwide economic growth and the generation of wealth are concerned.

A good guess at this point is that a major issue for the first part of the twenty-first century will be how the wealth generated by global capitalism will be distributed and shared. There is also likely to be increased emphasis on how capitalism can be managed so that it benefits the society as a whole, and not just a small number of capitalists. In the United States this is already an issue because of the growing income differences that have appeared. For much of the last part of the twentieth century, capitalism was restrained to some degree because of the competition with communism. With the absence of these ideologies as a restraining force, new issues are likely to arise around how large corporations and capitalism can be managed so that the maximum benefit is realized by society as a whole. Particularly central here is the issue of who will and can control global corporations.

As more and more global corporations appear, it is quite likely that corporate governance issues will develop that go far beyond issues concerned with the role of the board of directors. The typical large corporation is now primarily domiciled in one country, and the laws of that country act as an effective limitation on and guide to the company's behavior. It is not obvious, however, that this will still be true as organizations become more global and more flexible. If an organization can operate effectively in a large number of countries, and if it can easily move its operations and critical assets from one country to another, then it seems quite possible that no single country will be able to control the organization. This raises a significant problem for society because no corporation (or other kind of organization, for that matter) should be trusted to operate without effective checks and balances.

At this point, it is not clear what the best solution is to controlling major global corporations. One possibility is a multigovernment agreement that would allow governance of particular corporations to be given to one country and enforced by others. Another possibility would be an international organization like the United Nations that takes responsibility for controlling certain corporations. The obvious danger here is that a new governmental structure could render global corporations ineffective by creating a need for excessive bureaucracy; as a result, the advantages of being global could be lost. This should not discourage us, however, from debating the issue of how to govern global corporations and from working toward a solution.

Whether corporations are global or not, there clearly is a need for some changes in the way they are governed. This is particularly true at the board level, where, in most cases, the governance process tips the focus solely toward the interests of one stakeholder group: investors. The typical corporate board in the United States and in many other countries is made up of individuals who come from the corporate world and often are CEOs or major executives in other corporations. Missing are representatives of the communities that the corporations operate in, employees, and government officials. Having representatives of these stakeholder groups on boards might contribute to more balanced decision making, in which the interests of multiple stakeholders would be taken into account. Balanced stakeholder interests are likely to be an increasingly important issue in the twenty-first century as corporations are challenged with respect to their power and their impact on society.

The relationship between work organizations and the larger society has always been a fluid one warranting constant examination. Because of the many changes in the nature of organizations and in their demands on employees, this has never been more true. The typical large corporation can be conceptualized as having multiple stakeholders. The most obvious ones are its customers, its suppliers, its employees, the communities in which it operates, and, finally, its investors. A rather convincing argument can be made that the major organizational changes of the 1980s and 1990s were particularly advantageous for the investors, particularly in the United States, where stock prices soared. Senior managers, because of their incentive and stock-ownership plans, also profited tremendously from the increased effectiveness of their organizations. Perhaps the most unrewarded stakeholders in major corporations were the rank-and-file employees. They have gained a little financially and have augmented their skills, but their financial gains have been particularly small by comparison with the gains of investors and senior managers. Society needs to take a fresh look at the role of corporations and the consequences of creating organizational settings that are geared more to the creation of growth than to "hygiene" outcomes for employees. The intense commitment required for success in global business raises the need to make work more family-friendly.

We believe it is time to reexamine and change the treatment of employees by corporations. They need a new contract, one that gives them a more powerful stakeholder position and a greater claim on the performance gains of their corporations. Perhaps the best way to accomplish this is by putting them on an equal footing with investors. The easiest way to do this, of course, is to make them owners in their organizations. The new contract can be reinforced by putting them on the boards of directors of their corporations and by strengthening the laws that help protect their medical, insurance, retirement, and other benefits.

It is beyond the scope of this concluding chapter to go into specific details about the changes that are needed to adjust the balance between investors and employees as stakeholders. It is appropriate, however, to note that if the imbalance is not addressed, the foundations on which the organizations of the future need to be built will crumble. More than ever, organizational designs depend for their effectiveness on committed, learning-oriented employees. It is unreasonable to expect educated, knowledgeable employees to demonstrate the kind of commitment that is required to create a learning-oriented, reconfigurable organization if they do not have an appreciable piece of the action. These are not unskilled employees who have no choice but to take minimum-wage jobs—many of them have the ability to go out on their own and create new, competing organizations.

Overall, employee stakeholders need a better deal if organizations are going to be effective and satisfy their other stakeholders. We hope that this better deal will develop from major corporations' enlightened self-interest rather than from governmental action and legislation, which is almost always more cumbersome and dysfunctional, but that is what we may get if investors and corporate leaders do not soon realize that a balanced employment contract is critical to the health of organizations and to a meaningful society. In the end, corporations are only legal entities established to serve society by creating goods and services and providing work opportunities for members of the society. They are not created only to serve investors or senior managers.

The case of communities is much more complex. Some areas have struggled as a consequence of the globalization and reconfiguration of major corporations, and others have prospered. For example, Singapore and Taiwan have clearly prospered, whereas Germany and France have not done so well.

There are a number of challenges that go well beyond the confines of the organization and demand community and societal changes. As organizations shrink the size of their core workforces and deal increasingly with contractors, part-time employees, and vendors, they cease playing many of their traditional roles in the lives of their employees. Many employees will not be with any company long enough to have vested pensions. Societal approaches need to emerge to facilitate job changes; the time-consuming and costly process of job searches needs to be made easier and faster through the emergence of new services that gather information and link people to opportunities. Health insurance and retirement will have to become portable. The disappearance of well-paying low-skill jobs and the emergence of an employment arena that demands technological and educational sophistication as a ticket to success raises difficult issues for educational institutions and the government. New approaches are needed for linking employees to development opportunities. Organizational flexibility requires an infrastructure to support the fluid movement and development of people and jobs.

There is already evidence that the role of corporations in addressing some issues is being redefined. Concerted efforts by companies to hire employees off welfare, establish literacy programs, take family-friendly approaches, establish diversity programs, and undertake health care insurance reform are all small steps in establishing a new balance. The new competitive rules have created new forms of organization and placed new requirements on employees. Fundamental change in organizations will inevitably lead to the fundamental redrawing of the contours of work and society. A key organizational challenge is for corporations to help craft the contours that enable the legitimate concerns of multiple societal stakeholders to be addressed.

References

Introduction

Cooper, R. *When Lean Enterprises Collide: Competing Through Confrontation.* Boston: Harvard Business School Press, 1995.

D'Aveni, R. A. *Hypercompetition: Managing the Dynamics of Strategic Maneuvering.* New York: Free Press, 1994.

Galbraith, J. R. *Competing with Flexible Lateral Organizations.* Reading, Mass.: Addison Wesley Longman, 1994.

Galbraith, J. R. *Designing Organizations: An Executive Briefing on Strategy, Structure, and Process.* San Francisco: Jossey-Bass, 1995.

Halal, W. *The New Capitalism.* New York: Wiley, 1993.

Hamel, G., and Prahalad, C. K. *Competing for the Future.* Boston: Harvard Business School Press, 1994.

Lawler, E. E., III. *From the Ground Up: Six Principles for Building the New Logic Corporation.* San Francisco: Jossey-Bass, 1996.

Prahalad, C. K., and Hamel, G. "The Core Competence of the Corporation." *Harvard Business Review,* 1990, *68*(3), 79–91.

Ulrich, D. W., and Lake, D. *Organizational Capability.* New York: Wiley, 1990.

Werther, W. B., and Kerr, J. F. "The Shifting Sands of Competitive Advantage." *Business Horizons,* May–June 1995, pp. 11–17.

Williams, J. R. "How Sustainable Is Your Competitive Advantage?" *California Management Review,* 1992, *34,* 1–23.

Womack, J. P., Jones, D. T., and Roos, D. *The Machine That Changed the World.* Old Tappan, N.J.: Macmillan, 1990.

Chapter One

American Society of Corporate Secretaries, Inc. *Current Board Practices.* New York: American Society of Corporate Secretaries, Inc., 1996.

Bainbridge, S. M. "Independent Directors and the ALI Corporate Governance Project." *George Washington Law Review,* 1993, *61,* 1034–1083.

Bhagat, S., and Black, B. "Do Independent Directors Matter?" Unpublished manuscript. University of Colorado and Columbia Law School, Feb. 1996.

Budnitz, M. E. "Chapter 11 Business Reorganizations and Shareholder Meetings: Will the Meeting Please Come to Order, or Should the Meeting Be Canceled Altogether?" *George Washington Law Review,* 1990, *58,* 1214–1267.

Cochran, P. L., Wood, R. A., and Jones, T. B. "The Composition of Boards of Directors and Incidence of Golden Parachutes." *Academy of Management Journal,* 1985, *28,* 664–671.

Committee on the Financial Aspects of Corporate Governance and Gee & Co., Ltd. *The Financial Aspects of Corporate Governance* ("The Cadbury Report"). London: Gee & Co., Ltd./Professional Publishing, 1992.

Daily, C. M., and Dalton, C. R. "Outside Directors Revisited: Prescriptions for CEOs and Directors." *Journal of Small Business Strategy,* 1994, *5,* 57–68.

Dewar, J. A., Builder, C. H., Hix, W. M., and Levin, M. H. *Assumption-Based Planning: A Planning Tool for Very Uncertain Times.* Santa Monica, Calif.: RAND Corp., 1993.

Fama, E., and Jensen, M. "Separation of Ownership and Control." *Journal of Law and Economics,* 1983, *26,* 301–325.

Finkelstein, S., and D'Aveni, R. A. "CEO Duality as a Double-Edged Sword: How Boards of Directors Balance Entrenchment Avoidance and Unity of Command." *Academy of Management Journal,* 1994, *37,* 1079–1108.

Hautaluoma, J., Donkersgoed, W., and Kaman, V. *Governing Boards: The Most Important Work Teams.* Vol. 2: *Advances in Interdisciplinary Studies of Work Teams.* Greenwich, Conn.: JAI Press, 1995.

Jensen, M., and Meckling, W. "Theory of the Firm: Managerial Behavior, Agency Costs, and Ownership Structure." *Journal of Financial Economics,* 1976, *3,* 305–360.

Johnson, J. L., Daily, C. M., and Ellstrand, A. E. "Boards of Directors: A Review and Research Agenda." *Journal of Management,* 1996, *22,* 409–438.

Kaplan, R. S., and Norton, D. P. *The Balanced Scorecard: Translating Strategy into Action.* Boston: Harvard Business School Press, 1996.

Kesner, I. F. "Directors' Stock Ownership and Organizational Performance: An Investigation of Fortune 500 Companies." *Journal of Management,* 1987, *13,* 499–507.

Korn/Ferry International. *Board Meeting in Session: 23rd Annual Board of Directors Study.* New York: Korn/Ferry International, 1996.

Lawler, E. E., III. *Strategic Pay: Aligning Organizational Strategies and Pay* Systems. San Francisco: Jossey-Bass, 1990.

Lawler, E. E., III. *The Ultimate Advantage: Creating the High-Involvement Organization.* San Francisco: Jossey-Bass, 1992.

Lawler, E. E., III. *From the Ground Up: Six Principles for Building the New Logic Corporation.* San Francisco: Jossey-Bass, 1996.

Lear, R. W., and Yavitz, B. "The Best and Worst Boards of 1995: Evaluating the Boardroom." *Chief Executive,* Nov. 1995, pp. 24–32.

Lorsch, J. W., and MacIver, E. *Pawns or Potentates: The Reality of America's Corporate Boards.* Boston: Harvard Business School Press, 1989.

Mohrman, S. A., Cohen, S. G., and Mohrman, A. M., Jr. *Designing Team-Based Organizations: New Forms for Knowledge Work.* San Francisco: Jossey-Bass, 1995.

National Association of Corporate Directors. *Performance Evaluation of Chief Executive Officers, Boards, and Directors.* Washington, D.C.: National Association of Corporate Directors, 1994.

National Association of Corporate Directors. *The 1995 Corporate Governance Survey.* Washington, D.C.: National Association of Corporate Directors, 1995a.

National Association of Corporate Directors. *Performance Evaluation of Chief Executive Officers, Boards, and Directors.* Washington, D.C.: National Association of Corporate Directors, 1995b.

National Association of Corporate Directors. *Purposes, Principles, and Best Practices.* Washington, D.C.: National Association of Corporate Directors, 1995c.

Pearce, J. A., II, and Zahra, S. A. "Board Composition from a Strategic Contingency Perspective." *Journal of Management Studies,* 1992, *29,* 411–438.

Pfeffer, J., and Salancik, G. R. *The External Control of Organizations: A Resource Dependence Perspective.* New York: HarperCollins, 1978.

Schellenger, M. H., Wood, D. D., and Tashakori, A. "Board of Director Composition, Shareholder Wealth, and Dividend Policy." *Journal of Management,* 1989, *15,* 457–467.

Thain, D. H., and Leighton, D.S.R. "The Director's Dilemma: What's My Job?" *Business Quarterly,* 1992a, *56,* 75–88.

Thain, D. H., and Leighton, D.S.R. "Improving Board Effectiveness by Evaluating Director Performance." *Business Quarterly,* 1992b, *57,* 23–33.

Useem, M. *Executive Defense: Shareholder Power and Corporate Reorganization.* Cambridge, Mass.: Harvard University Press, 1993.

Vance, S. C. *Boards of Directors: Structure and Performance.* Eugene: University of Oregon Press, 1964.

Zahra, S. A., and Pearce, J. A., II. "Boards of Directors and Corporate Financial Performance: A Review and Integrative Model." *Journal of Management,* 1989, *15,* 291–334.

Chapter Two

Davis, S., and Lawrence, P. *Matrix.* Reading, Mass: Addison Wesley Longman, 1977.

Galbraith, J. R. *Competing with Flexible Lateral Organizations.* Reading, Mass.: Addison Wesley Longman, 1994.

Galbraith, J. R. *Designing Organizations: An Executive Briefing on Strategy, Structure, and Process.* San Francisco: Jossey-Bass, 1995.

Womack, J. P., Jones, D. T., and Roos, D. (1990). *The Machine That Changed the World.* Old Tappan, N.J.: Macmillan.

Chapter Three

Contractor, F. J., and Lorange, P. *Cooperative Strategies in International Business.* San Francisco: New Lexington Press, 1988.

Dyer, J. H. "How Chrysler Created an American Keiretsu." *Harvard Business Review,* 1996, *74*(6), 42–56.

Gerlach, M. L. *Alliance Capitalism.* Berkeley: University of California Press, 1992.

Killing, J. P. *Strategies for Joint Ventures Success.* New York: Praeger, 1983.

Killing, J. P. "The Design and Management of International Joint Ventures." In P. W. Beamish, J. P. Killing, D. J. Lecraw, and A. J. Morrison (eds.), *International Management* (2nd ed.). Burr Ridge, Ill.: Irwin, 1994.

Miles, R. E., and Snow, C. C. "Network Organizations: New Concepts for New Forms." *California Management Review,* 1986, *28,* 62–73.

Nohria, N., and Eccles, R. G. *Networks and Organizations.* Boston: Harvard Business School Press, 1992.

Chapter Four

Bartlett, C. A., and Ghoshal, S. *Managing Across Borders.* Boston: Harvard Business School Press, 1989.

Doz, Y. *Government Control and Multinational Strategic Management.* New York: Praeger, 1988.

Eccles, R. G., and Crane, D. B. *Doing Deals.* Boston: Harvard Business School Press, 1988.

Galbraith, J. R. *Competing with Flexible Lateral Organizations.* Reading, Mass.: Addison Wesley Longman, 1994.

Galbraith, J. R. *Designing Organizations: An Executive Briefing on Strategy, Structure, and Process.* San Francisco: Jossey-Bass, 1995.

Lorenz, C. "Global Webs Still Spun from Home." *Financial Times,* Aug. 18, 1995.

Mankin, D., Cohen S. G., and Bikson, T. K. *Teams and Technology: Fulfilling the Promise of the New Organization.* Boston: Harvard Business School Press, 1996.

Mohrman, S. A., Cohen S. G., and Mohrman, A. M., Jr. *Designing Team-Based Organizations: New Forms for Knowledge Work.* San Francisco: Jossey-Bass, 1995.

O'Hara-Devereaux, M., and Johansen, R. *Globalwork: Bridging Distance, Culture, and Time.* San Francisco: Jossey-Bass, 1994.

Patel, P. "Localized Production of Technology for Global Markets." *Cambridge Journal of Economics,* 1995, *19,* 141–153.

Porter, M. "The Competitive Advantage of Nations." *Harvard Business Review,* 1990, *68*(2), 73–93.

Prahalad, C. K., and Doz, Y. *The Multinational Mission.* New York: Pergamon Press, 1987.

Ruigrok, W., and van Tulder, R. *The Logic of International Restructuring.* New York: Routledge, 1996.

Stopford, J., and Wells, L. *Managing the Multinational Enterprise.* New York: Basic Books, 1972.

Yu, Y.-S. "Global or Stateless Corporations Are National Firms with International Operations." *California Management Review,* 1992, *34,* 107–125.

Yu, Y.-S. "The International Transferability of the Firm's Advantages." *California Management Review,* 1995, *37,* 73–88.

Chapter Five

American Compensation Association. *Raising the Bar: Using Competencies to Enhance Employee Performance.* Scottsdale, Ariz.: American Compensation Association, 1996.

Andrews, T. *The Manchester Interview: Competency-Based Teacher Education.* Washington, D.C.: American Association of Colleges for Teacher Education, 1972.

Ash, R. A., Levine, E. L., and Sistrunk, F. "The Role of Jobs and Job-Based Methods in Personnel and Human Resources Management." In K. Rowland and G. Ferris (eds.), *Research in Personnel and Human Resources Management.* Greenwich, Conn.: JAI Press, 1983.

Bowen, D. E., Ledford, G. E., Jr., and Nathan, B. R. "Hiring for the Organization, Not the Job." *Academy of Management Executive,* 1991, *5*(4), 35–51.

Boyatzis, R. E. *The Competent Manager: A Model of Effective Performance.* New York: Wiley, 1982.

Bridges, W. *Job Shift: How to Prosper in a Workplace Without Jobs.* Reading, Mass.: Addison Wesley Longman, 1994.

Capelli, P., and Crocker-Hefter, A. "Distinctive Human Resources as Firms' Core Competencies." *Organizational Dynamics*, 1996, *24*(3), 7–22.

Finegold, D. L. *Making Apprenticeships Work*. Santa Monica, Calif.: RAND Corp., 1993.

Galbraith, J. R. *Designing Complex Organizations*. Reading, Mass.: Addison Wesley Longman, 1973.

Galbraith, J. R. *Competing with Flexible Lateral Organizations*. Reading, Mass.: Addison Wesley Longman, 1994.

Hamel, G. "The Concept of Core Competence." In G. Hamel and A. Heene (eds.), *Competence-Based Competition*. New York: Wiley, 1994.

Hamilton, S. *Apprenticeship for Adulthood: Preparing Youth for the Future*. New York: Free Press, 1990.

Handy, C. *The Age of Unreason*. Boston: Harvard Business School Press, 1990.

Handy, C. *The Age of Paradox*. Boston: Harvard Business School Press, 1994.

Hoachlander, G., and Rahn, M. "National Skill Standards." *Vocational Education Journal*, Jan. 1994, pp. 20–22.

Jenkins, G. D., Jr., Ledford, G. E., Jr., Gupta, N., and Doty, D. H. *Skill-Based Pay: Practices, Payoffs, Pitfalls, and Prospects*. Scottsdale, Ariz.: American Compensation Association, 1992.

Jessup, G. *Outcomes: NVQs and the Emerging Model of Education and Training*. London: Falmer Press, 1991.

Keltner, B., Finegold, D. L., and Pager, C. *Institutional Supports for a High-Performing Skill Standards System: Evidence from Germany, the UK and Australia*. Santa Monica, Calif.: RAND Corp., 1996.

Klerman, J., and Karoly, L. "Young Men and the Transition to Stable Employment." *Monthly Labor Review*, 1994, *117*(8), 31–48.

Lado, A. A., and Wilson, M. C. "Human Resource Systems and Sustained Competitive Advantage: A Competency-Based Perspective." *Academy of Management Review*, 1994, *19*, 699–727.

Lawler, E. E., III. *Strategic Pay: Aligning Organizational Strategies and Pay Systems*. San Francisco: Jossey-Bass, 1990.

Lawler, E. E., III. "From Job-Based to Competency-Based Organizations." *Journal of Organizational Behavior*, 1994, *15*, 3–15.

Lawler, E. E., III. *From the Ground Up: Six Principles for Building the New Logic Corporation*. San Francisco: Jossey-Bass, 1996.

Lawler, E. E., III, and Ledford, G. E., Jr. "A Skill-Based Approach to Human Resource Management." *European Management Journal*, 1992, *10*, 383–391.

Lawler, E. E., III, and Ledford, G. E., Jr. "New Approaches to Organizing: Competencies, Capabilities, and the Decline of the Bureaucratic Model." In C. L. Cooper and S. E. Jackson (eds.), *Creating Tomorrow's*

Organization: A Handbook for Future Research in Organizational Behavior. New York: Wiley, 1997.

Lawler, E. E., III, Mohrman, S. A., and Ledford, G. E., Jr. *Creating High-Performance Organizations: Practices and Results of Employee Involvement and Total Quality Management in Fortune 1000 Companies.* San Francisco: Jossey-Bass, 1995.

Leavitt, H. "Applied Organizational Change in Industry." In J. March (ed.), *Handbook of Organization.* Skokie, Ill.: Rand McNally.

Ledford, G. E., Jr. "Paying for the Skills, Knowledge, and Competencies of Knowledge Workers." *Compensation and Benefits Review,* 1995, *27*(4), 55–62.

Mohrman, S. A., Cohen, S. G., and Mohrman, A. M., Jr. *Designing Team-Based Organizations: New Forms for Knowledge Work.* San Francisco: Jossey-Bass, 1995.

National Alliance of Business. "Report to the Nation: Business Perspectives on Voluntary Skill Standards." *Skill Standards,* Apr. 1995.

National Center on Education and the Economy and National Alliance of Business. *A Guide for Benchmarking International Skill Standards.* Washington, D.C.: U.S. Department of Labor, 1994.

O'Neal, S. "Competencies: The DNA of the Corporation." *ACA Journal,* 1993–1994, *2*(3), 6–13.

Osterman, P. *Employment Futures.* Oxford, England: Oxford University Press, 1988.

Prahalad, C. K., and Hamel, G. "The Core Competence of the Corporation." *Harvard Business Review,* 1990, *68*(3), 79–93.

Reich, R. B. *The Work of Nations: Preparing Ourselves for Twenty-First-Century Capitalism.* New York: Random House, 1991.

Rumelt, R. P. "Foreword." In G. Hamel and A. Heene (eds.), *Competence-Based Competition.* New York: Wiley, 1994.

Spencer, L. M., and Spencer, S. M. *Competence at Work.* New York: Wiley, 1993.

Stalk, G., Evans, P. E., and Shulman, L. E. "Competing on Capabilities: The New Rules of Corporate Strategy." *Harvard Business Review,* 1992, *70*(2), 57–69.

Streeck, W. "Skills and the Limits of Neo-Liberalism: The Enterprise of the Future as a Place of Learning." *Work, Employment, and Society,* 1989, *3,* 89–104.

Tucker, M. "Skill Standards, Qualification Systems, and the American Workforce." In L. B. Resnick and J. G. Wirt (eds.), *Linking School and Work: Roles for Standards and Assessment.* San Francisco: Jossey-Bass, 1996.

Tucker, S. A., and Cofsky, K. M. "Competency-Based Pay on a Banding Platform." *ACA Journal,* 1994, *3*(1), 30–45.

Ulrich, D. W., Brockbank, W., Yeung, A. K., and Lake, D. "Human Resource Competencies: An Empirical Assessment." *Human Resource Management,* 1995, *34,* 473–495.

Ulrich, D. W., and Lake, D. *Organizational Capability.* New York: Wiley, 1990.

Vickers, M. *Skill Standards and Skill Formation: Cross-National Perspectives on Alternative Training Strategies.* Cambridge, England: Jobs for the Future, 1994.

Wills, J. *Skill Standards Systems in Selected Countries.* Vol. 4. Washington, D.C.: Institute for Educational Leadership, 1994.

Wolf, A. *Competence-Based Assessment.* Philadelphia: Open University Press, 1995.

Zingheim, P., Ledford, G. E., Jr., and Schuster, J. "Competencies and Competency Models: One Size Fits All?" *ACA Journal,* 1996, *5*(1), 56–65.

Chapter Six

Bott, E. "Internet Lies." *PC Computing,* Oct. 1996, 189–196.

Capelli, P., and Rogovsky, N. "New Work Systems and Skill Requirements." *International Labour Review,* 1994, *133,* 205–220.

Chatterjee, P. "ULSI: Market Opportunities and Manufacturing Challenges." *Digest, IEEE International Electron Device Meeting, 1991,* pp. 11–17.

Cohen, S. G. "New Approaches to Teams and Teamwork." In J. R. Galbraith, E. E. Lawler III, and Associates, *Organizing for the Future: The New Logic for Managing Complex Organizations.* San Francisco: Jossey-Bass, 1993.

Davis, D. D. "Form, Function, and Strategy in Boundaryless Organizations." In A. Howard (ed.), *The Changing Nature of Work.* San Francisco: Jossey-Bass, 1995.

Dodd-Thomas, J. *Executive Summary of the Pacific Bell Telecommuting Survey, 1994.* San Francisco: Pacific Bell, 1994.

Dougherty, D. "Interpretive Barriers to Successful Product Innovation in Large Firms." *Organization Science,* 1992, *3,* 179–202.

Gordon, J. "Work Teams: How Far Have They Come?" *Training,* Oct. 1992, pp. 59–65.

Kahn, W. "Psychological Conditions of Personal Engagement and Disengagement at Work." *Academy of Management Journal,* 1990, *33,* 692–724.

Kanter, R. M. *The Change Masters: Innovation for Productivity in the American Workplace.* New York: Simon & Schuster, 1985.

Katzenbach, J., and Smith, D. *The Wisdom of Teams: Creating the High-Performance Organization.* Boston: Harvard Business School Press, 1993.

Lawler, E. E., III. *From the Ground Up: Six Principles for Building the New Logic Corporation.* San Francisco: Jossey-Bass, 1996.

Lawler, E. E., III, Mohrman, S. A., and Ledford, G. E., Jr. *Creating High-Performance Organizations: Practices and Results of Employee Involvement and TQM in Fortune 1000 Companies.* San Francisco: Jossey-Bass, 1995.

Mankin, D., Cohen, S. G., and Bikson, T. K. *Teams and Technology: Fulfilling the Promise of the New Organization.* Boston: Harvard Business School Press, 1996.

Mankin, D., Cohen, S. G., and Bikson, T. K. "Teams and Technology: Tensions in Participatory Design." *Organizational Dynamics,* 1997, *26,* 63–76.

Mohrman, S. A., and Cohen, S. G. "When People Get Out of the Box: New Relationships, New Systems." In A. Howard (ed.), *The Changing Nature of Work.* San Francisco: Jossey-Bass, 1995.

Mohrman, S. A., Cohen, S. G., and Mohrman, A. M., Jr. *Designing Team-Based Organizations: New Forms for Knowledge Work.* San Francisco: Jossey-Bass, 1995.

Nadler, D. A., Gerstein, M. S., Shaw, R. B., and Associates. *Organizational Architecture: Designs for Changing Organizations.* San Francisco: Jossey-Bass, 1992.

Neff, D. B., and Thrasher, T. S. "Technology Enhances Integrated Teams' Use of Physical Resources." *Oil and Gas Journal,* May 31, 1993, pp. 29–35.

Neisser, U. "Toward a Skillful Psychology." In D. Rogers and J. A. Sloboda (eds.), *The Acquisition of Symbolic Skills.* New York: Plenum, 1983.

Nilles, J. *Making Telecommuting Happen: A Guide for Telemanagers and Telecommuters.* New York: Van Nostrand Reinhold, 1994.

Orr, J. "Sharing Knowledge, Celebrating Identity: War Stories and Community Memory in a Service Culture." In D. S. Middleton and D. Edwards (eds.), *Collective Remembering: Memory in Society.* Thousand Oaks, Calif.: Sage, 1990.

Pinchot, G., III. *Intrapreneuring.* New York: HarperCollins, 1985.

Schrage, M. *No More Teams! Mastering the Dynamics of Creative Collaboration.* New York: Doubleday, 1995.

Sproull, L., and Kiesler, S. *Connections: New Ways of Working in the Networked Organization.* Cambridge, Mass.: MIT Press, 1991.

Stalk, G., and Hout, T. *Competing Against Time.* New York: Free Press, 1990.

Stein, B., and Kanter, R. M. "Building the Parallel Organization: Creating Mechanisms for Permanent Quality of Work Life." *Journal of Applied Behavioral Science,* 1980, *16,* 371–386.

Stewart, T. A. "Managing in a Wired Company." *Fortune,* July 11, 1994, pp. 44–56.

Stewart, T. A. "What Information Costs." *Fortune,* July 10, 1995, pp. 119–121.

Taninecz, G. "Team Players." *IW,* July 15, 1996, pp. 28–32.

Van der Spiegel, J. "New Information Technologies and Changes in Work." In A. Howard (ed.), *The Changing Nature of Work.* San Francisco: Jossey-Bass, 1995.

Wenger, E. "Communities of Practice: Where Learning Happens." *Benchmark,* Fall 1991, pp. 82–84.

Zuboff, S. *In the Age of the Smart Machine: The Future of Work and Power.* New York: Basic Books, 1984.

Chapter Seven

Bashein, B., Markus, M. L., and Riley, P. "Preconditions for BPR Success." *Information Systems Management,* 1994, *11*(2), 7–13.

Davenport, T. H. *Process Innovation: Reengineering Work Through Information Technology.* Boston: Harvard Business School Press, 1993.

Davidson, W. H. "Beyond Reengineering: The Three Phases of Business Transformation." *IBM Systems Journal,* Jan. 1993, pp. 65–69.

Deming, W. E. *Out of the Crisis.* Cambridge, Mass.: Center for Advanced Engineering Study, Massachusetts Institute of Technology, 1982.

Galbraith, J. R. *Designing Organizations: An Executive Briefing on Strategy, Structure, and Process.* San Francisco: Jossey-Bass, 1995.

Hackman, J. R. "The Design of Work Teams". In J. W. Lorsch (ed.), *Handbook of Organizational Behavior.* Upper Saddle River, N.J.: Prentice Hall, 1987.

Hackman, J. R., and Lawler, E. E., III. "Employee Reactions to Job Characteristics." *Journal of Applied Psychology,* 1971, *55,* 259–286.

Hackman, J. R., and Oldham, G. R. *Work Redesign.* Reading, Mass.: Addison Wesley Longman, 1980.

Hammer, M. "Reengineering Work: Don't Automate, Obliterate." *Harvard Business Review,* 1990, *90*(4) 104–113.

Hammer, M. *Beyond Reengineering.* New York: HarperBusiness, 1996a.

Hammer, M. "You Get What You Deserve." *CFO,* 1996b, *12*(9), 9.

Hammer, M., and Champy, J. *Reengineering the Corporation: A Manifesto for Business Revolution.* New York: HarperCollins, 1993.

Hill, S., and Wilkinson, A. "In Search of TQM." *Employee Relations,* 1995, *17*(3), 8–25.

Juran, J. M. *Juran on Leadership for Quality.* New York: Free Press, 1989.

Lawler, E. E., III. "The New Plant Revolution." *Organizational Dynamics,* 1978, *6*(3), 2–12.

Lawler, E. E., III. *High-Involvement Management: Participative Strategies for Improving Organizational Performance.* San Francisco: Jossey-Bass, 1986.

Lawler, E. E., III. *Strategic Pay: Aligning Organizational Strategies and Pay Systems.* San Francisco: Jossey-Bass, 1990.

Lawler, E. E., III. *The Ultimate Advantage: Creating the High-Involvement Organization.* San Francisco: Jossey-Bass, 1992.

Lawler, E. E., III. *From the Ground Up: Six Principles for Building the New Logic Corporation.* San Francisco: Jossey-Bass, 1996.

Lawler, E. E., III, and Mohrman, S. A. "Quality Circles After the Fad." *Harvard Business Review,* 1985, *63*(1), 64–71.

Lawler, E. E., III, Mohrman, S. A., and Ledford, G. E., Jr. *Employee Involvement and Total Quality Management: Practices and Results in Fortune 1000 Companies.* San Francisco: Jossey-Bass, 1992.

Lawler, E. E., III, Mohrman, S. A., and Ledford, G. E., Jr. *Creating High-Performance Organizations: Practices and Results of Employee Involvement and TQM in Fortune 1000 Companies.* San Francisco: Jossey-Bass, 1995.

Mohrman, S. A., Cohen, S. G., and Mohrman, A. M., Jr. *Designing Team-Based Organizations: New Forms for Knowledge Work.* San Francisco: Jossey-Bass, 1995.

Mohrman, S. A., and Cummings, T. G. *Self-Designing Organizations: Learning How to Create High Performance.* Reading, Mass.: Addison Wesley Longman, 1989.

Mohrman, S. A., Tenkasi, R. V., and Mohrman, A. M., Jr. *An Organizational Learning Framework for Understanding Business Process Redesign: A Case Study from the Financial Services Industry.* Working paper, Center for Effective Organizations, Jan. 1997.

Pasmore, W. A. *Designing Effective Organizations: The Sociotechnical Systems Perspective.* New York: Wiley, 1988.

Peters, T., and Waterman, R. H., Jr. *In Search of Excellence.* New York: HarperCollins, 1982.

Schneider, B., and Bowen, D. E. *Winning the Service Game.* Boston: Harvard Business School Press, 1995.

Schonberger, R. J. "Human Resource Management Lessons from a Decade of Total Quality Management and Reengineering." *California Management Review,* 1994, *36*(4), 109–123.

Thach, L., and Woodman, R. W. "Organizational Change and Information Technology: Managing on the Edge of Cyberspace." *Organizational Dynamics,* Summer 1994, 30–46.

Walton, R. E. "From Control to Commitment: Transformation of Workforce Management Strategies in the United States." In K. B. Clark, R. H. Hayes, and C. Lorenz (eds.), *The Uneasy Alliance: Managing the Productivity-Technology Dilemma.* Boston: Harvard Business School Press, 1985.

Womack, J. P., Jones, D. T., and Roos, D. *The Machine That Changed the World.* Old Tappan, N.J.: Macmillan, 1990.

Chapter Eight

Evans, P. "Business Strategy and Human Resource Management: A Four-Stage Framework." Working paper, INSEAD, Fontainebleau, France, 1994.

Galbraith, J. R. "The Value-Adding Corporation: Matching Structure with Strategy." In J. R. Galbraith, E. E. Lawler III, and Associates, *Organizing for the Future: The New Logic for Managing Complex Organizations.* San Francisco: Jossey-Bass, 1993.

Galbraith, J. R. *Competing with Flexible Lateral Organizations.* Reading, Mass.: Addison Wesley Longman, 1994.

Galbraith, J. R., Lawler, E. E., III, and Associates. *Organizing for the Future: The New Logic for Managing Complex Organizations.* San Francisco: Jossey-Bass, 1993.

Hall, D. T., and Mirvis, P. H. "Careers as Lifelong Learning." In A. Howard, *The Changing Nature of Work.* San Francisco: Jossey-Bass, 1995.

Handy, C. *The Age of Unreason.* Boston: Harvard Business School Press, 1990.

Lawler, E. E., III. *The Ultimate Advantage: Creating the High-Involvement Organization.* San Francisco: Jossey-Bass, 1992.

Lawler, E. E., III. "Strategic Human Resources Management: An Idea Whose Time Has Come." In B. Downie and M. L. Coates (eds.), *Managing Human Resources in the 1990s and Beyond: Is the Workplace Being Transformed?* Kingston, Ontario: IRC Press, 1995.

Lawler, E. E., III. *From the Ground Up: Six Principles for Building the New Logic Corporation.* San Francisco: Jossey-Bass, 1996.

Mohrman, A. M., Jr., and Mohrman, S. A. "Performance Management *Is* 'Running the Business.'" *Compensation and Benefits Review,* 1995, 27, 69–75.

Mohrman, S. A., and Cohen, S. G. "When People Get Out of the Box: New Relationships, New Systems." In A. Howard (ed.), *The Changing Nature of Work.* San Francisco: Jossey-Bass, 1995.

Mohrman, S. A., Cohen, S. G., and Mohrman, A. M., Jr. *Designing Team-Based Organizations: New Forms for Knowledge Work.* San Francisco: Jossey-Bass, 1995.

Mohrman, S. A., and Cummings, T. G. *Self-Designing Organizations: Learning How to Create High Performance.* Reading, Mass.: Addison Wesley Longman, 1989.

Mohrman, S. A., Lawler, E. E., III, and McMahan, G. C. *New Directions for the Human Resources Organization: An Organization Design Approach.* Los Angeles. Center for Effective Organizations, 1996.

Nadler, D. A., Gerstein, M. S., Shaw, R. B., and Associates. *Organizational Architecture: Designs for Changing Organizations.* San Francisco: Jossey-Bass, 1992.

Pasmore, W. A. *Designing Effective Organizations: The Sociotechnical Systems Perspective.* New York: Wiley, 1988.

Rousseau, D. M., and Wade-Benzoni, K. A. "Changing Individual-Organization Attachments: A Two-Way Street." In A. Howard (ed.), *The Changing Nature of Work.* San Francisco: Jossey-Bass, 1995.

Savage, C. *Fifth Generation Management: Integrating Enterprises Through Human Networking.* Waltham, Mass.: Digital Press, 1990.

Trist, E. *The Evolution of Sociotechnical Systems.* Toronto: Quality of Working Life Centre, 1981 (photocopied).

Ulrich, D. W., Brockbank, W., and Yeung, A. K. "Human Resource Competencies in the 1990s." *Personnel Administrator,* Nov. 1989, pp. 91–93.

Chapter Nine

Adler, N. J. *International Dimensions of Organizational Behavior.* Cincinnati, Ohio: Southwestern College Publishing, 1997.

Adler, N. J., and Bartholomew, S. "Managing Globally Competent People." *Academy of Management Executive,* 1992, *6*(3), 52–65.

American Compensation Association Competencies Research Team. "The Role of Competencies in an Integrated HR Strategy." *ACA Journal,* Summer 1996, pp. 6–21.

Attewell, P. "Information Technology and the Productivity Paradox." In National Research Council (ed.), *Organizational Linkages: Understanding the Productivity Paradox.* Washington, D.C.: National Academy Press, 1994.

Bassi, L., and Cheney, S. *Results from the 1996 Benchmarking Forum.* Alexandria, Va.: American Society for Training and Development, 1996.

Becker, G. *Human Capital.* Chicago: University of Chicago Press, 1962 .

Birch, D. "Entrepreneurship and Job Generation in the 1990s." Presentation to the Milken Institute, Santa Monica, Calif., Jan. 21, 1997.

Bishop, J. H. *What We Know About Employer-Provided Training: A Review of the Literature.* Ithaca, N.Y.: Center for Advanced Human Resource Studies, Cornell University, 1996.

Bowen, D. E., and Lawler, E. E., III. "The Empowerment of Service Workers: What, Why, How, and When." *Sloan Management Review,* 1992, *33*(3), 31–39.

Finegold, D. L., and Mason, G. "National Training Systems and Industrial Performance: U.S.-European Matched-Plant Comparisons." Paper presented at ILR–Cornell Institute for Labor Market Policies Conference, Cornell University, Nov. 1996.

Finegold, D. L., and Schechter, S. "International Models of Management Development: Lessons for Australia." In *Enterprising Nation: Renewing*

Australia's Managers to Meet the Challenges of the Asia-Pacific Century: Research Report. Vol. 2: *Industry Task Force on Leadership and Management Skills.* Canberra, Australia: Australian Government Publishing Service, 1995.

Finegold, D. L., and others. *Closing the Knowledge Gap for Transit Maintenance Employees: A Systems Approach.* Santa Monica, Calif.: RAND Corp., 1996.

Flanigan, J. "Big Bonus Is Nice, but It's Thought That Counts." *Los Angeles Times,* Dec. 22, 1996, p. D-1.

Fletcher, J. K. "Personal Development in the New Organization: Developing the Protean Worker." In D. T. Hall and Associates (eds.), *The Career Is Dead—Long Live the Career: A Relational Approach to Careers.* San Francisco: Jossey-Bass, 1996.

Fruin, W. M., and Nishiguchi, T. *The Toyota Production System: Its Organizational Definition and Diffusion in Japan.* Cambridge, Mass.: Massachusetts Institute of Technology, 1990 (mimeograph).

Galbraith, J. R., Lawler, E. E., III, and Associates. *Organizing for the Future: The New Logic for Managing Complex Organizations.* San Francisco: Jossey-Bass, 1993.

Hall, D. T. "Protean Careers of the 21st Century." *Academy of Management Executive,* 1996, *10*(4), 8–16.

Hamel, G., and Prahalad, C. K. *Competing for the Future.* Boston: Harvard Business School Press, 1994.

Hollenbeck, K. "Employer Motives for Investing in Training." Paper presented at ILR–Cornell Institute for Labor Market Policies Conference, Cornell University, Nov. 1996.

Jagmin, N. "Designing a Competency-Based Promotion System." In *Competency-Based Pay for Knowledge Workers: The State of the Art.* Los Angeles: Center for Effective Organizations, 1995.

Keltner, B., and Finegold, D. L. "Adding Value in Banking: Human Resource Innovations for Service Firms." *Sloan Management Review,* 1996, *38*(1), 57–68.

Lawler, E. E., III, Mohrman, S. A., and Ledford, G. E., Jr. *Creating High-Performance Organizations: Practices and Results of Employee Involvement and TQM in Fortune 1000 Companies.* San Francisco: Jossey-Bass, 1995.

Ledford, G. E., Jr. "New Directions in Competency-Based Pay." In *Competency-Based Pay for Knowledge Workers: The State of the Art.* Los Angeles: Center for Effective Organizations, 1995.

Lillard, L. A., and Tan, H. W. *Private Sector Training: Who Gets It and What Are Its Effects?* Santa Monica, Calif.: RAND Corp., 1986.

London, M. "Hard Lessons and Positive Examples from the Downsizing Era." *Academy of Management Executive,* 1996, *10*(4), 67–79.

MacDuffie, J. P., and Krafcik, J. "Integrating Technology and Human Resources for High Performance Manufacturing: Evidence from the International Auto Industry." In T. A. Kochan and M. Useem (eds.), *Transforming Organizations.* New York: Oxford University Press, 1992.

Mason, G., and Finegold, D. L. *Skills, Machinery and Productivity in Precision Metalworking and Food Processing: A Pilot Study of Matched Establishments in the U.S. and Europe.* London: National Institute of Economic and Social Research, 1995.

Mohrman, S. A., Cohen, S. G., and Mohrman, A. M., Jr. *Designing Team-Based Organizations: New Forms for Knowledge Work.* San Francisco: Jossey-Bass, 1995.

Mohrman, S. A., Lawler, E. E., III, and McMahan, G. C. *New Directions for the Human Resources Organization: An Organization Design Approach.* Los Angeles: Center for Effective Organizations, 1996.

Mohrman, S. A., and Mohrman, A. M., Jr. "Organizational Change and Learning." In J. R. Galbraith, E. E. Lawler III, and Associates, *Organizing for the Future: The New Logic for Managing Complex Organizations.* San Francisco: Jossey-Bass, 1993.

National Center on the Educational Quality of the Workforce. *The EQW National Employer Survey.* Washington, D.C.: National Center for the Educational Quality of the Workforce, 1995.

Nicholson, N. "Information Age." *Academy of Management Executive,* 1996, *10*(4), 40–51.

Paye, J. C. "Policies for a Knowledge-Based Economy." *OECD Observer,* 1996, *200,* 1–4.

Reich, R. B. *The Work of Nations: Preparing Ourselves for Twenty-First-Century Capitalism.* New York: Random House, 1991.

Rousseau, D. M. *Psychological Contracts in Organizations: Written and Unwritten Agreements.* Thousand Oaks, Calif.: Sage, 1995.

Schaffer, D. "Measuring Customer Satisfaction Using Level 4 Results." In L. P. Grayson (ed.), *Learning Organizations for the 21st Century: Education on Demand.* Proceedings of the 1995 College Industry Education Conference. New Orleans: American Society for Engineering Education, 1995.

Schlesinger, L., and Heskett, J. L. "The Service-Driven Company." *Harvard Business Review,* 1991, *69,* 71–81.

Schneider, B., and Bowen, D. E. *Winning the Service Game.* Boston: Harvard Business School Press, 1995.

Schopp, W. "Evolution of Competency-Based Pay at Monsanto." In *Competency-Based Pay for Knowledge Workers: The State of the Art.* Los Angeles: Center for Effective Organizations, 1995.

Snow, C., and others. "Use Transnational Teams to Globalize Your Company." *Organizational Dynamics,* Spring 1996, pp. 50–67.

Spreitzer, G. M., McCall, M. W., Jr., and Mahoney, J. D. *The Early Identification of International Executive Potential.* Los Angeles: Center for Effective Organizations, 1994.

Ulrich, D. W., and Greenfield, H. "The Transformation of Training and Development to Development and Learning." *American Journal of Management Development,* 1995, *1*(2), 11–22.

U.S. Bureau of Labor Statistics. *Employer-Provided Formal Training.* Washington, D.C.: U.S. Department of Labor, 1996.

Waterman, R. H., Jr., Waterman, J. A., and Collard, B. A. "Toward a Career-Resilient Workforce." *Harvard Business Review,* 1994, *72,* 87–95.

Womack, J. P., Jones, D. T., and Roos, D. *The Machine That Changed the World.* Old Tappan, N.J.: Macmillan, 1990.

Chapter Ten

Bolt, J. F. "Achieving the CEO's Agenda: Education for Executives." *Management Review,* 1993, *82*(5), 44–48.

Cairns-Lee, H. M. "Demonstrating the Impact of Management Development: Current Practice of Evaluation in International Companies." Unpublished master's thesis, Lancaster University, 1996.

Clark, R. "How the Cognitive Sciences Are Shaping the Profession." In H. Stolovitch and J. Keeps (eds.), *Handbook of Human Performance Technology: A Comprehensive Guide for Analyzing and Solving Performance Problems in Organizations.* San Francisco: Jossey-Bass, 1992.

Conger, J. A., and Xin, K. R. "Adult Learning and Executive Education." Paper presented at the International Consortium for Executive Development Research Conference, Charlottesville, N.C., Apr. 1996.

D'Aveni, R. A. *Hypercompetition: Managing the Dynamics of Strategic Maneuvering.* New York: Free Press, 1994.

Fulmer, R. M., and Vicere, A. A. *Executive Education and Leadership Development: The State of the Practice.* University Park: Pennsylvania State Institute for the Study of Organizational Effectiveness, 1995.

Noel, J., and Charan, R. "Leadership Development at GE's Crotonville." *Human Resources Management,* 1988, *27*(4), 433–447.

Ready, D. A. *In Charge of Change: Insights into Next-Generation Organizations.* Lexington, Mass.: International Consortium for Executive Development Research, 1995.

Saari, L. M., Johnson, T. R., McLaughlin, S. D., and Zimmerle, D. M. "A Survey of Management Training and Education Practices in U.S. Companies." *Personnel Psychology,* 1988, *41,* 731–743.

Tichy, N. M., and Sherman, S. *Control Your Destiny or Someone Else Will.* New York: Doubleday, 1993.

Weiss, H. M. "Learning Theory and Industrial and Organizational Psychology." In M. D. Dunnette and L. M. Hough (eds.), *Handbook of Industrial and Organizational Psychology.* Palo Alto, Calif.: Consulting Psychologists Press, 1992.

Chapter Eleven

Blinder, A. S. *Paying for Productivity.* Washington, D.C.: Brookings Institution, 1990.

Gerhart, B., and Milkovich, G. T. "Employee Compensation: Research and Practice." In M. D. Dunnette and L. M. Hough (eds.), *Handbook of Industrial and Organizational Psychology.* Palo Alto, Calif.: Consulting Psychologists Press, 1992.

Heneman, R. L. *Merit Pay.* Reading, Mass.: Addison Wesley Longman, 1992.

Jenkins, G. D., Jr., Ledford, G. E., Jr., Gupta, N., and Doty, D. H. *Skill-Based Pay: Practices, Payoffs, Pitfalls, and Prospects.* Scottsdale, Ariz.: American Compensation Association, 1992.

Kerr, S. "On the Folly of Rewarding A While Hoping for B." *Academy of Management Journal,* 1975, *18,* 769–783.

Lawler, E. E., III. *Pay and Organizational Effectiveness: A Psychological View.* New York: McGraw-Hill, 1971.

Lawler, E. E., III. *Strategic Pay: Aligning Organizational Strategies and Pay Systems.* San Francisco: Jossey-Bass, 1990.

Lawler, E. E., III. "The New Pay: A Strategic Approach." *Compensation and Benefits Review,* 1995, *27*(4), 14–22.

Lawler, E. E., III, and Jenkins, G. D. "Strategic Reward Systems." In M. D. Dunnette and L. M. Hough (eds.), *Handbook of Industrial and Organizational Psychology.* Palo Alto, Calif.: Consulting Psychologists Press, 1992.

Lawler, E. E., III, Mohrman, S. A., and Ledford, G. E., Jr. *Employee Involvement and Total Quality Management: Practices and Results in Fortune 1000 Companies.* San Francisco: Jossey-Bass, 1992.

Lawler, E. E., III, Mohrman, S. A., and Ledford, G. E., Jr. *Creating High-Performance Organizations: Practices and Results of Employee Involvement and TQM in Fortune 1000 Companies.* San Francisco: Jossey-Bass, 1995.

Lawrence, P. R., and Lorsch, J. W. *Organization and Environment: Managing Differentiation and Integration.* Burr Ridge, Ill.: Irwin, 1967.

Ledford, G. E., Jr. "Designing Nimble Reward Systems." *Compensation and Benefits Review,* 1995a, *27*(4), 46–54.

Ledford, G. E., Jr. "Paying for the Skills, Knowledge, and Competencies of Knowledge Workers." *Compensation and Benefits Review,* 1995b, *27*(4), 55–62.

Schuster, J. R., and Zingheim, P. K. *The New Pay.* San Francisco: New Lexington Press, 1992.

Vroom, V. H. *Work and Motivation.* New York: Wiley, 1964.

Chapter Twelve

Attewell, P. "Information Technology and the Productivity Paradox." In National Research Council (ed.), *Organizational Linkages: Understanding the Productivity Paradox.* Washington, D.C.: National Academy Press, 1994.

Bikson, T. K., and Eveland, J. D. *New Office Technology: Planning for People.* New York: Pergamon Press, 1986.

Bikson, T. K., Stasz, C., and Mankin, D. A. *Computer-Mediated Work: Individual and Organizational Impact in One Corporate Headquarters.* Santa Monica, Calif.: RAND Corp., 1985.

Carey, J. M., and Currey, J. D. "The Prototyping Conundrum." *Datamation,* 1989, *35,* 29–33.

Cascio, W. S. *Guide to Responsible Restructuring.* Washington, D.C.: Office of the American Workplace, U.S. Department of Labor, 1995.

Ciborra, C. U. "From Thinking to Tinkering: The Grassroots of Strategic Information Systems." In *Proceedings of the 12th Internal Conference on Information Systems.* New York: Association for Computing Machinery, 1991.

Davenport, T. H. "Will Participative Makeovers of Business Processes Succeed Where Reengineering Failed?" *Planning Review,* 1995, *23*(1), 24–29.

Drucker, P. F. "The Age of Social Transformation." *Atlantic,* Nov. 1994, pp. 53–80.

Dumaine, B. "The Trouble with Teams." *Fortune,* Sept. 5, 1994, pp. 86–92.

Johnson, B. M., and Rice, R. E. *Managing Organizational Innovation.* New York: Columbia University Press, 1986.

Kantor, B. "Iterative Prototyping Model: How to Use Iterative Prototyping When Developing Lotus Notes Applications." *Workgroup Computing Report,* 1994, *17*(1), 14–25.

Keen, P. *Shaping the Future: Business Design Through Information Technology.* Boston: Harvard Business School Press, 1991.

Klein, K. J., and Ralls, R. S. "The Organizational Dynamics of Computerized Technology Implementation: A Review of the Empirical Literature." In L. R. Gomez-Mejía and M. W. Lawless (eds.), *Advances in Global High Technology Management.* Greenwich, Conn.: JAI Press, 1995.

Lawler, E. E., III. *From the Ground Up: Six Principles for Building the New Logic Corporation.* San Francisco: Jossey-Bass, 1996.

Lawler, E. E., III, Mohrman, S. A., and Ledford, G. E., Jr. *Creating High-Performance Organizations: Practices and Results of Employee Involvement and TQM in Fortune 1000 Companies.* San Francisco: Jossey-Bass, 1995.

Ledford, G. E., Jr., and Mohrman, S. A. "Self-Design for High Involvement: A Large-Scale Organizational Change." *Human Relations,* 1993, *46*(2), 143–173.

Leonard-Barton, D. "Implementation as Mutual Adaptation of Technology and Organization." *Research Policy,* 1988, *17*, 251–267.

Mankin, D., Cohen, S. C., and Bikson, T. K. *Terms and Technology: Fulfilling the Promise of the New Organization.* Boston: Harvard Business School Press, 1996.

Markus, M. L., and Robey, D. "Business Process Reengineering and the Role of the Information Systems Professional." In V. Grover and W. Kettinger (eds.), *Business Process Reengineering: A Strategic Approach.* Middletown, Pa.: Idea Group Publishing, 1995.

Mohrman, S. A., and Cummings, T. G. *Self-Designing Organizations: Learning How to Create High Performance.* Reading, Mass.: Addison Wesley Longman, 1989.

National Research Council. *Information Technology in the Service Sector: A Twenty-First-Century Lever.* Washington, D.C.: National Academy Press, 1994.

Rice, R. E., and Rogers, E. M. "Reinvention in the Innovation Process." *Knowledge,* 1980, *1*, 499–514.

Seybold, P. *How to Leapfrog Your Organization into the 21st Century: Highlights from Patricia Seybold's 1994 Technology Forum.* Boston: Patricia Seybold Group, 1994.

Stewart, T. A. "What Information Costs." *Fortune,* July 10, 1995, pp. 119–121.

Takeuchi, H., and Nonaka, I. "The New New Product Development Game." *Harvard Business Review,* 1986, *64*, 137–146.

Tyre, M. J., and Orlikowski, W. J. "Windows of Opportunity: Temporal Patterns of Technology Adaptation in Organizations." *Organization Science,* 1994, *5*, 98–118.

Von Hippel, E. *The Sources of Innovation.* New York: Oxford University Press, 1988.

Chapter Thirteen

Argyris, C., and Schön, D. A. *Organizational Learning: A Theory of Action Perspective.* Reading, Mass.: Addison Wesley Longman, 1978.

Bennis, W. G., and Nanus, B. *Leaders: Strategies for Taking Charge.* New York: HarperCollins, 1985.

Boland, R. J., Tenkasi, R. V., and Te'eni, D. "Designing Information Technology to Support Distributed Cognition." *Organization Science,* 1994, 5(3), 456–475.

Brand, S. *How Buildings Learn: What Happens After They're Built.* New York: Penguin Books, 1994.

Brown, J. S., and Duguid, P. "Organizational Learning and Communities-of-Practice: Toward a Unified View of Working, Learning, and Innovation." *Organization Science,* 1991, 2(1), 40–57.

Ciborra, C. U. "The Platform Organization: Recombining Strategies, Structures and Surprises." *Organization Science,* 1996, 7(2), 103–118.

Ciborra, C. U., and Schneider, L. S. "Transforming the Routines and Contexts of Management, Work and Technology." In P. S. Adler (ed.), *Technology and the Future of Work.* New York: Oxford University Press, 1992.

Dougherty, D. "Interpretive Barriers to Successful Product Innovation in Large Firms." *Organization Science,* 1992, 3(2), 179–202.

Drazin, R., and Sandelands, D. "Autogenesis: A Perspective on the Process of Organizing." *Organization Science,* 1992, 3(2), 230–249.

Dykstra, E. A., and Carasik, R. P. "Structure and Support in Cooperative Environments: The Amsterdam Conversation Environment." *International Journal of Man-Machine Studies,* 1991, 34, 419–434.

Friedlander, F. "Patterns of Individual and Organizational Learning." In S. Srivastava (ed.), *The Executive Mind: New Insights on Managerial Thought and Action.* San Francisco: Jossey-Bass, 1984.

Galbraith, J. R. *Organization Design.* Reading, Mass.: Addison Wesley Longman, 1977.

Gerstein, M. S. "From Machine Bureaucracies to Networked Organizations: An Architectural Journey." In D. A. Nadler, M. S. Gerstein, R. B. Shaw, and Associates, *Organizational Architecture: Designs for Changing Organizations.* San Francisco: Jossey-Bass, 1992.

Keidel, R. *Seeing Organizational Patterns: A New Theory and Language of Organizational Design.* San Francisco: Berrett-Koehler, 1995.

Kolb, D. A. Problem Management: Learning from Experience. In S. Srivastava (ed.), *The Executive Mind: New Insights on Managerial Thought and Action.* San Francisco: Jossey-Bass, 1984.

Ledford, G. E., Jr., Mohrman, S. A., Mohrman, A. M., Jr., and Lawler, E.E., III. "The Phenomenon of Large-Scale Change." In A. M. Mohrman, Jr., and others, *Large-Scale Organizational Change.* San Francisco: Jossey-Bass, 1989.

Levitt, B., and March, J. G. "Organizational Learning." *Annual Review of Sociology,* 1988, *14,* 319–340.

Malone, T. W., Lai, K. Y., and Fry, C. "Experiments with OVAL: A Radically Tailorable Tool for Cooperative Work." In J. Turner and R. Kraut (eds.), *Proceedings of the Association of Computing Machinery Conference on Computer-Supported Cooperative Work.* Toronto: ACM Books, 1992.

March, J. G. "Exploration and Exploitation in Organizational Learning." *Organization Science,* 1991, *2*(3), 71–87.

Marjchzak, A., and Gasser, L. "HITOP: A Tool to Facilitate Interdisciplinary Manufacturing Systems Design." *International Journal of Human Factors in Manufacturing,* 1992, *2*(3), 255–276.

Maruyama, M. *Mindscapes in Management: Use of Individual Differences in Multicultural Management.* Brookfield, Vt.: Dartmouth, 1994.

McGill, M. E., Slocum, J. W., and Lei, D. "Management Practices in Learning Organizations." *Organizational Dynamics,* 1993, *22*(1), 5–17.

Mohrman, S. A., and Cummings, T. G. *Self-Designing Organizations: Learning How to Create High Performance.* Reading, Mass.: Addison Wesley Longman, 1989.

Mohrman, S. A., Cohen, S. G., and Mohrman, A. M., Jr. *Designing Team-Based Organizations: New Forms for Knowledge Work.* San Francisco: Jossey-Bass, 1995.

Nadler, D. A. "Introduction: Organizational Architecture: A Metaphor for Change." In D. A. Nadler, M. S. Gerstein, R. B. Shaw, and Associates, *Organizational Architecture: Designs for Changing Organizations.* San Francisco: Jossey-Bass, 1992.

Nadler, D. A., Gerstein, M. S., Shaw, R. B, and Associates. *Organizational Architecture: Designs for Changing Organizations.* San Francisco: Jossey-Bass, 1992.

Perlmutter, H. V., and Trist, E. "Paradigms for Societal Transition." *Human Relations,* 1986, *39*(1), 1–27.

Quinn, J. B., Anderson, P., and Finkelstein, S. "Leveraging Intellect." *Academy of Management Executive,* 1996, *10*(3), 7–27.

Rasmussen, S. E. *Experiencing Architecture.* Cambridge, Mass.: MIT Press, 1991.

Roth, G. L., and Senge, P. M. "From Theory to Practice: Research Territory, Processes and Structure at an Organizational Learning Center." *Journal of Organizational Change Management,* 1996, *9*(1), 92–106.

Sandelands, L., and Stablein, R. E. "The Concept of Organizational Mind." In S. Bacharach and N. DiTomaso (eds.), *Research in the Sociology of Organizations.* Greenwich, Conn.: JAI Press, 1987.

Senge, P. M. *The Fifth Discipline: The Art and Practice of the Learning Organization.* New York: Doubleday, 1990.

Thompson, J. D., and Tuden, A. "Strategies, Structures, and Processes of Organizational Decision Making." In J. D. Thompson (ed.), *Comparative Studies in Organizations.* Pittsburgh, Pa.: University of Pittsburgh Press, 1959.

Tichy, N. M., and Devanna, M. *The Transformational Leader.* New York: Wiley, 1986.

Turner, B. "Failed Artifacts." In P. Gagiliardi (ed.), *Symbols and Artifacts: Views of the Corporate Landscape.* Hawthorne, N.Y.: Aldine de Gruyter, 1992.

Ulrich, D. W., Von Glinow, M. A., and Jick, T. "High-Impact Learning: Building and Diffusing Learning Capability." *Organizational Dynamics,* 1993, 22(1), 52–66.

Weick, K. E. "Organizational Redesign as Improvisation." In G. P. Huber and W. H. Glick (eds.), *Organizational Change and Redesign: Ideas and Insights for Improving Performance.* New York: Oxford University Press, 1993.

Weick, K. E., and Westley, F. "Organizational Learning: Affirming an Oxymoron." In S. R. Clegg, C. Hardy, and W. R. Nord (eds.), *Handbook of Organization Studies.* Thousand Oaks, Calif.: Sage, 1996.

Chapter Fourteen

Davenport, T. H. *Process Innovation: Reengineering Work Through Information Technology.* Boston: Harvard Business School Press, 1993.

Deming, W. E. *Out of the Crisis.* Cambridge, Mass.: Center for Advanced Engineering Study, Massachusetts Institute of Technology, 1986.

Galbraith, J. R. *Competing with Flexible Lateral Organizations.* Reading, Mass.: Addison Wesley Longman, 1994.

Galbraith, J. R., and Lawler, E. E., III. "Challenges to the Established Order." In J. R. Galbraith, E. E. Lawler, III, and Associates, *Organizing for the Future: The New Logic for Managing Complex Organizations.* San Francisco: Jossey-Bass, 1993.

Hammer, M., and Champy, J. *Reengineering the Corporation: A Manifesto for Business Revolution.* New York: HarperCollins, 1995.

Katz, D., and Kahn, R. *The Social Psychology of Organizations.* New York: Wiley, 1978.

Kuhn, T. S. *The Structure of Scientific Revolutions.* Chicago: University of Chicago Press, 1970.

Ledford, G. E., Jr., Mohrman, S. A., Mohrman, A. M., Jr., and Lawler, E. E., III. "The Phenomenon of Large-Scale Change." In A. M. Mohrman, Jr., and others, *Large-Scale Organizational Change*. San Francisco: Jossey-Bass, 1989.

Lundberg, C. "On Organizational Development Interventions: A General Systems-Cybernetic Perspective." In T. G. Cummings (ed.), *Systems Theory for Organization Development*. New York: Wiley, 1980.

Massarik, F. "'Mental Systems': Toward a Practical Agenda for a Phenomenology of Systems." In T. G. Cummings (ed.), *Systems Theory for Organization Development*. New York: Wiley, 1980.

Mohrman, A. M. Jr., and Lawler, E. E., III. "The Diffusion of QWL as a Paradigm Shift." In W. G. Bennis, K. D. Benne, and R. Chin (eds.), *The Planning of Change*. (4th ed.) Austin, Tex.: Holt, Rinehart and Winston, 1985.

Mohrman, A. M. Jr., Mohrman, S. A., and Lawler, E. E., III. "The Performance Management of Teams." In W. J. Bruns Jr., *Performance Measurement, Evaluation, and Incentives*. Boston: Harvard Business School Press, 1992.

Mohrman, A. M., Jr., Mohrman, S. A., and Worley, C. "High Technology Performance Management." In M. A. Von Glinow and S. A. Mohrman (eds.), *Managing Complexity in High Technology Organizations*. New York: Oxford University Press, 1990.

Mohrman, A. M., Jr., Resnick-West, S., and Lawler, E. E., III. *Designing Performance Appraisal Systems: Aligning Appraisals and Organizational Realities*. San Francisco: Jossey-Bass, 1989.

Mohrman, S. A., Cohen, S. G. and Mohrman, A. M., Jr. *Designing Team-Based Organizations: New Forms for Knowledge Work*. San Francisco: Jossey-Bass, 1995.

Mohrman, S. A., and Cummings, T. G. *Self-Designing Organizations: Learning How to Create High Performance*. Reading, Mass.: Addison Wesley Longman, 1989.

Mohrman, S. A., and Mohrman, A. M., Jr. "Fundamental Organizational Change as Organizational Learning: Creating Team-Based Organizations." In W. A. Pasmore and R. W. Woodman (eds.), *Research in Organizational Change and Development*. Vol. 10. Greenwich, Conn.: JAI Press, 1997.

Murphy, K. R., and Cleveland, J. N. *Performance Appraisal: An Organizational Perspective*. Needham Heights, Mass.: Allyn & Bacon, 1991.

Nadler, D. A., Gerstein, M. S., Shaw, R. B., and Associates. *Organizational Architecture: Designs for Changing Organizations*. San Francisco: Jossey-Bass, 1992.

Pfeffer, J. *Organizations and Organizational Theory*. Marshfield, Mass.: Pitman Press, 1982.

Savage, C. *Fifth Generation Management: Integrating Enterprises Through Human Networking.* Waltham, Mass.: Digital Press, 1990.

Senge, P. M. *The Fifth Discipline: The Art and Practice of the Learning Organization.* New York: Doubleday, 1990.

Taylor, M. S., Fisher, C. D., and Ilgen, D. R. "Individuals' Reactions to Performance Feedback in Organizations: A Control Theory Perspective." In K. M. Rowland ad G. R. Ferris (eds.), *Research in Personnel and Human Resources Management.* Vol. 2. Greenwich, Conn.: JAI Press, 1984.

Conclusion

Barnard, C. *Functions of the Executive.* Cambridge, Mass.: Harvard University Press, 1938.

Mohrman, S. A., and Tenkasi, R. V. Unpublished document, Center for Effective organizations, University of Southern California, 1997.

Rousseau, D. M. *Psychological Contracts in Organizations: Understanding Written and Unwritten Agreements.* Thousand Oaks, Calif.: Sage, 1995.

Rousseau, D. M., and Wade-Benzoni, K. A. "Changing Individual-Organizational Attributes: A Two-Way Street." In A. Howard (ed.), *The Changing Nature of Work.* San Francisco: Jossey-Bass, 1995.

Waterman, R. H. Jr., Waterman, J. A., and Collard, B. A. "Toward a Career-Resilient Workforce." *Harvard Business Review,* 1994, 72, 87–95.

Zuboff, S. *In the Age of the Smart Machine: The Future of Work and Power.* New York: Basic Books, 1984.

Name Index

A

Adler, N. J., 258, 259
Anderson, P., 357, 359
Andrews, T., 142
Argyris, C., 332
Ash, R. A., 145
Attewell, P., 259, 309

B

Bainbridge, S. M., 24, 31, 35
Barnard, C., 401
Bartholomew, S., 259
Bartlett, C. A., 105, 107, 111, 123
Bashein, B., 199, 205
Bassi, L., 260
Becker, G., 249
Benetton, L., 15
Bennis, W. G., 331
Bhagat, S., 32
Bikson, T. K., 120, 154n, 173, 259,
    309, 310n, 312n, 316n, 323, 325
Birch, D., 233, 237
Bishop, J. H., 140, 249, 262
Black, B., 32
Blinder, A. S., 290
Boland, R. J., 359
Bolt, J. F., 264
Bott, E., 155
Bowen, D. E., 149, 202, 236, 253, 256
Boyatzis, R. E., 136
Brand, S., 338
Bridges, W., 137, 145
Brockbank, W., 136, 224
Brown, J. S., 337–338, 360
Budnitz, M. E., 24
Builder, C. H., 39

C

Cairns-Lee, H. M., 272, 280, 282
Capelli, P., 18–19, 151, 165
Carasik, R. P., 359
Carey, J. M., 320
Cascio, W. S., 327
Champy, J., 187–188, 192, 205, 371
Charan, R., 270
Chatterjee, P., 155
Cheney, S., 260
Ciborra, C. U., 326, 336, 358
Clark, R., 276–277
Cleveland, J. N., 369
Cochran, P. L., 31
Cofsky, K. M., 148
Cohen, S. G., 29, 39, 47, 120, 138, 145,
    154, 161, 166, 168, 169, 171, 172,
    173, 202, 214, 217, 238, 259, 309,
    310n, 312n, 316n, 331, 364, 371, 390
Collard, B. A., 234, 404
Conger, J. A., 23, 264, 281
Contractor, F. J., 81
Cooper, R., 1, 2
Crane, D. B., 119
Crocker-Hefter, A., 151
Crosby, P. B., 184
Cummings, T. G., 182, 222, 317, 340,
    342, 371, 387
Currey, J. D., 320

D

Daily, C. M., 24, 31, 34
Dalton, C. R., 31
D'Aveni, R. A., 3, 31, 227
Davenport, T. H., 187–188, 192, 196,
    316, 371

Davidson, W. H., 201
Davis, D. D., 163
Davis, S., 63
Deming, W. E., 184, 185, 186, 371
Devanna, M., 331
Dewar, J. A., 39
Dodd-Thomas, J., 163
Donkersgoed, W., 31
Doty, D. H., 148, 289, 299
Dougherty, D., 172, 344, 359
Doz, Y., 107, 108, 109
Drazin, R., 336
Drucker, P. F., 310
Duguid, P., 337–338, 360
Dumaine, B., 309
Dyer, J. H., 93
Dykstra, E. A., 359

E

Eccles, R. G., 76, 119
Ellstrand, A. E., 24, 34
Evans, P. E., 135, 220, 221
Eveland, J. D., 323

F

Fama, E., 24
Finegold, D. L., 23, 133, 141, 143, 231, 238, 241, 242, 246, 248, 249, 251, 252, 260
Finkelstein, S., 31, 357, 359
Fisher, C. D., 368, 387
Flanigan, J., 236
Fletcher, J. K., 238
Ford, H., 93
Friedlander, F., 349
Fruin, W. M., 245
Fry, C., 359
Fulmer, R. M., 269, 271, 272

G

Galbraith, J. R., 1, 6, 8, 9n, 51, 54, 63, 76, 103, 118, 120, 125, 144, 150, 173, 178, 206, 212, 213, 214, 221, 227, 240, 333, 364, 369, 371
Gasser, L., 360
Gerhart, B., 293

Gerlach, M. L., 93
Gerstein, M. S., 173, 213, 333, 357, 371
Gerstner, L., 52
Ghoshal, S., 105, 107, 111, 123
Gordon, J., 165
Greenfield, H., 238, 240
Gupta, N., 148, 289, 299

H

Hackman, J. R., 181, 196, 201
Halal, W., 12
Hall, D. T., 214, 217, 232, 240
Hamel, G., 2, 6, 133, 134, 135, 231, 239
Hamilton, S., 141
Hammer, M., 187–188, 192, 205, 371
Handy, C., 151, 214
Hautaluoma, J., 31
Heneman, R. L., 290
Heskett, J. L., 253
Hill, S., 184
Hix, W. M., 39
Hoachlander, G., 141
Hollenbeck, K., 249
Hout, T., 167

I

Ilgen, D. R., 368, 387
Ishikawa, K., 184

J

Jagmin, N., 257
Jenkins, G. D., Jr., 148, 286, 289, 299
Jensen, M., 24
Jessup, G., 141
Jick, T., 332
Johansen, R., 128
Johnson, B. M., 325
Johnson, J. L., 24, 34
Johnson, T. R., 280
Jones, D. T., 2, 57, 184, 245
Jones, T. B., 31
Juran, J. M., 184

K

Kahn, R., 373
Kahn, W., 171
Kaman, V., 31

Kanter, R. M., 161, 168
Kantor, B., 315
Kaplan, R. S., 40
Karoly, L., 140
Katz, D., 373
Katzenbach, J., 171
Keen, P., 329
Keidel, R., 333
Keltner, B., 133, 143, 252
Kerr, J. F., 2
Kerr, S., 290
Kesner, I. F., 31
Kiesler, C., 165
Killing, J. P., 86, 88
Klein, K. J., 313
Klerman, J., 140
Kolb, D. A., 332
Krafcik, J., 239
Kuhn, T. S., 373, 375, 376

L

Lado, A. A., 135
Lai, K. Y., 359
Lake, D., 6, 135, 136
Lawler, E. E., III, 1, 6, 23, 29, 33, 45,
    133, 135–136, 144, 145, 148, 149,
    153, 161, 163, 165, 168, 175, 178,
    179, 180, 181, 182, 183, 184, 190,
    191, 192, 195, 196, 200, 201, 202,
    204, 207, 211, 212, 215, 217, 220,
    221, 222, 224, 225, 229, 233, 236,
    240, 248, 286, 287, 289, 292, 293,
    294, 299, 302, 309, 327, 331, 363,
    364, 370, 371, 373, 375, 376, 379,
    385, 394
Lawrence, P. R., 63, 295
Lear, R. W., 23–24
Leavitt, H., 144
Ledford, G. E., Jr., 133, 137, 138,
    144, 145, 148, 149, 153, 165, 180,
    183, 190, 191, 193n, 196, 200,
    202, 204, 207, 233, 257, 287, 289,
    299, 309, 318, 331, 363
Lei, D., 332
Leighton, D.S.R., 25, 48
Leonard-Barton, D., 323
Levin, M. H., 39

Levine, E. L., 145
Levitt, B., 331, 345
Lillard, L. A., 238
London, M., 233
Lorange, P., 81
Lorenz, C., 104
Lorsch, J. W., 24, 25, 34, 35, 42, 295
Lundberg, C., 368

M

MacDuffie, J. P., 239
MacIver, E., 24, 25, 34, 35, 42
Mahoney, J. D., 259, 261
Malone, T. W., 359
Mankin, D. A., 120, 154, 173, 259,
    309, 310n, 312n, 316n, 325
March, J. G., 331, 345, 355
Marjchzak, A., 360
Markus, M. L., 199, 205, 329
Maruyama, M., 357–358
Mason, G., 238, 260
Massarik, F., 388
McCall, M. W., Jr., 240, 259, 261
McGill, M. E., 332
McKinsey, J. O., 144
McLaughlin, S. D., 280
McMahan, G. C., 224, 225, 229
Meckling, W., 24
Miles, R. E., 76
Milkovich, G. T., 293
Mirvis, P. H., 214, 217
Mohrman, A. M., Jr., 29, 39, 47, 120,
    138, 145, 168, 169, 192, 202, 204,
    217, 223, 238, 240, 330, 331, 362,
    363, 364, 370, 371, 379, 385, 387,
    390
Mohrman, S. A., 29, 39, 47, 120, 138,
    145, 148, 149, 161, 165, 168, 169,
    171, 172, 179, 180, 182, 183, 184,
    190, 191, 192, 196, 200, 202, 204,
    207, 211, 214, 217, 222, 223, 224,
    225, 229, 233, 238, 240, 248, 287,
    289, 299, 309, 317, 318, 330, 331,
    340, 342, 362, 363, 364, 371, 373,
    375, 376, 379, 385, 387, 390, 394,
    403n
Murphy, K. R., 369

N

Nadler, D. A., 173, 213, 330, 333, 357, 371
Nanus, B., 331
Nathan, B. R., 149
Neff, D. B., 167
Neisser, U., 159–160
Nicholson, N., 234
Nilles, J., 162
Nishiguchi, T., 245
Noel, J., 270
Nohria, N., 76
Nonaka, I., 322
Norton, D. P., 40

O

O'Hara-Devereaux, M., 128
Oldham, G. R., 181, 196
O'Neal, S., 148
Orlikowski, W. J., 323–324
Orr, J., 161
Osterman, P., 140

P

Pager, C., 133, 143
Pasmore, W. A., 181, 216
Patel, P., 123
Paye, J. C., 232
Pearce, J. A., II, 24, 31, 32, 40
Perlmutter, H. V., 347
Peters, T., 179
Pfeffer, J., 24, 32, 373
Pinchot, G., III, 161
Porter, M., 123
Prahalad, C. K., 2, 6, 107, 108, 133, 134, 135, 231, 239

Q

Quinn, J. B., 357, 359

R

Rahn, M., 141
Ralls, R. S., 313
Rasmussen, S. E., 333
Ready, D. A., 264, 272
Reich, R. B., 139, 232

Resnick-West, S., 370
Rice, R. E., 323, 325
Riley, P., 199, 205
Robey, D., 329
Rogers, E. M., 323
Rogovsky, N., 165
Roos, D., 2, 57, 184, 245
Roth, G. L., 360
Rousseau, D. M., 214, 218, 219, 234, 401, 405
Ruigrok, W., 122
Rumelt, R. P., 135

S

Saari, L. M., 280
Salancik, G. R., 24, 32
Sandelands, L., 336
Savage, C., 216, 371
Schaffer, D., 260
Schechter, S., 242, 246, 249, 251
Schellenger, M. H., 32
Schlesinger, L., 253
Schneider, B., 202, 253, 256
Schneider, L. S., 336, 358
Schön, D. A., 332
Schonberger, R. J., 197
Schopp, W., 257
Schrage, M., 162
Schuster, J. R., 137, 138, 287
Senge, P. M., 330, 332, 352, 353, 354, 360, 371
Seybold, B., 315, 319
Shaw, R. B., 173, 213, 333, 357, 371
Sheldon, S., 98
Sherman, S., 271
Shulman, L. E., 135
Sistrunk, F., 145
Slocum, J. W., 332
Smith, D., 171
Snow, C. C., 76, 259
Spencer, L. M., 136
Spencer, S. M., 136
Spreitzer, G. M., 259, 261
Sproull, L., 165
Stablein, R. E., 336
Stalk, G., 135, 167

Stasz, C., 325
Steel, D., 98
Stein, B., 168
Stein, G., 166
Stewart, T. A., 155, 309
Stopford, J., 109
Streeck, W., 140

T

Takeuchi, H., 322
Tan, H. W., 238
Taninecz, G., 167
Tashakori, A., 32
Taylor, M. S., 368, 387
Te'eni, D., 359
Tenkasi, R. V., 192, 204, 330, 359, 403n
Thach, L., 197
Thain, D. H., 25, 48
Thompson, J. D., 351
Thrasher, T. S., 167
Tichy, N. M., 271, 331
Trist, E., 216, 347
Tucker, M., 140, 141, 142
Tucker, S. A., 148
Tuden, A., 351
Turner, B., 333
Tyre, M. J., 323–324

U

Ulrich, D. W., 6, 135, 136, 224, 238, 240, 332
Useem, M., 23

V

Van der Spiegel, J., 156, 160, 161
van Tulder, R., 122
Vance, S. C., 31
Vicere, A. A., 269, 271, 272
Vickers, M., 142

Von Glinow, M. A., 332
Von Hippel, E., 323
Vroom, V. H., 293

W

Wade-Benzoni, K. A., 214, 218, 219, 405
Walton, R. E., 183
Waterman, J. A., 234, 404
Waterman, R. H., Jr., 179, 234, 404
Weick, K. E., 331, 338, 347, 351
Weiss, H. M., 278–279
Wells, L., 109
Wenger, E., 161
Werther, W. B., 2
Westley, F., 331, 351
Wilkinson, A., 184
Williams, J. R., 3, 4n
Wills, J., 140, 141, 142
Wilson, M. C., 135
Wolf, A., 141, 142
Womack, J. P., 2, 57, 184, 245
Wood, D. D., 32
Wood, R. A., 31
Woodman, R. W., 197
Worley, C., 379, 385

X

Xin, K. R., 264, 281

Y

Yavitz, B., 23–24
Yeung, A. K., 136, 224
Yu, Y.-S., 112, 122, 123

Z

Zahra, S. A., 24, 31, 32, 40
Zimmerle, D. M., 280
Zingheim, P. K., 137, 138, 287
Zuboff, S., 157, 159, 160, 397

Subject Index

A

Acer Computer: global nature of, 108; reward system at, 18

Advantage, competitive: and human resources, 221; and learning contract, 242–243; sustaining and disrupting, 2–5, 12

Allfast Corporation, and learning, 242–243

Alliances, and networks, 83–84, 85, 87, 88

Amazon Books, and value chain, 98

American Airlines, and change, 322

American Compensation Association, 139, 257

American Management Association, 251

American Society of Corporate Secretaries, 45–46, 48

Anderson Consulting: and change, 322; and reengineering, 188

Apple, network of, 78, 85, 95, 100, 101

Aramco, and competitive advantage, 3–4

Argentina: and customer-product structure, 61; and global organizations, 117

Asea Brown Boveri (ABB), global nature of, 116–118, 121, 122, 127

Asia, and global organizations, 106

Assessment, of executive education, 280–282, 285. *See also* Performance appraisal

AT&T: and change management, 20; and human resources, 231; and management team, 168

Australia, competencies in, 141, 142, 143

Automatic Data Processing, network of, 80

Automaticity, and learning, 278

Automobile industry, value chain for, 92–94

B

Banking industry, and learning contract, 252–257

Behaviors, and organizational learning, 337, 343–344, 346

Benetton: and competitive advantage, 6, 14–16; network of, 77–78, 79, 80, 95, 96, 98, 101

Boards: aspects of, 23–50; background on, 23–24; and CEO development and evaluation, 27–28, 41–42, 44–45; and committees, 45–46; conclusion on, 50; and crisis management, 29, 39–40; development for, 38–39; effectiveness of, 29–31; evaluations of, 47–48; in future, 409–410; and information, 30, 40–42; and knowledge, 30, 32–35, 37–40; and legal and ethical issues, 28–29, 41; membership on, 31–37; and motivation, 30, 46–49; for networked organizations, 90; operations of, 37–50; and opportunity/time, 30, 36–37, 49–50; peer CEOs on, 33, 36; and performance issues, 23–24, 40–42; and power, 30, 35–36,

42–46; roles of, 24–29; and senior management development, 28, 41–42; and strategy, 26–27

Boeing: and information technology, 167; and learning, 242; and networking, 16, 81, 94

Bonus plans, 297

Boys, The, and customer-product structure, 74

Braking-system supplier, customer-product structure for, 57–61

Brazil: and customer-product structure, 61; and global organizations, 117

Bundling, in customer-product structure, 56

Business-process reengineering. *See* Reengineering

C

California: banking and learning in, 252–257; customer-product structure in, 74; telecommuting in, 163

California at Los Angeles, University of, Anderson School of Management of, 251

California Federal Bank, and learning, 254–255

Canada, competencies in, 141

Canon, network of, 95

Capabilities. *See* Competencies

Capitalism, and wealth, 408–409

Category management, 11

Center for Effective Organizations, 402

Change: action-learning approach to, 317–318; approaches to, 314–328; architectural, 332–338; to business-unit organization, 338–345; challenge of, 1–20; and competencies, 145; culture of, 322–323, 329; deterred, 377–381; and employee involvement, 182–183; enabled, 381–387; and executive education, 266; funda-

mental, 412; future challenge of, 406–407; and human resources, 222; impact of, 203–204; and information technology, 173–175; large-scale, 363–364, 368, 403, 406; and management approaches, 19–20, 195, 197–204; mutuality of, 312; and organizational learning, 330–361; and performance management, 363–364, 368, 377–387; and reinvention, 323–328; spiral work flow model of, 319; systems development approaches to, 318–322; waterfall metaphor of, 315–316

ChemTeam, and performance management, 382–383, 387

China: competition from, 272; and global organizations, 112, 125; joint ventures in, 14; learning in, 249–250; and network, 95

Chrysler: and customer-product structure, 57–61; and learning, 239; network of, 93–94, 95, 99–100

CIGNA, and change, 322

Citibank: customer-product structure at, 64; and learning, 254–255

Coca-Cola: and competencies, 151; direct delivery by, 10; network of, 100–101

Cognitions, and organizational learning, 336–337, 342–343, 346

Collaborative environments, in telecommuting, 162–163

Committee on the Financial Aspects of Corporate Governance, 44

Communications, on reward system, 292, 301–302

Communities of practice, and information technology, 161

Compaq: global nature of, 108; network of, 78, 80

Competencies: aspects of, 133–153; background on, 133–134; for career ladders, 253–254, 261–262;

characteristics of, 135; conclusion on, 152–153; conflicting approaches to, 142–143; core, 134–136; and employment stability, 150–151; and fit, 152; in future, 396–397, 404–405; and human resources, 136–139, 147–151, 217–218; individual, 136–139, 145–146; individual linked to organizational, 239–240; internal training for, 245–247; national systems of, 139–142, 153; organizational design for, 143–152, 153; partnerships for building, 231–263; and processes, 147–148; responsibility for, 248–251; and reward systems, 148–149, 298–300; types of, 135

Competitive organizations: advantage in, 1–20; boards of, 23–50; customer-product structure for, 51–75; designing, 21–129, 395–398; future challenges of, 394–412; global, 103–129; and human resources, 18–19, 209–305, 401–406; and motivations, 17–18; networked, 14–16, 76–102; performance of, 131–207; societal challenges for, 407–412; strategies for, 1–7; structures for, 7–17; transforming, 307–412; transition challenge for, 406–407; trends for, 4; and work changes, 398–401

Conflict: in customer-product structure, 64–65; in teams, 171–172

Consumer goods manufacturer, customer-product structure for, 71–75

Contracting. See Networked organizations

Contracts. See Learning contracts; Psychological contract

Corning, network of, 87, 92

Cost: effectiveness of, and human resources, 227–228; reduction of,

and management approaches, 200–201; and reward system, 295

Creative Artists Agency, and networking, 99

Credibility, and networked organizations, 99–100

Crisis management, and boards, 29, 39–40

Cross-selling, in customer-product structure, 56

Culture, organizational: of change, 322–323, 329; and organizational learning, 335–336, 342, 351, 360; and performance management, 383–385; and reward system, 294, 300

Cummins Engine, network of, 84

Customer-product structure: aspects of, 51–75; background on, 51–52; conclusion on, 75; contention in, 64–65; examples of, 65–75; form of, 52–54; management of, 62–65; in practice, 57–62; and quality, 185; reasons for, 54–57; regional teams for, 66–68, 72–74; reward system in, 69–70, 71; roles and responsibilities in, 63–64

D

Decision making: group, 38–39, 202; in reward system, 292, 302–303

Delta Airlines, network of, 84

Denmark, internal marketing in, 13–14

Design. See Organizational design

Development: for boards, 38–39; of executives, 27–28, 41–42, 44–45; SPORT model of, 243–244. See also Learning contract

Dialogue, in organizational learning, 352–353

Digital, and customer-product structure, 56

Downsizing, and management approaches, 199–200, 203

Dun & Bradstreet, internal marketing at, 13

DuPont: global nature of, 123; and telecommuting, 163

E

Earnings gap, and learning, 262

Education. *See* Executive education; Learning contracts

Effectiveness: and boards, 23–50; and competencies, 133–153; of learning contracts, 259–261; models of, 6–7, 143–145, 177, 286; and reward system, 295–300; of teams, 29–30

Employee involvement: approach of, 180–183; and change, 201, 202; comparisons with, 193, 198; future for, 205; and reengineering, 192; and TQM, 190–191

Employees: attracting and retaining, 293; empowered, 186–187, 202; interests of, 401–402, 407, 410–411; organization related to, 366–367; stability for, 150–151. *See also* Workforce

Equity, in networks, 84–85

Ethical and legal issues, for boards, 28–29, 41

Europe: competencies in, 138; and global organizations, 106, 107, 111, 112; TQM in, 184; workers on boards in, 34

European Economic Community, 111

Evaluation: of boards, 47–48; of executive education, 280–282, 285. *See also* Performance appraisal

Executive education: aspects of, 264–285; assessment of, 280–282, 285; background on, 264–265; and boards, 27–28, 41–42, 44–45; changing nature of, 265–272, 274–275; components of, 267–268; conclusion on, 284–285; and content, 269, 278–279; future issues for, 272–283; integrating mechanisms for, 271–272,

282–283, 285; and needs, 268–269, 272–273, 284; objectives of, 266–268; participants in, 270–271, 279–280, 285; and pedagogy, 270, 276–278, 284–285; sponsors of, 273, 276, 284

F

Federal Express, network of, 80

Feedback: in organizational learning, 348, 349, 353; and performance management, 368, 388–390

Fiat: and customer-product structure, 57–61; and learning, 246

Film industry, value chain of, 98–99

Financial services, customer-product structure for, 65–71

Financing, in networked organizations, 98–99

First Federal Bank, and learning, 254, 255–256, 257

Fit: and competencies, 152; and reward system, 304

Ford: global nature of, 106; and learning, 247–248; network of, 83, 84, 89–90, 93

Front-back approach. *See* Customer-product structure

France, and global organizations, 119, 123, 125, 126, 411

Frito-Lay: direct delivery by, 10; and learning, 257

G

Gee & Co., Ltd., 44

Gemini, and reengineering, 188

General Electric: and executive education, 264, 270, 271; global nature of, 110; and learning, 246; strategic business unit at, 53–54

General Motors: and change, 322; and customer-product structure, 56; network of, 88–89, 93

Germany: competencies of, 141; and global organizations, 110,

111, 119, 125, 411; reward system in, 18

Glendale Community College, and learning, 242–243

Global organizations: aspects of, 103–129; and business diversity, 109–110; conclusion on, 129; and cross-border coordination, 107–109; design factors for, 103–111; future for, 126–129, 409; history for, 111; and home-country market, 110; and host governments, 109; and international development, 103–106; with international or geographic divisions, 111–113; with lateral networking, 118–123; and learning, 258–259, 261; models of, 111–126; as multibusiness, 115–118; as multidimensional, 113–123; with single business, 114–115; as transnational, 123–126

Goals 2000 Act, 140

Group processes, and boards, 38–39

GTE, and change, 322

H

Harley-Davidson: and change management, 20; and reengineering, 194

Harris Bank, and learning, 255–256

Hewlett-Packard: and change management, 20; customer-product structure at, 61–62; global nature of, 116, 121, 122, 125; and information technology, 155, 163, 168–169

Hitachi Data Systems, and telecommuting, 164

Human capital theory, 249

Human resources: aspects of, 209–305; background on, 211–212; challenges for, 214–220; and competencies, 136–139, 147–148, 149–151, 217–218; and competitive organizations, 18–19, 209–305; and cost effectiveness, 227–228; cross-skilling and rotation in, 227; and deployment, 216–217; designing, 225–229; and executive education, 264–285; expertise and functions in, 226; future of, 221, 229–230, 401–406; and internal marketing, 14; issues for, 228–229; and learning contracts, 231–263; management of, 209–305; in networked organizations, 91–92; and organizational design, 212–215, 222; and organizational learning, 218; and performance, 215–216, 223; and psychological contract, 219–220; responsibilities in, 226–227; and reward system, 286–305; strategic partnerships for, 211–230, 251–252; and teams, 313; time given to, 224; and value-adding function, 220–225

I

IBM: and change management, 20; customer-product structure of, 52–53, 55–56; and human resources, 231; network of, 84

Index, and reengineering, 188

India: and global organizations, 126; reward system in, 18

Indonesia, and network, 95

Industry ecosystem concept, 273

Information technology (IT): age of, 155–156; aspects of, 154–178, 309–329; as boundary spanning, 172–173, 328–329; and change, 173–175; and competencies, 147–148, 150; conclusions on, 175–178, 328–329; in customer-product structure, 70; future challenges for, 397, 398, 399, 406–407; and global organizations, 128; and knowledge-based work, 156–161; and learning,

259; and mutual design and implementation, 313; and organizational learning, 358–360; and reengineering, 188–189, 195, 204, 206; scale of, 315; and teams, 165–172, 309–329; and telecommuting, 162–165

Infosys, reward system of, 18

Intel, global nature of, 108–109

Involvement. *See* Employee involvement

Italy: customer-product structure in, 60; networked organization in, 77, 98

J

Jaguar, and size, 77

Japan: architecture in, 358; competencies in, 141; competitive advantage in, 3, 5, 14; and global organizations, 110, 111, 112; lean enterprise in, 2; reward system in, 18, 290; and TQM, 183, 184

Joint ventures, and networks, 84, 88–89

K

Kingston Technologies, and employment security, 236

Knowledge: as basis for work, 150–161; and boards, 30, 32–35, 37–42; bridges for, 355; and customer-product structure, 56–57; expert, distributed, 359; in future, 396–397, 405; in networked organizations, 78, 85, 92, 96–98; organizational, 218; and reward system, 294; tacit, 159–161; and teams, 309–310

Korea: competition from, 272; and networks, 95

Korn/Ferry International, 24, 25, 33, 35, 36, 43, 44, 45, 46, 47, 48, 49

L

Latin America, and global organizations, 106

Learning: action, 270, 276–278, 284–285, 317–318; continuous, 241–242; experiential, 353, 358–359; and global organizations, 258–259, 261; open-loop, 354–355. *See also* Organizational learning

Learning contracts: aspects of, 231–263; background on, 231–232; basis for, 234–237; and competencies, 138; and competitive advantage, 242–243; for development, 237–243; effectiveness of, 259–261; future issues for, 257–263, 404; and internal promotion, 255–256; implementing, 243–252, 258; in practice, 252–257; and public policy, 262; and skill demands, 232–233, 235; tuition reimbursement for, 250–251, 260–261

Leverage, and networked organizations, 94–95

Levi Strauss, and executive education, 264, 283

Linkages, in customer-product structure, 65

M

Management: approaches to, 179–207; background on, 179–180; brand, 101; with business-process reengineering, 187–189; category, 11; and change, 19–20, 195, 197–204; of crises, 29, 39–40; cross-functional, 225–226, 227; of customer-product structure, 62–65; development for senior, 28, 41–42; differences in, 192–197; with employee involvement, 180–183; future for, 204–207, 399–400, 401; of human resources, 209–305; similarities in, 190–192; teams for, 168; of telecommuting, 164–165; total quality approach to, 183–187. *See also* Performance management

Market position, and reward system, 290–291, 299–300

Marketing: in customer-product structure, 63, 68–69; internal, 12–14; and networked organizations, 82

Mazda: network of, 84, 89–90; and size, 77

McDonald's, global nature of, 112

Meaning, shared, 350–351, 352–353, 356

Measurement, and competencies, 147

Medco, performance management at, 377–379, 385

Merck, internal marketing at, 13

Merit pay system, 290

Merrill Lynch, and organizational learning, 359

Mexico: and customer-product structure, 61; and global organizations, 117

Microsoft: and ecosystem shift, 273; network of, 78, 85, 95

Mitsubishi Trading Company, global nature of, 116

Modules, concurrent development of, 320–321

Monsanto, and learning, 257

Motivation: and boards, 30, 46–49; and competitive organizations, 17–18; and employee involvement, 181, 196; and reward system, 17–18, 293–294

Motorola: and executive education, 264; global nature of, 108; and learning, 239, 246–247, 248, 260; network of, 84; and TQM, 184–185

Mutual design and implementation (MDI) process, and teams, 311–314

N

National Academy of Sciences, 315

National Alliance of Business, 133, 140

National Association of Corporate Directors, 24, 44, 48

National Center on Education and the Economy, 133

National Center on the Educational Quality of the Workforce, 232, 238, 239

National Research Council, 315

National Skills Standards Board, 140

NEC, global nature of, 108

Nestlé, global nature of, 105, 109, 110, 115, 119, 122, 125

Netherlands, executive education in, 271

Networked organizations: aspects of, 76–102; autonomous model of, 91; brand management in, 101; contracting relationships for, 82–83; designing, 79–92; drawbacks of, 78–79; external relationships for, 81–86; financing in, 98–99; future of, 102; human resources in, 91–92; integrating, 80–81, 92–102; knowledge in, 78, 85, 92, 96–98; and leverage, 94–95; merits of, 76–78; operator model of, 88–89; responsibility for, 100–101; shared-responsibility model of, 89–90; strategy for, 79–81

Networks: ad hoc, 168–169; and competitive organizations, 14–16; equity in, 84–85; internal, 8–9; lateral, 118–123; multidimensional, 113–123; self-organizing, 119; and telecommuting, 164

New Zealand, competencies in, 141

Nike: and competitive advantage, 6; and information technology, 173; network of, 80, 94, 95, 101

Nintendo, network of, 101

Nippon Telephone and Telegraph (NTT), and competitive advantage, 3

Nissan, and human resources, 231

North Carolina, technical college training in, 252

Novelty, and learning, 279

O

Oilco, performance management at, 383–385

Organizational design: and architectural change, 332–338; for competencies, 143–152, 153; future challenges for, 395–398; and human resources, 212–215, 222; and management approaches, 194; network approach to, 6, 51–75

Organizational learning: accelerated, 330–361; and architectural change, 332–338; background on, 330–331; and behaviors, 337, 343–344, 346; challenges in, 338–345; and cognitions, 336–337, 342–343, 346; concept of, 332; conclusion on, 361; domains of, 336–337; dynamics of, 350–357; embedded in work, 356–357; experimentation for, 360; future challenges for, 357–361, 406; as iterative, 347–348; and learning contracts, 240–241; and local structuring, 337, 344, 346; and market architecture, 334, 336, 339, 346, 358; memory encoded for, 359–360; model of, 345–350; open-systems view of, 387–392; and performance, 349–350; processes in, 352–357; resources for, 356; and social architecture, 335, 336, 339, 346, 358; system view in, 354; and technical architecture, 334–335, 336, 339, 346, 358–360

Organizations: business-unit, 338–345; capabilities of, 4–6; flexible, 174, 178; functional, 340; greenfield, 183, 318; hypercompetitive, 3, 4–5, 8, 14; internal marketing in, 12–14; lateral, 8–9, 399; multistructuring, 10–12; nested systems of, 356, 365–366, 371–372, 377; platform, 358; reconfigurable, 357–361, 396; and reinvention, 326–328; schools or universities of, 246–247; size of, 77; stakeholders of, 410; virtual, 76–102, 216. *See also* Competitive organizations; Culture, organizational; Global organizations; Networked organizations

Oticon, internal marketing at, 13–14

Ownership, and networks, 85

P

Pacific Bell: and learning, 260; and telecommuting, 163

Partners: for human resources, 211–230, 251–252; for learning, 238–239; selecting, 86–87; structures for, 87–91; strategy for, 79–81

Pay: for job or person, 289; merit, 290; for performance, 256–257, 290, 296–297; skill-based, 299. *See also* Reward system

PepsiCo: and competencies, 151; direct delivery by, 10

Performance: aspects of, 131–207; and boards, 23–24, 40–42; and competencies, 133–153; and human resources, 215–216, 223; and information technology, 154–178; and management approaches, 179–207; and organizational learning, 349–350; pay for, and learning, 256–257, 290, 296–297; and performance management, 365–366

Performance appraisal: by peers, 381–383, 391; and performance management, 369–370, 372, 378–379, 380, 384, 388–390

Performance management: and anomalies, 375–376; aspects of, 362–393; background on, 362–363; centrality of, 364–368, 385–386; and change, 363–364,

368, 377–387; concept of, 362; conclusion on, 392–393; and employee relationship to organization, 366–367; and feedback, 368, 388–390; in future, 407; new models of, 371–374; open-systems view of, 387–392; and paradigm shift, 373–387; and performance, 365–366; traditional models of, 369–370, 374

Phamaceuticals industry, global nature of, 114–115

Philips Corporation: and executive education, 271–272; global nature of, 127

Poland, customer-product structure in, 60–61

Post, Telephone and Telegraph (PTT) (Switzerland), and competitive advantage, 3

Power: and boards, 30, 35–36, 42–46; and teams, 169–170

PPG, and customer-product structure, 56

Pratt & Whitney, and learning, 250, 262

Processes: and competencies, 147–148; group, 38–39; in organizational learning, 352–357

Procter and Gamble, global nature of, 107

Products. See Customer-product structure

Promotion, internal, 255–256

Prototyping, iterative, 320

Psychological contract: in future, 401–402; and human resources, 219–220; hygiene factors in, 401–402; and learning, 231–263

Publishing industry, value chain in, 97–98

Q

Quality. See Total quality management

R

Rapid application development (RAD), for change, 318–322

Raychem, and learning, 261

Reebok, and competitive advantage, 6

Reengineering: approach of, 187–189; and change, 197–199, 201, 203; comparisons with, 193, 198; and competencies, 147; and employee involvement, 192; future for, 205–207; and human resources, 228; and TQM, 196–197

Reinvention: issues of, 326–328; job, 324–325, 327–328; task, 324; team, 325; tool, 323–324, 326–327; user, 323

Reward system: aspects of, 286–305; background on, 286–288; centralization of, 291, 303–304; communications on, 292, 301–302; and competencies, 148–149, 298–300; conclusion on, 304–305; and costs, 295; in customer-product structure, 69–70, 71; design of, 287–292; and effectiveness, 295–300; and employee involvement, 182; and executive education, 283; and fit, 304; in future, 404; and hierarchy, 291–292, 300; and information technology, 177–178; and market position, 290–291, 299–300; and motivation, 17–18, 293–294; in networked organizations, 92; objectives of, 292–295; operating effectiveness of, 301–304; and organizational structure, 294–295; and performance management, 372, 380, 390–391; and teams, 327–328, 329

Rhône-Poulenc, global nature of, 125

Roadway Express, and networking, 16

Rowntree, global nature of, 125

Russia, and global organizations, 112

S

Saab, and size, 77
SAP (Germany), reward system in, 18
Saudi Arabia, competitive advantage in, 3–4
Schwinn, network of, 78, 86
SCI, network of, 79–80
Securities and Exchange Commission, 36
Shareholders, and boards, 23, 46–47
Siemens, network of, 84
Singapore, and global organizations, 126, 411
Singapore Airlines, network of, 84
Skandia, and executive education, 282
Skills: intellective, 159–161; and learning contracts, 232–233, 235; and pay, 299
Softboy, reward system at, 18
Sony: competencies of, 134–135, 239; global nature of, 127; network of, 95
Sotheby's, and competitive advantage, 4
Sourcing, by networked organizations, 78, 83, 85, 88
South Carolina, technical college training in, 252
Strategy: actionable, 17; and boards, 26–27; for competitive organizations, 1–7; concept of, 2; and human resources, 222; for networked organizations, 79–81
Structuring, and organizational learning, 337, 344, 346
Sweden, executive education in, 282
Swiss Air, network of, 84
Switzerland: competitive organizations in, 3, 4; and global organizations, 123, 125
Systems development approaches, and change, 318–322

T

Taiwan: competition from, 272; and global organizations, 125, 411; and networked organizations, 78, 86, 95; reward system in, 18
Tandem Computer, and telecommuting, 163
Teams: ad hoc, 168–169; aspects of technology and, 309–329; background on, 309–311; boards as, 23–50; and change approaches, 314–328; and competencies, 145–146; conclusions on, 328–329; conflict in, 171–172; effectiveness of, 29–30; and employee involvement, 181, 194; in future, 399–400; in global organizations, 119–121; and information technology, 165–172, 309–329; and interdependence, 170–171, 178; in lateral organizations, 8–9; learning for, 238; management, 168; and multistructuring, 10, 12; and mutual design and implementation process, 311–314; and organizational learning, 331, 352; parallel, 168; and performance management, 379, 382–383, 388–392; and power, 169–170; project and development, 167; regional, 66–68, 72–74; and reinvention, 325; and reward system, 18; stakeholders on, 312–314; and TQM, 194; work, 166–167
Techco, performance management at, 388–390
Technology. See Information technology
Telecommuting, impact of, 162–165
Telephone company, reengineering at, 157, 158, 159
Texaco, and learning, 260
Toshiba, network of, 84
Total quality management (TQM): approach of, 183–187; and

change, 200–201, 202–203; comparisons with, 193, 198; and competencies, 147; and employee involvement, 190–191; future for, 205; and learning, 239; and reengineering, 196–197

Toyota: competencies of, 135; as lean enterprise, 2; and learning, 239, 245; network of, 88–89; and reengineering, 188

Training: customized, 251–252, 269; internal, 245–247; modular, 254–255; priority setting for, 243–245; as revenue generator, 247–248. *See also* Learning contract

TRW: internal marketing at, 13; network of, 83

Tuition reimbursement, for learning contracts, 250–251, 260–261

Turkey: and customer-product structure, 61; joint ventures in, 14

U

United Auto Workers, and partnering, 88

United Kingdom: boards in, 44; competencies in, 141, 142, 143; and global organizations, 125

United Nations, 409

U.S. Bureau of Labor Statistics, 260

UPS, and change, 322

V

Value-adding activities: and customer-product structure, 56; and human resources, 220–225

Value chain, in networked organizations, 92–94, 97–99

Values, and organizational learning, 335–336, 353

Verifone, global nature of, 125–126, 128

Virtual corporation. *See* Networked organizations

Von's, and customer-product structure, 74

W

Wal-Mart: competencies of, 135, 136, 239; and distribution, 78

Waldenbooks, and value chain, 98

Wells Fargo Bank, and customer-product structure, 55–56

Westinghouse, global nature of, 106

William Morris Agency, and networking, 99

Work: abstract nature of, 156–161; as boundary spanning, 400–401; changing nature of, 176–177, 398–401; design of, and motivation, 17; future challenges for, 398–401; and information technology, 154–178; intellective, 159–161; knowledge-based, 156–161; learning embedded in, 356–357; self-managed, 157–158; upgrading, 157

Workforce: competencies for, 139–142; development for, 238–239; in future, 405–406, 411–412; variety in, 214. *See also* Employees

X

Xerox: and change management, 20; and learning, 246; and organizational learning, 337–338; and TQM, 184–185

XYZ, Inc., and team reinvention, 325